The Khārijites in Early Islamic Historical Tradition

Edinburgh Studies in Classical Islamic History and Culture
Series Editor: Carole Hillenbrand

A particular feature of medieval Islamic civilisation was its wide horizons. The Muslims fell heir not only to the Graeco-Roman world of the Mediterranean, but also to that of the ancient Near East, to the empires of Assyria, Babylon and the Persians; and beyond that, they were in frequent contact with India and China to the east and with black Africa to the south. This intellectual openness can be sensed in many inter-related fields of Muslim thought, and it impacted powerfully on trade and on the networks that made it possible. Books in this series reflect this openness and cover a wide range of topics, periods and geographical areas.

Titles in the series include:

The Body in Arabic Love Poetry: The ʿUdhri Tradition
Jokha Alharthi

The Books of Burhān al-Dīn: Literacy and Book Ownership in Mamluk Jerusalem
Said Aljoumani and Konrad Hirschler

Arabian Drugs in Early Medieval Mediterranean Medicine
Zohar Amar and Efraim Lev

Towards a History of Libraries in Yemen
Hassan Ansari and Sabine Schmidtke

The Abbasid Caliphate of Cairo, 1261–1517: Out of the Shadows
Mustafa Banister

The Medieval Western Maghrib: Cities, Patronage and Power
Amira K. Bennison

Christian Monastic Life in Early Islam
Bradley Bowman

Keeping the Peace in Premodern Islam: Diplomacy under the Mamluk Sultanate, 1250–1517
Malika Dekkiche

Queens, Concubines and Eunuchs in Medieval Islam
Taef El-Azhari

Islamic Political Thought in the Mamluk Period
Mohamad El-Merheb

The Kharijites in Early Islamic Historical Tradition: Heroes and Villains
Hannah-Lena Hagemann

Medieval Damascus: Plurality and Diversity in an Arabic Library – The Ashrafiya Library Catalogue
Konrad Hirschler

A Monument to Medieval Syrian Book Culture: The Library of Ibn ʿAbd al-Hādī
Konrad Hirschler

The Popularisation of Sufism in Ayyubid and Mamluk Egypt: State and Society, 1173–1325
Nathan Hofer

Defining Anthropomorphism: The Challenge of Islamic Traditionalism
Livnat Holtzman

Making Mongol History: Rashid al-Din and the Jamiʿ al-Tawarikh
Stefan Kamola

Lyrics of Life: Saʿdi on Love, Cosmopolitanism and Care of the Self
Fatemeh Keshavarz

Art, Allegory and The Rise of Shiism In Iran, 1487–1565
Chad Kia

The Administration of Justice in Medieval Egypt: From the 7th to the 12th Century
Yaacov Lev

The Queen of Sheba's Gift: A History of the True Balsam of Matarea
Marcus Milwright

Ruling from a Red Canopy: Political Authority in the Medieval Islamic World, From Anatolia to South Asia
Colin P. Mitchell

Islam, Christianity and the Realms of the Miraculous: A Comparative Exploration
Ian Richard Netton

The Poetics of Spiritual Instruction: Farid al-Din ʿAttar and Persian Sufi Didacticism
Austin O'Malley

Sacred Place and Sacred Time in the Medieval Islamic Middle East: An Historical Perspective
Daniella Talmon-Heller

Conquered Populations in Early Islam: Non-Arabs, Slaves and the Sons of Slave Mothers
Elizabeth Urban

edinburghuniversitypress.com/series/escihc

The Khārijites in Early Islamic Historical Tradition

Heroes and Villains

Hannah-Lena Hagemann

EDINBURGH
University Press

Edinburgh University Press is one of the leading university presses in the UK. We publish academic books and journals in our selected subject areas across the humanities and social sciences, combining cutting-edge scholarship with high editorial and production values to produce academic works of lasting importance. For more information visit our website: edinburghuniversitypress.com

Edinburgh University Press Ltd
The Tun – Holyrood Road
12 (2f) Jackson's Entry
Edinburgh EH8 8PJ

First published in hardback by Edinburgh University Press 2021

Typeset in 11/15 Adobe Garamond by
Servis Filmsetting Ltd, Stockport, Cheshire

A CIP record for this book is available from the British Library

ISBN 978 1 4744 5088 1 (hardback)
ISBN 978 1 4744 5089 8 (paperback)
ISBN 978 1 4744 5091 1 (webready PDF)
ISBN 978 1 4744 5090 4 (epub)

Contents

Note on Conventions vii
Abbreviations viii
Acknowledgements x
Map: The Near East in the Umayyad Period xii

PART I Preliminaries

Introduction 3
Sources, Genre, Authorship 24
Historical Setting 41

PART II Early Islamic Historiography and Literary Khārijism

1 Literary Approaches to Islamic Historiography and Khārijite History 59

2 Portraying Khārijism 86

3 Composing Khārijism 114

PART III The Portrayal of Khārijite History from Ṣiffīn to the Death of ʿAbd al-Malik

4 Narratives of Khārijite Origins 135

5 Khārijism during the Reign of Muʿāwiya b. Abī Sufyān 165

6 Khārijism from the Second Fitna until the Death of ʿAbd al-Malik 217

PART IV Observations and Conclusions

7 Observations Regarding the Historiographical Tradition on Khārijism 257

Conclusion 274

Bibliography 279
Index 310

Note on Conventions

The Arabic transliteration follows the system employed by the *Encyclopaedia of Islam, THREE.* Some place names are transliterated, but those familiar in English are rendered in their anglicised form (such as Medina, Iraq, Basra or Kufa). Arabic and technical terms are italicised, again with the exception of terms that are familiar in English usage (e.g., caliph, Islam) and those that describe political or religious factions (e.g., Sunnī, ʿUthmānī). Academic disciplines will be capitalised (e.g., Classics, History). Unless otherwise indicated, translations are my own. Longer quotes from al-Ṭabarī's *Taʾrīkh* usually follow the renderings given by the various translators of the SUNY series in Near Eastern Studies, with moderate alterations. They are provided in the format 'Al-Ṭabarī, *Taʾrīkh*, II, 18; Morony, *Muʿāwiyah*, 22'. Both the Islamic (H) and the Gregorian (CE) calendar are ordinarily used when introducing events. When only Common Era dating is used, the 'CE' will not appear (i.e. '35–40 H/656–61 CE' or '42 H', but '656' or 'ninth century').

Abbreviations

AHR	*American Historical Review*
AIUON	*Annali dell'Istituto Universitario Orientale di Napoli*
ASIA	*Asiatische Studien*
ASQ	*Arab Studies Quarterly*
BRIIFS	*Bulletin of the Royal Institute for Inter-Faith Studies*
BRISMES	*Bulletin (British Society for Middle Eastern Studies)*
BSOAS	*Bulletin of the School of Oriental and African Studies*
DMES	*Digest of Middle East Studies*
EI^2	*Encyclopaedia of Islam, Second Edition*
EI^3	*Encyclopaedia of Islam, Three*
GAL	C. Brockelmann, *Geschichte der arabischen Litteratur*
GAS	F. Sezgin, *Geschichte des arabischen Schrifttums*
ICMR	*Islam and Christian-Muslim Relations*
IJMES	*International Journal of Middle East Studies*
IOS	*Israel Oriental Studies*
ISL	*Der Islam*
JAAR	*Journal of the American Academy of Religion*
JAIS	*Journal of Arabic and Islamic Studies*
JAL	*Journal of Arabic Literature*
JAOS	*Journal of the American Oriental Society*
JESHO	*Journal of the Economic and Social History of the Orient*
JIMS	*Journal of Islamic and Muslim Studies*
JIS	*Journal of Islamic Studies*
JNES	*Journal of Near Eastern Studies*
JQS	*Journal of Qur'anic Studies*
JRAS	*Journal of the Royal Asiatic Society*
JSAI	*Jerusalem Studies in Arabic and Islam*
Lane	Edward W. Lane, *An Arabic-English Lexicon*
MW	*Muslim World*
Occhialì	*Rivista sul Mediterraneo Islamico*
ONS	*Oriental Numismatic Society Newsletter*

REMMM	*Revue des mondes musulmans et de la Méditerranée*
RSO	*Rivista degli studi orientali*
SI	*Studia Islamica*
StIr	*Studia Iranica*
StOrE	*Studia Orientalia Electronica*
ʿUW	*al-ʿUṣūr al-Wusṭā*
WO	*Die Welt des Orients*
ZAL	*Zeitschrift für Arabische Linguistik*
ZDMG	*Zeitschrift der Deutschen Morgenländischen Gesellschaft*

Acknowledgements

It takes a village to write a book. I am accordingly indebted to a great many people for their support, both during the four years of writing the PhD dissertation that this book is based on and during the months of intense revision leading to the present monograph. Going in chronological order, I want to start by expressing my gratitude to the Edinburgh friends and colleagues who accompanied the original PhD project from its inception in 2011 to the viva in early 2015. First and foremost, I am deeply grateful to Andrew Marsham, who supervised my PhD and offered unfailing guidance in all matters academic, giving generously of his time and advice. My heartfelt thanks also go to Andreas Görke, who acted as second supervisor: I have benefitted greatly from his expertise and friendship. My PhD colleague Faisal al-Wazzan provided invaluable assistance during the frustrating undertaking of making sense of the poetry contained in the less than reliable edition of Ibn Aʿtham's *Kitāb al-Futūḥ* available to me. My fellow PhD students and wonderful friends Lina Aylott, Jehan al-Azzawi and Emily Goetsch were then and remain to this day a great source of support and comfort, patiently nudging me along and happily commiserating whenever the mood struck (or indeed strikes). My former office-mates Yousef, Lizzie and Charlie created the most intellectually stimulating and companionable workspace anyone could hope for. Last but most definitely not least among my academic debts, my eternal gratitude to the Centre for the Advanced Study of the Arab World (CASAW) for providing the three-year scholarship without which I would not have been able to pursue my PhD.

Returning to the thesis after five years of leaving it to languish was not an easy undertaking. I have been encouraged and sustained along the way by a great number of people who offered advice, read and commented on parts of the revised manuscript, counteracted library closures with an endless supply of literature and over the years allowed me to challenge and refine my ideas about Khārijism. My wonderful friend and colleague Stefanie Brinkmann patiently worked her way through some truly verbose and over-annotated writing to offer her signature sound advice, encouragement, sense of humour and much-needed suggestions for simplified prose. I am also very grateful to Adam Gaiser for his insightful comments on my work, for providing a sounding board (hard to come by in the tiny field of Khārijism Studies!) and for generously sharing his research – where we disagree, I have always found myself benefiting from his ideas and challenges to my own approach. Complacency is poisonous, after all! My thanks also go to my fellow tea devotee Antonia Bosanquet for discussing issues of authorship with me. My Edinburgh (and now Taipei) friend and colleague Su I-Wen, in her usual sharp-witted fashion, likewise helped me make (more) sense of pre-modern authorship and generously shared her then unpublished work with me. When libraries closed in March 2020, I was in the midst of reworking the manuscript – I cannot express enough how grateful I am to May Shaddel, ever-generous, for sending me what probably amounts to half his private library.

When I moved back to Hamburg in 2014, it was to take up a position as research associate with Stefan Heidemann's ERC project 'The Early Islamic Empire at Work'. Working alongside the fantastic team put together by Stefan (Peter Verkinderen, Simon Gundelfinger, José Haro Peralta, Antonia Bosanquet, Katharina Mewes and Ahmad Khan) made me a much better academic and led to some wonderful friendships. Gratitude is due to my colleague Natalie Kontny-Wendt as well, for offering advice and encouragement, but primarily for being a brilliant friend.

Over the years, I have had opportunity to discuss various aspects of my work with many a colleague. In addition to those already mentioned, I would like to thank Teresa Bernheimer, Majied Robinson, Ryan Lynch, Carole Hillenbrand and Jürgen Paul for providing feedback, exchanging ideas and otherwise inspiring my work. I am also very grateful to Carole for including my book in EUP's Edinburgh Studies in Classical Islamic History and Culture series, and I would like to extend my thanks as well to the anonymous reader for their insightful comments. All remaining errors of fact or interpretation are most certainly my own.

Above all, I owe my greatest debt of gratitude to my wonderful mother. Her strength (and multi-tasking skills) as a single working mum will always be an inspiration to me.

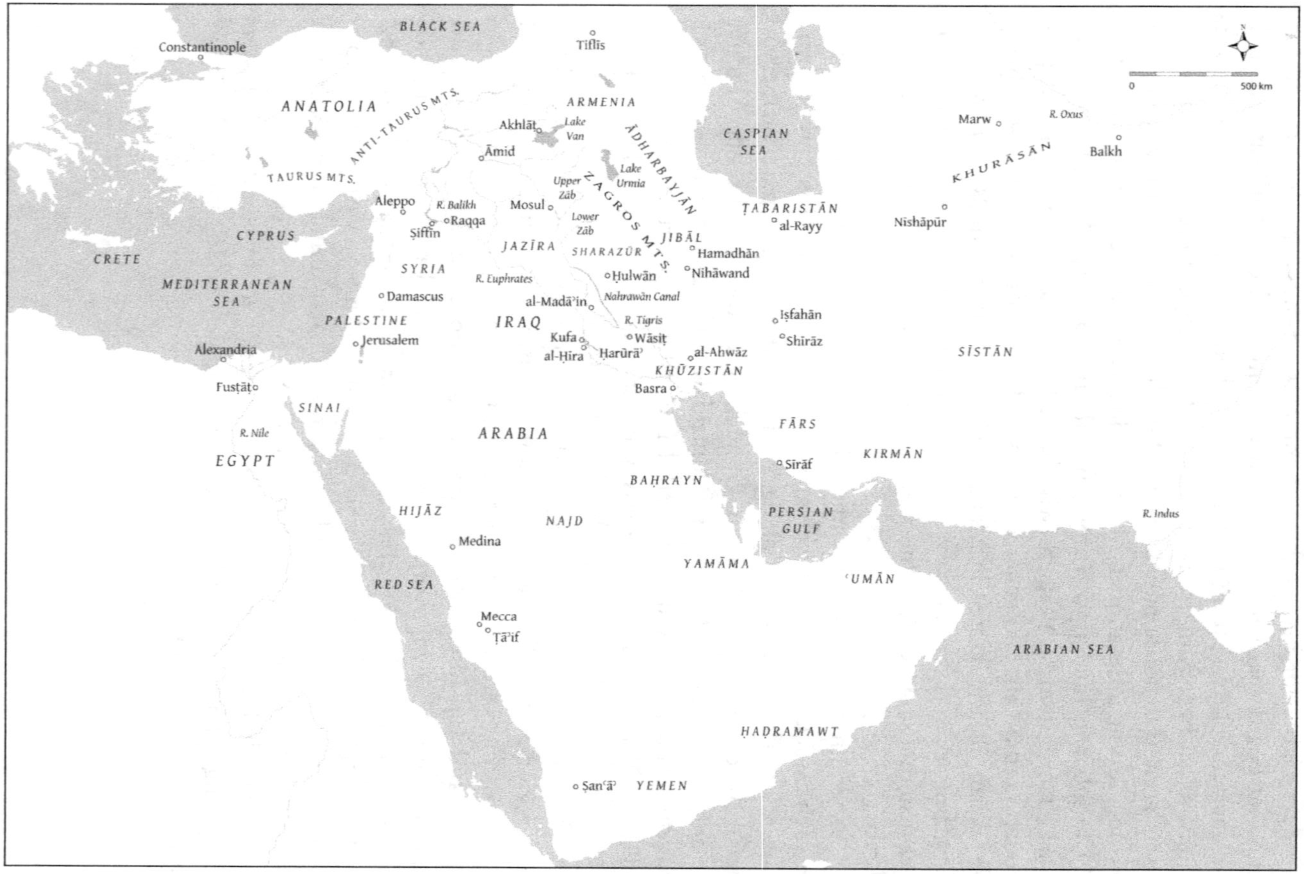

The Near East in the Umayyad Period

PART I

PRELIMINARIES

Introduction

The Khārijites (in Arabic al-Khawārij) are regarded in the Islamic tradition as the first schismatics to appear within the Muslim community. Their origin is commonly located in the first civil war (*fitna*; 35–40 H/656–61 CE), specifically in the Battle of Ṣiffīn (37 H/657 CE), following which they repudiated both parties to the conflict and subsequently engaged in countless revolts against the caliph ʿAlī b. Abī Ṭālib, the Umayyads and then later the ʿAbbāsids. Early Islamic literature abounds with reports of the uncompromising piety and unparalleled violence of the Khawārij, a volatile combination that seems to have led to the obliteration of most Khārijite groups before the end of the ninth century. Their particular brand of militantly pious opposition was encompassed in the watchword *lā ḥukma illā li-llāh* ('judgement is God's alone') and left a lasting impression on early Islamic history as it was remembered over time. It is not a surprise that the Khawārij continue to both fascinate and horrify modern-day Muslims and historians alike: the label '(neo-)Khārijite' has become a common appellation for (and thus a useful tool against) groups such as Daesh, Boko Haram, al-Qa'ida or the Muslim Brotherhood as well as inconvenient political opponents.[1]

The study of Khārijite history and thought is, however, fraught with fundamental difficulties. For instance, scholars have long recognised that Muslim heresiographers, who provide the bulk of information on the tenets of the Khawārij, had a more schematic than historical interest in the factions they described, Khārijite or otherwise. The arbitrary creation of 'heretical' groups and the equally indiscriminate attribution of doctrines to one party or another constitute only the most basic problems associated with the study of Islamic heresiography.[2] Early Islamic historiography, on the other hand, offers much contradictory information concerning the sequence and exact dates of events or the identities of the participants. Moreover, these sources are so riddled with literary *topoi* and rhetorical devices that since the 'sceptic turn' in the 1970s and 1980s, the reliability of the early Islamic tradition as a whole has been called into question.[3]

These challenges are not peculiar to the study of Khārijism, of course. But the problem is particularly pronounced because little research has been carried out on the Khawārij to date. The scholarship that does exist is sometimes sharply divided over how best to understand their origins and motivations[4] – some historians follow the classical Islamic sources, while others reject the traditional story of Khārijism largely or wholly in favour of offering their own interpretations of the background and intentions of the early Khārijites.[5] Unlike studies of many other episodes in the history of early Islam, however, scholarship on Khārijism has so far not systematically approached the sources as *texts* that are subject to the rhetorical embellishment and narrative strategies so important to understanding the formation of early Islamic historical memory: for the most part, research on Khārijism remains dedicated to (re) constructing history.

Over the past few decades, some research has been undertaken on the place and representation of Khārijites in Islamic heresiography and *adab*.[6] Less attention has been paid to how the early historical tradition approaches Khārijism. This goes particularly for those works that, unlike al-Ṭabarī's *Ta'rīkh* or al-Balādhurī's *Ansāb al-Ashrāf*, are not part of the standard Islamicist canon. Considered more 'sober' than heresiography, poetry or *adab*, historiographical works are usually mined for hard facts of Khārijite history and (less so) doctrine.

In contradistinction to this tendency, the present study will offer an analysis of the portrayal of Khārijite origins that asks about the narrative role and function of Khārijism in early Islamic historical writing. The focus is thus on 'literary' rather than 'historical' Khārijism. The analysis is based on a representative selection of historiographical sources from the early period of Islam, that is, works that were compiled during the second to fourth centuries H/eighth to tenth centuries CE. In taking this approach, the book pursues two goals: first and foremost, it seeks to fill a gap in the study of Khārijism and argue for the need to approach the subject from different perspectives that will take fuller account of this phenomenon in its contemporary settings. Narrative analysis, it is hoped, will serve here as a precursor to a new historical analysis. Second, such an investigation will further our understanding of early Islamic historiography and tell us something about the concerns and interpretative frameworks of individual historians as well.[7]

For the purpose of this study, 'Khārijite origins' refers to the period from the Battle of Ṣiffīn until the death of the second Marwānid caliph ʿAbd al-Malik (d. 86 H/705 CE). This time span is divided into three parts: the rule of ʿAlī from Ṣiffīn until his assassination (by a Khārijite) in 40 H/661 CE; the subsequent reign of Muʿāwiya b. Abī Sufyān (r. 41–60 H/661–80 CE); and, finally, the era of the second civil war (60–73 H/680–92 CE) and the reign of ʿAbd al-Malik (c. 73–86 H/c. 692–705 CE).[8]

By 'narrative analysis', I do not mean a narratological or poetic study of these sources – while of course a valuable and indeed a necessary endeavour, my interest here is in content over form.[9] Elements of narratological analysis such as emplotment, placement strategies or narrative conventions will feature throughout this study, but recourse to literary or narrative theory is not my concern. Instead, I will focus on identifying (some of) the themes and concerns emerging from our sources' depictions of Khārijism when we read these accounts not as 'hard facts' but as contributions to a discourse on the correct interpretation and remembrance of the early Islamic past, and thus as lines of argument. I am fully aware that this kind of excavation work is highly subjective, shaped by my own intellectual formation and so informed by distinct underlying assumptions about the meanings, purposes and processes of history-writing. This is always the case in reading, writing and interpreting history, however, even if it often goes unacknowledged in the construction of grand historical master narratives. We will return to this issue in Chapter One.

My approach to early Islamic historiography is based on an understanding of historical writing as the casting of past events in a manner that highlights their relevance for contemporary affairs, and thus as having a decidedly discursive function. Najam Haider has recently argued for the influence of a particular form of late antique history-writing on early Islamic historiography that is concerned with "narrative logic, credibility devices, and emotive persuasion".[10] These elements indeed characterise the early historical tradition rather well and we will come across them at various points in the present book. Chapter One will look in more detail at the challenges of Islamic historiography, the question of historiography as literature and the importance of studying Khārijism from a literary perspective. For now, the premise of this book as the point of departure for what follows is that

> these [early Muslim] historians employed literary devices and stylistic elaborations that both made a story more edifying and conveyed some type of moral lesson. At the same time, they wove stories into interpretive frameworks that inscribed meaning onto an event or biography. This suggests that the literary characteristics of the material . . . were only one component of a larger historical project mainly centered on interpretation.[11]

Over the course of this study, I will argue two main points: first, that there is little narrative substance[12] to the Khawārij as they are presented in the sources and that their identity is both static and largely collective. This effect is created by a range of techniques that will be examined over the subsequent chapters, among them the 'silencing' of Khārijite actors by denying them an equal (or sometimes any) share in discourse, almost always granting their opponents the last word and having them express themselves in the same terms over and over again with little sense of development or individuality. Khārijism thus often appears as a collection of stock phrases without any real connection to specific historical circumstances.

This leads us to the second point: early Islamic historiography approaches Khārijism not necessarily as an end in itself, but as a narrative tool with which to illustrate and discuss other issues. The accounts may have a historical core, but they have been shaped and reshaped to reflect contemporary concerns. This is a common and expected function of history-writing, part and parcel of the "larger historical project mainly centered on interpretation".[13] Combined, these two points emphasise the pitfalls inherent in even a critically positivist approach to Khārijite (and much early Islamic) history: what 'the' Khārijites' 'real' intentions were and what they hoped to achieve 'in actuality' is very difficult to extract from a standardised and thus dehistoricised portrayal. This is not to say that we should abandon history as a positivist discipline altogether, of course, but research of that kind needs to recognise and acknowledge these challenges before attempting to unearth what historical Khārijism was really all about.

The remainder of the Introduction will establish the basic framework for the analysis to follow. It will review the scholarly literature on early Khārijism as a point of departure for the approach adopted here and then outline the basic premises underlying the book's take on pre-modern Islamic historiography. It will conclude with a brief summary of the book's structure and main findings. The remaining two sections of Part I will briefly comment on the source selection as well as the tricky questions of genre and authorship, and then provide an historical overview of the events referenced in the narratives we will come to discuss.

The Study of Khārijism

Let us turn to scholarly interpretations of how Khārijism came to be. Over the past 130 years or so, a broad range of theories regarding Khārijite origins and intentions have been advanced. Despite this interest in the rise and development of Khārijism, Western scholarship has remained limited. Published monographs are in the single digits; two of these are over a century old,[14] another two are dedicated to the modern perception of Khārijism and its perceived relation to militant Islamist movements.[15] The remaining works are several decades old as well; some of them tend to be descriptive rather than analytical and are based rather uncritically on the Islamic tradition.[16] There are also a handful of MA and PhD dissertations that deal with Khārijism, mostly with Khārijite poetry and oratory or the treatment of Khārijism in Islamic heresiography. With one exception, these remain unpublished.[17] The articles and book chapters that have been published on the Khārijites mostly follow the same tendency of addressing either Khārijite poetry[18] or heresiographical concerns,[19] with only a few focusing on other matters such as Khārijite coinage.[20]

The study of Ibāḍism, a moderate offshoot of Khārijism, is a whole other matter. Due to the considerable success in Oman and North Africa of the group itself as well as the survival of archives of Ibāḍī literature, there is now an increasing interest in the past and present of Ibāḍī communities.[21] Engagement with hitherto unstudied works of Ibāḍī scholarship promises fresh insights into – or at least different perspectives on – the history and development of Islam and thus constitutes an enticing incentive for Islamicists to explore Ibāḍism.[22] Increasing access to Ibāḍī source material also offers some more unconventional takes on early Khārijism. Ibāḍī communities throughout history have had a complex and often problematic relationship with the Khawārij, and modern Ibāḍī intellectuals in particular tend to deny more than a passing acquaintance with the Khārijites of early Islamic history.[23] Some Islamicists – chief among them Adam Gaiser – have nevertheless studied not just the Ibāḍī depiction of and attitude to Khārijism, but have also illuminated the ways in which (mostly pre-modern) Ibāḍī scholarship utilised and adapted narratives of Khārijite rebels and martyrs in the course of their own processes of identity formation.[24] Such analyses tell us much about Ibāḍism, but rather little about historical Khārijism.

The quality and quantity of Ibāḍī material are unfortunately not matched in the material available for the study of Khārijite history. The only allegedly Khārijite sources that have come down to us consist of poems and speeches attributed to them in the works of Muslim scholars unsympathetic to their cause. This explains both the preoccupation with Khārijite poetry and oratory and the perseverance of positivist approaches to Khārijism. The problem is two-fold: because poetry is the only genuinely Khārijite material we (appear to) have, scholars tend to focus on it disproportionately; and as we want to make statements about the historical Khawārij, the material needs to be considered authentic in the first place. Among other issues, this sometimes results in methodological inconsistency. In an article on Khārijite poetry, for example, Donner laments the late, fragmentary and biased source base for early Islamic history, but argues in the next paragraph that Khārijite poetry "may have been subjected at least to a different kind of editing than those accounts transmitted within the "orthodox" or "Sunni" community" because of "the fact that the poetry of the early Khārijites was (initially, at least) circulated and preserved especially among the Khārijites themselves".[25] How he knows this for a "fact" remains unclear, particularly because Khārijite poetry is preserved in much the same sources as the "orthodox" or "Sunni" accounts he contrasts it with.[26]

This approach is not unusual. Islamicists and Muslim scholars happily revisit the same narratives of Khārijism and employ the same, often contradictory, methods and approaches in the quest for Khārijism 'as it really was'. Interestingly, they often arrive at radically different interpretations. One reason for this disparity of opinion is that there is no consensus on precisely why the Khārijites protested against the arbitration and what was meant by 'judgement is God's alone'.[27] Many studies of Khārijism tend to follow the (later) Islamic tradition, which views Khārijism as an expression of religious zealotry turned into rebellion and heresy. Van Ess, for example, has argued that the Khārijites

> considered themselves the only true Muslims . . . [Their] schism resulted from the claim to exclusive sanctity. Hence, the Khārijites abhorred intermarriage with non-Khārijite Muslims. They also battled their coreligionists everywhere they could. They believed they were dealing not with Muslims of lesser quality but quite simply with unbelievers . . . As a result, not only were they convinced that all other Muslims would go to hell, but they even felt justified in conducting a jihad against them.[28]

Along the same lines, Watt declared one particular Khārijite faction "a body of rebels and terrorists",[29] and Foss suggested that "[b]y this time [689–99], terrorism had made the Khārijites deeply unpopular with mainstream Islam".[30] Morony summarised them as follows:

> "They were militant, fundamentalist, self-righteous, homicidal, and suicidal; they were likely to raise the *taḥkīm* (Ar.) in a crowded *masjid* and be instantly torn to pieces by the panicked crowd.[31]

Others have taken a different, sometimes more nuanced, approach to the question of Khārijite origins. Donner, in his *Narratives of Islamic Origins*, for instance, acknowledges the tendentious nature of the Islamic tradition, which has done much to establish the heretical nature of Khārijism:

> The tendency to view the Khawārij as a "sect" and to emphasize doctrinal issues that eventually led them to be considered "unorthodox" has sometimes obscured the fact that their motivation – which was to establish communities of truly pure Believers – appears to be an exact continuation of the original mission of Muhammad.[32]

This statement acknowledges the difficulties in basing our understanding of early Khārijism on Islamic heresiography. At the same time, however, it is also a good example of the desire to discover 'what really happened' to cause the Khawārij to break so violently with their coreligionists. The following overview illustrates the range of theories of Khārijite origins scholars have advanced, which will serve to position my own approach to the question more clearly.[33]

We can discern broadly three strands in scholarly approaches to the early Khawārij. One focuses on a tribal, sometimes nomadic framework for the emergence of Khārijism that is considered irreconcilable with the demands of a centralising polity.[34] The second regards excessive piety, based perhaps on expectations of the imminent end of the world, as the motivating factor behind Khārijite protest and rebellions.[35] Despite their differences, both of these interpretative frameworks sometimes include arguments to the effect that Khārijism was ultimately an expression of anarchism.[36] The third strand emphasises pragmatic, 'rational' interests such as economic or political status. The various interpretations of Khārijism often combine elements from different frameworks,[37] though a primary strand can usually be determined. The following survey exemplifies the range of opinions; virtually all other studies that engage with the question of how Khārijism came to be can be located somewhere along this spectrum. The overview will proceed chronologically rather than thematically in order to trace the development of scholarly theories on the subject, which in their overall transition from largely faithful retellings of the sources to sceptical and occasionally radical reinterpretations we can also read as a reflection on the development of the field of early Islamic Studies more generally.[38]

The first academic study of Khārijism was the doctoral thesis of Rudolf Ernst Brünnow, a scholar of Semitic philology, which was published in 1884 under the title *Die Charidschiten unter den ersten Omayyaden*. He argued that the parties who emerged from the first *fitna* – the "orthodox faction", the Shīʿa and the Khawārij – were at that point political factions. Religious developments only occurred at a later stage. The Khārijites, according to Brünnow, were former Bedouins who were "by nature" opposed to the rule of townspeople.[39] They were veterans of the conquest of Iran who had settled in Basra and Kufa, but nevertheless clung to their Bedouin roots. While the *qurrāʾ* – reciters of the Qurʾān or perhaps more generally those 'knowledegable in religion' – were an important faction among the first Khārijites, Brünnow argued that the most significant group comprised the veterans, who elected one of their own as caliph after ʿAlī had lost their respect at Ṣiffīn. As they had shown no particular loyalty to ʿAlī even before his opponents' call for arbitration, they had no qualms about leaving him. For all that, Brünnow also argued that the Khārijite protest at Ṣiffīn was based on religious reasons: judgement should not be left to mere mortals but was God's domain only.[40] Brünnow did not comment further on this apparent two-fold nature of these earliest Khawārij, or on how to reconcile the distinction between political and religious motivations made elsewhere in his study. His final assessment of Khārijite origins thus remains uncertain.

In 1901, Julius Wellhausen published *Die religiös-politischen Oppositionsparteien im alten Islam*, in which he arrived at a slightly different conclusion regarding the nature of Khārijism. According to him, the Khārijites originated in the *qurrāʾ*, whom he understood to be reciters of the Qurʾān and hence particularly pious scholars. Wellhausen concluded that their protest at Ṣiffīn was exclusively based on religious reservations. Like Brünnow, he detected a political dimension to their actions, but this dimension was dominated by religious objections, which eventually led to a break with the community:

> In diesem Widerspruch zwischen Din und Gamâa, zwischen der Pflicht, Gott und das Recht über Alles zu stellen, und der Pflicht, bei der Gemeinschaft zu bleiben und dem Imâm zu gehorchen, treten die Chavârig entschlossen auf die Seite des Din.[41]

These two studies remained the only detailed scholarly engagements with the Khārijites until, 70 years after the publication of Wellhausen's *Oppositionsparteien*, M. A. Shaban published his 'new interpretation' of Islamic History in 1971.[42] His portrayal of the Khawārij is radically different. Throughout his work, Shaban calls for the rational, logical interests of the Arab Muslims to be taken into account. He identifies the predecessors of the Khārijites as those tribesmen who had been loyal to the Islamic polity during the *ridda* wars that ensued after Muḥammad's death and thus occupied a privileged socio-economic position under ʿUmar I as governors of the fertile *sawād* lands of the former Sasanian Empire. With the accession of ʿUthmān they lost this position and, in their anger, joined the groups of malcontents that eventually murdered the caliph. These (proto-)Khawārij first supported ʿAlī because they hoped he would reinstate their former privileges, but in the wake of his agreement to the arbitration these hopes were disappointed and they separated from him.[43] The motives behind the Khārijite protest before, at and after Ṣiffīn are hence presented as purely socio-economic.[44]

In his assessment of Khārijism, Shaban raised two issues that had not been seriously considered before: first, that the Khawārij may not have come into being in the context of the battle and arbitration agreement of Ṣiffīn;

and second, that the factors which motivated Khārijite protest were not at all religious in nature.

Similar ideas were expressed in an article that was published in the same year but independently from Shaban. Martin Hinds' "Kufan Political Alignments and Their Background in the Mid-Seventh Century AD" (1971) contends that the predecessors of the Khārijites were early converts to Islam who lost their privileged position during the caliphate of ʿUthmān. Unlike Shaban, however, Hinds argued that this privileged position was based on *sharaf* ('honour, dignity, eminence'), which in the Islamic system was earned through early conversion (*sābiqa*; 'priority, preference') and participation in the *ridda* and *futūḥ* expeditions rather than membership in a prominent tribe. This last aspect was particularly important to the Khārijites-to-be, who mainly belonged to tribal splinter groups and whose social standing hence depended on *sābiqa*.[45] They opposed ʿUthmān's reforms and later the arbitration at Ṣiffīn not because of religious zealotry, but because they associated the undivided authority of the Qurʾān with the rule of ʿUmar, under whom they had been favoured and whose example they expected ʿAlī to follow. In other words, political and economic grievances were expressed in religious language without necessitating a purely religious motive for discontent.

W. Montgomery Watt offered yet another explanation of Khārijism in his 1973 work *The Formative Period of Islamic Thought*. Like Brünnow, he opined that the Khawārij had originated in a nomadic milieu and attempted to recreate the tribal structures of ancient Arabian Bedouin society on an Islamic basis: Khārijite groups were small in number, outsiders were regarded as enemies and basic equality prevailed among the group members. Watt interpreted the fact that Khārijite revolts continued after ʿAlī's death as confirmation that the Khawārij were in fact opposed to the whole system of rule and government established by the Islamic proto-state, which to him supported his thesis of nomadic origins. Unlike the pre-Islamic Arabian Bedouin, he argued, Khārijite communities were based on Islamic precepts – only the most pious man was eligible for leadership – and in Watt's opinion, their insistence that the caliphate should rest on the same precepts was an important Khārijite contribution to Islamic doctrine.[46]

Yet another, somewhat different approach to the question of Khārijite origins was advanced in Gerald Hawting's 1978 article on "The Significance of the Slogan "Lā ḥukma illā li-llāh" and the References to the "Ḥudūd" in the Traditions about the Fitna and the Murder of ʿUthmān". Hawting suggested that a better understanding of terms and slogans such as *lā ḥukma* could be achieved through drawing parallels between the events of the first civil war among the Muslims and similar conflicts in Jewish communities.

As he pointed out, certain contemporary Jewish groups had accused others of allowing human beings to partake in God's divine legislation through the use of Oral Law (i.e. human interpretation of divine provisions and the use of legislative sources other than Scripture), which for them equalled idolatry. Hawting thus concluded that the first *fitna* was essentially a clash over the authority of Scripture (here, the Qur'ān) in relation to Oral Law (here, the appointment of arbiters and their use of *sunna*). The Khārijite *lā ḥukma* slogan, he suggested, may have been influenced by these parallel inner-Jewish conflicts, concluding that "there are grounds, then, for thinking that the *lā ḥukma* slogan is a summary of the scripturalist position and a protest against the Oral Law rather than a reaction to the arbitration agreement made at Ṣiffīn".[47] Hawting's article was published a year after Crone and Cook's *Hagarism*, one of the first and to this day most radical engagements with Islamic history through the lens of non-Muslim and especially Jewish sources. The authors were among the earliest and most prominent representatives of the so-called sceptical approach to early Islam that flourished from the 1970s to the early 1990s in particular.[48] Hawting's take on the Khawārij can be read within this context, as can much of his later work.[49]

A focus on religious factors is also observable in Fred Donner's 1997 article on "Piety and Eschatology in Early Khārijite Poetry". His analysis turns on poetry attributed to Khārijite rebels before the year 65 H/685 CE. Based on his understanding of these poems, he concluded that the rebels were extremely pious believers who expressed their religious devotion "in an activist, indeed militant, way" and in this followed the Qur'ānic understanding of godliness.[50] This led him to suggest "that the early Khārijites may represent the real "true Believers" of the early community, that is, the truest guardians of the values enshrined in the Qur'ān".[51] According to Donner, Khārijite piety was rooted in the imminent expectation of the eschaton. This *Naherwartung* caused their reckless and violent behaviour: they courted death in this world in order to escape God's wrath in the next. While Donner acknowledged that Khārijite poetry did not actually mention the End Times specifically, he posited that the Khawārij may have considered contemporary events such as the *ridda* wars and the early conquests as evidence that the end of days was already upon them. Consequently, "it was urgently important for them to make whatever sacrifices were required in the furtherance of the goal of spreading the hegemony of the righteous community of Believers".[52] Political, economic or social concerns were thus of no consequence to the Khārijites, whose sights were firmly set on the Hereafter.[53]

Chase Robinson came to yet another conclusion about the nature of Khārijism in his *Empire and Elites after the Muslim Conquest*, which was published in 2000. Referring to Hobsbawm's concepts of social banditry and rebellion,[54] Robinson identified the Khārijites of the Jazīra (Northern Mesopotamia) as tribesmen opposed to the rule of the Islamic state and Khārijism as "the Islamic form of that politicised and revolutionary edge of social action towards which banditry, given the appropriate conditions, can move".[55] In this, his argument resembled that of Watt and Brünnow, although Robinson discussed tribesmen in general, who do not necessarily have to be Bedouins. Unlike them, however, he maintained that Khārijism probably did not originate in the events of the first civil war: a monolithic group of Muslims from whom the Khawārij then separated is unlikely to have existed at this early stage; for the same reason, he considers the date around which the Khārijites are said to have divided into distinct subgroups (c. 684) to be too early. He claimed that the Khārijite rebels in the Jazīra had a political programme (which he does not describe; nor does he outline his understanding of 'programme' in this context)[56] and thus could only be explained in the more politicised Marwānid period: for the Jazīra at least, Robinson contended that no Khārijites should be expected prior to the caliphate of ʿAbd al-Malik, as there were no state structures in the region to rebel against.[57]

Finally, Donner's ideas about the significance of eschatology for early Khārijism were explicitly taken up and adapted by Paul Heck in his "Eschatological Scripturalism and the End of Community: The Case of Early Kharijism" (2005). He combined these ideas with Hawting's arguments about Oral Law vs. Scripture, but Heck's overall assessment of early Khārijism remains somewhat unclear and contradictory. His main argument is that "Khārijite eschatology, twinned to their own shame at being in the world and on its margins . . . offered a framework wherein such shame could be transformed into both hatred and despair of this world as foreign to the reign of God",[58] but this not explained further in any detail (for example, why were they ashamed in the first place?). He also seems to offer several different explanations for who the early Khārijites were: "a band of marauders";[59] proponents of the principle that "the community was bound together by scripture, the Qurʾan being its effective and exclusive leader (*imām*)";[60] and "a coalescence of tribal elements and an intensely qurʾano-centric piety attributable in large part to the *qurrāʾ*".[61] It was apparently "proto-Khārijite tendencies" that led to the murder of ʿUthmān, who had been accused of "having introduced innovations into the divinely sanctioned system of distributing the proceeds of conquest".[62] Essentially, Heck's article presents an amalgamation of previous interpretations of and different interpretative frameworks for Khārijite origins, but the mixture does not work all that well and leaves the reader wondering about his precise understanding of early Khārijism.

Research Approach and Sources

The many different interpretations of early Khārijite history reveal the lack of a simple (or single) satisfactory answer – the origins of the Khawārij are certainly not "clear in the main".[63] Despite the diversity concerning approach, use of sources and ultimate conclusions, however, the above explanations have three things in common: they all work reasonably well within their own frame of reference, i.e. taken on their own they all sound plausible to a greater or lesser extent;[64] they are all based on some form of source or tradition criticism which is then applied to a particular selection from the immense corpus of available source material; and they are all of a positivist bent in that they attempt to unearth the 'true' story of how Khārijism emerged.[65]

The first of these characteristics can only be achieved by sidelining evidence that does not accord with one's frame of reference to avoid contradictions. If, for instance, the Khārijites were focused primarily on the Hereafter and had no interest in territorial gains,[66] how do we explain the coins minted by the historical figure Qaṭarī b. al-Fujāʾa, who is associated in the sources with the most violent and most puritanical of Khārijite factions? The coins make a clear claim to worldly rule not just in declaring an intention to stay in and govern a region, but also in calling him *amīr al-muʾminīn*, which is the caliphal title. The Persian legends are clearly directed at the local population in telling the elites, at least, about the change in power.[67]

This last point is paradigmatic. Much scholarship on early Islamic history still remains largely faithful to the sources, in part certainly because dismissing what they have to say would have some rather irksome consequences for the writing of said history.[68] This is particularly true for comprehensive surveys and textbooks of Islamic history.[69] But dismissal is not the only alternative; in fact, it is no real alternative at all.[70] Moreover, acknowledging the literary nature of (Islamic) historiography does not diminish its usefulness as a source. It has been argued that historical events do not have intrinsic meanings in the way literary texts do, that it is the historian (modern or pre-modern) who endows them with a particular meaning by casting them in one literary mould or another.[71] This approach turns history-writing into "essentially a literary, that is to say fiction-making, operation", true, but this "in no way detracts from the status of historical narratives as providing a kind of knowledge".[72] On the contrary: "If we view history as a literary composition, as a textual construction rather than a reconstruction, we are not limiting history but emancipating it".[73] In order to achieve this, we have to dispense with the notion that historiography can provide scientific knowledge in the same way as that attained by the study of the natural sciences,[74] which is based on a modern understanding of History as an objective discipline belonging to the realm of science rather than the arts.[75] But "there is no such thing as pure fiction and no such thing as history so rigorous that it abjures the techniques of fiction".[76] Many Islamicists remain sceptical regarding this despite much criticism of the Islamic Tradition: "Virtually to a man and woman, we [historians of Islam] are all unreconstructed positivists, determined to reconstruct texts or the reality we take them to reflect."[77] Ultimately, then, both the faithful and the critical approach "share a common ground in their attempt to differentiate between fact and fiction".[78]

In addressing issues of textual representation, the present book departs from the works discussed in the preceding literature review: it has no aspirations as to the provision of yet another interpretation of what Khārijism was, or where and why it began. Of interest here is not the plausibility of one particular interpretation or the differentiation between 'factual' and 'fictional' accounts of Khārijism. As this study focuses on the narrative role and functions of the Khawārij in the early Islamic historical tradition, it will set aside positivist concerns.

This approach allows us to circumvent the problems posed by the pursuit of factual history and to look at the historiographical tradition more fully rather than only focusing on those individual author-compilers that appear to provide a more plausible picture of Khārijite history. This way we will arrive at a more profound and more fully developed grasp of what Khārijism came to signify, how the Khawārij were remembered and how (if at all) this memory was contested in the sources. This improved understanding of how the Khārijite legacy was construed will in turn serve as the foundation for a more sophisticated approach to historical Khārijism that pays as close attention to *how* something is being said as it does to *what* is being said. And finally, the juxtaposition of divergent accounts of Khārijism in the sources also sheds light on the debates regarding the history of the Muslim community more generally and on the process in which the past was negotiated and reformulated.

The book is divided into four parts. Part I introduces the subject and sets up the parameters of the study to follow. Part II (Chapters 1–3) is concerned with early Islamic historiography more generally, makes the case for a literary approach to Khārijite history and elucidates the core themes emerging from the portrayal of Khārijism in the selected sources. Part III (Chapters 4–6) analyses the narratives of Khārijite origins pertaining to specific periods and teases out motifs and concerns particular to the individual eras. Part IV then returns to the sources and asks what the analysis can tell us about the early historical tradition, particularly about issues like the distinction between proto-Sunnī and proto-Shīʿī works.

Chapter One gives an introductory overview of the challenges inherent in both the 'genre' and the research field of early Islamic historiography. It addresses methods of and approaches to historical writing prominent in other disciplines that may prove useful for improving Islamicist approaches to our source material. The main part of the chapter reviews some of the literature that has highlighted the rhetorical features of the early Islamic (historical) tradition and then argues for the application of similar methods to Khārijite history.

Chapter Two discusses the core themes and *topoi* in the depiction of Khārijism that recur over the entire time period under study, i.e. from Ṣiffīn until ʿAbd al-Malik's death. These themes include the motifs of Khārijite piety, longing for *jihād* and the resulting excessive violence that was considered one of their trademarks. The continuous presence of these particular themes indicates their importance not only for the characterisation of Khārijism but also for the development of Islamic doctrine, which largely came to condemn the kind of militant piety exhibited by the Khawārij as they were remembered by the early Islamic tradition.

Chapter Three argues for the conspicuous absence of a palpable Khārijite identity in the selected sources, focusing primarily on two case studies: the use of Khārijite language by non-Khārijite Muslims, many of them directly opposed to the rebels; and the replication of events and narrative content associated with the Khawārij. The analysis will show that literary Khārijism is defined by a series of constantly reiterated stock phrases that are often not unique to the Khawārij, either. The replication of certain events, such as the appointment of Khārijite leaders, according to particular narrative conventions further illustrates the distinctly rhetorical character of such accounts.

Chapter Four engages with the specific themes discernible in the portrayal of Khārijism during the caliphate of ʿAlī b. Abī Ṭālib. It maintains that the relevant accounts are primarily concerned with providing an apologia for ʿAlī by providing various justifications for his agreement to the arbitration requested by Muʿāwiya at Ṣiffīn as well as for his subsequent slaughter of Khārijite opponents at Nahrawān a year later. The overwhelming interest that the sources show in this affair indicates its centrality for the formation of a consensus on the events of early Islamic history in the classical and post-classical tradition, particularly concerning the status of ʿAlī and with regard to the development of ʿAlid/Shīʿī positions over time. Connected to this is the second main theme, the relationship between ʿAlī and Ibn ʿAbbās. In his capacity as an eminent Companion, a scholar of Arabic and the Qurʾān and of course as an important ancestor of the ʿAbbāsids, Ibn ʿAbbās occupies a prominent position in the narratives of early Islam. The analysis shows that while the selected sources stress the close and cordial relationship between ʿAlī and Ibn ʿAbbās, on the whole they confirm ʿAlī's superiority.

Chapter Five looks at the narratives of Khārijism during the caliphate of Muʿāwiya. It departs from the structure of the previous chapters by focusing not on overarching themes directly, but instead on two specific works and their treatment of Khārijite history in this period. This is because there is a marked decrease in the amount of Khārijite material transmitted by the sources for this period: al-Balādhurī and al-Ṭabarī alone preserve enough narrative material – sermons, speeches, poems, letters, and the like – to allow for a meaningful analysis. This analysis reveals that while they transmit much of the same material, their interpretations are rather different. They both engage with the topic of Khārijite piety, but where al-Ṭabarī uses it to discredit militant forms of devotion, al-Balādhurī employs it as a foil for Umayyad injustice and immorality. This is a thread that weaves through their depictions of early Khārijite history more generally.

Chapter Six examines the material on the Khārijites pertaining to the second civil war and the caliphate of ʿAbd al-Malik. It returns to the structure established in Chapter Four by proceeding thematically. Five main concerns are identified, four of which permeate the majority of our sources: (1) the reputation of al-Muhallab and his family as formidable warriors and saviours of the *umma* from the menace of the most violent Khārijite faction, the Azāriqa; (2) the volatility of Khārijism as antithesis for the importance of communal togetherness; (3) criticism of the Umayyads and their agents, especially the Iraqi governor al-Ḥajjāj b. Yūsuf; and (4) Ibn al-Zubayr's interactions with the Khārijites. A fifth theme is peculiar to al-Ṭabarī, who seems to utilise accounts of Khārijite military prowess to fashion a military manual of sorts for the prudent field commander.

Chapter Seven returns to the early historical tradition. It asks what the portrayal of Khārijism in the selected sources can tell us about its formation, whether we can actually speak of an historiographical 'tradition' on Khārijism. The chapter also discusses potential differences between so-called 'proto-Sunnī' and 'proto-Shīʿī' works on the basis of their outlines of Khārijite history, concluding that it makes little sense to distinguish between them during the early period. A particular spotlight is put on Ibn Aʿtham and his *Kitāb al-Futūḥ*, whose work is quite distinct from the other examined sources.

The Conclusion will briefly revisit the book's main premises and findings. It will close with some remarks on potential future avenues of research intended to encourage renewed interest in and engagement with the Khārijites and thereby to narrow at least some of the gaps in the study of Khārijite history and thought.

Notes

1. One of the earliest pieces of research to apply the term 'neo-Khārijite' was Martin's study of ʿUthman dan Fodio, who at the turn of the nineteenth century used *jihād* to establish the so-called Sokoto Caliphate (Martin, "Unbelief"). The term has since found widespread usage and comparisons between modern militant groups and the Khārijites abound. See, for example, Kenney, *Muslim Rebels* and "Jews, Kharijites"; Timani, *Modern Intellectual Readings*, esp. chapter five; Kelsay, "Al-Qaida"; Wagemakers, " 'Seceders' and 'Postponers'?"; Ansari, "Non-Violent Social Activism"; Antúnez and Tellidis, "The Power of Words"; Cascio, "Il Kharigismo"; Lahoud, *Jihadi's Path*, esp. chapter one.
2. See, for example, Watt, "Development of the Islamic Sects", "Significance of the Sects", and "The Great Community"; Lewis, "Significance of Heresy"; Knysh, " 'Orthodoxy' and 'Heresy' ". On the Khārijites in Islamic heresiography, see, for example, Pampus, "Historische Minderheitenforschung"; Lewinstein, *Studies*; Kenney, *Heterodoxy and Culture*.
3. Robinson, *Islamic Historiography*, 50.
4. Timani, *Modern Intellectual Readings*, 1 argues that pre-modern Islamic historical writing on the Khārijites was "strictly narrative", whereas modern historiography is "interpretive". I agree with the latter, but disagree regarding the former: not only does this disregard the strong discursive element in pre-modern (Islamic) historiography, but part of the reason why modern scholarly interpretations of the origins of Khārijism diverge to such an extent (as we shall see shortly) is also precisely because the sources are so very interpretive in their depictions. They may often advance their claims in subtle ways, but that does not mean that they are limited to mere description. For more on this issue in the present book, see especially section three of Part I ('Sources, Genre, Authorship') and Chapter One, but, really, *passim*.
5. See below.
6. Lewinstein, *Studies*, and the articles based thereon ("Azāriqa", "Eastern Ḥanafite Heresiography", and "Making and Unmaking"); Kenney, *Heterodoxy and Culture*; Crone and Zimmerman, *Epistle*; Pellat, "Djāḥiẓ".
7. On an author's interpretive framework as "the superstructure for the stitching together of narrative elements", see Haider, *Rebel and Imām*, 8. The term 'historian' is anachronistic in a way because there was no such discipline or professional category in the early Islamic period – those who wrote works we categorise as history were jurists and *ḥadīth* transmitters, court secretaries, tutors or administrators, among other things. The first mention of 'historian' – *akhbārī* – is made in Ibn al-Nadīm's *Fihrist*, which dates to the very end of the tenth century and thus several decades after the death of the youngest scholar considered here, al-Masʿūdī, who was also the first to expound on methods of historical inquiry.

See Leder, "Literary Use", 314 n. 165 (for Ibn al-Nadīm); Khalidi, *Islamic Historiography*, 28 (for al-Mas'ūdī; Khalidi's study is an exploration of these methods of historical inquiry as embraced in al-Mas'ūdī's work). Nevertheless, all of these scholars were engaged in collecting and interpreting accounts of the past; their activities were thus both history-writing and history-making. With all the necessary caveats in mind, we shall therefore refer to them as historians.

8. The reign of 'Abd al-Malik is often dated to 685–705, but for much of the period from c. 684–92, 'Abdallāh b. al-Zubayr controlled (to varying degrees) most Muslim-dominated territories. It was only after Ibn al-Zubayr's defeat and death in 692 that 'Abd al-Malik managed to unite the Islamic Empire under his rule. For further details and references, see the historical overview below.
9. One example of such a narratological study of an early Islamic text is Shoshan, *Poetics*.
10. Haider, *Rebel and Imām*, 2.
11. Ibid., 3.
12. By this I mean that the contents of reports on Khārijite activities chiefly consist of structural components – dates, names, locations and such like – and particular *topoi* associated with Khārijism. The distinction between topical and non-topical material is not straightforward, of course, and topical material does not automatically signal ahistoricity or inauthenticity. The focus of this study is on literary Khārijism, however, and so it asks different questions. See Part II for a discussion of literary Khārijism and its general markers.
13. Haider, *Rebel and Imām*, 3.
14. Brünnow, *Charidschiten* and Wellhausen, *Oppositionsparteien*; the latter has a broader focus and is thus not limited to Khārijism.
15. Timani, *Modern Intellectual Readings* and Kenney, *Muslim Rebels*. See also Lahoud's 2010 book *Jihadi's Path*, which attempted to prognosticate the fate of modern jihadis on the basis of Khārijite history.
16. This applies particularly to Salem, *Political Theory*. An older, but still useful, introduction to Khārijism is Pampus, *Über die Rolle*. See also W. Thomson, "Kharijitism".
17. Kenney, "Emergence of the Khawārij" and *Heterodoxy and Culture*; Higgins, *Qur'ānic Exchange* (her PhD dissertation; a revised version under the title *Secession and Identity in Early Islam: Redefining the Khārijites and Their Challenge to the Umayyads* was listed as forthcoming by I. B. Tauris for several years, but Higgins sadly died suddenly in September 2014 and so the work will presumably remain unpublished); Bathish, *Discourse Strategies*; Lewinstein, *Studies*; Spannaus, "Azāriqa"; al-Ṣāliḥī, *Society, Beliefs and Political Theory*; Zarrou, *Les thèmes réligieux*; R. Thomson, "Khawārij"; Ahsan, "Qaṭarī b. al-Fujā'ah".
18. See, for example, Donner, "Piety and Eschatology"; Khalidi, "Poetry of the Khawārij"; al-Qāḍī, "Limitations of Qur'ānic Usage"; Gabrieli, "La poesia Ḫārigita"; Higgins, "Faces of Exchangers"; Masullo, "Laylà bint Ṭarīf's *rithā'*"; Sanagustin, "Poésie de combat".

19. In addition to the works cited at note 6, see, for example, Watt, "Wāṣil", "Significance of Khārijism" and "Khārijite Thought"; Crone, "Statement by the Najdiyya".
20. For example Gaiser, "What Do We Learn"; Sears, "Umayyad Partisan"; Foss, "The Kharijites" and "Kharijite Dirham"; Warden, "Khārijite Propaganda".
21. Ibāḍīs today make up about 1% of Muslims globally. For an introduction to the field, see Van Ess, "Ibadi Studies"; al-Sālimī, "Ibadi Studies and Orientalism"; and the four chapters in the section on "Contributions of Western Scholarship to the Reconstruction of Ibāḍī History" in Eisener, ed., *Today's Perspectives.*
22. Scholarship on Ibāḍism continues to grow. See, for example, Ennami, *Studies*; Schwartz and Ibn Yaʿqūb, *Kitāb Ibn Sallām*; Savage, *Gateway to Hell* and "Survival through Alliance"; Hoffman, *Essentials of Ibāḍī Islam* and, for an overview of recent scholarship, "Ibāḍism"; Wilkinson, "Early Development" and *Ibadism*; Crone and Zimmermann, *Epistle*; Francesca, "Formation and Early Development"; Gaiser, *Muslims, Scholars, Soldiers*; Love, *Ibadi Muslims*; Muranyi, *First Compendium of Ibadi Law*; Ziaka, ed., *On Ibadism*; Aillet, ed., *L'ibadisme*; Francesca, ed., *Ibadi Theology*. M. Custers has compiled a comprehensive bibliography of primary and secondary works on Ibāḍism: Custers, *Al-Ibadiyya*.
23. Hoffman, "Historical Memories"; al-Ṣallābī, *al-Ibāḍiyya*; Aṭfayyish, *al-Farq*; Ghazal, "Politics and Polemics".
24. See, for example, Gaiser, *Shurāt Legends*, *Ibāḍī Identities*, "Good Models" and "Tracing the Ascetic Life".
25. Donner, "Piety and Eschatology", 13.
26. This approach to Khārijite poetry is prevalent among Islamicists, who either do not acknowledge the problematic provenance of the material or, if they do, tend to ignore the implications and operate on the assumption of authenticity. See, for example, Higgins, "Faces of Exchangers"; Salem, *Political Theory*; decidedly more cautious, but at times inconsistent in his take on Khārijite poetry: Gaiser, *Shurāt Legends*, e.g., 12, 46, 50–2, 58, 69, 75 n. 173, 79–86, 88, 89–90.
27. Crone, *Medieval Islamic Political Thought*, 54.
28. Van Ess, *Flowering of Muslim Theology*, 30–1.
29. Watt, *Formative Period*, 21.
30. Foss, "Islam's First Terrorists", 15. As implied by the title, this article is a piece of popular science and thus lacks a critical analysis of its subject matter. Instead it gives a purely descriptive account of Khārijite history based on the Islamic tradition.
31. Morony, *Iraq*, 472.
32. Donner, *Narratives*, 102; restated briefly in his *Muhammad*, 164. In a similar vein, Crone, *Medieval Islamic Political Thought*, 59 argued that the Khārijites tried to "systematiz[e] the principles behind the early caliphate in Medina". See also Morony, *Iraq*, 470. Lahoud, "Early Kharijites", 301: "They were idealists in living up to teachings of the Qurʾan."

33. For another detailed, though differently weighted overview of Western scholarship on Khārijism, see Timani, *Modern Intellectual Readings*, 49–76. He also surveyed modern Arab scholarship on the Khawārij, for which see ibid., 25–48.
34. In addition to the references below, see, for example, Lewis, *Arabs*, 78.
35. A representative of this strand is Lahoud, "Early Kharijites", which looks at Khārijism through the lens of 'holy war' and the jurists' later development of a theory of *jihād*. See also her *Jihadi's Path*, esp. chapter two.
36. See, for example, Lewis, *Arabs*, 78, 113; Lahoud, *Political Thought*, 61–3; Crone, "Ninth-Century" (on Najdī Khārijites, the only subdivision she considers anarchists).
37. See, for example, Morony, *Iraq*, 468: "The Khārijī movement developed out of religiously justified opposition to the growing socioeconomic polarization in the garrison cities of Iraq."; 470: "In opposition to the new elite of the garrison cities, the early Khawārij stood for the original Islam of equality and brotherhood, including women, and for a community based on faith instead of kinship."
38. For western academic approaches to early Islamic history and its sources, see the excellent overviews by Donner, *Narratives*, 1–31 and "Modern Approaches"; on the Qurʾān, Motzki, "Collection of the Qurʾān". This trajectory is not linear, of course: one can find representatives of all approaches to Khārijism among contemporary scholars of early Islam. Refer to the notes at the end of this section.
39. Brünnow, *Charidschiten*, 9.
40. Ibid., 1–15.
41. Wellhausen, *Oppositionsparteien*, 14.
42. Shaban, *Islamic History*.
43. Ibid., 66–8, 76.
44. In a similar vein, the Marxist scholar Ḥusayn Muruwwa understood the conflicts within the early Islamic community as a struggle over resources (among other factors) and the Khārijites as peasants who revolted against the landowning class. See the discussion in Timani, *Modern Intellectual Readings*, chapter four.
45. Hinds, "Kufan Political Alignments", 359–60.
46. Watt, *Formative Period*, 20 and "Khārijite Thought", 217. For a brief critique of his position see Morony, *Iraq*, 474.
47. Hawting, "Significance", 461. On Khārijites as scripturalists, see also M. Cook, "ʿAnan and Islam", esp. 172.
48. Donner, *Narratives*, 19–30 (including a critique of hyper-scepticism). For the legacy of the sceptics, see Robinson, "Crone" and Segovia, "John Wansbrough".
49. See the works listed in the bibliography.
50. Donner, "Piety and Eschatology", 14.
51. Ibid.,16.
52. Ibid.,19.
53. Ibid.,13–19.

54. Hobsbawm, *Primitive Rebels*. Hobsbawm further developed his ideas in a subsequent monograph (*Bandits*) and various articles (for example, "Social Banditry").
55. Robinson, *Empire and Elites*, 113.
56. He does not explain either what exactly he understands 'Khārijism' to be beyond a mode of expressing opposition, where its origins lay, or how, where and why the accounts locating the Khārijite origins at Ṣiffīn came into being.
57. Robinson, *Empire and Elites*, 110–13. The idea that an Islamic state proper only developed with ʿAbd al-Malik is one of the core tenets of Robinson's 2007 monograph on this caliph (Robinson, *ʿAbd al-Malik)*.
58. Heck, "Eschatological Scripturalism", 150; see also 137, 139, 148, 149–50, 152.
59. Ibid., 137.
60. Ibid.,139.
61. Ibid.,141.
62. Ibid.,139.
63. Ibid.
64. Commenting on the merits and shortcomings of individual theories is both beyond the scope of this introduction and beside the point, as will be shown below.
65. On this, see also the brief remarks in Leube, *Kinda*, 12.
66. Donner, "Piety and Eschatology"; Lahoud, "Early Kharijites", 292, 299. Lahoud's article spends some time explaining why the references to the distribution of the spoils in Khārijite rhetoric do not contradict their religious devotion and motivation, which is a good example of attempting to reconcile seemingly diverging pieces of information, but also misunderstands the religious connotations of the *fayʾ*. See EI³, "Fayʾ" (A. Marsham).
67. On Qaṭarī's coins, see below, 50 and n. 76 thereto. He was not the only Khārijite to mint coins, for which see Gaiser, "What Do We Learn" and Foss, "The Kharijites".
68. As Wansbrough put it, "the vague but enduring conviction that the record has got to be readable." Wansbrough, "Res Ipsa Loquitur", 17.
69. Donner, "Modern Approaches", 629, 633. See also Crone, *Slaves* 13, 14–15; El-Hibri, *Reinterpreting Islamic Historiography*, 12; Brockopp, "Islamic Origins", 32. However, even scholars approaching Islamic history from a sceptical or literary-critical point of view cannot escape positivist statements. See, for example, Cobb, "Review", 110.
70. For the same dilemma as it pertains to ancient history, see Averil Cameron's introductory remarks to Rich, "Dio", 86–7.
71. Robinson, "History and Heilsgeschichte". See also Watt's distinction between a person's external acts and the internal motives ascribed to them in *Muḥammad at Mecca*, xiv.
72. White, *Tropics of Discourse*, 85.
73. Munslow, "Authority and Reality", 85.

74. White, *Tropics of Discourse*, 23.
75. Iggers, "Intellectual Foundations"; Lingelbach, "Institutionalization and Professionalization"; Potter, *Literary Texts*, 102–3, 126–8; Robinson, *Historiography*, 5–6, 83–4.
76. Shoshan, *Poetics*, xxi. See also Cooperson, "Probability", 69. The distinction between considering an early Islamic work as 'fiction' (as Leder has done, for instance) and identifying 'techniques of fiction' used in such a work is important – as Haider argues, "fiction is a modern construct whose projection into earlier periods risks anachronism" (Haider, *Rebel and Imām*, 14).
77. Robinson, "Reconstructing", 115. See also Montgomery, "Editor's Introduction", 6. Verisimilitude was a major objective of the early Muslim historians, which contributes to the challenges of recognising rhetorical and literary devices. Hoyland, "History, Fiction and Authorship", 17–18, 21–2.
78. Shoshan, *Poetics*, xxv. See also Hoyland, "History, Fiction and Authorship", 18, 19. For practical examples of this, see, for example, Leder and Kilpatrick, "Classical Arabic Prose", 14, 16; Lang, "Review of Tayeb El-Hibri", 112; Rippin, "Review of *Islamic Revolution and Historical Memory*", 553, where Rippin forcefully criticises Lassner's approach to ʿAbbāsid historiography: "Behind all the words it is hard to avoid the sense of seeing a traditional historian being a bit more cautious than in the 'good old days' when positivism was rampant. The change, at least in this instance, would seem to be more cosmetic than paradigmatic."

Sources, Genre, Authorship

This book is based on a representative selection of chronicles from the formative period of the Islamic written tradition (ninth to tenth century) as major vehicles of historical knowledge and knowledge transmission within the 'genre' of early Islamic historiography. These works are all of Iraqi or broadly 'eastern' provenance; the extant pre-eleventh century non-Iraqi historiography is limited, on the whole not on the same level in terms of both volume and scale and thus unsuited to the kind of comparative narrative analysis pursued here.[1] More to the point, it tends to gloss over the Khawārij or at least does not discuss them in sufficient detail for inclusion in this study. Examples of this tendency are the *Taʾrīkh* of the Syrian scholar Abū Zurʿa (d. 281 H/895 CE)[2] or Ibn Ḥabīb's (d. 238 H/853 CE) *Kitāb al-Taʾrīkh*, the earliest extant piece of Andalusi historical writing.[3] Khārijism, whatever its precise nature, was largely an eastern phenomenon (unlike Ibāḍism), and as early Syrian, Egyptian and Andalusi historiography largely focuses on the west, it is perhaps not surprising that Khārijites do not feature much in these works.

The main chronicles selected for analysis in this book are Khalīfa b. Khayyāṭ (d. 241 H/854 CE), *Taʾrīkh*; Abū Ḥanīfa al-Dīnawarī (d. c. 281 H/894 CE), *al-Akhbār al-Ṭiwāl*; Ibn Aʿtham al-Kūfī (fl. 3rd/late ninth–early tenth century),[4] *Kitāb al-Futūḥ*; al-Yaʿqūbī (d. c. 286 H/908 CE), *Taʾrīkh*; al-Ṭabarī (d. 310 H/923 CE), *Taʾrīkh al-Rusul wa-l-Mulūk*; and al-Masʿūdī (d. 345 H/956 CE), *Murūj al-Dhahab wa-Maʿādin al-Jawhar*. For Chapter Four, an important additional source is *Waqʿat Ṣiffīn* ascribed to Naṣr b. Muzāḥim al-Minqarī (d. 212 H/827 CE), a (reconstructed)[5] monograph on the battle and arbitration of Ṣiffīn. These works are supplemented by literature generally classified as biography such as Ibn Saʿd's *Ṭabaqāt*.

Another major source for this study is the *Ansāb al-Ashrāf* of al-Balādhurī (d. c. 279 H/892 CE). The *Ansāb* is not a work of history-writing in the sense of al-Ṭabarī or al-Yaʿqūbī's *Taʾrīkh*, some have argued. It does not follow a chronological format but is instead structured according to important tribal groups and families like the ʿAlids and ʿAbbāsids, sub-divided into individual and often rather lengthy biographies. The work is a combination of biography and historiography, a curious mixture of *ṭabaqāt*, *nasab* and *taʾrīkh*, with the latter frequently overshadowing the former two in the narrating of reports that have little to do with the biographee in question but are important in the context of another event discussed within that particular biographical section.[6] Because of al-Balādhurī's interest in edifying and entertaining tales – he himself was a poet, storyteller and translator of Persian literature – and his position at court as both boon companion to the ʿAbbāsid caliph al-Mutawakkil (r. 232–47 H/847–61 CE) and secretary (*kātib*), his work has also been identified as an example of *adab*.[7] Indeed, his Khārijite material overlaps considerably with such works as al-Mubarrad's *Kāmil*, which contains several Khārijite episodes preserved by al-Balādhurī alone among the works considered in this study.[8] Nevertheless, while there are "distinctive functions of biographical as opposed to historical discourse",[9] there is a great deal of overlap between the two forms of literature, so much so that it is often difficult to draw a line between biographical and historical writing 'proper'.[10] Because of this, and because the *Ansāb* covers much of the material that features in the selected chronicles and therefore allows for comparative analysis, the work has been included.

The difficulties in attempting to (somewhat artificially) distinguish between different types or categories of writing apply to early Islamic literature in general. Genres were not sharply delineated and often shared narrative conventions as well as material, not to mention personnel.[11] This is particularly true concerning historiography and *adab*,[12] but initially most, if not all, scholars and storytellers (the categories overlap) "drew upon the same material. Thus one and the same report could appear in a number of different contexts."[13] Genre classifications advanced by both later medieval and modern scholarship can therefore appear anachronistic.[14] Indeed, we might best understand genre in this early period of Islamic writerly culture as a particular mode of framing narrative material that influenced the selection and ordering of the available material. There was significant overlap between such 'frames', but within individual frames heterogeneity was the norm as well, not just regarding the content of selected accounts but also in terms of scope and narrative technique. For instance, some of the works to be examined in the following are universal chronicles, in that they begin with Creation and/or the history of ancient peoples (for example, al-Yaʿqūbī's and al-Ṭabarī's *Taʾrīkh*).[15] Others, at least in their extant form, focus on the nearer pre-Islamic past or begin with the Islamic period (for example, Ibn Khayyāṭ's *Taʾrīkh* or Ibn Aʿtham's *Futūḥ*). Some adhere to an 'atomistic' narrative structure by transmitting individual *akhbār* complete with *isnād*s (for example, al-Ṭabarī's *Taʾrīkh*), while others harmonise various reports into one flowing narrative largely uninterrupted by *isnāds* and other interjections (for example, al-Dīnawarī's *Akhbār*).[16] The titles of early works further contribute to the confusion over genre among both later medieval Islamic and modern scholars. Ibn Aʿtham's work is entitled *Kitāb al-Futūḥ*, for instance, but its scope far exceeds the early conquests and it is arranged chronologically, like the *taʾrīkh* works.[17] The title of al-Balādhurī's *Ansāb* likewise implies a different genre, but as noted the work actually transmits much the same material, as does Ibn Saʿd's *Ṭabaqāt*. Moreover, pre-modern Islamic texts, especially from the early period, often did not have fixed titles; modern editions, as helpful as they are, require these, however, and thus obscure the fluidity of medieval titling.[18] Historiography as a distinct frame (as opposed to *ḥadīth* or *adab*, for example) and chronicles as a particular form of historical writing are nonetheless sufficiently cohesive to function as a case study within the broader context of the Islamic written tradition.

The sources examined in this study, or rather the scholars associated with these texts, do not post-date the mid-tenth century. The early period of Islamic historical writing (late eighth to tenth century) witnessed the compilation, collection and reworking of older narratives. It is at this time that the first annalistic works and universal histories were composed through the collation, (re-)combination and creation of narrative material.[19] Following the tenth century, the consensus regarding the early history of the *umma* "ceased to be actively worked out and reworked" because "a suitable position was already present in existing works", and because the classical issues of succession, *fitna* and legitimate rule were no longer of immediate importance to the *umma*.[20] While later works do engage in the reformulation and renegotiation of these fundamental themes, the extent of this is limited, and post-tenth-century texts that deal with the early period of Islam are mainly based on the works of the formative period.[21] In some cases they preserve what appears to be early material, Ibn ʿAsākir's *Taʾrīkh Madīnat Dimashq* being a case in point.[22] However, the provenance and transmission process – and thus the actual age and original form – of this material are often uncertain.[23] As this study focuses primarily on the representation of Khārijism in the emerging historical tradition, these later sources will not be included in the discussion.

Another source corpus that is largely excluded from the analysis is Ibāḍī historiography. The Ibāḍī tradition is without doubt an important counterpart to the (proto-)Sunnī tradition in particular, offering complementary and often conflicting depictions of early Islamic history. At the same time, Ibāḍī and non-Ibāḍī scholars of the early Islamic period exchanged ideas and frequented much the same pool of source material, although the framing of events and actors can be quite different. The reason for not systematically including Ibāḍī sources in the analysis is two-fold: first, the book's primary interest is in the *early* Islamic *historical* tradition. Ibāḍī sources are now being made increasingly accessible to Islamicists, but the bulk of (supposedly) very early material consists of creeds, epistles, heresiographical and other doctrinal material that is mostly inward looking, i.e. focused on an evolving Ibāḍī identity. Ibāḍī historiography, in a form comparable to the selected sources, largely postdates the tenth century, which is the cut-off date here.[24] While later Ibāḍī sources, like their Sunnī and Shīʿī equivalents, contain older fragments, the same difficulties in identifying and assessing these fragments apply, even if they are not always acknowledged. Gaiser has argued that "Ibadi writings [beginning in the early eighth century] remain historically closer in composition to the era of the early Kharijites",[25] but these very early writings – and can we be sure that the narratives in question were in fact written down? – almost exclusively survive in the form of quotations in much later sources,[26] which renders this problematic. The collection of epistles edited by S. I. Kāshif, for instance, contains numerous texts attributed to very early Ibāḍī scholars, but the manuscript is tentatively dated to the year 1600[27] and many of the pieces included in this collection are not attested elsewhere. There is no way to be sure about the original shape of these texts (assuming there was an authoritative version to start with) or the transmission process of the fragments that survived in later works.[28] As Landau-Tasseron so astutely observed, false ascriptions and text modification over time are only two of the issues that seriously affect such attempts to excavate earlier layers of material.[29]

Second, as mentioned already, considerable research is now being done on Ibāḍī portrayals of early Islamic and thus also Khārijite history. On the other hand, a detailed investigation of the ways in which the non-Ibāḍī historical tradition depicts early Khārijism is still a desideratum, one that this study seeks to redress. The few examples of pre-tenth century Ibāḍī historiography that do not just survive as fragmentary quotations in later works will therefore not be considered here.

Now, anyone working on early Islamic history and historiography faces two fundamental challenges: the problematic nature of our source material, i.e. its provenance, 'original' form, reliability and authenticity, and the related question of authorship. Most of the material that the large compilations and chronicles of the ninth and tenth century incorporated is not extant independently. Scholarly efforts have resulted in the reconstruction and study of the corpus of work attributed to authorities like Abū Mikhnaf or al-Haytham b. ʿAdī,[30] but, as outlined above, there are significant caveats to consider – most importantly, we do not know whether such reconstructions are close to the 'original', both because there is usually no way to tell how much is lost and thus missing from the reconstructed corpus and because an increasing number of studies have shown that early Islamic texts largely did not have a stable written form well into the third/ninth century and beyond. Neither was it unusual for scholars to revise their works and circulate different versions.[31] The persistence of orality[32] and later adaptations and interpolations in the transmission of early texts are two factors that further complicate the matter.[33] The very notion of a fixed original is thus deeply problematic.[34] This applies not only to the earliest identifiable layers of the Islamic historical tradition but also, though less dramatically, to the ninth- and tenth-century works examined here. For instance, there is often a substantial gap between the composition dates of our sources and the earliest manuscript evidence at our disposal. The *Taʾrīkh* of Ibn Khayyāṭ, a Basran *muḥaddith* who died in the mid-ninth century, is known from a single manuscript copied in al-Andalus in the late eleventh century,[35] in the recension of his student Baqī b. Makhlad (d. 276 H/889 CE). We know there was at least one other recension that has not survived but that appears to have differed somewhat from Baqī's version.[36] And this is a fairly close correspondence of composition period and copied manuscript. In contrast, the two extant manuscripts of al-Yaʿqūbī's *Taʾrīkh* were copied in the mid-14th and late 17th centuries, respectively.[37] The earliest manuscript evidence for Ibn Aʿtham's *Futūḥ* dates from the fifteenth century, a gap of half a millennium, and there are significant variations in the surviving Arabic and Persian versions.[38]

Research on the manuscript tradition of a particular work alongside studies of a text's recensions and quotations in later works can help us gain insight into the relative stability of that text as it was transmitted over time. Scholarship has made some inroads,[39] but overall much more research of this kind is needed. Even that can only take us so far, however: we do not have manuscripts dating to the lifetimes (or shortly thereafter) of the historians under study here, often only a few are extant (barring new discoveries) and some works – like al-Yaʿqūbī's *Taʾrīkh* – were not particularly popular, so there are few quotations in later texts that could be used for comparison.

On the other hand, while texts were fluid and scholars operated in a cultural environment that favoured the "free transmission of texts",[40] transmission was in fact not (or not always) entirely free. The two recensions of Khalīfa b. Khayyāṭ's *Taʾrīkh*, for instance, did vary, but the differences are minor and did not produce two entirely different works – the broad outline and arrangement seem to go back to Khalīfa.[41] We do not have complete manuscripts of al-Ṭabarī's *Taʾrīkh*, but the several incomplete ones we do have indicate that the text, which unlike Khalīfa's *Taʾrīkh* had been put down in writing by al-Ṭabarī himself, was transmitted in rather stable form.[42]

Nevertheless, the modern obsession with stable texts codified as books is anachronistic and has at times hindered our understanding of the very nature of our sources and early Islamic writerly culture more generally.[43] These observations are one reason why the analysis to follow will not focus primarily on identifying the provenance of the reports on Khārijism or discussing the evolution of individual accounts, especially at the level of the predecessors of Ibn Khayyāṭ and his colleagues. Another is that the main purpose of this book is to study the literary portrayal of Khārijism in the early historical tradition as a precursor to a renewed engagement with the historical Khawārij, rather than employing Khārijism as a case study of early Islamic historiographical production processes. These issues are of course intertwined, but while research on the evolution of Islamic historiography and particularly on individual texts and authors is still sorely needed, this is beyond the scope of the study at hand.

Finally, the question of authorship requires some consideration. Little research exists on this issue in an early Islamic context.[44] Older scholarship on the whole did not consider early Islamic historians as authors but as compilers and sometimes mere scribes slavishly copying whatever material they could find of the great authorities of old.[45] The individual genius of an inspired author creating an entirely new composition was absent from the large-scale compilations of al-Balādhurī and his colleagues, it was argued. That this is a very modern, post-Enlightenment and specifically Romantic concept of authorship[46] that does not do justice to pre-modern notions of historical (and other) writing is increasingly recognised in Islamic Studies,[47] but the field is behind other disciplines in this regard, Medieval European Literature or Classics being a case in point.[48] The matter is complicated, of course, not least owing to the particular features of early Islamic (historical) literature, such as its compilatory nature and the peculiarities of the *khabar*, that make the identification of where, when, with whom and under what circumstances a particular account or series of accounts originate very difficult.[49] The uncertainty is observable, for instance, in the many different terms in which modern scholars describe what al-Ṭabarī and his colleagues were doing, variously: authors, compilers, author-compilers, editors, commentators, transmitters or some combination of those terms. This is not just a matter of terminology but an expression of serious questions regarding our source material: how do we distinguish between a poet's creation and his *rāwī*'s contribution to it, for example, and does such a distinction make sense in the first place?[50] In the transition from a largely oral to a substantial written tradition, does the compilation and arrangement of material not include characteristics commonly ascribed to the realm of authorial creativity? To whom should we attribute the authorship of those many texts that are available to us only in the recension of a scholar's students or of the students' students?[51]

Over the past several decades, scholarship across many fields has increasingly dealt with re-definitions of the term 'author', most radically among them the works of Michel Foucault and Roland Barthes. Some of these new approaches have, in good old postmodernist and poststructuralist fashion, declared the author dead.[52] Others have argued the inherent impracticality of such a concept and its impoverishing effect on the understanding of textual creations,[53] setting out to find a more workable notion of what it means to be an author in modern and pre-modern settings alike. Such studies are not yet fully utilised within Islamic Studies, even though the imposition of modern categories such as the inspired genius author on pre-modern processes and mechanisms of knowledge and text production is bound to distort our perception of 'what really happened' more than acknowledging the customs of pre-modern intellectual cultures ever could.[54] Bayreuth University's 2012 workshop on "Rethinking Authorship in Islamic Literature" was a step in the right direction, but only a starting point.[55] It is certainly telling in this regard that none of the three editions of the Encyclopaedia of Islam has entries on 'author' or 'authorship', 'compilation' or 'text production' – hopefully some will eventually be added to the third edition.[56]

My own approach to the question of authorship in early Islamic historiography is rooted in the insights of scholars of medieval European literature. Based on their findings, I propose that we consider pre-modern authorship not as an expression of solitary genius but rather as an umbrella term that combines the features of (modern) author, compiler, editor, commentator, scribe, copyist, transmitter, translator and so forth, even if not all of these functions were performed by each individual to the same extent in every work. Instead of unitary authorship, we thereby arrive at a concept of 'distributed authorship',[57] which fits medieval literary production, both European and Islamic, much better.

A prerequisite of this notion is the understanding that compilation is an inherently creative authorial process.[58] This is not just a modern insight: Ibn ʿAbd Rabbih (d. 328 H/940 CE) in the introduction to *al-ʿIqd al-Farīd* lays out all the various methods and source materials he employed in the compilation of his anthology, justifying his decision to omit *isnād*s and explaining the logic behind the work's title and chapter headings.[59] As was customary at the time,[60] he states that he merely put together already existent accounts transmitted from the learned authorities, but he emphasises very strongly that this does not decrease the work's value or his own contribution:

> Selection of speech is more difficult than composing it [*ikhtiyār al-kalām aṣʿab min taʾlīfihi*]. They say, "A man's selection demonstrates his mind."
> A poet said:
> We have known you by your selection,
> For one's selection shows one's intelligence.
> Plato said, "People's minds are recorded on the tips of their pens and are evident in their selection."[61]

In the context of this book, this means that the very inclusion as well as the overall structure of a particular narrative section are considered a conscious choice and indicative of a particular framing of early Islamic/Khārijite history. Whether or not the historian to whom a particular work is ascribed also originated (the specific phrasing of) an account does not have much impact on his authorial status.

The term 'distributed authorship' refers not just to a multiplicity of authors, as is often the case when applied to certain phenomena on the Internet (Wikipedia, for example); rather, distributed authorship describes a network of individuals and groups over time who contribute to a narrative by interacting with each other and meddling with each other's texts, amending, excising and constantly negotiating the particular shape of a narrative unit, not least to "improve the text in accordance with the tastes and interests of their day".[62] Authorship in this conception is a series of conversations; every participant makes a (greater or lesser) contribution, but no single individual is responsible for the development of the whole from start to finish.[63] This phenomenon has certainly been appreciated in studies of pre-modern Islamic literature, but has not been systematically related to the question of authorship.[64]

Medievalists, on the other hand, increasingly acknowledge the authorial role of archivists, scribes, compilers and librarians[65] and in turn recognise various functions embedded in the person(s) of the author, such as that of scribe, mediator, reporter, imitator and editor.[66] A pertinent question that scholars of medieval European literature tackle is, "who should be credited with creativity – the talented individual, tradition/society, or the creative process itself?"[67] Moreover, "When can the creative moment be pinpointed in the lengthy process from telling a story to having a neatly written, illuminated manuscript ready to be read out loud to an audience, possibly several copies removed from the hypothetical "original"?"[68] One answer is that authorship "includes *both* tradition and individual talent",[69] while notions of authorship as a unitary phenomenon cause more problems than they solve.[70] In the words of a medievalist working on Icelandic sagas:

> If only we could free our thinking from the romantic notion of the author with a quill in hand as the single mastermind behind a literary work, then there is nothing in particular that would speak against the project-model of writing . . . It would also relieve scholars of the burdensome concept of a lost original and open up ways to treat medieval texts as the product of the fluid, multi-voiced tradition of which they once were a part.[71]

Such utilisation of insights produced from analyses of medieval European writerly conventions and mechanisms is valid because of the many similarities between pre-modern Islamic and European literary production. Both were scribal cultures with a dynamic approach to text and knowledge production and characterised by the enduring importance of oral tradition.[72] We shall see that the combination of tradition and individual talent applies as well to the works selected for this study: our authors compile and transmit much the same material on early Kharijite history, but also shape it in distinctly individual ways. By way of example, Chapter Five (on the reign of Muʿāwiya) will demonstrate that the works of al-Balādhurī and al-Ṭabarī both focused on the same main theme (Khārijite piety) and transmitted similar material, but achieved different effects. Much of al-Ṭabarī's material on Khārijism is based on Abū Mikhnaf (d. 157 H/774 CE), whose ʿAlid sympathies probably influenced his take on the Khawārij;[73] but is al-Ṭabarī's work more critical of Khārijites because of his use of Abū Mikhnaf, or did he use Abū Mikhnaf because of his own critical stance on Khārijism? Al-Balādhurī, on the other hand, who quotes Abū Mikhnaf extensively in his *Futūḥ al-Buldān* and other parts of the *Ansāb*, does not seem to use him much for his portrayal of Khārijism in that period, perhaps because the tenor of Abū Mikhnaf's accounts did not serve his purpose as well as other sources. Differences in how the two scholars assessed Khārijism are thus not just a matter of source material (the origin of which is often difficult to determine), but of personal and professional choice.

This combination of creative input and simultaneous dependence on pre-formed materials reflects the notion of distributed authorship and renders a sharp distinction between author, editor and compiler largely inapplicable. It is also not that different from what modern scholars do: we cast our materials in (hopefully) new and original forms, but in the process we build on a vast foundation of pre-existing research and primary sources. We quote, paraphrase, rephrase, reference and allude to, and we follow our own writerly and academic conventions while doing so. In some ways, the modern obsession with novelty and originality (claims of which are advanced in virtually every piece of scholarship, including this one) is an inversion of pre-modern conventions, neither perfectly implemented at all times and each as much a function of academic rhetoric as the other.[74]

This is not to say that the work of modern scholars is by its very nature derivative, of course. Quite the contrary: all this to emphasise that I hold the early Islamic scholars who are credited with the works we will study to be part of a chain of authorial presences rather than 'mere' compilers without creative agency or agendas of their own. The following chapters will mainly refer to them as author-compilers to underline that the creation of their texts was subject to a process of collation and resulted in multivalent and polyphonic compositions. The term 'author' will also appear, not least to simplify the prose in places, but mainly to underline the creative agency of Ibn Khayyāṭ and his colleagues. Referring to 'scholar x' as an author is also intended here as a cipher subsuming not just the historical person and their particular background, but also the cultural and scholarly milieu, impacted by socio-political developments, in which they moved. For instance, al-Ṭabarī's background as an affluent, independent scholar and jurist influenced the shape of his work, but so did the conventions of *ḥadīth* scholarship and the crumbling authority of the ʿAbbāsid Empire. The latter certainly impacted the overall agenda of his chronicle, while the former affected his choice of source materials and narrative structure as he, too, sought to appeal to his particular scholarly communities.[75] The resulting text is thus a combination of both tradition and individual input in more than one sense. Any reference to 'al-Ṭabarī's *Taʾrīkh*' accordingly refers both to the individual scholar and to the text as part of the Islamic tradition.

To conclude, this book is not a study of an individual text and its manuscript history; it does not seek to uncover or reconstruct 'original' works, either. Its objective is a study of how the early Islamic historical tradition remembered and portrayed Khārijism. Unless we succumb to some kind of conspiracist thinking, the texts examined here can stand as parts of this tradition. Further, until there is conclusive evidence to the contrary, and allowing for some alterations (omissions, additions, some restructuring) over time, I hold the texts studied in this book to reflect, broadly, the aural and/or written body of work of the historians they are associated with.

Notes

1. The predominance of Iraqi material can perhaps be explained with the region's significance for the development of religious scholarship. Hawting, *First Dynasty*, 2–3. On the scarcity of early Islamic historical works from Syria, see Rotter,

"Abū Zurʿa ad-Dimašqī"; Khalek, *Damascus*, chapter two and 142–3; Donner, "Problem"; and Borrut, "Future". The mid-tenth-century *Kitāb al-Badʾ* by the Sīstānī (?) scholar al-Maqdisī likewise gives only the barest details of Khārijite history; the drawn-out rebellion of the Azāriqa under first Nāfiʿ and then Qaṭarī in Iran as well as the uprising of Shabīb b. Yazīd in the Jazīra in the 690s, for instance, are summarised on three pages and lack the narrative substance (conveyed through letters, speeches and the like) necessary for the analysis attempted here. Al-Maqdisī, *Kitāb al-Badʾ*, VI, 31–4 [Arabic text].

2. Abū Zurʿa, for example, only says of the first *fitna* that after ʿUthmān's death the people were divided for five years until they reunited under Muʿāwiya. He mentions a date for the Battle of the Camel and Ṣiffīn, but does not give any further information; ʿAlī does not appear at all. Abū Zurʿa, *Taʾrīkh*, 41. The primary section on the Umayyad caliphs (Abū Zurʿa, *Taʾrīkh*, 41–7) is scarce in detail and the Khārijites are altogether absent. Later chapters revisit Umayyad, but not Khārijite, history.
3. Unlike Abū Zurʿa, Ibn Ḥabīb mentions ʿAlī's reign and provides some information on Ṣiffīn, but the Khārijites do not appear; the Battle of Nahrawān is not covered, either. Ibn Ḥabīb, *Taʾrīkh*, 114–16. The note on ʿAlī's murder gives the name of his assassin, but does not identify him as a Khārijite (Ibn Ḥabīb, *Taʾrīkh*, 116). Likewise, the extant sections on Umayyad history until after the death of ʿAbd al-Malik are silent on the Khawārij.
4. There has been an extended debate over Ibn Aʿtham *floruit*. I follow Lindstedt, "Biography", in assuming a tenth-century death date for Ibn Aʿtham, which appears to me to fit better in terms of the scope, narrative complexity and rhetorical style of Ibn Aʿtham's work. Chapter Seven will discuss the issue of dating Ibn Aʿtham's life and work in more detail.
5. The question of whether it is possible to reconstruct lost or only partially extant sources from later works has been subject to controversial debate. Fuat Sezgin (*GAS*, I, 79–84, 237–56) argued explicitly that this could in fact be done, proposing a method that was based on his particular understanding of transmitters as authors of written works. This was in turn rooted in his belief that material from all genres had begun to be written down from the death of Muḥammad at the latest and thus survived basically unchanged in the later, still extant, sources (for exegesis, see ibid., 19–20; for *ḥadīth*, ibid., esp. 55–61, 77). Schoeler's studies of the development of the written Islamic tradition and the relationship between oral and written transmission have cast doubt on Sezgin's method and ideas (see Schoeler's various articles in German in the bibliography; a German summary can be found in Schoeler, "Gesprochenes Wort". An English translation of his main ideas is available in Schoeler, *Genesis of Literature*. See also n. 32 below). Attempts at reconstruction still continue, however, and in all genres. Examples are U. Sezgin, *Abū Miḫnaf*; Rotter, "Zur Überlieferung"; Gwynne, *Tafsir*; Stauth, *Überlieferung*; and of course the *Waqʿat Ṣiffīn* attributed to Naṣr b. Muzāḥim. Landau-Tasseron's discussion of the pitfalls and challenges of such

reconstructions is perhaps the most cogent engagement with this topic despite its age (Landau-Tasseron, "Reconstruction"; her 2004 article was originally submitted to a different publication in 1989 and eventually published essentially unchanged; see also Leder, "Grenzen der Rekonstruktion"). For similar issues pertaining to Graeco-Roman histories, see Potter, *Literary Texts*, 70–8. Challenges notwithstanding, I have opted to include *Waqʿat Ṣiffīn* because the question of the 'original', while of import, is not the central concern of this book.

6. EI², "al-Balādhurī" (C. H. Becker and F. Rosenthal). Al-Qāḍī explicitly does not count the *Ansāb* among works of that genre precisely because its primary organisational principle is not the biography, but the tribe and the family; she considers it "an indirect history". Al-Qāḍī, "Biographical Dictionaries", 96. Similarly, Khalidi, *Arabic Historical Thought*, 58: the work is "more like a comprehensive history loosely arranged around prominent families than a work of strict genealogy".
7. See Hasson, "Ansāb al-ašrāf". There are many different definitions of *adab*, reflecting the complex history and meanings of the term. On *adab* as a literary genre and intellectual concept, for instance, see Bonebakker, "*Adab*". For *adab* as an approach to writing rather than a genre, see Kilpatrick, "Adab". A brief overview of scholarly approaches is provided in Alshaar, "Introduction", 6–11; Alshaar argues strongly in favour of reconciling the secular and religious dimensions of *adab*. The question of 'history or *adab*?' has also been asked of al-Masʿūdī's work: Pellat, "al-Masʿūdī". Khalidi in his *Islamic Historiography* rejects Pellat's reading, contending that, while an '*adabī* spirit' is noticeable, it "subserves rather than dominates" al-Masʿūdī's "main historical theme" (ibid., 23). Similar confusion over the classification of al-Balādhurī's *Futūḥ*, which contains material from several different 'genres', is discussed in Lynch, *Arab Conquests*, 130–1, 151–87, esp. 154–69. For al-Balādhurī's biography see ibid., 36–43, 173–6.
8. Compare e.g. al-Balādhurī, *Ansāb*, IV/1, 389–90 with Rescher, *Kharidschitenkapitel*, 102–4, and al-Balādhurī, *Ansāb*, IV/1, 392–3 with Rescher, *Kharidschitenkapitel*, 105–6.
9. Cooperson, *Classical Arabic Biography*, 22.
10. On the similarities, differences and interconnectedness of history and biography, see Cooperson, *Classical Arabic Biography*, 18–23, 192; Andersson, *Early Sunnī Historiography*, 90–103.
11. Al-Maqdisī, al-Masʿūdī and al-Ṣūlī are cases in point.
12. Leder, "Composite Form", 126–7; Khalidi, *Islamic Historiography*, 14–15 and the references in 14 n. 2.
13. Hoyland, "History, Fiction and Authorship", 19. On the challenges of defining genre, see Robinson, *Historiography*, 56–7; he lists both prosopography and biography under historiography (55–79 and *passim*). Montgomery, "Serendipity" demonstrates the fluid boundaries of *adab* and 'non-literary' works, while Rippin, "Place of the Qurʾan", 219 argues that different types of literature "tend to blend together in early works"; see also ibid., 228–9. Ibn al-Nadīm in his

Fihrist includes al-Balādhurī in the section on *akhbārīs* and genealogists (chapter three, section one, 125–6).

14. Lynch, *Arab Conquests*, 180 n. 23.
15. For a concise comparative overview of Christian and Islamic universal chronicles, see Marsham, "Universal Histories".
16. On different conventions of early Islamic history writing over time, see Robinson, *Historiography*, 20–38 (esp. 35–6), 92–5; Hagler, *Echoes of Fitna*, 15–17; Donner, *Narratives*, 255–60; Leder, "Literary Use"; Hoyland, "History, Fiction and Authorship", 25 and *passim*.
17. For a discussion of the complex relationship between the 'genre' of conquest literature and texts entitled *Futūḥ*, see Lynch, *Arab Conquests*, 156–60, esp. 157–8.
18. Lynch, *Arab Conquests*, 179 n. 13.
19. Donner, *Narratives*, 280–1; Robinson, *Historiography*, 24–38.
20. Donner, *Narratives*, 291. See also Borrut, *Entre mémoire et pouvoir*, 97–108; Lynch, *Arab Conquest*, 123.
21. See, for example, Keaney, "First Islamic Revolt", 398–400 as well as her *Medieval Islamic Historiography*, esp. chapters three to five; Hagler, *Echoes of Fitna* demonstrates that the basic building blocks of the Ṣiffīn story remain virtually unchanged even if there are differences in the presentation and interpretation of the material; Ibn Kathīr (d. 744 H/1373 CE) is the last historian to engage with Ṣiffīn in detail – the role ascriptions of the involved characters had largely found acceptance among the Muslim (scholarly) community by then. See also Hagemann, "Muṭarrif", for a case study involving the later historical tradition's reliance on the renderings of al-Balādhurī and in particular al-Ṭabarī.
22. See the collected articles in Lindsay, ed., *Ibn ʿAsākir*, in particular Lindsay's own contribution, "Ibn ʿAsakir, His Taʾrīkh madinat Dimashq and its Usefulness for Early Islamic History"; briefly, Eisener, *Faktum und Fiktion*, 249–50.
23. Landau-Tasseron, "Reconstruction", 57–82.
24. Gaiser, *Muslims, Scholars, Soldiers*, 16–18. Rare exceptions are the *Kitāb* of Ibn Sallām (written after 273 H/886 CE) and the *Akhbār al-āʾimma al-rustumiyyīn* by Ibn al-Saghīr (d. late third/ninth century). Neither work is suitable for the comparative analysis undertaken in this book, however. Ibn Sallām's *Kitāb*, for instance, contains only a fraction of the material preserved in the selected chronicles. More importantly, it does not mention the constitutive events of early Khārijite history. Ṣiffīn is mentioned twice (ibid., 75, 106), but not in connection with the Khārijite protest; in fact, terms like *shurāt* or *khawārij* are absent, as are references to Nahrawān, Ḥarūrāʾ, the Azāriqa and other Khārijite subdivisions (except the Ibāḍīs, of course). The only 'Khārijite' protagonist who appears briefly is Abū Bilāl (ibid., 110–11), on whom see Chapter Five. Ibn al-Saghīr's *Akhbār* is concerned with the Rustamid *imāms* of Tāhart and so sketches the early history of that dynasty from the mid-eighth century, but remains silent on early Khārijite history.

25. Gaiser, "Tracing the Ascetic Life", 68.
26. Gaiser, "Tracing the Ascetic Life", 59–61 and *Muslims, Scholars, Soldiers*, 16–8. This confident approach to the recovery of now lost early Ibāḍī texts may be due to a somewhat more positivist interest in early Ibāḍī political and doctrinal history, meaning that his overall approach to the sources is different from the one adopted here, although he, too, acknowledges the story-telling and identity-formation aspects of Ibāḍī narratives.
27. Kāshif, *al-Siyar*, I, 18. The editor rightfully urges caution regarding this date, however, as it is not clear whether it applies to the whole manuscript or just the final treatise it contains.
28. Gaiser himself appears wary at times (e.g., "Tracing the Ascetic Life", 63).
29. Landau-Tasseron, "Reconstructing", 47–82.
30. U. Sezgin, *Abū Mikhnaf*; Leder, *Korpus*.
31. For a mid-tenth-century example of this process as narrated in Ibn al-Nadīm's *Fihrist*, see Mez, *Renaissance*, 171–2.
32. A pioneer in this field is Gregor Schoeler, for whom see also n. 5 above (esp. his "Zur Frage"). He demonstrated that throughout the first centuries of Islamic scholarship, knowledge was transmitted both aurally and in writing, with the former predominant well into the ninth century. The term *kitāb*, he showed, should not be understood as reference to a codified book in the modern sense (as advocated by Sezgin and Nabia Abbott, for instance) but rather as signalling a scholar's expertise in a certain field, the body of material attributed to their authority, a notebook or *aide-memoire*; only rarely did it refer to a stable text written down or passed on through oral/aural transmission. On the many versions of the *sīra* attributed to Ibn Isḥāq and the recension of Ibn Hishām, for instance, see al-Samuk, *Die historischen Überlieferungen*; Görke, "Authorship", 79–80. Robinson, "Reconstructing", 117–18 addresses the keen focus on written texts as a modern phenomenon. The continuing importance of the oral transmission of knowledge after the tenth century is shown e.g. by Vajda, "Oral Transmission". For the complex relationships between 'original' narratives (written or oral), their subsequent transformations as part of an oral tradition and (re-)recording in writing in other cultural settings, see Vansina, *Oral Tradition*, 33–67, esp. 48–67. On the entanglement of oral tradition and written text in non-Islamicate contexts, see also Oskarsdottir, "Resourceful Scribe", 325; Sigurdsson, "Poet", 231–4.
33. Günther, *Quellenuntersuchungen*, 34–6. An example of how difficult authorship and text composition can be to determine is Rippin's discussion of a work attributed to Abū ʿUbayd al-Qāsim b. Sallām. See Rippin, "Place of the Qurʾan", 222–4.
34. Montgomery, "Serendipity", 200 warns that assuming the existence of an *Ur-Text* is anachronistic for the ninth century and calls on scholars to "treat with extreme caution our post-Guttenberg concept (idealisation?) of the book". Günther, *Quellenuntersuchungen*, 34 suggests "Unterrichts- oder Sinneinheiten"

('teaching units' or 'units of meaning') as terms preferable to 'texts', presumably because of the latter's modern connotation of fixedness.

35. EI², "Ibn Khayyāṭ al-ʿUṣfurī" (S. Zakkar).
36. Andersson, *Early Sunnī Historiography*, 16–17. On the transmission of Ibn Khayyāṭ's *History* see ibid., 15–44.
37. Rowson, "Manuscripts", 23.
38. See the discussion in Chapter Seven. Balʿamī's (d. 363 H/974 CE) *Tārīkhnāma* is another example of a complex transmission history, with the text (or possibly texts) extant in many, often highly divergent, manuscripts. Peacock, *Medieval Islamic Historiography*, esp. 48–72.
39. An excellent example of the fruitfulness of this approach is Peacock, *Medieval Islamic Historiography*, which nevertheless also illustrates how difficult it is to grapple with these issues. The book demonstrates very convincingly that a reconstruction of Balʿamī's original version of the *Tārīkhnāma* is virtually impossible due to the many interpolations and alterations made by later scribes, editors and translators. At the same time, the study frequently refers to Balʿamī's creative authorial agency, suggesting that what we have in front of us in fact reflects Balʿamī's own work, a notion seriously challenged in other parts of the book.
40. Peacock, *Medieval Islamic Historiography*, 48.
41. As emerges from Andersson, *Early Sunnī Historiography*, 15–44.
42. Peacock, *Medieval Islamic Historiography*, 63.
43. Leube, *Kinda*, 134; see also the next following discussion.
44. As pointed out e.g. by Franz, *Kompilation*, 271; Rubanovich, "Metaphors of Authorship", 127, 133; Görke, "Authorship", 64.
45. See, for example, Rosenthal, *Muslim Historiography*, 61; Von Grunebaum, *Medieval Islam*, 281; Friedlaender, "Geschichtskonstruktionen", 18; Crone, *Slaves*, 10; Khalidi, *Arabic Historical Thought*, 30: "they [ʿUrwa b. al-Zubayr and al-Zuhrī] are *authors* who speak with the historian's voice, and not mere collectors or editors." Similarly, ibid., 24, 32, 36, 52. This notion – and its criticism – is not unique to Islamic Studies. See, for example, Sonnesyn, "Obedient Creativity", 116–17 (117 specifically for a critique of monks as unthinking copyists); Klein, "Abhängigkeit und Autonomie", 15–17.
46. An important piece on the development of modern notions of authorship over the course of the eighteenth century is Martha Woodmansee's 1984 article "The Genius and the Copyright", in which she relates the emergence of the 'inspired author' to disputes between publishers and writers over salaries and royalties, another result of which was the introduction of copyright. For a discussion of the relationship between authorship and copyright, see also the review article by Bently, "Copyright". My thanks to Andreas Görke for pointing out Woodmansee's work to me.
47. See, for example, Leder, "Authorship and Transmission" and "Features of the Novel"; Chamberlain, *Knowledge*, 141–5; Franz, *Kompilation*; Hirschler, *Medieval Arabic Historiography*; Görke, "Authorship".

48. The research output here is vast. I have found helpful the collection of articles in Rankovic, ed., *Modes of Authorship*; the chapters by Klein, Schmid and Laude in Schlesier and Trinca, eds, *Inspiration und Adaptation*; Burrow, *Medieval Writers*; Stillinger, *Multiple Authorship*; and the contributions of Wenzel, Suerbaum, Gärtner, Hellgardt, Holznagel and Flood in Andersen et al., eds, *Autor und Autorschaft*.
49. Görke, "Authorship", esp. 63–4.
50. An eloquent exploration of early Arabic poetry as "the scene of successive incarnations and subtle reincarnations" is offered by Kilito, *Author and His Doubles*, 9–23 (quote on 16).
51. On some of these issues, see Motzki, "The Author".
52. Most famously in Barthes' 1967 essay "The Death of the Author". See also the brief comments in Kittang, "Authors", 17–18. For the author as a socially constructed 'discursive function', see Foucault, "What is an Author?". On Barthes, Foucault and like-minded theorists, see briefly Clark, *History, Theory, Text*, 132–5.
53. See, for example, Hirsch, *Validity*, chapter one ("In Defense of the Author"); Stillinger, *Multiple Authorship*, 3–24.
54. For the same argument but focused on approaches to early Islamic historical writing based on modern concepts of history, see Haider, *Rebel and Imām*, 256–62, esp. 259–62; Cooperson, "Probability", 69.
55. The proceedings were published in 2015 (Behzadi and Hämeen-Anttila, eds, *Concepts of Authorship*). See now also the contributions to *JSAI* 45 (2018), a themed issue on authorship in medieval Arabic and Persian literature.
56. The EI[2] entry for "Kitāb" (R. Sellheim) has nothing on the first two and only touches on the latter two in passing. The EI[3] entry ("Book", H. Touati) passes over these issues very quickly.
57. For the concept of 'distributed authorship', see Rankovic, *The Distributed Author*, 97–100. Concerning the early Islamic case, Görke, "Authorship" advocates for a study of all the individuals who were involved in the creation and compilation of *akhbār*, here specifically the *sīra* literature, instead of "following a specific definition of 'author' and then determining who would qualify" (71), especially because there are several equally valid notions of authorship (for example, responsibility for the content of a given account, responsibility for the ultimate form of an account, and so forth) (86).
58. For the early Islamic case, see Conrad, "Ibn Aʿtham", 102 and "Conquest of Arwād", 391–5; Leder, *Korpus*, 8–14; Cooperson, *Classical Arabic Biography*, 22–3; Hoyland, "History, Fiction and Authorship", 32–9, 40; Robinson, *Historiography*, 154–5; Gruendler, "Pardon", 191–2, 200–4; Haider, *Rebel and Imām*, 17–18, 113, *passim*. For non-Islamic contexts, see Burnyeat, "Wrenching the Club" and "*Córugud* and *compilatio*", esp. 360–5; Sonnesyn, "Obedient Creativity", esp. 123–4; Conti, "Scribes as Authors", esp. 267, 288; Sigurdsson, "Poet", 231.
59. Ibn ʿAbd Rabbih, *al-ʿIqd*, I, 4–8. On the question of Ibn ʿAbd Rabbih's

authorship, his methods and the originality of this work, see also Alshaar, "Qur'an", esp. 382–3.

60. See Chapter Four, 191.
61. Ibn ʿAbd Rabbih, *al-ʿIqd*, I, 4–5; trans. Boullata, *Unique Necklace*, I, 2.
62. Peacock, *Medieval Islamic Historiography*, 57; see also his extended discussion on 137–45, 166.
63. The notion of 'distributed authorship' corresponds here to Stillinger's 'multiple authorship'. See also Görke's summary of the multiple authorship of the *sīra* in his "Authorship", 86–7; for a non-Islamic example, see Lethbridge, "Authors and Anonymity", 364.
64. Among the few exceptions are Abdelfattah Kilito's masterful *Author and His Doubles* as well as the works of Stefan Leder (see, for example, his *Korpus*, 283). See also the references in n. 47 above.
65. E.g., Conti, "Scribes as Authors", 267; Fisher, *Scribal Authorship*, esp. 14–58. For scribal agency in the pre-modern Islamic world, see Peacock, *Medieval Islamic Historiography*, esp. 57–72.
66. See, for example, Vollmann, "Autorenrollen"; Burrow, *Medieval Writers*, 32; O'Connor, "Irish Narrative Literature", 17.
67. Rankovic, "Introduction", 1–2.
68. Sigurdsson, "Poet", 231.
69. Drout, "Medieval Author", 51. See also Sonnesyn, "Obedient Creativity", 115.
70. Drout, "Medieval Author", 33.
71. Sigurdsson, "Poet", 233–4.
72. For medieval Europe, see Conti, "Scribes as Authors"; Sigurdsson, "Poet". Görke, "Authorship", 67–8 argues that pre-modern Arabic terms for those involved in the production of writing differ from the terminology employed by their late antique and medieval European counterparts, but this does not necessarily mean that the functions themselves were all that different. Certainly someone like al-Ṭabarī was imbued with *auctoritas* even in the absence of corresponding terms. For a brief example of this last point, see B. Radtke, *Weltgeschichte*, 161.
73. EI[3], "Abū Mikhnaf" (K. Athamina).
74. Some justifications given by (late) ancient and early Muslim scholars as to why they felt it necessary to compose their works should still sound familiar to the modern academic, from 'existing scholarship has neglected this subject' to 'previous scholarship got it wrong' to 'long have I been interested in this subject'. See the detailed discussion in Freimark, *Vorwort*, 36–50 and – for very similar tropes in ancient historiography – Marincola, *Authority and Tradition*, esp. 43–62, 112–17.
75. On al-Ṭabarī's education and intellectual milieu (a "milieu of sages"), see Gilliot, "Scholarly Formation" (quote on 143).

Historical Setting

This section will give a historical overview of the period under study. The analysis in Parts II and III will make frequent reference to protagonists and events in early Islamic and Khārijite history. For reasons of space and ease of reading, however, it will refrain from rehashing said history unless absolutely necessary. The reader is therefore directed to the following survey for orientation and to help contextualise literary Khārijism as discussed over the subsequent chapters.

Khārijite History from the Battle of Ṣiffīn to the Death of ʿAbd al-Malik

The following summary of key dates and events in early Khārijite history is based on the depiction given in the Islamic tradition and accepted by most scholarship. This is not to say that the historicity of this portrayal should be accepted at face value, but neither will there be an attempt to evaluate the truth value of one account or another. The analysed sources operate within this common framework of Khārijite and early Islamic history, which therefore requires some elucidation. Moreover, they often only allude to historical events and their meanings, knowledge of which was presupposed among the contemporary audience but might not be quite as firmly entrenched in the mind of the modern reader. Early Islamic historiography shares this feature with late antique conventions of history-writing, which enabled the historians in question to "construct accounts with subtle differences that the audience could discern without difficulty".[1] We will see this in action over the course of the subsequent chapters.

The early historical tradition often differs concerning details such as the exact sequence of events, which Khārijite revolts are mentioned, and occasionally also the identity of the actors involved. Only with regard to a few major Khārijite figures can we observe some consistency in the structural components that make up the relevant accounts. Overall, however, our author-compilers agree in their identification of the major events of early Khārijite history and provide a more or less consistent picture of these, even if they differ in their interpretations.[2] Consensus alone should certainly not be understood as an indicator of historicity, of course, but (also) as a "phenomen[on] of discourse".[3] However, it does point to the formation of dominant narratives within Islamic historiography that illustrate the evolution of a communal memory of Khārijism. This book will thus focus on these 'grand narratives' rather than the variations in the structural components of each and every account. Of course, noticeable differences in the sources' presentation of Khārijism or the rendering of a particular episode will be discussed over the course of the individual chapters.

According to the Islamic tradition, the Khārijite movement originated in the first civil war (*fitna*) of the early Muslim community, specifically the conflict between Muḥammad's fourth successor, ʿAlī b. Abī Ṭālib, and Muʿāwiya, governor of Syria and relative of the murdered third caliph, ʿUthmān b. ʿAffān (r. 644–56).[4] When ʿAlī succeeded ʿUthmān as caliph after the latter's assassination, Muʿāwiya refused to swear allegiance to him and the two opponents finally met in battle at Ṣiffīn in 657. The depictions of the events at Ṣiffīn are confusing and often contradictory,[5] but the sources largely agree that ʿAlī was about to win the confrontation when Muʿāwiya, under advice from the shrewd tactician ʿAmr b. al-ʿĀṣ, called for negotiations by ordering his troops to hoist leaves with verses from the Qurʾān (*maṣāḥif*, sg. *muṣḥaf*) onto their lances. The ensuing arbitration agreement (*taḥkīm*) concluded between ʿAlī and Muʿāwiya is understood to have instigated the emergence of the Khārijites, who protested against the adjudication on religious grounds and held that judgement was God's alone (*lā ḥukma illā li-llāh*).

The circumstances under which the caliph agreed to the arbitration are central to the later debates between ʿAlī and the Khārijites as these are rendered by the sources. Let us therefore take a closer look at how early Islamic historiography presents the decision process leading to ʿAlī's acceptance of the adjudication.

According to the historical tradition, ʿAlī initially rejected Muʿāwiya's call for arbitration because he suspected treachery on the part of the Syrians.[6] The sources all agree and indeed stress that ʿAlī was forced to accept adjudication by his own supporters.[7] When Muʿāwiya offered a ceasefire agreement, certain elements in ʿAlī's own army urged him to accept the offer, perhaps assuming that the former intended to proclaim his surrender and acknowledge ʿAlī as *amīr al-muʾminīn* (Commander of the Faithful).[8] These insubordinate subjects of the caliph are variously described as "the people", "the *qurrāʾ*" (sg. *qārī*)[9] or "the (future) Khawārij". However, the one person identified in all sources as the major culprit is al-Ashʿath b. Qays, chief of the tribe of Kinda in Kufa.[10] Al-Yaʿqūbī is the only one to go so far as to explicitly accuse him of working for Muʿāwiya,[11] but he is vilified in all of the other sources as well: al-Ashʿath and his followers among ʿAlī's troops reportedly threatened the caliph with withdrawal from his camp should he insist on fighting the Syrians and not agree to the arbitration. They even threatened to "kill you [ʿAlī] like we killed [ʿUthmān] Ibn ʿAffān" if he did not give in to their demands.[12] This portrayal accords with the controversial status of al-Ashʿath in Islamic historiography, which comes down on the negative side of his reputation overall, a tendency that is sometimes also extended to his family.[13] The depiction of al-Ashʿath as instigator of ʿAlī's (Khārijite?) troubles at Ṣiffīn is brought to a fitting conclusion in the accusation that he later hosted ʿAlī's murderer, his fellow tribesman Ibn Muljam, the night (or month) before the caliph's assassination.[14]

To add insult to injury, the (future) Khawārij also forced ʿAlī's hand in the selection of his arbiter. Led by al-Ashʿath and against ʿAlī's explicit protest, they insisted on Abū Mūsā al-Ashʿarī[15] because they considered him impartial; he had not taken part in the conflict between ʿAlī and Muʿāwiya and was thus expected to treat both sides with equal fairness.[16] ʿAlī objected to this choice, arguing that Abū Mūsā "incited the people to abstain from aiding me (*khadhdhala al-nās ʿannī*)",[17] but to no avail – al-Ashʿath and the *qurrāʾ* insisted on him.

Shortly afterwards, however, we find the same group of people calling upon ʿAlī to resume battle against Muʿāwiya, citing objections to the idea of two mere humans deciding such serious matters not exclusively on the basis of the Qurʾān but also of their own judgement, as had been stipulated in the arbitration document.[18] They even assaulted al-Ashʿath b. Qays when he informed them of the precise content of the arbitration document, crying out *lā ḥukma illā li-llāh*, which would become the Khārijite maxim.

The events are muddled and, as noted, the whole Ṣiffīn story is chaotic and at times contradictory. It is unclear why a group of ʿAlī's supporters should have first forced him into the arbitration only to then condemn him for agreeing to it. Different explanations have been offered, some – as stated in the preceding paragraph – focusing on the adjudication document that stipulated the conditions for the arbiters, and others identifying the eventual outcome of the arbitration as the breaking point. Regarding the latter, it has been argued, for instance, that those among ʿAlī's troops who demanded the resumption of armed conflict were concerned with the question of whether or not ʿUthmān had been killed legitimately. According to them, he had been guilty of transgressing Qurʾānic directives, meaning his caliphate had become illegitimate, threatening to lead the entire *umma* astray. Hence, his assassination had not only been a lawful act, but a necessity.[19] Discussing the issue was therefore superfluous and even dangerous, as Muʿāwiya obviously did not intend to obey God's law.

It may not be possible to ascertain what really happened, but the Islamic tradition agrees that ʿAlī decided not to resume hostilities. He abided by his reluctant acceptance of the arbitration and settled on awaiting the decision of the arbiters. In response to this, those of ʿAlī's followers who disagreed with him left his camp after the army's return to Kufa to 'go out' (*kharaja*; whence al-Khawārij) to Ḥarūrāʾ, a nearby village, where they chose a leader and prepared for armed conflict with the caliph.[20]

At first, ʿAlī successfully convinced these 'Ḥarūrites' to return to his camp, but a contingent of a few thousand fighters left his ranks anew when he showed no signs of renouncing his agreement to the arbitration meeting despite their protests.[21] Shortly before their second departure from Kufa, the dissidents elected ʿAbdallāh b. Wahb al-Rāsibī, a man renowned for his bravery and piety, as their leader. As we shall see, the early Islamic tradition highlights the connection between the Khawārij and piety and so it is unsurprising that their doctrinal 'ancestors' and early leaders are portrayed as particularly devout believers as well.[22]

Following months of negotiations and a fruitless exchange of letters and messengers, ʿAlī finally fought his former supporters at Nahrawān – a town in what is now eastern Iraq – in Ṣafar 38 H/July 658 CE and defeated them utterly. Of the approximately 3,000 men under Ibn Wahb's command, only a few managed to escape, and he himself was killed.[23] Some 400 Khārijites were wounded and later pardoned by ʿAlī.[24]

The Battle of Nahrawān marked the end of organised large-scale Khārijite activities during the reign of ʿAlī. The historical tradition records a number of small, isolated and short-lived uprisings by rebels accused of Khārijism. The only revolt about which we have a little more information is that led by a certain Abū Maryam al-Saʿdī in 38 H/658–9 CE. All of these insurgencies were easily countered and their leaders put to death, either by ʿAlī himself or by one of his agents.[25] However, the Khawārij would prove to be his downfall: in 40 H/661 CE, ʿAlī was killed by the Khārijite assassin Ibn Muljam.

After ʿAlī's death, the Iraqis gave their allegiance to his oldest son, al-Ḥasan b. ʿAlī. It is unclear whether al-Ḥasan's rule was accepted anywhere outwith Iraq, or even in all of Iraq, but the sources are agreed that in Kufa at least he was recognised as caliph without opposition.[26] The exact length of al-Ḥasan's rule is uncertain, but it does not seem to have exceed one year. The historical tradition has al-Ḥasan relinquish his position to Muʿāwiya in 41 H/661–2 CE,[27] under undetermined circumstances. Muʿāwiya is said to have essentially bought the caliphate by issuing guarantees of safe-conduct to al-Ḥasan and his most important companions, among them his younger brother al-Ḥusayn as well as ʿAbdallāh b. ʿAbbās, while also granting al-Ḥasan a substantial amount of money from the state treasury.[28] The sources put forward various explanations for al-Ḥasan's submission to Muʿāwiya: the latter's superior military strength; al-Ḥasan's aversion to bloodshed and preference for a peaceful solution to the conflict between his family and Muʿāwiya; the realisation on al-Ḥasan's part that the divisions among his own followers made it impossible for him to rule effectively without running the risk of meeting the same unfortunate end as his father.[29] This diversity of opinion testifies to the debates al-Ḥasan's decision must have encouraged – his renunciation of the caliphate was rather ill received, at least as remembered by later historians.[30] An Iraqi pro-ʿAlid/proto-Shīʿī tradition may be reflected in two Syriac works that name al-Ḥasan and/or his brother al-Ḥusayn as legitimate caliphs before or instead of Muʿāwiya.[31] Almost every other source is in agreement, however, that al-Ḥasan settled in Medina with al-Ḥusayn and their cousin ʿAbdallāh b. Jaʿfar, where he remained until his death in 50 H/669–70 CE.[32]

Having reached an agreement with ʿAlī's immediate family and established his rule over the territories under Muslim rule, Muʿāwiya appointed al-Mughīra b. Shuʿba and ʿAbdallāh b. ʿĀmir as governors of Kufa and Basra, respectively.[33] During the preparations for his return to Syria, however, a group of about 500 Khārijites under the command of Farwa b. Nawfal al-Ashjāʿī gathered at al-Nukhayla to oppose Muʿāwiya.[34] At first, Muʿāwiya sent Syrian troops against the rebels, who had relocated to Kufa in the meantime. These troops failed, however, so Muʿāwiya apparently resorted to another means of attacking the Khārijites that illustrates his (reputation for) political cunning: he told the Kufans that he would only grant them a guarantee of safe-conduct for their siding with ʿAlī if they agreed to take on the problem of the Khārijite rebels themselves. The Kufans obliged and mounted an attack against the Khārijites, who attempted to avoid the confrontation by arguing that they had a common enemy in Muʿāwiya. Their reasoning fell on deaf (or coerced) ears, however – they were all killed by the Kufan army.[35]

Having solved this particular Khārijite problem, Muʿāwiya finally returned home to Syria. From Damascus, he ruled the burgeoning Islamic Empire until his death in 60 H/680 CE, firmly establishing Umayyad power and Syrian predominance over the Iraqis.[36] There are no reports of Khārijite revolts in Syria at all and Muʿāwiya himself does not appear to have been personally involved in dealing with Khārijite rebels. We shall therefore leave him in Damascus and focus on events in Iraq and Iran, the main *loci* of Khārijite activities during his reign.

Al-Mughīra b. Shuʿba, a member of the tribe of Thaqīf from Ṭāʾif and a Companion, was appointed as governor of Kufa in 41 H/661–2 CE, a position he retained until his death in 50 or 51 H/670–1 CE.[37] Besides a number of smaller Khārijite uprisings, he had to deal with probably the largest Khārijite revolt during Muʿāwiya's reign, the rebellion headed by al-Mustawrid b. ʿUllafa in 43 H/663–4 CE. Al-Mughīra did not personally engage with the dissidents but sent out troops who succeeded in quelling the revolts and killing, imprisoning or exiling the Khārijites.[38]

As the main Khārijite rebel in this period, al-Mustawrid warrants closer examination. He was a prominent representative of the Khawārij in Kufa, who in 42 H/662–3 CE decided to rebel against al-Mughīra and elected al-Mustawrid as their commander. Before they were able to set their plans in motion, however, the governor arrested and imprisoned a large number of them. Al-Mustawrid was the only one among the leadership not to be taken prisoner, whereupon he decided to leave Kufa. He settled near al-Ḥīra but returned to Kufa to seek refuge with a member of the ʿAbd al-Qays tribal group, to whom he was related by marriage. When al-Mustawrid's presence there endangered the life and property of his host, the Khārijite left the town once again and took his supporters towards al-Madāʾin,[39] whose governor refused to let them pass.[40] The rebels relocated towards al-Madhār, a town in the territory of Basra, but ultimately turned back towards Kufa to avoid being caught between the Kufan troops sent by al-Mughīra and the army dispatched by the Basran governor.[41] Along the way, there were several skirmishes with al-Mughīra's troops, but the final battle took place at Bahurasīr, a former Sasanian city west of the Tigris that formed the western part of al-Madāʾin. Al-Mustawrid and the Kufan leader, Maʿqil b. Qays, killed each other in a duel. The army under the command of Maʿqil's successor then killed the remaining Khārijites.[42]

As governor of Basra, Muʿāwiya appointed ʿAbdallāh b. ʿĀmir, who had already held this office under the third caliph, ʿUthmān b. ʿAffān. However, Ibn ʿĀmir was removed from his position in 44 H/664 CE and replaced with Ziyād b. Abīhi, who was also appointed governor over Khurāsān, Sīstān, Baḥrayn and ʿUmān.[43] Ziyād, later also known as Ziyād b. Abī Sufyān after Muʿāwiya acknowledged him as his half-brother, held the position of governor until his demise in 53 or 54 H/673–4 CE. Following al-Mughīra's death three years prior, Ziyād had also been granted the governorship of Kufa, in principle uniting all of Iraq as well as parts of Iran, the Arabian Peninsula and Central Asia under his command.[44]

Ziyād is notorious in the historical tradition for his strict demands for obedience from his subjects and harsh treatment of rebels.[45] Unlike al-Mughīra and ʿAbdallāh b. ʿĀmir, he is also reported to have personally dealt with Khārijite insurgents. He apparently engaged in verbal confrontations with Khārijites, most notably with the Basran Khārijite Abū Bilāl Mirdās b. Udayya, and he personally saw to the persecution and crucifixion of several Khārijite insurgents.[46]

Ziyād was succeeded in all of his offices by his son ʿUbaydallāh, who may have surpassed his father in the cruel treatment of (suspected) Khārijite rebels.[47] He is said to have offered a group of Khārijite rebels their freedom if one half of them killed the other half,[48] which some of the prisoners agreed to, and he had no qualms about killing women along with the men.[49] His torture and crucifixion of a female Khārijite reportedly led to the famous uprising of Abū Bilāl Mirdās,[50] either in the last year of Muʿāwiya's reign or the first year of Yazīd's caliphate.[51]

Muʿāwiya died in 60 H/680 CE and was succeeded by his son Yazīd I, allegiance to whom he had (tentatively) secured against considerable resistance several years before his death. Notwithstanding that, upon Muʿāwiya's passing opposition to Yazīd was widespread and eventually led to the second civil war (c. 680–92). Eminent figures of the Muslim community openly opposed Yazīd's accession to the caliphate, among them al-Ḥusayn b. ʿAlī, the Prophet's grandson, but successful resistance was achieved only by ʿAbdallāh b. al-Zubayr, the grandson of the first caliph Abū Bakr.

As early as c. 61 H/680–1 CE, Ibn al-Zubayr had managed to acquire a large following made up of various different elements united by their opposition to Yazīd and the Umayyads. Ibn al-Zubayr was based in the Ḥijāz, with Mecca and Medina his primary bases of operation. In 63 H/682–3 CE, Yazīd sent a large Syrian army against Ibn al-Zubayr that took Medina and then marched onto Mecca, where open hostilities broke out after all attempts at negotiation had failed. The threat posed to Mecca and the Kaʿba by the Umayyad forces besieging Ibn al-Zubayr led many Muslims from all walks of life to flock to the city in order to protect the Sanctuary of God. Among them were also several Khārijites, including the future chiefs of the Azāriqa and Najdiyya factions of the Khawārij, Nāfiʿ b. al-Azraq and Najda b. ʿĀmir, respectively,[52] as well as al-Mukhtār b. Abī ʿUbayd,[53] who would revolt in Kufa in the name of ʿAlī's son Muḥammad b. al-Ḥanafiyya only a few years later. While the Syrian forces were engaged in attacking the Kaʿba, news of the sudden death of Yazīd in 64 H/683 CE reached Mecca and saved Ibn al-Zubayr from dire straits.[54] However, this also led to a split between him and the Khārijites, who are said to have disagreed with his opinion on ʿUthmān b. ʿAffān and thus abandoned him once it had become clear that Mecca was no longer under threat.[55]

The death of Yazīd led to a succession crisis in Umayyad Syria, although some of the seeds of discord had already been sown when his father had secured the oath of allegiance (*bayʿa*) for him, and his own short reign appears to have caused considerable discontent:

> In the first year [of Yazīd's rule], al-Ḥusayn b. ʿAlī and the People of the House of God's Messenger were killed; in the second, the *ḥaram* of God's Messenger was attacked and the sanctity of al-Madīna was violated; and in the third, blood was shed in the *ḥaram* of God and the Kaʿba was burned.[56]

Yazīd's son succeeded him but died after a few short weeks. Yazīd had left no other sons who were of age; other factions both within the Umayyad family and among the Syrian tribes now vied for the office of the caliphate, plunging Syria into civil war. Ibn al-Zubayr and the Khārijites, in turn, used the Umayyads' internal strife to strengthen their own positions. Following Yazīd's death, "the mass of people turned to Ibn al-Zubayr".[57] With the exception of Syria, he managed to successfully bring all of the core territories of the nascent Islamic Empire under his control, and they were more or less securely governed by Zubayrid governors throughout the 680s.[58] It has been argued that it is thus inaccurate to describe Ibn al-Zubayr as an anti-caliph[59] – for years, Ibn al-Zubayr was the effective ruler of most of the empire, relegating his Umayyad opponents in Syria to the rank of (increasingly successful) rebels.[60] This also meant that the Khārijites' main foe in the period of the second civil war was Ibn al-Zubayr – Zubayrid forces fought the Najdiyya and were also responsible for the death of Nāfiʿ b. al-Azraq. The man who eventually caused the downfall of the Azāriqa entire, the general al-Muhallab b. Abī Ṣufra, was first appointed as commander-in-chief by Ibn al-Zubayr.[61]

The early years of the second *fitna* (c. 683–5) saw the formation of the four main Khārijite factions, the *uṣūl al-Khawārij*: the Najdiyya, the Azāriqa, the Ṣufriyya and the Ibāḍiyya.[62] All of them reportedly originated in Basra and it is from there that many of them left for Mecca to support Ibn al-Zubayr against Yazīd's army. Upon their separation from Ibn al-Zubayr, many Khārijites returned to Basra, which Yazīd's death had left torn by civil strife. Various tribal factions were in open conflict with one another, wresting control of the city from its resident governor, ʿUbaydallāh b. Ziyād, who fled to Syria in 683 or 684[63] and was subsequently killed in 686 when he attempted to return to Iraq and regain control of the province for ʿAbd al-Malik.[64] In this chaotic environment, the Basran Khārijites managed to free those of their brethren who had been imprisoned by ʿUbaydallāh,[65] turning into a formidable force that inspired terror in their non-Khārijite neighbours. The two militant Khārijite groups present in Basra, the Azāriqa under Nāfiʿ

and the followers of Nadja, soon left the city, however. The Azāriqa was initially active mostly in Iraq, where they are said to have indiscriminately murdered anyone who disagreed with them, including fellow Khārijites, until Nāfiʿ's death in battle against Zubayrid forces in 685. The surviving Azraqīs withdrew to Iran, specifically to Fārs, Kirmān and Sīstān, which remained their primary areas of activity until the destruction of the group in the late 70s H/690s CE.[66]

The Najdīs, on the other hand, successfully – if only briefly – gained control over a large territory and established themselves in Yemen, Baḥrayn and Ḥaḍramawt. Their relative moderation in comparison with the Azāriqa, frequently remarked upon by the sources, might be due to their military and political success and the ensuing need for pragmatism in everyday affairs.[67] Like all Khārijite groups, however, the Najdiyya was prone to internal conflict: in 72 H/692 CE, Najda was deposed and killed by a rival who afterwards broke from the main body of the group and established his own Khārijite faction.[68] Only a year later, forces of the Iraqi governor, al-Ḥajjāj b. Yūsuf (d. 95 H/714 CE), destroyed the remainder of the Najdiyya.[69] It is possible, however, that parts of the group survived into the ninth century.[70]

Returning to the mid-680s, a member of the Umayyad family eventually emerged victorious from the civil war in Syria in 64 H/684 CE: Marwān b. al-Ḥakam. With him, power was transferred from the Sufyānid branch of the family to the Marwānid line that would remain in power until the Umayyads were overthrown by the Hāshimiyya movement in 132 H/749–50 CE, putting the ʿAbbāsids in power. Marwān himself died only a year after his accession, but this time there was no succession crisis.[71] His son ʿAbd al-Malik, whose importance for the development of the Islamic state can hardly be overstated, took office without much noteworthy opposition from the Syrian factions. He consolidated his power through a combination of shrewd politics and brute military force, culminating in the defeat and death of Ibn al-Zubayr in 73 H/692 CE. While the killing of an eminent Companion like Ibn al-Zubayr and the preceding siege of Mecca, which led to the destruction of the Kaʿba, certainly left a bitter aftertaste in the Islamic tradition,[72] ʿAbd al-Malik nevertheless managed to unite the Muslim-ruled territories under his authority and initiate a series of reforms that had long-lasting effects on the structure and shape of the Islamic Empire.[73]

Having secured the territories previously ruled by Ibn al-Zubayr, ʿAbd al-Malik turned to the problem of fighting the Khārijite rebels, who had so far proved to be rather resilient.[74] Probably the most important figure in the battle against the various Khārijite groups wreaking havoc in Iraq and Iran in the 690s was al-Ḥajjāj b. Yūsuf. Al-Ḥajjāj had led the Umayyad troops in battle against Ibn al-Zubayr in 692 and had afterwards shown himself very adept at quelling the last remnants of revolt in the Ḥijāz. He was notorious for meting out harsh discipline and punishment, a quality that apparently endeared him to ʿAbd al-Malik, who appointed al-Ḥajjāj as governor of ever-rebellious Iraq in 694.[75] In this capacity, al-Ḥajjāj was responsible for eradicating the Khārijite problem. ʿAbd al-Malik had confirmed al-Muhallab as commander of the troops in pursuit of the Azāriqa, who, now led by Qaṭarī b. al-Fujāʾa, were active in Iran.[76] While al-Ḥajjāj at first seems to have doubted al-Muhallab's suitability for the position, he later came to revise his opinion.[77]

A Khārijite threat much more immediate to Iraq and al-Ḥajjāj were the revolts of the Jazīran (Northern Mesopotamian) tribesmen Ṣāliḥ b. Musarriḥ and Shabīb b. Yazīd from 76 H/695 CE onwards. It is unclear whether there was any direct connection between the two and, if so, how exactly they were related.[78] Shabīb is perhaps the most famous Khārijite rebel of the late seventh century; his story is an epic tale of adventure and irreverence in the face of largely helpless authorities. Al-Ṭabarī transmits by far the longest account of Shabīb, although the material is jumbled and contradictory in places.[79] The outline of Ṣāliḥ and Shabīb's revolts is broadly the same in the sources that discuss it, although none is as detailed as al-Ṭabarī's report.

The early historical tradition knows Ṣāliḥ as an ascetic, a pious and humble Muslim whose disgust with the actions of the Umayyads and their agents led him to revolt. He was killed by al-Ḥajjāj's troops soon after he 'went out' in the Jazīra. Some accounts have Shabīb take over command immediately and lead Ṣāliḥ's remaining Khārijites to safety. Over the next two years or so, he successfully defeated every army al-Ḥajjāj sent against him, despite being greatly outnumbered; he even managed to enter Kufa brazenly under al-Ḥajjāj's nose. His reputation appears contradictory: accounts of his involvement in indiscriminate killing are balanced with reports of his unwavering piety, reluctance to kill Companions and superior military skills; the Christians of Mosul apparently held him in much higher regard than the Umayyads due to his fair treatment of them.[80] He mainly roamed Iraq and the Jazīra, never staying long in one place, uninterested in ruling any of the cities or regions he invaded. Shabīb eventually engaged al-Ḥajjāj and his troops in combat directly. It was during this battle outside Kufa that he suffered a severe defeat and lost both his brother and his wife, who had accompanied him. He escaped with a number of his supporters but died not long after. His end, when it came, was rather inglorious: he did not fall in battle but was thrown off his horse and drowned while trying to escape al-Ḥajjāj's troops.[81]

The Shabīb story in al-Ṭabarī has strong legendary overtones and contains miraculous material, particularly with regard to Shabīb's birth.[82] The statements uttered by Shabīb's mother are reminiscent of the visions ascribed to the Prophet's mother in the *sīra* of Ibn Isḥāq as edited by Ibn Hishām.[83] Such embellishments are a good indication of the importance Shabīb's story took on over time; that he was a literary and historical figure of some stature is further confirmed by the fact that he appears in non-Muslim sources.[84] These are by no means entirely independent from the Islamic tradition, of course,[85] but their discussion of Islamic history tends to focus on major actors and events only. The fact that Shabīb's adventures made it into non-Muslim literary traditions as well is noteworthy: while Khārijites do feature in these works in a general sense, only a handful of them appear by name.

The almost simultaneous defeats of Shabīb and the Azraqī leader Qaṭarī rang in the end of large-scale Khārijite uprisings during the caliphate of ʿAbd al-Malik. Al-Ḥajjāj continued to persecute Khārijites in Iraq and elsewhere, including those who did not necessarily express their opposition to the Umayyads in violent terms. A famous example of this is al-Ḥajjāj's pursuit of the well-known Khārijite poet and scholar ʿImrān b. Ḥiṭṭān, who reportedly endured much hardship on his prolonged flight from the Umayyad authorities until his death in 84 H/703 CE.[86] Larger revolts by militant Khārijites remained a comparatively rare phenomenon in the first half of the eighth century, however, and did not pose a threat to the caliphs and their governors until the last few years of Umayyad rule, when the upheaval of the third *fitna* (c. 743–7/50) provided ample space for malcontents of all persuasions.

Notes

1. Haider, *Rebel and Imām*, 4. On early Islamic history-writing as "rhetoricized historiography" sharing a number of commonalities with (late) antique conventions of historical writing, see ibid., 1–6; for a brief definition of the term, 14.
2. On this phenomenon of early Islamic historiography generally, see Humphreys, "Qurʾānic Myth", 275. Haider, *Rebel and Imām* shows that while historians embellish their materials in distinct ways to achieve certain effects, the core structure of a story is the same across the board. See Chapter One below for a brief summary.
3. Conrad, "Conquest of Arwād", 395. See also Khalidi, *Arabic Historical Thought*, 43: "veracity had been linked [by the ninth century] to consensus to the point where one might speak of a consensual theory of truth to be employed by *Hadith* scholars and historians".
4. The assassination of ʿUthmān and the ensuing events of the first civil war are well-covered in modern scholarship. See, for example, Crone, *Medieval Islamic Political Thought*, 17–32; Kennedy, *Prophet*, 69–81; Hinds, "Murder";

Madelung, *Succession to Muḥammad*, 78–310. For a critical assessment of the early historians' treatment of 'Uthmān's reign, see Humphreys, *Islamic History*, 98–103 and "Qur'ānic Myth". For the memory of 'Uthmān's murder in Islamic chronicles up to the Middle Period, see Keaney, *Medieval Islamic Historiography*, "First Islamic Revolt" and "Confronting the Caliph".

5. For a brief discussion of this issue, see EI², "Ṣiffīn" (M. Lecker). For a detailed study of the various Ṣiffīn narratives in early and medieval Islamic historiography, see Petersen, *'Alī and Mu'āwiya*, 20–45 and *passim*; Hagler, *Echoes of Fitna* as well as his "Repurposed Narratives" and "Unity through Omission".
6. See al-Ya'qūbī, *Ta'rīkh*, II, 188; al-Balādhurī, *Ansāb*, II, 312, 324; Ibn Muzāḥim, *Waq'at Ṣiffīn*, 560, 561; al-Dīnawarī, *Akhbār*, 221; al-Ṭabarī, *Ta'rīkh*, I, 3330; Ibn Sa'd, *Ṭabaqāt*, III, 32; al-Mas'ūdī, *Murūj*, I–II, 390–1, 402; Ibn A'tham, *Futūḥ*, III, 306, 307, 319 and IV, 96.
7. See, for example, al-Dīnawarī, *Akhbār*, 221; al-Ya'qūbī, *Ta'rīkh*, II, 189; al-Balādhurī, *Ansāb*, II, 308, 312, 314; Ibn Muzāḥim, *Waq'at Ṣiffīn*, 560–2; al-Ṭabarī, *Ta'rīkh*, I, 3330–1; al-Mas'ūdī, *Murūj*, I–II, 390–1; Ibn A'tham, *Futūḥ*, III, 307, 312, 313, 314, 321 and IV, 1–4.
8. This is the interpretation of Martin Hinds in "Kufan Political Alignments", 364.
9. The precise meaning of the term *qurrā'* and the identity of the members of this group have been subject to debate. Compare, for example, the approach of Juynboll, "Qurrā'" and "Qur'ān Reciters", with Sayed, *Revolte*. For a general overview, see Shah, "Quest".
10. On al-Ash'ath and his family, see Leube, *Kinda*, 48–50, 91–2, 106–10, 210–19; EI², "al-Ash'ath, Abū Muḥammad Ma'dīkarib b. Ḳays b. Ma'dīkarib" (H. Reckendorf). For al-Ash'ath's involvement at Ṣiffīn and his family's lasting relationship with the *qurrā'*, see Leube, *Kinda*, 172–4.
11. Al-Ya'qūbī, *Ta'rīkh*, II, 188–9. For 'Alī's assassin, Ibn Muljam, staying with al-Ash'ath in Kufa before killing 'Alī, see ibid., 212 and also Ibn Sa'd, *Ṭabaqāt*, III, 36.
12. Ibn Muzāḥim, *Waq'at Ṣiffīn*, 561; al-Ṭabarī, *Ta'rīkh*, I, 3330, 3331; al-Mas'ūdī, *Murūj*, I–II, 391; Ibn A'tham, *Futūḥ*, III, 312, 314. This statement will be discussed in Chapter Four, section on 'Apologia for 'Alī'.
13. Leube, *Kinda*, 57–63, 95–6, 107–10, esp. 118–23, 126–9, 161–2.
14. See for a brief discussion Leube, *Kinda*, 192–3.
15. See, for example, al-Balādhurī, *Ansāb*, II, 293; al-Dīnawarī, *Akhbār*, 205; Ibn Muzāḥim, *Waq'at Ṣiffīn*, 572–3; al-Ya'qūbī, *Ta'rīkh*, II, 189; al-Ṭabarī, *Ta'rīkh*, I, 3333; al-Mas'ūdī, *Murūj*, I–II, 391; Ibn A'tham, *Futūḥ*, IV, 2, 94.
16. Ibn Muzāḥim, *Waq'at Ṣiffīn*, 572. See also al-Ṭabarī, *Ta'rīkh*, I, 3333; al-Balādhurī, *Ansāb*, II, 293; al-Dīnawarī, *Akhbār*, 205; Ibn A'tham, *Futūḥ*, IV, 2, 3.
17. Al-Balādhurī, *Ansāb*, II, 293. See also al-Ya'qūbī, *Ta'rīkh*, II, 189; al-Ṭabarī, *Ta'rīkh*, I, 3333; al-Mas'ūdī, *Murūj*, I–II, 391; al-Dīnawarī, *Akhbār*, 205; Ibn A'tham, *Futūḥ*, IV, 2.

18. See, for example, al-Balādhurī, *Ansāb*, II, 295, 296; al-Ṭabarī, *Ta'rīkh*, I, 3339–40; al-Mas'ūdī, *Murūj*, I–II, 393; al-Ya'qūbī, *Ta'rīkh*, II, 190; Ibn Muzāḥim, *Waq'at Ṣiffīn*, 588, 589, 594; Ibn Sa'd, *Ṭabaqāt*, III, 32, 37.
19. Watt, *Islamic Political Thought*, 54–5.
20. Morony, *Iraq*, 469.
21. Ibid. There is considerable confusion as to the precise dates and number of the arbitration meeting(s). EI[2], "Taḥkīm" (M. Djebli).
22. For example al-Dīnawarī, *Akhbār*, 204, 215, 223; al-Balādhurī, *Ansāb*, II, 298, 317; al-Ṭabarī, *Ta'rīkh*, I, 3330, 3332; Ibn Muzāḥim, *Waq'at Ṣiffīn*, 560; al-Mas'ūdī, *Murūj*, I–II, 391; Ibn A'tham, *Futūḥ*, III, 312. See also the discussion in Chapter Two.
23. Watt, *Formative Period*, 13.
24. EI[2], "al-Nahrawān" (M. Morony).
25. See, for example, al-Balādhurī, *Ansāb*, II, 424–9.
26. Al-Ṭabarī, *Ta'rīkh*, II, 1, 2; al-Ya'qūbī, *Ta'rīkh*, II, 214; Ibn Khayyāṭ, *Ta'rīkh*, I, 228; Ibn A'tham, *Futūḥ*, IV, 148; al-Mas'ūdī, *Murūj*, I–II, 426 and *Tanbīh*, 260; al-Dīnawarī, *Akhbār*, 230; al-Balādhurī, *Ansāb*, II, 466, 467, 468.
27. Al-Mas'ūdī, *Murūj*, I–II, 426 and *Tanbīh*, 260–1; al-Dīnawarī, *Akhbār*, 230–2; al-Ṭabarī, *Ta'rīkh*, II, 1, 5–7; Ibn Khayyāṭ, *Ta'rīkh*, I, 234; al-Balādhurī, *Ansāb*, II, 484. Al-Ya'qūbī, *Ta'rīkh*, II, 216 gives the year 40 H as Mu'āwiya's accession date.
28. Al-Ṭabarī, *Ta'rīkh*, II, 1–4, 5–6, 7; al-Balādhurī, *Ansāb*, II, 474, 489–90 (where Mu'āwiya sends al-Ḥasan a blank document to write down his demands in return for his abdication). Al-Ṭabarī, *Ta'rīkh*, II, 6 and al-Balādhurī, *Ansāb*, II, 490 (a shorter version) finish their accounts with a short speech by al-Ḥasan that attempts to vindicate his decision to surrender and maintains his moral superiority over Mu'āwiya. Al-Ya'qūbī and al-Mas'ūdī both transmit this episode almost verbatim (apart from a few additions and re-wordings), but they omit the reports of al-Ḥasan accepting money and/or a guarantee of safe-conduct for himself and his supporters included by al-Ṭabarī. Al-Ya'qūbī, *Ta'rīkh*, II, 215; al-Mas'ūdī, *Murūj*, I–II, 430–1.
29. Al-Dīnawarī, *Akhbār*, 233–4; al-Ṭabarī, *Ta'rīkh*, II, 1, 3, 5; al-Ya'qūbī, *Ta'rīkh*, II, 215; al-Balādhurī, *Ansāb*, II, 468.
30. See particularly al-Mas'ūdī, *Tanbīh*, 260 and Ibn A'tham, *Futūḥ*, IV, 154, who state that al-Ḥasan was "the first caliph to remove himself" (*awwal khalīfa khala'a nafsahu*). See also al-Balādhurī, *Ansāb*, II, 474–6; al-Dīnawarī, *Akhbār*, 233–4; al-Ṭabarī, *Ta'rīkh*, II, 1–2, 3, 9; al-Ya'qūbī, *Ta'rīkh*, II, 216.
31. Tillier, "Règne du calife Ḥasan".
32. His exact death date is controversial. See EI[2], "al-Ḥasan b. 'Alī b. Abī Ṭālib" (L. Veccia Vaglieri).
33. Al-Balādhurī, *Ansāb*, II, 478–9, 490; al-Dīnawarī, *Akhbār*, 232; al-Ṭabarī, *Ta'rīkh*, II, 10–11, 15.
34. Al-Nukhayla was a town in Iraq, near al-Kufa and on the road to Syria. EI[2],

"al-Nukhayla" (E. Honigmann). The exact timing of this revolt is not clear. Al-Balādhurī, *Ansāb*, IV/1, 163 states that it took place after al-Ḥasan had already left Kufa for Medina, in 41 H/661–2 CE. Al-Ṭabarī, *Taʾrīkh*, II, 10 places it in the same year, but claims that al-Ḥasan was still in Kufa. Al-Yaʿqūbī, *Taʾrīkh*, II, 217 has 40 H/660–1 CE, but does not mention al-Ḥasan at all. Ibn Khayyāṭ, *Taʾrīkh*, I, 234 places a revolt against Muʿāwiya at al-Nukhayla in 41 H/661–2 CE, but he puts a certain ʿAbdallāh b. Abī al-Ḥawsāʾ in charge of the rebels and mentions neither Farwa b. Nawfal nor Khārijites. Ibn Abī al-Ḥawsāʾ, in turn, is mentioned by the other sources in connection with a different Khārijite revolt (see below).

35. Al-Ṭabarī, *Taʾrīkh*, II, 10; al-Yaʿqūbī, *Taʾrīkh*, II, 217; al-Balādhurī, *Ansāb*, IV/1, 163–4.
36. On the history of the Umayyad dynasty, see Hawting, *First Dynasty*; Marsham, *Umayyad Empire*; and the collection of articles in Marsham, ed., *Umayyad World*.
37. Al-Ṭabarī, *Taʾrīkh*, II, 87 and Ibn Khayyāṭ, *Taʾrīkh*, I, 247 give as his death date the year 50 H. Al-Yaʿqūbī has 51 H.
38. See, for example, al-Yaʿqūbī, *Taʾrīkh*, II, 221–2; Ibn Khayyāṭ, *Taʾrīkh*, I, 246; al-Ṭabarī, *Taʾrīkh*, II, 28–9.
39. The former Sasanian capital Ctesiphon, about 35 km southeast of modern Baghdad. In the early Islamic period, it was part of the territory governed from Kufa.
40. The governor of al-Madāʾin at this time was Simāk b. ʿUbayd.
41. At the time of al-Mustawrid's revolt, Basra was governed by ʿAbdallāh b. ʿĀmir.
42. For all this, see al-Ṭabarī, *Taʾrīkh*, II, 20–64; al-Yaʿqūbī, *Taʾrīkh*, II, 221; al-Balādhurī, *Ansāb*, IV, 169–70.
43. Al-Ṭabarī, *Taʾrīkh*, II, 73; Ibn Khayyāṭ, *Taʾrīkh*, I, 241, who gives the year 45 H.
44. Al-Yaʿqūbī, *Taʾrīkh*, II, 229; Ibn Khayyāṭ, *Taʾrīkh*, I, 247. Ibn Khayyāṭ places Ziyād's death in the year 50 H.
45. See, by way of example, al-Ṭabarī, *Taʾrīkh*, II, 73–6, 83, 91, 185; al-Yaʿqūbī, *Taʾrīkh*, II, 232.
46. For example, al-Ṭabarī, *Taʾrīkh*, II, 76, 83–4; Ibn Khayyāṭ, *Taʾrīkh*, I, 241, 246, 264; al-Balādhurī, *Ansāb*, IV/1, 173.
47. Morony, *Iraq*, 472.
48. This episode is discussed in Chapter Five, 175–6.
49. For example, al-Ṭabarī, *Taʾrīkh*, II, 186–8. Al-Balādhurī, *Ansāb*, IV/1, 176, 177 already ascribes this practice to ʿUbaydallāh's father Ziyād.
50. Al-Balādhurī, *Ansāb*, IV/1, 181–2. On Abū Bilāl's revolt, see Chapter Five.
51. The exact date is unclear. See the remarks in Chapter Five, 200 n. 192.
52. Ibn Khayyāṭ, *Taʾrīkh*, I, 248; al-Ṭabarī, *Taʾrīkh*, II, 425–6, 513–15, 529; al-Balādhurī, *Ansāb*, IV/1, 394–5 and IV/2, 372–3, 455.
53. Al-Ṭabarī, *Taʾrīkh*, II, 529.

54. Kennedy, *Prophet*, 90.
55. Al-Ṭabarī, *Taʾrīkh*, II, 516; al-Balādhurī, *Ansāb*, IV/1, 395 and IV/2, 373.
56. Al-Yaʿqūbī, *Taʾrīkh*, II, 252.
57. Ibid., 255.
58. Kennedy, *Prophet*, 90–1; Hawting, *First Dynasty*, 46–57. For a detailed study of the second *fitna*, see Rotter, *Umayyaden*. For ideological aspects of Ibn al-Zubayr's claims to power, see Shaddel, "ʿAbd Allāh ibn al-Zubayr"; Lynch, "Sons of the Muhājirūn".
59. As in EI[2], "ʿAbd Allāh b. al-Zubayr" (H. A. R. Gibb).
60. Robinson, *ʿAbd al-Malik*, 31–48.
61. See the references in Chapter Six, in the section on al-Muhallab.
62. Crone, *Medieval Islamic Political Thought*, 55 argues that the Ṣufriyya and the Ibāḍiyya only appeared with the third *fitna* in the later 740s. Lewinstein, "Making and Unmaking" maintains that the Ṣufriyya was a category, invented much later, for otherwise unspecified Khārijites.
63. Al-Ṭabarī, *Taʾrīkh*, II, 461, 516–18, 581; al-Balādhurī, *Ansāb*, IV/1, 396–427 and IV/2, 106, 401.
64. Kennedy, *Prophet*, 94.
65. Al-Ṭabarī, *Taʾrīkh*, II, 459, 513, 517–18; al-Balādhurī, *Ansāb*, VI/1, 401, 413 and VI/2, 401, 417.
66. See especially the lengthy, if confusing, accounts in Ibn Aʿtham, *Futūḥ*, VI, 1–47 (in the Zubayrid era), 298–322 (during ʿAbd al-Malik's reign) and VII, 1, 17–83; al-Ṭabarī, *Taʾrīkh*, II, 517–20, 580–91, 753–65, 821–8, 855–80, 1003–19. See also EI[2], "Azāriḳa" (R. Rubinacci).
67. Schwartz, *Ǧihād*, 71.
68. Al-Balādhurī, *Ansāb*, IV/2, 453, 462–3; al-Ṭabarī, *Taʾrīkh*, II, 829; Ibn Khayyāṭ, *Taʾrīkh*, I, 263–4; EI[2], "Nadjadāt" (R. Rubinacci).
69. Watt, *Formative Period*, 23.
70. Crone, "Statement by the Najdiyya", 56.
71. Kennedy, *Prophet*, 91–3.
72. See, for example, al-Balādhurī, *Ansāb*, IV/2, 386–7 for Ibn al-Zubayr's mother Asmāʾ cursing al-Ḥajjāj.
73. Robinson, *ʿAbd al-Malik*, esp. chapter 4; Hawting, *First Dynasty*, 58–71.
74. Bacharach even argued that the Khārijites posed such a challenge to ʿAbd al-Malik that his coinage reforms of 72–8 H/692–8 CE should primarily be understood as an attempt to counter their claims to the caliphate. Bacharach, "Signs of Sovereignty", 9–14.
75. EI[2], "al-Ḥadjdjādj b. Yūsuf" (A. Dietrich).
76. Coin finds from the period 691–5 confirm Qaṭarī's presence in Iran and that he claimed the title of *amīr al-muʾminīn* for himself. Madelung, *Religious Trends*, 56–7. See also Gaiser, "What Do We Learn", 174–7; Bernheimer, "'Kharijism' and 'the Kharijites'". Nevertheless, apart from the *lā ḥukma* slogan, there is little distinctly Khārijite about these coins and the slogan in itself is not problematic

for Muslims *per se*. Moreover, it was also used on Zanj coinage (Gaiser, "Source-Critical Methodologies", 1382), and scholarship has called into question the Khārijī motivation of the Zanj rebellion (for example, Berkey, *Formation of Islam*, 141; Gaiser, "What Do We Learn", 169 n. 10). Qaṭarī is explicitly identified as a Khārijite by the written sources only. On this, see also Hagemann and Verkinderen, "Kharijism".

77. On al-Muhallab's role in the conflict with the Azāriqa and his initial difficulties with al-Ḥajjāj, see Chapter Six.
78. Robinson, *Empire and Elites*, 117–19 and the references cited there.
79. See Chapter Six. It is difficult to tell whether this issue is due to al-Ṭabarī's ordering of the material, a feature of his sources or a result of the transmission process of his *Taʾrīkh*.
80. Robinson, *Empire and Elites*, 120 and the references in n. 94.
81. Al-Ṭabarī, *Taʾrīkh*, II, 880–978; Ibn Khayyāṭ, *Taʾrīkh*, I, 272–4; al-Yaʿqūbī, *Taʾrīkh*, II, 274–5; al-Masʿūdī, *Murūj*, III–IV, 139–40, but note that here Shabīb does not drown but is fished out, sent to al-Ḥajjāj and subsequently executed; Ibn Aʿtham, *Futūḥ*, VII, 84–92.
82. Al-Ṭabarī, *Taʾrīkh*, II, 976–8.
83. Compare e.g. al-Ṭabarī, *Taʾrīkh*, II, 976 with Ibn Hishām, *Sīra*, I, 180–1.
84. Robinson, *Empire and Elites*, 117; Palmer et al., *Seventh Century*, 79, 205; Hoyland, *Seeing Islam*, 650 and the references listed in n. 114.
85. Conrad, "Theophanes"; Hoyland, "Arabic, Syriac and Greek"; Vacca, "Fires of Naxčawan"; Heijer and Pilette, "Transmission".
86. On ʿImrān, see EI², "ʿImrān b. Ḥiṭṭān, al-Sadūsī al-Khāridjī" (J. Fück); Rubinacci, "Political Poetry", 188; Sezgin, *GAS*, II, 352–3. See also the introduction to ʿAbbās' collection of Khārijite poems as well as his notes on the poems attributed to ʿImrān. ʿAbbās, *Diwān*, 18–24, 140–73.

PART II

EARLY ISLAMIC HISTORIOGRAPHY AND LITERARY KHĀRIJISM

1

Literary Approaches to Islamic Historiography and Khārijite History

The Challenges of Early Islamic Historical Writing

Considering that early Islamic historiography is the bedrock upon which our understanding of the origins and development of Islam as a civilisation is built, the research that has been done on this 'genre' as a whole is limited. Studies on Islamic history vastly outnumber those on historiography, especially with regard to the early period.[1] Rosenthal's *A History of Muslim Historiography*, published in 1952, was the first comprehensive survey and analysis of that section of the Islamic written tradition. It was followed by a handful of monograph-length studies of the early Islamic historical tradition,[2] but Robinson's 2003 *Islamic Historiography* is the most recent at the time of writing. Partial studies are much more numerous, and we are now finally seeing an uptick of research on individual authors and texts,[3] but compared with other fields, we still know rather little about the scholars and texts that inform our view of the early Islamic period.

The existing scholarship on Islamic historiography has nevertheless done much to improve our grasp of the evolution of historical writing. Robinson, as the most recent to study it, postulated a development from rudimentary lists (of caliphs or governors, for example) to thematic monographs (on certain events, groups or individuals) to the large syntheses of the ninth and tenth century (like al-Ṭabarī's *Taʾrīkh*) that combined much of this earlier material and cast it in new forms.[4] We now also have a much better understanding of the building blocks of early (historical) literature thanks to the works of Stefan Leder on the *khabar* (report; pl. *akhbār*), the core unit of much early historiography (written and aural), its features and utilisation.[5] A *khabar* is usually of paragraph length, but can range from a single sentence to a few pages. It is typically prefaced by an *isnād*, although these are sometimes dropped or combined into a collective *isnād* for ease of reading or memorising. The narrator of a *khabar* is absent as a rule – the content of an account is commonly traced back to an eyewitness (for events) or important authority (for example, in the case of Prophetic pronouncements), who are mainly quoted in direct speech in the form of dialogues. These characteristics create an impression of factuality and reliability[6] that can be seriously misleading.

Most recently, Najam Haider has suggested in a major study that early Islamic historical writing follows a three-step model that includes (1) a core structure, which is shared by all sources, and (2) the rhetorical elaboration of this core in order to (3) create an interpretive framework relevant to the contemporary context.[7] He clarifies that the creation of his model "is marked by a degree of reductionism and simplification"[8] and also addresses some potential issues, especially with regard to the compilatory nature of the surviving works.[9] Nevertheless, Haider's work is great food for thought, especially on aspects that need further consideration like the question of whether/how the interpretive framework identified for a particular event in a particular source relates to the interpretive framework of the source on the whole. If I am not mistaken, Haider does not address this last point, which is in any case extremely difficult to investigate considering the volume and complexity of our sources. It is not attempted in detail here either for precisely this reason, and also because I approach my subject from a different direction. Where I study historiography to learn something about the historical memory of the Khawārij, Haider seems to utilise his rebellions primarily to learn something about the mechanisms of historiography. Two sides of the same coin, of course, but guided by somewhat different questions. In any case, his model will surely prove immensely helpful for scholars seeking to understand the conventions and work processes of early Islamic historiography.[10]

There are of course many divergent ideas on how, when, why, where and in what form Islamic historiography began and then continued to evolve,[11] but the very existence of this diversity of opinion represents a vast improvement in a long-neglected field. The more scholars of early Islam began to engage not just with the historical tradition, but also with other genres like *ḥadīth*, however, the more obvious it became that this literature is subject to serious pitfalls and challenges.[12] These were anticipated in the works of Ignaz Goldziher and a few others,[13] but, as noted above, such studies only gained serious momentum in the 1970s with the publications of Crone, Cook, Wansbrough and Hawting, among others. While some have argued that the use of writing was a systematic feature of Islamic intellectual production from the beginning, it is now widely acknowledged that this is a later development – accounts of the history of the early community were routinely written down only from the ninth century on, but even then aurality remained highly important.[14] Our sources are overwhelmingly at a considerable remove (at least 150–200 years) from the events they purport to describe; they are fragmentary, contradictory, subject to partisan perspectives and frequent reworkings by scholars and storytellers;[15] and they show clear signs of the influence of salvation history – notions of an idealised past that present the success of Islam as proof of its divine sanction, of history as "*gesta Dei per homines*" or *ʿibra* (monition, object lesson).[16] Moreover, the socio-political, legal, religious, economic and military context had changed so much from the seventh/early eighth to the ninth/tenth century that new questions were being asked which could not be answered with recourse to what was remembered of the early community's conduct. This led, on the one hand, to the 'reconstruction' of supposedly authentic material that was then attributed to eminent figures of the earliest periods of Islamic history to legitimate it; on the other, this tendency resulted in the massive growth of material over time, an evolution "from uncertainty to profusion of precise detail".[17] Crone once called the early historical tradition "debris of an obliterated past",[18] and while this is an overstatement, "the consensus about how to reconstruct this [early Islamic] period – indeed, about the prospect that it *can* be reconstructed in any real detail – has broken down almost completely".[19]

Historiography as Literature[20]

In the face of these challenges, Islamicists have devised several strategies with which to circumvent or counterbalance the problematic nature of the source material. Few have opted to reject the Islamic sources altogether; much more common are approaches that look for ways to differentiate between historical and ahistorical reports or that use additional sources (material culture, non-Muslim texts) to contextualise the Islamic written tradition. Others engage with the literary dimension of our sources and pursue issues such as authorship and poetic analysis, although the focus here is often on poetry, *adab* and other forms of *belles-lettres* rather than historical writing.[21] This last point is characteristic of much (Islamicist) research: as noted, historiography is frequently considered different from literature 'proper' in that it is assumed to "be free of fictivity" and employ "a special kind of language whose determining characteristic is its aim to be truthful"; literary-historical analyses of such texts are thus less common.[22] This constitutes a marked difference to how the complex relationship between history and literature is understood in other disciplines,[23] especially following the 'linguistic turn' of the early twentieth century that has profoundly influenced fields as diverse as Philosophy of Language, Anthropology and Psychoanalysis.

The 'linguistic turn' began with a new approach to the relationship between philosophy and language that emphasised the latter as "constitutive of intellectual and social life"[24] and has had an immense impact on the field of History since the WWII era.[25] Its proponents challenge the Rankean notion of history as a description of the past 'as it really was'[26] and argue that this past does not exist outside its representation in/by texts.[27] At the most fundamental level lies the acknowledgement that "the historical record consists of nothing more or less than human utterance" and thus requires elucidation based on literary criticism.[28] Building on the insights gained in the above-mentioned fields, historians have produced an ever-growing mass of scholarship that has substantially changed the way in which the relationship between history, narrative and literature is viewed.[29]

The findings of this research have been slow to permeate the field of Islamic Studies,[30] which is still often characterised by a "fetish for fact".[31] There has been a marked increase in studies that pursue a literary approach to Islamic historiography and other genres,[32] but overall the idea that "texts designed as "history" cannot be treated simply as databanks, but are legitimate candidates for linguistic inquiries and literary analyses" is still rather novel;[33] this despite the fact that treating our sources as *texts* rather than "mere mines for fact" had already been advocated by Marshall Hodgson[34] and (to a lesser extent) Franz Rosenthal.[35] There are obvious advantages to such an approach – for instance, by reading the sources as literary constructs, we are more likely to get a sense of how author-compilers conceptualised their works and what textual strategies they used to create certain effects.[36] This also gets us closer to the conventions of knowledge production in the early Islamic period:

> Modern texts possess a sheer facticity that no pre-modern *ʿālim* would have granted, steeped as he was in a culture of audition and orality, one in which authority lay not in the inert written word, but in an interplay between text on the one hand, and its reader and commentator on the other, one where multiple meanings were not merely accommodated, but in some measure even encouraged: if anything was fetished [*sic*], it was *ikhtilāf* – agreeing to disagree – rather than facts.[37]

Reluctance to approach historiography as literature is by no means restricted to Islamicists.[38] On the contrary, they are in good and plentiful company. Historians in general and medievalists in particular often reject the 'linguistic turn'

> because in treating documents as texts rather than sources, it suggests the instability and opacity of all and any knowledge of the past, while at the same time (perhaps more important?) attacking the very foundations on which medievalists had constructed their professional legitimacy, involved as it had always been with mastery of highly technical (rather opaque) fields such as palaeography, diplomatics, codicology, and so on, not to mention all those "dead" languages.[39]

Of course, applying some of the implications of the linguistic turn to early Islamic history is not to say that the entire Islamic tradition should be disregarded as pure discourse, or worse, mere invention. The idea that the Muslim (and non-Muslim!) scholars of the first several centuries, ranging from the Iberian Peninsula to the Indian subcontinent, somehow all secretly agreed to replace the history of their community with a wholly fictitious story is preposterous and disregards the highly complex, often conflicting and overwhelmingly multivalent and polyphonic character of early Islamic (historical) writing.[40] In short, "serious historians do not hold conspiracy theories about the rise of Islam".[41] Increasing scholarly engagement with early Islamic material culture – coins, inscriptions, papyri, textiles, archaeology and the like – has also shown this evidence to complement or modify, but not all-out falsify, the basic outlines of Islamic history as told by the written tradition.[42]

The devil is in the detail, however, and it cannot be denied that, much to the detriment of our understanding of precisely the details that make up the narrative bulk of early Islamic history, the literary dimension of Islamic historical writing is still often neglected beyond a superficial acknowledgement that the early sources are problematic. This is all the more unfortunate as what is now broadly accepted in Classics or Medieval European History – that historiography was not primarily intended to record facts but to convey truth and meaning[43] – most definitely applies to pre-modern Islamic historiography as well.[44] And it goes without saying that the modern historian is no "neutral reader"[45] either but is just as influenced by their own beliefs, background, education and politics[46] as their pre-modern counterpart, with such influences readily observable in their own works; the imposition of modern categories of analysis on pre-modern texts and authors is but one example of this.[47] As Marshall Hodgson observed, "careful studies have shown the degree to which even leading Islamicists have been determined, in their approach to the products of Islamicate culture, by their several Western allegiances, religious or cultural".[48] And this is not even to mention the fact that modern historians are of course just as enmeshed in processes of text production as their historical subjects and objects of study:

> Whether or not most historians will wish to engage themselves in these literary and philosophical battles [of modern theory], the whole debate does bring to the fore the extent to which the writing of a historical work is itself a 'text upon text'. For history is a matter of interpretation. In order to write history – to generate a text – the historian must interpret existing texts . . . But he will interpret, or 'read', his texts in accordance with a set of other texts, which derive from the cultural code within which he works himself; and he will go on to write his text, that is, his history, against

the background of and within the matrix of this larger cultural text. Thus history-writing is not a simple matter of sorting out 'primary' and 'secondary' sources; it is inextricably embedded in a mesh of text.[49]

A Literary Approach to Khārijite History

As stated in the Introduction, this book is an exercise in setting aside positivist ambitions and looking at Khārijism as a literary phenomenon. It is the first sustained study to do so, with two partial exceptions: the late Thomas Sizgorich's *Violence and Belief in Late Antiquity* and Tayeb El-Hibri's *Parable and Politics in Early Islamic History*. However, the present book also departs from these studies in some key respects.

Sizgorich studied the connections between Khārijite piety and militance as narrative tropes without explicitly seeking to reconstruct the emergence of Khārijism or the intentions of its proponents. Nevertheless, his approach to the portrayal of the Khawārij in the Islamic tradition is not wholly consistent: at times, he read the relevant accounts as narratives intended to convey and contrast certain ideas and ideals,[50] while elsewhere he apparently accepted some of these reports as historical fact.[51] This oscillation between a historicising and a literary take on Khārijism leaves the reader somewhat unsure about his understanding of the Khārijites: were they in actual fact violent pietists in the late antique tradition of saints and martyrs analysed in his book, or were they *remembered* as such by the early Islamic tradition as a tool with which to illustrate and condemn "the potential for discord, disunity, and bloodshed that resided in the volatile mix of revelation, ascetic rigor, and an evolving mythology of righteous raiding"?[52]

By contrast, Tayeb El-Hibri very clearly rejects the historicity of much of what we find in the early Islamic tradition: "the story preserved in the early Islamic narratives was neither real in its details nor intended to be factual".[53] He argues for "an alternative reading of [early Islamic] history as a largely parabolic cycle of literary narrative".[54] His book does not focus on Khārijites specifically, but the author makes some intriguing observations on the narrative function of Khārijism in the portrayal of ʿAlī that are relevant to the discussion in Chapter Four and will be addressed there. In arguing for an analysis of literary Khārijism, however, two other studies had a much more fundamental impact on the methodological approach pursued in this book. We will look at them shortly.

Many studies of early Islamic history and historiography still 'do' factual history: they attempt to reconstruct 'what actually happened' by reinterpreting the data provided by the Islamic tradition without questioning its basic framework.[55] Scholarship on Khārijite history is no exception to this, as we have seen. The present study will show that such an approach is not sustainable, at least not without a complementary literary analysis, because the accounts that deal with Khārijism largely marginalise it in order to discuss a variety of other actors and topics that often reflect late-eighth to tenth-century concerns rather than seventh to early-eighth-century realities. Again, this is not to say the sources are useless for historical reconstruction. But there is no getting past the acknowledgment that whatever historical 'truth' has survived is woven into and often buried underneath a complex construct of rhetorical elements and references many of whose subtleties and double entendres had already been lost to the passage of time when these stories finally found their way into the written record of the early Islamic historical tradition. For the modern reader, the challenge is infinitely greater.[56] What we may be able to discern, on the other hand, are the main threads forming this construct, the predominant topics and themes that lay at the heart of the accounts that were passed on and refashioned over time to finally take on their familiar form in the extant sources. This is not to say that the same narrative patterns apply everywhere, of course, but as I will demonstrate over the course of this book, there are enough commonalities in the material to identify some of the concerns that were of prime importance to the early Muslim scholars and (perhaps) the community at large.

That we are confronted with a distinctly literary Khārijism is apparent not only in the content of the literary forms (letters, speeches and sermons, for instance) that make up the relevant accounts, but also with regard to their structural components. These structural components consist of the dates, names, sequence of events or places that are used as pieces of evidence for the various theories of Khārijite origins. Taking a closer look at this data, however, shows that it can be as problematic as the story content of letters, speeches and poems. Much of this data belongs to various different *topoi* and *schemata*, concepts of literary analysis that were introduced to the field of early Islamic history and literature in the mid-1960s. This renders the use of this information for the purpose of (re)constructing Khārijite history highly problematic.

Topoi and *Schemata* in Early Islamic Historiography

The earliest and to-date most comprehensive studies of the literary forms that abound in early Islamic (historical) writing are the works of Eckart Stetter and Albrecht Noth.[57] In his 1965 PhD dissertation on *Topoi und Schemata im Ḥadīṯ*,[58] Stetter analysed the formal structure and thematic content of *ḥadīth*s preserved in al-Bukhārī's *Ṣaḥīḥ* and came to the following conclusion: "Eine auch nur oberflächliche Lektüre des Ḥadīṯ . . . [führt] zur Feststellung nicht allein inhaltlicher Klischees, sondern auch formaler Gesetzmäßigkeiten."[59] These clichés of content he called *topoi*; the formal organisation of that content, which follows well-established and oft-repeated patterns, he called *schemata*. His work was based on studies of antique and medieval European as well as Biblical and Jewish literature, such as Curtius' *Europäische Literatur und lateinisches Mittelalter*, which introduced the term *topos* to the study of medieval literature,[60] and Bultmann's *Die Geschichte der synoptischen Tradition*. As these works focus mostly on *schemata*, Stetter's dissertation also dedicated more space to them than to the analysis of the *topoi* in *ḥadīth* literature.[61]

The section on *topoi* is concerned with the situational introduction at the beginning of the *matn* of a *ḥadīth*, where the scene is set for the particular statement or action that forms the tradition's central point. Stetter focused mostly on aspects related to the Prophet's facial expressions, gestures and postures, identifying a host of oft-repeated descriptions such as Muḥammad resting his head on someone's thighs,[62] laughing out loud[63] and sitting in a mosque or *majlis*.[64] Other *topoi* include the negative reputation of Bedouins[65] and the frequent repetition of particular phrases that are meant to enhance the impression of a transmitter's reliability.[66] This feature of the *ḥadīth* literature, Stetter argued, can be explained by the very act of collecting and editing the traditions:

> Typisierte Situationen, floskelhafte Wendungen, bestimmte Motive und stereotype Formeln und Ausdrücke weisen auf einen Schatz traditioneller Elemente hin, auf den die Redaktoren für ihre vielfältigen Zwecke zurückgreifen konnten.[67]

In short: far from describing historical events, Stetter held the *ḥadīth* literature to be characterised by a limited number of themes that were inserted into individual traditions at the collectors' discretion.

Stetter's investigation of the *schemata* that abound in *ḥadīth* literature was much more extensive. This is at least in part due to the comprehensive stylisation of this type of literature, which is not restricted to the words and deeds of the Prophet himself: "Mehr oder weniger alles Reden und Tun, das sich in Traditionsberichten niedergeschlagen hat, vollzieht sich in stilisierter Form."[68] Much more so than the section on *topoi*, Stetter's examination of *schemata* was based on studies of ancient Hebrew and Biblical literature, implying an explicit influence of the Jewish and Christian traditions on the formation of Islamic thought and literature. Stetter identified a variety of formal structures in the organisation of *ḥadīth* content, dealing mostly with basic literary elements such as rhetorical questions, prayers and admonitions.

His analysis drew attention to the use of *Zahlensprüche*,[69] parallelism in form and content,[70] sequential ordering of words and formulae[71] and particularly the triplication of narrative content.[72] In addition to these scriptural features of *ḥadīth* literature, Stetter also pointed out a number of aural elements, such as the use of rhyme and assonance.[73] These aural elements, along with other factors, led him to conclude that the oral tradition persisted for quite some time after the emergence of Islam.[74]

Stetter's dissertation was the first systematic literary analysis that pointed out the presence of *topoi* and *schemata* in a particular subset of the Islamic tradition; its neglect by recent scholarship in particular is unwarranted. Still, of much greater significance to the subject of this study is the work of the late Albrecht Noth, who did not focus on *ḥadīth* but on the historical tradition. In 1968, he published an article on the depiction of the conquest of Iṣfahān in a report transmitted by various different sources and concluded that this account consisted almost entirely of distinct narrative motifs (*Erzählmotive*) that were by no means particular to the conquest of Iṣfahān but recurred in several other *futūḥ* traditions, most prominently on the conquest of Nihāwand. This latter account, he argued, in fact represented the origin of the Iṣfahān tradition, which owes its existence entirely to the Nihāwand narrative.[75] In Noth's view, the substitution of Iṣfahān for Nihāwand occurred because of the indifference of the report's narrative motifs: they lacked a specific relation to a particular conquest and could thus be recycled for use in other conquest narratives.[76] In short:

> man [komponierte] Traditionen . . ., indem man eine Reihe von mehr oder weniger selbstständigen Erzählmotiven, die zum eisernen Bestand der *futūḥ*-Überlieferung gehörten, zu einem größeren Ganzen zusammensetzte.[77]

Neither tradition should therefore be used for a historical reconstruction of how the conquest of either city was accomplished.[78]

In the conclusion of this article, Noth stated that he was working on a larger study of the historical tradition to investigate the occurrence of *topoi* beyond the case study of the conquest of Iṣfahān/Nihāwand. He submitted this study as his *Habilitationsschrift* under the title *Quellenkritische Studien zu Themen, Formen und Tendenzen frühislamischer Geschichtsüberlieferung* in two volumes, only the first of which was ever published, in 1973.[79] An English translation of the revised and updated first volume (on *Themen und Formen*) of this groundbreaking work was published in 1994. The English translation, entitled *The Early Arabic Historical Tradition: A Source-Critical Study*,[80] has become one of the standard works in the field of Arabic and Islamic historiography, despite some criticism of issues such as its almost exclusive focus on *futūḥ* material.[81]

Like Stetter, Noth drew attention to the issue of *topoi* and *schemata*, which feature extensively in early Islamic historiography.[82] However, Noth's work encompassed a much larger range of source material, paid significantly more attention to *topoi* and went into much greater detail than Stetter's analysis had done. Noth's study was also more systematic than Stetter's, who mostly refrained from providing definitions of key terminology or discussing his methodological approach – Stetter's introduction covers only two and a half pages, his conclusion is a mere two pages long. Beyond the investigation of *topoi* and *schemata*, Noth's work also offered important findings for the study of Islamic historical writing in general, such as his refutation of the theory of historical 'schools' first developed by Wellhausen[83] or his recognition of the impact of Islamic law on the formation of the historical tradition and vice versa.[84]

Noth distinguished two forms of rhetorical devices, the *topos* and the *schema*. He defined a *topos* as "a narrative motif which has as its primary function the specification of *content*, and aims to elaborate matters of fact".[85] Such *topoi* may be grounded in fact but turn into rhetorical devices when they become transferable. It is important to note that this topological "drift"[86] is a common characteristic of early Islamic historiography,[87] beyond the *futūḥ* accounts upon which Noth's analysis was based in the main. We shall return to this issue in the following chapters, which will provide ample documentation of the mobility of narrative content across all selected sources. An important observation regarding the emergence of *topoi* as literary commonplaces[88] or clichés of content is that they signal a consensus regarding the interpretation, significance and collective remembrance of a particular subject: "*topoi* will not circulate about issues that remain controversial; for opinions that are controversial cannot be commonplace".[89]

The *schema* Noth defined as "a narrative motif that is first and foremost concerned with matters of *form*, with connecting, relating, and organizing matters of content".[90] Unlike a *topos*, a *schema*'s grounding in fact is "purely coincidental" – in fact, it emerges precisely in situations whose "genuine interpretative connections and relations are not known. Its raison d'etre is to fill such voids, and since the point of departure is lack of knowledge, this process is a completely arbitrary one".[91]

A cursory look at the accounts of Khārijite history in the historiographical sources suffices to reveal a whole array of *topoi* and *schemata*. One of the most prominent literary forms in the source material on Khārijism that function as a *schema* is the issue of *awāʾil*;[92] concerning *topoi*, particularly pertinent to the portrayal of Khārijite history is the use of personal names in the order of battle.[93] By way of example, the following section will discuss the bearing of such rhetorical devices on the question of Khārijite origins to further illustrate the premises that underlie the approach adopted in this study.

Schemata in the Source Material: *Awāʾil*

The early Islamic tradition displays a marked interest in *awāʾil* ('firsts') – the question of who was the first to perform a certain act, use a certain phrase, establish a certain custom, compose poetry in a certain metre, and so on.[94] This fascination with 'firsts' can also be observed in the reports of the emergence of the Khārijites at Ṣiffīn. These specifically Khārijite *awāʾil* focus on issues such as who was the first to proclaim *lā ḥukma*, whose sword was the first to be drawn on account of the Khārijite protest against the *taḥkīm*, and who was the first to 'go out'.

There are two main versions of the origin of the Khārijite slogan *lā ḥukma illā li-llāh* and the question of who was first to draw his sword in reaction to the Ṣiffīn arbitration agreement read out by al-Ashʿath b. Qays. The less popular variant names two otherwise unknown brothers of the ʿAnaza tribe, who, having exclaimed in protest, are said to have charged the Syrian army and fought until they were killed.[95] It is not explicitly stated that their swords were the first to be drawn, but these are the first hostilities on account of the *taḥkīm* described by the sources in question. This report can thus be taken as crediting the brothers with coining the phrase as well as commencing the Khārijite tradition of resorting to violence to uphold their principles.

The second, more prevalent, version ascribes the origin of this phrase to ʿUrwa b. Udayya al-Tamīmī, the brother of Abū Bilāl Mirdās b. Udayya, who plays an important part in the narratives of Khārijism just before the second civil war (discussed in Chapter Five). The precise sequence of events is a little muddled. Widespread Khārijite protest is mentioned *after* the decision of the arbiters and the announcement of the judgement: "The people became divided, and the Khawārij proclaimed: 'The two judges have become unbelievers, *lā ḥukma illā li-llāh*!'"[96] However, al-Balādhurī, al-Ṭabarī, al-Yaʿqūbī and al-Masʿūdī also preserve several accounts which place ʿUrwa's protest *before* the arbitration meeting, in the same situation as the first version of the two brothers: the arbitration document having been composed, al-Ashʿath is on his way through ʿAlī's camp to read it out to the caliph's followers. When he walks past a group of Banū Tamīm, ʿUrwa says to him: "Do you appoint men as judges over the religion of God? . . . Judgement is God's alone!"[97] The report concludes with the remark: "And he [ʿUrwa] was the first to say *lā ḥukma*."[98]

ʿUrwa as a representative of the Banū Tamīm and their protest against the arbitration document also features prominently in the sources that do not credit him with coining the *lā ḥukma* phrase. Both Ibn Muzāḥim and al-Dīnawarī's work include accounts according to which he was most vehemently opposed to the arbitration document, and his objections are portrayed rather more articulately and extensively than those of the two brothers of ʿAnaza.[99] In fact, ʿUrwa is the only protagonist explicitly named as opposing the arbitration across almost all of the sources examined here.[100] Other names are mentioned as well, but they differ from source to source, and objections in the form of the Khārijite slogan are more often attributed to an undefined group of people ('they', 'the people', 'the Tamīmīs').[101] ʿUrwa is clearly the main figure associated with the first protest. Most sources continue the accounts of his objections with the story of how he followed up his verbal attack on al-Ashʿath with a physical one and drew his sword against him, whereupon al-Ashʿath fled back to his men. The Tamīmī leaders subsequently apologised to him on behalf of ʿUrwa.[102] Al-Balādhurī's report concludes that "ʿUrwa's sword was the first that was drawn on account of the arbitration".[103] The expression of dissent by tongue and hand characterises the portrayal of activist Khārijism and is here perfectly embodied in ʿUrwa's proto-Khārijism.

Given ʿUrwa's prominence in these narratives, it is somewhat surprising that he is not otherwise mentioned in the stories of Khārijism during the reign of ʿAlī. We neither encounter him at Ḥarūrāʾ nor at Nahrawān, neither as leader of his own group of insurgents nor among those who returned to ʿAlī. For the moment, ʿUrwa's role in the emergence of the Khawārij appears limited to his violent opposition to the arbitration document. He reappears at a later stage, during the caliphate of Muʿāwiya b. Abī Sufyān, as victim of an Umayyad governor, but it is his brother Abū Bilāl who came to occupy a prominent place within the early Islamic tradition.[104]

Al-Balādhurī preserves yet another, somewhat curious account of the first Khārijite to 'go out,' whom he identifies as Shurayḥ b. Awfā.[105] The report states that Shurayḥ rebelled at the time of the morning prayer, reciting Q 4:75: 'O Lord, take us away from this town whose people are oppressors.' His people attempted to hold him back but let him go when he threatened to attack them.[106] This report is not embedded in the Ṣiffīn narratives; instead, it is placed after a description of the battle at Nahrawān, in the course of which Shurayḥ was killed. The circumstances of Shurayḥ's morning *khurūj* are not quite clear in al-Balādhurī's work – there is no explicit connection to Ṣiffīn, but a different date and location do not fit the usual narrative as the sources commonly place the break between ʿAlī and the Khārijites at Ṣiffīn, either before or after the arbiters met. It is possible that this report was intended as a retrospective look at Shurayḥ's beginnings as a Khārijite and that the Ṣiffīn connection was so obvious that it did not need to be stated. But as we saw, al-Balādhurī also names ʿUrwa as the originator of the *lā ḥukma* phrase and as the first Khārijite to rebel by sword, and so while it was entirely common to preserve different versions of an event, there are other possibilities.

For instance, al-Ṭabarī preserves a report that might place this particular account of al-Balādhurī. According to al-Ṭabarī's version, Shurayḥ cited (albeit different) verses from the Qurʾān not at Ṣiffīn but afterwards, when the Khārijites left Kufa for Nahrawān, which appears to be a better fit.[107] It is possible that al-Balādhurī's account lost its original context, or at least the context of al-Ṭabarī's version, during the transmission or compilation process. Removing it from that context could have also been editorial choice: al-Balādhurī's Shurayḥ story is embedded in a series of related reports concerning the relationship between those who rebelled as Khārijites and their families and tribes.[108] The point here might therefore not have been to contribute to *awāʾil* but to add to the corpus of accounts detailing the breaking of social ties that becoming a Khārijite necessitated.[109] The Shurayḥ narrative thus seems to exemplify the *schema* as a literary form organising content where "genuine interpretative connections and relations are not known"[110] or have been deliberately dropped for specific narrative purposes.

Topoi in the Source Material: The 'Order of Battle'

Descriptions of violent conflict permeate the accounts of Khārijite history. This is particularly so regarding the last period investigated in this book, the era of the second *fitna* and of ʿAbd al-Malik's reign. However, the first and most famous battle between the Khārijites and their supreme enemy, ʿAlī, was the Battle of Nahrawān. Noth identified six distinct but related *topoi* connected to the use of personal names in a battle context: order of battle; persons who kill or capture well-known enemies; victory messages sent to the caliph (and in the Khārijite case, the governor); arranging the succession of command; appointing deputies; and reinforcements.[111] Motifs that are connected with names might have originated in lists that seem to have survived from the earliest period and among other things specify participants in battles and campaigns.[112] Such lists may have contributed to or perhaps originated in the early historians' "onomatomania", the "obsession for providing names",[113] or in Crone's words, "*horror anonymitatis*".[114] Without exception, all *topoi* related to names can be observed in the narratives of Khārijite history. In what follows, I will illustrate this using the example of the 'order of battle' *topos*.

The source material on the *ridda*, *futūḥ* and various other conflicts contains a wealth of details on the composition of the armies involved. This information belongs to the "basic stock" of military narratives and is "characteristic of all the early historical compilations".[115] The battle order *topos* usually takes one of two major forms, either naming the leader of a particular unit of the army ("the leader of [formation or unit] (*wa-ʿalā* . . .) was [name]") or reporting the appointment of a certain commander by a superior ("[high-ranking person] gave command of [formation or unit] to [name] (*wa-kāna ʿalā; jaʿala ʿalā*)").[116] And there are plenty of army units to choose from: starting with the left and right flank (*maysara* and *maymana*, respectively) on to the infantry (*rajjāla*, *rajl*), the cavalry (*khayl*, *mujarrada*) and the vanguard (*muqaddima*, *muqaddama*), among others.[117] The reports of who was in charge of which unit are often contradictory, and Noth contends that there are "no valid criteria" for choosing one version over another.[118] In fact, the very ubiquity of this *topos* indicates that the information it purports to transmit is difficult to use for a reliable historical reconstruction of events.

The battle order *topos* is a frequent feature of the stories that detail the clashes between the Khawārij and their opponents, and indeed, we are confronted with often-contradictory information: Ibn Khayyāṭ, al-Dīnawarī, al-Balādhurī and al-Ṭabarī all name different Khārijite sub-commanders at Nahrawān, for instance.[119] The *topos* usually follows certain conventions irrespective of the context in which it is employed (*ridda*, *futūḥ*, Khārijite rebellion or civil war, for instance) and shows remarkable consistency. Two examples shall suffice here:

> They [the Khārijites] put in command over their right flank Yazīd b. Ḥusayn and over their left flank Shurayḥ b. Abī Awfā al-ʿAbsī, who belonged to their ascetics; they appointed over the infantry Ḥurqūṣ b. Zuhayr, and ʿAbdallāh b. Wahb was in command over the cavalry (*fa-jaʿala ʿalā maymanatihim Yazīd b. Ḥusayn wa-ʿalā maysaratihim Shurayḥ b. Abī Awfā al-ʿAbsī wa-kāna min nussākihim wa-ʿalā al-rajjāla Ḥurqūṣ b. Zuhayr wa-ʿalā al-khayl ʿAbdallāh b. Wahb*).[120]

> Ibn al-Azraq put in command over his right flank ʿUbayda b. Hilāl al-Yashkurī and over his left flank al-Zubayr b. al-Māḥūz al-Tamīmī (*wa-jaʿala Ibn al-Azraq ʿalā maymanatihi ʿUbayda b. Hilāl al-Yashkurī wa-ʿalā maysaratihi al-Zubayr b. al-Māḥūz al-Tamīmī*).[121]

In addition to such detailed statements, there is also frequent mention of both Khārijite commanders and their counterparts among the caliphal troops gathering and readying their armies for battle (*ʿaskara; ʿabbā*).[122] It appears that this has evolved into a stock *topos* as well – arranging one's army is one of the ingredients of proper battle as described in the sources. The fact that this is also an eminently reasonable thing to do before engaging in combat is precisely why it is all the more important to be aware of the standardisation of this particular theme. Taken on their own, such accounts read like sober descriptions of a specific battle. It is only when studying a sizeable number of these reports that recurring patterns are fully revealed and that sober descriptions of specific battles appear as little more than an accumulation of motifs lacking any grounding in a specific event. This does not mean that all such information should be considered false, of course, but disagreements over issues like the Khārijite sub-commanders at Nahrawān are plentiful. The sources do not agree on the individual at whose house Ibn Wahb was elected leader, for example, and at a basic level there is even some confusion over who was or was not a Khārijite. This is evident, for instance, in the figure of the Kufan Tamīmī leader Shabath b. Ribʿī, who appears to have been a particularly contested personality. We variously encounter him as one of ʿAlī's supporters and commanders at Nahrawān,[123] as a Khārijite at Ḥarūrāʾ who eventually returns to ʿAlī but is not mentioned at Nahrawān,[124] or as a Khārijite whose fate is not disclosed.[125] It thus needs to be borne in mind that while *topoi* are stable, their purpose is often the "arbitrary filling in of blank formulae",[126] and so the information they transmit needs to be regarded with caution.[127]

Conclusions

The preceding discussion suggests that both the structural components and the story content of the reports that narrate Khārijite history – names, dates, chronology, events – frequently belong to sets of rhetorical devices characteristic of early Islamic historiography in general. It has also addressed the confusion regarding these components in the sources. This challenges positivist reconstructions of Khārijite history, but the problem goes further.

That the historicity of Khārijite endeavours as preserved in the early historical tradition is problematic is further confirmed by reports placing otherwise identical episodes at different points in time or different localities. For instance, in one of the debates between ʿAlī's envoys and the Khārijites, the former group admonish the rebels not to "hasten the *fitna* this year fearing the next".[128] Al-Ṭabarī's account places this particular phrase in the context of the first withdrawal of the Khawārij, at Ḥarūrāʾ, when ʿAlī's (nameless) agents attempt to reconcile the dissenters. Now, al-Balādhurī places this argument in the context of similar debates between Ibn ʿAbbās and Ṣaʿṣaʿa b. Ṣūḥān on ʿAlī's side and the Khārijites at Nahrawān. Such "wandering passages" seem to be the result of the transmission process the texts underwent and indicate the "surprising freedom" the author-compilers enjoyed in editing their sources.[129] As noted in Noth's analysis of the conquest stories concerning Iṣfahān/Nihāwand, such recyclable narrative content was a recurrent feature of early Islamic historiography,[130] but we also encounter this phenomenon in other genres, such as *ḥadīth*.[131] This is because the same basic narration techniques prevailed within the early Islamic tradition: "Die Erzähltechnik arbeitete mit Modulen, die immer wieder ausgewechselt und anders zusammengesetzt wurden."[132] On what grounds, then, should we decide which accounts convey historical information and which ones are fictitious? Is this even a workable distinction or does it not perhaps distort the nature of (early Islamic) historiography?[133] To repeat, pre-modern practices of history-writing were different from modern notions of history as objective, factual reporting, however much modern historians fall short of their ideals:

> The historian remained faithfully within the epistemological borders of the discipline when he altered details, elaborated speeches, and related encounters that *could have* occurred in order to make a larger point. This was an integral and accepted component in the vocation of historical writing.[134]

But even if we insist on separating fact from fiction, the absence of hard criteria on the basis of which such a distinction could securely be made remains a challenge.[135] Favouring any one particular narrative merely because it sounds more plausible seems haphazard,[136] especially because plausibility (as contingent on context) was the benchmark against which the acceptability of historiographical accounts was measured.[137] Noth's contention that the identification of *topoi* could serve as a means of distinguishing 'authentic' from 'inauthentic' reports is equally problematic.[138] The articulation of narrative content in the form of a *topos* does not necessarily mean that the account is ahistorical, although often there is no reliable way of determining whether a particular motif does reflect real events.[139] Conversely, the (apparent) absence of *topoi* does not necessarily mean that a report can be accepted at face value.

The interchangeability of phrases and their contexts emphasises an intriguing tendency in the accounts of Khārijite origins: when we turn from the structural frame of these reports to their contents (speeches, debates, deeds, creeds . . .), we find that they are much less confused. There might not be a consensus regarding the individual in whose house the Khārijites met to elect their leader, or which rebel gave a speech on that occasion, but the subject matter of such speeches and the issues discussed are largely uncontested and significantly more stable than the external circumstances detailed in a given report, which can differ greatly.[140] The admonition not to "hasten the *fitna*", for instance, may be impossible to anchor in a particular historical moment, but the line clearly belongs in a debate context – which debate exactly does not seem to have mattered much as long as the narrated exchange appeared fitting, that is, plausible.

The importance of such narratives thus lies in the representation of Khārijism as a set of ideas that could then be used to throw other matters into relief. This mechanism underlines Noth's observations regarding the historical method of early Islamic scholars:

> [Es] folgt für die Geschichtsauffassung einiger muslimischer Überlieferer, die sich mit der Frühzeit beschäftigten, dass es ihnen weniger um korrekte Berichterstattung ging als um die Zeichnung ansprechender und einprägsamer Bilder.[141]

Even though a similarly generalising tendency has been recognised in the case of Khārijite doctrine as portrayed by Islamic heresiography,[142] studies of Khārijite origins based on the supposedly more sober historiographical material have so far mostly failed to acknowledge this. A thorough examination of literary Khārijism in fact reveals several themes that are of particular importance to the historians. The remaining two chapters of this section (Part II) will illustrate these with a particular view to understanding their function in the construction of Khārijism as a literary phenomenon. Chapter Two will study its main element, militant piety, to argue for a standardised characterisation of the Khawārij that has little historical but considerable argumentative value for early Islamic discourse. The resulting impression of literary Khārijism as repetitive, monotonous and therefore ultimately insubstantial is the subject of Chapter Three, which will examine how this effect is created before returning to the importance of pursuing a literary approach to Khārijite history, the main focus of Part III.

Notes

1. Mamlūk historiography, for instance, has recently begun to attract significantly more attention. See, for example, the contributions in Conermann, ed., *Mamlūk Historiography*; Guo, "Mamluk Historiographic Studies"; Hirschler, "Studying Mamluk Historiography"; Munt, "Mamluk Historiography"; Van Steenbergen, "Truth and Politics".
2. Al-Dūrī, *Rise of Historical Writing* (1960, translated into English in 1983); Khalidi, *Arabic Historical Thought* (1994); Donner, *Narratives* (1998); Meisami, *Persian Historiography* (1999). B. Radtke, *Weltgeschichte* (1992) focuses on universal histories in several languages (among them Syriac, Greek and Latin) and his study includes later periods of Islamic historiography as well. Cheddadi, *Les arabes* (2004) likewise looks at Islamic historiography from the second to the eighth century H.

3. Andersson, *Early Sunnī Historiography*; Lynch, *Arab Conquests*; M. R. J. Bonner, *Historiographical Study*; Gordon et al., *Works of Ibn Wāḍiḥ*, I, 1–27 (comments on al-Yaʿqūbī's biography and the two extant manuscripts of his *Taʾrīkh*, prefacing the three-volume translation of his surviving works); Wurtzel and Hoyland, *Khalifa b. Khayyat's History*; Lindstedt, *Transmission*; Deghani, *Text und Kontext*; Heck, *Construction of Knowledge*.
4. Robinson, *Historiography*, 18–38. For lists, see also n. 112.
5. Note especially his "Literary Use" and "Composite Form", and for a brief overview, "Conventions", 37–9. See also Osti, "Tailors of Stories".
6. This was equally the case among medieval European scholars, who considered eyewitness testimony the most truthful form of evidence. Fulton, "History and *Historia*", 41–2. For third-person 'impersonal' narration as a criterion of objectivity and thus truthfulness in ancient historiography, see Marincola, *Authority and Tradition*, 6–7, 9–12; Wheeldon, '"True Stories"', 45–50.
7. Haider, *Rebel and Imām*, 6–9 (for a schematic overview).
8. Ibid., 16.
9. Ibid., 16–17.
10. Haider's assertion that historiography should be studied across communal boundaries and his criticism of the exclusion of non-Sunnī sources from much scholarship, for example, are particularly on target.
11. See, for example, Robinson's review article, "Study of Islamic Historiography", in which he discusses Khalidi's *Arabic Historical Thought* and Noth's *Early Arabic Historical Tradition*; and Robinson, *Historiography*, 43–54, esp. 43–50.
12. For a forceful yet cogent articulation of these challenges, see Crone, *Slaves*, 3–17 and *Meccan Trade*, 203–30 (mainly on the value of the Qurʾān, *ḥadīth* and *tafsīr* for historians of early Islam); much more reader-friendly but equally compelling, Cook, *Muhammad*, 61–76.
13. See esp. Goldziher, *Muhammedanische Studien*, II, 1–274. Other important early studies that adumbrate the sceptic trend of the 1970s and 1980s are Widengren, *Muhammad* and Schacht, *Origins*.
14. As argued convincingly by Schoeler. See above, 34 (n. 5) and 37 (n. 32), on the opposing views of Schoeler and Sezgin regarding this; also Schoeler, "Theorien zu den Quellen", where he discusses Sezgin's (and Fleischhammer's) approach to the relationship between (written) sources, transmitters and authors.
15. On storytellers, see now Armstrong, *Quṣṣāṣ*, who challenges the prevalent negative image of early Islamic storytellers.
16. On the impact of salvation history on the early Islamic (historical) tradition and possible Jewish/Christian connections, see Wansbrough, *Sectarian Milieu*, esp. 1–49; B. Radtke, *Weltgeschichte*, 160–8 (the quote is on p. 163); Robinson, "History and Heilsgeschichte".
17. Cook, *Muhammad*, 64.

18. Crone, *Slaves*, 10. See also her *Meccan Trade*, 230: "Spurious information can be rejected, but lost information cannot be regained."
19. Robinson, *Historiography*, 50. For an eloquent – and rather entertaining – summary of some of the challenges involved in studying early Islamic history and historiography, see also Lassner, "'Doing" Early Islamic History".
20. Meisami, "History as Literature", 15 correctly points out that neither Arabic nor Persian had a word for 'literature' corresponding to Western notions of the term. Nevertheless, early Islamic historiography certainly exhibits traits and structures associated with 'literature': ibid., 15–16, 29 (Meisami focuses on Persian historical writing, but her observations apply to the early Arabic tradition as well).
21. Prime examples of this are the incisive works of the Moroccan literary critic Abdelfattah Kilito on authorship, storytelling, narrativity and translation as they pertain to Arabic literature, which examine poetry, *adab* works, philosophy and on rare occasions even *ḥadīth*, but not history-writing. See, for example, his *Author and His Doubles* as well as *Arabs and the Art of Storytelling* and *Thou Shalt Not Speak My Language*.
22. One of the first to address this issue was Waldman, *Toward a Theory*. See ibid., 17 for the quotes.
23. See, for example, Fulton, "History and *Historia*", 46; O'Connor, "Irish Narrative Literature", 21: "Historiography in the Middle Ages was plainly a branch of high literature, composed using the same technical skills and poetic devices and with the aim of entertaining as well as instructing." O'Connor rejects the distinction between literary and non-literary narratives, at least as it is applied to medieval Irish literature (ibid.).
24. Surkis, "Linguistic Turn", 704. A milestone in the history of the term 'linguistic turn' was the publication in 1967 of Rorty, *Linguistic Turn*, a collection of essays on analytical philosophy that simultaneously criticised the notion of a single, cohesive turn.
25. There are many different narratives of the beginnings and further development of the linguistic turn in the various fields that it has affected. For one interpretation of the linguistic turn in History, see Spiegel, "Task" and "Introduction". For a critical assessment of Spiegel's take on this issue and a 'genealogical' approach to the historiography of the linguistic turn, see Surkis, "Linguistic Turn". The general concept of 'turns' in historiography as cohesive and circumscribed phenomena is criticised by Surkis as well as other contributors to the *AHR Forum* in the issue of *American Historical Review* in which Surkis' article appeared. See also Schöttler, *Nach der Angst*, 11–27 and the brief but eminently readable overview of approaches to history as a "linguistic discourse" in Potter, *Literary Texts*, 6–9 (quote on 6).
26. On Ranke, see the studies in Mommsen, ed., *Leopold von Ranke*, esp. the contribution by Nipperdey on the question of Ranke's criteria for objectivity

in history; Potter, *Literary Texts*, 122–6; Clark, *History, Theory, Text*, 9–28, esp. 9–17.

27. This is a broad generalisation, of course. Proponents of the 'linguistic turn' in History have been criticised for their (supposed) total rejection of the notion of objectivity and positivism in favour of a purely discursive framework. See, for example, Toews, "Intellectual History", 906, who is concerned about "word-makers who claim to be the makers of reality". The spectrum is very broad indeed, however, and many historians have embraced tenets of the 'linguistic turn' (or rather, turns) without succumbing to the notion that 'everything is (only) discourse'. Vernon, "Who's Afraid of the 'Linguistic Turn'?"; Schöttler, *Nach der Angst*, esp. chapters three and four; Sewell, *Logics of History*, 23; Eley, "Is All the World a Text?".
28. Wansbrough, "Res Ipsa Loquitur", 10.
29. On the linguistic turn as it pertains to the field of History, see, for example, Clark, *History, Theory, Text*, esp. 156–85 (on the (potential) benefits of literary theory to her particular field, early Christianity); Lindorfer, "Diskurs der Geschichte"; Schöttler, *Nach der Angst*; and the contributions in Spiegel, ed., *Practicing History*. Seminal works that utilise and augment the notion of history as/and discourse are White, *Content of the Form*, 'Discourse of History' and *Tropics of Discourse*; Spiegel's essay collection, *Past as Text*; Tyler and Balzaretti, eds, *Narrative and History*; Hen and Innes, eds, *Uses of the Past*; Althoff et al., eds, *Medieval Concepts*; Geary, *Phantoms of Remembrance*; McKitterick, *The Carolingians*.
30. An early example is Wansbrough, "Res Ipsa Loquitur".
31. Robinson, "Reconstructing", 116. See also Wansbrough, "Res Ipsa Loquitur", esp. 4–5, 10; Meisami, "History as Literature", 15–16, 18; Humphreys, "Qur'ānic Myth", 272; Hoyland, "History, Fiction and Authorship", 19. Like Hoyland's piece itself, however, many studies that do address the literary features of Islamic historiography are still focused on the question of 'fact' vs. 'fiction', which ultimately serves a positivist purpose. On this issue, see also Robinson, "Reconstructing", 115, 118; Haider, *Rebel and Imām*, 10, 14.
32. See, for example, Shoshan, *Poetics*; El-Hibri, *Reinterpreting Islamic Historiography* and *Parable and Politics*; Leder, "Features of the Novel" and "Literary Use"; Noth, *Early Arabic Historical Tradition*; Meisami, *Persian Historiography*; Malti-Douglas, "Texts and Tortures"; Beaumont, "Hard-Boiled"; Franz, *Kompilation*; Hirschler, *Medieval Arabic Historiography*; Haider, *Rebel and Imām*. See also the contributions in Bray, ed., *Writing and Representation* and in Leder, ed., *Story-Telling*.
33. Shoshan, *Poetics*, xxiv. See also Robinson, "History and Heilsgeschichte", 119; Meisami, "Masʿūdī on Love", "History as Literature" and "Masʿūdī and the Reign", 149–50.
34. Hodgson, "Pre-Modern Muslim Historians", esp. 57, 62–3. The quote is on 65.

35. Rosenthal, *Muslim Historiography*, 67, 70.
36. Meisami, "Masʿūdī on Love", 270.
37. Robinson, "Reconstructing", 117.
38. For instance, Clark's discussion of the rather hesitant engagement with literary theory (as opposed to social theory) in Early Christian Studies will sound quite familiar to the historian of (in particular, early) Islam. Clark, *History, Theory, Text*, 156–61, 165–6. Fifteen years earlier, in 1989, Averil Cameron had already urged the application of literary theory to ancient and early Christian history: "But, lest anyone should be thinking otherwise, literature and history must go together. History is not *just* rhetoric, it is true . . . But rhetoric in the wide sense, that is, all that is implied by textuality, is as much a part of all but the most technical historical writing as it is of literature itself." Cameron, "Introduction", 1–10 (quote on 10).
39. Spiegel, "Mirror's Eye", 73–4. For this issue among Islamicists, see Cobb, "Review", 109.
40. "Just as there may have been many versions of a given text in circulation, so any one text, or any one version, can have a multiplicity of purposes. Early ʿAbbasid prose texts are truly polysemous and we should not restrict them by tying them to one reading at the expense of others which may be equally appropriate or plausible." Montgomery, "Serendipity", 223–4. The few pre-modern Muslim scholars who rejected the notion of multivalence, such as Ibn Kathīr or Ibn Taymiyya, sat "very uneasily in the mainstream pre-modern tradition". Robinson, "Reconstructing", 120 n. 88.
41. Robinson, *Historiography*, 53. See also Donner, *Narratives*, 26–9.
42. See, for example, Donner, *Narratives*, 3; Johns, "Archaeology"; Hoyland, "New Documentary Texts", esp. 410–11.
43. Spiegel, "Political Utility", esp. 85–6, 89–90, and "History, Historicism"; Sonnesyn, "Obedient Creativity", 130–1; Potter, *Literary Texts*, 150: "Historical narrative and the recording of facts are not, and were not in antiquity, the same thing." See also Clark, *History, Theory, Text*, 167–9.
44. Hodgson, "Pre-Modern Muslim Historians", 62, 63; Meisami, "History as Literature", 29–30; El-Hibri, *Reinterpreting Islamic Historiography*, 13; Haider, *Rebel and Imām*, 3, 4; Peacock, *Medieval Islamic Historiography*, 1–2; Robinson, *Historiography*, 11–13, 152.
45. As argued by El-Hibri, *Reinterpreting Islamic Historiography*, 53.
46. 'Politics' here means "the networks of power and authority, private and public, in which scholarship is produced". Robinson, "Reconstructing", 111.
47. Haider, *Rebel and Imām*, 1.
48. Hodgson, "Pre-Modern Muslim Historians", 64; see also his discussion on 65–7. Similarly, Robinson, "History and Heilsgeschichte", 119–20 as well as "Reconstructing", 111–15 and *Historiography*, 57–8, 154–5; Hoyland, "History, Fiction and Authorship", 18. Wansbrough, "Res Ipsa Loquitur",

addresses the "imaginative reconstruction" of the past (13, 19) that lies at the heart of the historian's task, a "creative licence" that historians nevertheless rarely acknowledge (9). Similarly, Meisami, "History as Literature", 29–30 n. 48. Nirenberg, "Rhineland Massacres" illustrates the same fundamental issue with regard to the reception of the 1096 massacre of German Jews in pre- and post-Holocaust Jewish history and historiography.

49. Cameron, "Introduction", 4–5.
50. See, for example, 17: "In the figure of the Khārijite, then, was embodied a seductive danger that resided in the consequences of the Muslim *umma*'s formative narratives and so in the imaginative basis for identity formation within that community"; 195: "It is necessary, then, that one proceed with a good deal of caution in approaching the . . . sources for Khārijī history. What these sources can tell us . . . is what . . . early Islamic authors thought of the Khawārij, how they imagined them and what they believed motivated them."
51. See, for example, 197: Khārijites were "men who had chosen rebellion and murder as the only way to preserve the one true community of God upon the earth"; 216: "The bonds of Islamic identity were no protection in these encounters [between Khārijites and non-Khārijites] as the Khawārij pounced upon their victims and hacked away with their swords"; 277: Ibn Ḥanbal and most of his contemporaries "vehemently rejected the behavior of the Khawārij, even as he closely adhered to what we know of their vision of the very early Islamic past and their notions of pious praxis."
52. Sizgorich, *Violence and Belief*, 167. A similar issue is apparent in some of Gaiser's otherwise highly thought-provoking work. See, for example, his "*Takfīr* Re-Examined" and *Shurāt Legends*; on the latter, briefly, Hagemann, "Review".
53. El-Hibri, *Parable and Politics*, 237.
54. Ibid., ix.
55. On this, see also Hawting, *Idea of Idolatry*, 9; Waldman, *Toward a Theory*, esp. 3–25.
56. Cooperson, "Probability", 78 makes a similar argument for a modern reader's (in)capability to recognise signals of veracity in pre-modern texts. See also Lassner, "'Doing' Early Islamic History", 5: "The author and medieval reader (or, in certain cases, the speaker and listener) were partners in the original act of transmission. Needless to say, the partnership has not survived . . . Confronting the medieval traditions, current readers, clever and learned as they are, might not even grasp the broad meaning of the apologists' message for want of access to the fine detail." Also ibid., 7. For the same problem as it pertains to medieval European literature, see Spiegel, "Political Utility", 98.
57. The *topoi* found in the prefaces of pre-modern works in Arabic were studied by Peter Freimark in his 1967 doctoral dissertation (Freimark, *Vorwort*). His analysis addressed mostly *adab* works, and Freimark was interested in the

preface as a 'literary form' displaying conventional motifs concerning authorial intentions, purposes of composition, structure, scope and related issues. His focus was thus different from Stetter's and Noth's studies.

58. Stetter, *Topoi und Schemata.*
59. Ibid., 35.
60. Ibid., 1.
61. The section on *topoi* covers pp. 4–34, the section on *schemata* pp. 35–122.
62. Stetter, *Topoi und Schemata,* 11, 16–17.
63. Ibid., 27.
64. Ibid., 5–7.
65. Ibid., 28–30.
66. Ibid., 31–3.
67. Ibid., 34.
68. Ibid., 35.
69. Ibid., 71–9. On numbers in Islamic historiography, see also Conrad, "Seven and the Tasbīʿ".
70. Stetter, *Topoi und Schemata,* for example 48–9, 51–9.
71. Ibid., 40–51 and *passim.*
72. Ibid., 36–43, 53–4 and *passim.*
73. Ibid., 41–3.
74. Ibid., 50. The work of Schoeler confirmed Stetter's arguments regarding this.
75. Noth, "Iṣfahān-Nihāwand", 276–7, 283. For similar instances of "argument over a void", see Conrad, "ʿUmar at Sargh" (quote on 526) and "Conquest of Arwād".
76. Noth, "Iṣfahān-Nihāwand", 278–9. He reached the same conclusion regarding the occurrence of *topoi* in the early historiographical tradition in his "Charakter" (see esp. 188).
77. Noth, "Iṣfahān-Nihāwand", 294.
78. Ibid.
79. Noth, *Quellenkritische Studien,* 3.
80. Noth, *Early Arabic Historical Tradition.*
81. Robinson, "Islamic Historiography"; El-Hibri, "Review"; Hoyland, "Review".
82. On *topoi* see also Conrad, "Abraha and Muhammad"; Donner, *Narratives,* 266–71; Leube, *Kinda,* esp. chapter 3.
83. Noth, *Early Arabic Historical Tradition,* 4–17, which expands on Noth, "Charakter". Against Wellhausen's concept of historical schools, compare also the remarks in Crone, *Slaves,* 10, 13 and Landau-Tasseron, "Sayf b. ʿUmar".
84. Noth, *Early Arabic Historical Tradition,* 22–3. See also his "Recht und Geschichte"; for a monograph-length study, A. Radtke, *Offenbarung,* esp. the case study in chapter two (97–168).
85. Noth, *Early Arabic Historical Tradition,* 109.
86. Ibid.

87. It is also a feature of pre-modern history-writing more generally, especially in the case of chronicles. For medieval European historiography, see Conti, "Scribes", 275.
88. This is the meaning of the Greek *topos koinós*, 'common place'; the single term *topos* is an ellipsis of this phrase.
89. Donner, *Narratives*, 268.
90. Noth, *Early Arabic Historical Tradition*, 109–10.
91. Ibid., 110.
92. On *awāʾil* as a literary form, see Noth, *Early Arabic Historical Tradition*, 104–8.
93. On "Topoi Connected with Personal Names" and their relevance for the description of battles and wars, see Noth, *Early Arabic Historical Tradition*, 109–29 and Noth, "Charakter", 191–3.
94. See EI^3, "Awāʾil" (M. Bernards) and the references cited there.
95. Ibn Muzāḥim, *Waqʿat Ṣiffīn*, 588; al-Dīnawarī, *Akhbār*, 210 (al-Dīnawarī's Ṣiffīn section from the first call to arbitration to the Khārijites' withdrawal from ʿAlī is essentially identical to the material preserved in the relevant section of *Waqʿat Ṣiffīn*).
96. Al-Yaʿqūbī, *Taʾrīkh*, II, 190.
97. Al-Balādhurī, *Ansāb*, II, 295, 296; al-Ṭabarī, *Taʾrīkh*, I, 3339–40; al-Masʿūdī, *Murūj*, I–II, 393; al-Yaʿqūbī, *Taʾrīkh*, II, 190.
98. Al-Balādhurī, *Ansāb*, II, 295. See also al-Masʿūdī, *Murūj*, I–II, 393; Ibn Qutayba, *al-Maʿārif*, 410. Al-Balādhurī also preserves a line on the same page according to which "they said" (*qālū*) that the first to proclaim *lā ḥukma* was a certain Yazīd b. ʿĀsim al-Muḥāribī.
99. Ibn Muzāḥim, *Waqʿat Ṣiffīn*, 588; al-Dīnawarī, *Akhbār*, 210.
100. Ibn Khayyāṭ does not mention the *lā ḥukma* slogan. Ibn Aʿtham transmits a unique report that ascribes the first protest against the arbitration to a follower of ʿAlī from Banū Yashkur, who is named as the first to dissociate from both ʿAlī and Muʿāwiya. Ibn Aʿtham, *Futūḥ*, IV, 17–19.
101. For example al-Dīnawarī, *Akhbār*, 210; al-Ṭabarī, *Taʾrīkh*, I, 3339–40; al-Yaʿqūbī, *Taʾrīkh*, II, 190, 191; al-Masʿūdī, *Murūj*, I–II, 395; Ibn Muzāḥim, *Waqʿat Ṣiffīn*, 588, 589; Ibn Saʿd, *Ṭabaqāt*, III, 32; Ibn Aʿtham, *Futūḥ*, IV, 89; al-Balādhurī, *Ansāb*, II, 301, 311.
102. Al-Balādhurī, *Ansāb*, II, 295, 296; al-Dīnawarī, *Akhbār*, 210; Ibn Muzāḥim, *Waqʿat Ṣiffīn*, 588; al-Ṭabarī, *Taʾrīkh*, I, 3338–9. Al-Masʿūdī, *Murūj*, I–II, 393 omits the apology.
103. Al-Balādhurī, *Ansāb*, II, 296.
104. For the stories of ʿUrwa and Abū Bilāl, see Chapter Five. On Abū Bilāl in the Islamic tradition and his memory among non-Khārijites, see Gaiser, "Tracing the Ascetic Life".
105. Al-Balādhurī, *Ansāb*, II, 322.
106. Ibid. For the depiction of Khārijite piety, see Chapter Two.

107. See below, 88–9 and ns. 19 and 20 thereto.
108. Al-Balādhurī, *Ansāb*, II, 322–34.
109. See below, 176–7, for more such examples.
110. Noth, *Early Arabic Historical Tradition*, 110.
111. Ibid., 109–29.
112. Ibid., 96–104, 114, 122. On the importance of lists, possibly some of the earliest fragments of the historical tradition to have survived into the eighth and ninth century, see Robinson, *Historiography*, 23, 47, 67–8; Leder, "Literary Use", 309–10; Crone, *Slaves*, 16–17. On the continued – and varied – use of lists in the creation and/or organisation of cultural memory in the ninth century, see Bray, "Lists and Memory".
113. Noth, *Early Arabic Historical Tradition*, 126.
114. Crone, *Slaves*, 16.
115. Noth, *Early Arabic Historical Tradition*, 111.
116. Ibid.
117. Ibid., 111–12.
118. Ibid.,113.
119. Al-Ṭabarī, *Taʾrīkh*, I, 3380; Ibn Khayyāṭ, *Taʾrīkh*, I, 224; al-Dīnawarī, *Akhbār*, 223; al-Balādhurī, *Ansāb*, II, 331.
120. Al-Dīnawarī, *Akhbār*, 223.
121. Al-Ṭabarī, *Taʾrīkh*, II, 581.
122. See, for example, Ibn Aʿtham, *Futūḥ*, IV, 121; VI, 310, 311; and VII, 23, 24, 26–7. See also al-Ṭabarī, *Taʾrīkh*, II, 904, 958, 966; al-Balādhurī, *Ansāb*, II, 330.
123. Al-Ṭabarī, *Taʾrīkh*, I, 3380; al-Balādhurī, *Ansāb*, II, 320, 330; al-Dīnawarī, *Akhbār*, 223.
124. Al-Ṭabarī, *Taʾrīkh*, I, 3349, 3387; Ibn Khayyāṭ, *Taʾrīkh*, I, 216; al-Balādhurī, *Ansāb*, II, 300.
125. See, for example, al-Yaʿqūbī, *Taʾrīkh*, II, 191–3, who mentions Shabath as a Khārijite leader but does not say whether he returned to ʿAlī before Nahrawān or not; al-Balādhurī, *Ansāb*, II, 301.
126. Noth, *Early Arabic Historical Tradition*, 120.
127. Confusion over someone's affiliation with Khārijism is a frequent occurrence that did not spare even such well-known and copiously cited scholars as al-Haytham b. ʿAdī (d. 207 H/822 CE) or Abū ʿUbayda Maʿmar b. al-Muthannā (d. c. 210 H/825 CE), and the debate continues. Affiliation with the Khawārij was and is a common and effective accusation, of course, but if it is also accurate here then the question is, what did being a Khārijite at that time entail? The focus is usually on violent forms of Khārijism, but clearly these two had nothing to do with the sword-wielding barbarians of early Islamic historiography and they also do not seem to have held particularly 'Khārijite' opinions and beliefs. On al-Haytham, see Leder, *Korpus*, 289, 307–8; on Abū ʿUbayda, see Madelung, "Abū ʿUbayda"; Lecker, "Biographical Notes".

128. Al-Ṭabarī, *Taʾrīkh*, I, 3388; al-Balādhurī, *Ansāb*, II, 313.
129. Landau-Tasseron, "New Data", 371. See also Donner, *Narratives*, 260–3; Osti, "Tailors", esp. 285–7; Haider, *Rebel and Imām*. The considerable degree to which later author-compilers were free to engage with their materials is demonstrated by Hirschler, *Historiography*; with regard to legal writing, Robinson, "Reconstructing", 117: "Third/ninth-century legal thinking and writing were far more dynamic, eclectic, adaptive and creative than we have been inclined to believe."
130. On such "topisch[e] Wandermotiv[e]" see also Leube, *Kinda*, 16, 57–63 (quote on 58).
131. Tillschneider, "*Asbāb wurūd al-ḥadīṯ*".
132. Van Ess, "Unfertige Studien I", 1403.
133. See Haider, *Rebel and Imām*, 10, 14, 259. Cooperson, "Probability", 69–70 also discusses the similarities between Arabic historiography and early Christian writings regarding truth claims; Meisami, "History as Literature", 16–18, 29–30. The question of 'factual' vs. 'fictional' accounts transcends historiography, of course: concerning early Arabic poetry, for instance, Jacobi identifies "keine Opposition, sondern eine ständige Grenzüberschreitung" between fictional (i.e., reflecting reality) and imaginary elements, with the latter demonstrating a very loose connection (or none at all) to reality. Jacobi, "Das Fiktive", 21–2 (quote on 22). See also Noth, "Fiktion", 472–3; Conrad, "ʿUmar at Sargh", esp. 520–4.
134. Haider, *Rebel and Imām*, 5. See also Cooperson, "Probability", 70: "In the Islamic tradition, plausibility was usually expressed in terms of probability: that is, the likelihood (rather than the mere possibility) that a certain event had occurred." The same principle was used in the evaluation of *ḥadīth*, which focused on greater or lesser credibility rather than conclusive veracity, on benefit to the audience and sound transmission (70–5); in fact, this principle generally applied to "a legal and ritual world shot through with systemic and pervasive indeterminacy" (77).
135. Leder, "Conventions", 34–5 gives a succinct summary of the problem as it relates to narrative structures. But where he sets out to define such criteria for recognising and eliminating fictional elements (for historiography, 52–5), I remain sceptical as to the feasibility of such an endeavour; Leder himself appears wary, too, at the end (ibid., 59–60).
136. See also El-Hibri, *Reinterpreting Islamic Historiography*, 12; Mattock, "History and Fiction", 95.
137. Cooperson, "Probability"; Haider, *Rebel and Imām*, 15.
138. Noth, "Iṣfahān-Nihāwand", 296. See also the remarks in Humphreys, "Qurʾānic Myth", 272.
139. Donner, *Narratives*, 267; Crone, *Slaves*, 12; Pratsch, *Topos*, 364–71.
140. On the dynamics of a stable "Motivkern" vis-à-vis contradictory details as a function of the inherent fluidity of early Islamic historiography,

see Leube, *Kinda*, 52–6 and *passim*; Van Ess, “Unfertige Studien I”, 1403–4.
141. Noth, “Iṣfahān-Nihāwand”, 294.
142. For example Kenney, *Muslim Rebels*, 46.

2

Portraying Khārijism

The main purpose of the portrayal of Khārijism in early Islamic historical writing is to illustrate, criticise and ultimately reject excessive forms of piety as cause for bloodshed and strife within the *umma*. The denunciation of militant piety is a commonality between Islamic historiography and other late antique/early medieval traditions, the figure of the violent Christian monk being a case in point.[1] Militant piety had its place in Islamic (and Christian[2]) society and thought, of course, and connoted laudable religious devotion in the right context, such as among Muslim frontier warriors. But directed inwards, militant piety was a threat to society. This primary concern can be observed across all time periods considered in this study. It is expressed through three interconnected recurring themes: (1) Khārijite piety and its ramifications; (2) longing for *jihād* and martyrdom; and (3) the Khawārij as indiscriminate killers and transgressors of the very same Islamic norms they claim to defend. The first two evolved into Khārijite-specific *topoi* denoting a particular brand of dissidence and – in the *firaq* literature at least – heresy. The third cannot be called a *topos* as such but rather represents the logical conclusion to the first two themes. This chapter will explore how the early historical tradition fleshed out these themes in the creation of a Khārijite master narrative that was then used to condemn Khārijite piety.

Khārijite Piety in Early Islamic Historiography

The Islamic historical tradition depicts the Khawārij as fundamentally pious men and, occasionally, women. This first becomes apparent in the accounts that draw a direct connection between the later Khārijites and the *qurrāʾ*[3]: "Misʿar b. Fadakī and Ibn al-Kawwāʾ and their group of the *qurrāʾ who later became Khawārij* were those who urged the people to respond to the judgement of the *muṣḥaf*".[4] A familial relationship between the two groups and the 'pious descent' of the Khārijites is thereby established and frequently reiterated.[5]

The most succinct expression of Khārijite godliness is their famous rallying cry *lā ḥukma illā li-llāh* as the foundation of their actions and beliefs. The sources abound with descriptions of the Khārijite commitment to upholding the will of God and their self-appointed mission to defend His rights against those who would violate the divine provisions. The depth of their commitment to following God's orders is illustrated by the fact that the Khawārij apply their strict standards to themselves as well. For instance, they are shown to freely admit their mistake in insisting on the arbitration. Subsequent repentance is considered a prerequisite for atonement; as they have seen reason, so are self-reproach and penitence expected from those who seek to (re-)enlist their support:

> *Lā ḥukma illā li-llāh*, judgement is for God, O ʿAlī, not for you. We do not agree to men judging over the religion of God . . . We erred when we accepted the two arbitrators, and we returned and repented. So return, O ʿAlī, as we returned, and repent towards God as we repented. If not, we will dissociate from you.[6]

Other than the *lā ḥukma* watchword, nothing is more inherently Khārijite than the idea of selling or 'exchanging' oneself, i.e. giving up one's life for God. This notion finds expression in the epithet *al-shurāt* ('sellers', 'exchangers'), one of the most common names for the Khawārij and indeed the term we find most often as a self-designation in the poetry attributed to them.[7] Exchange of one's worldly life for God's favour in the Hereafter is a Qurʾānic concept. It finds expression in a number of verses; the two most commonly cited to explain the Khārijite epithet *al-shurāt* are Q 2:207 ('Among people is one who sells his soul seeking the pleasure of God. God is Tender towards His worshippers.') and 9:111 ('God has purchased from the believers their souls and their wealth and, in exchange, the Garden shall be theirs. They fight in the cause of God, they kill and are killed – a true promise from Him in the Torah, the Evangel and the Qurʾan. Who is more truthful to his promise than God? So be of good cheer regarding that business deal you transact. That is the greatest of triumphs.').[8] The latter verse in particular emphasises the importance of fighting to uphold God's ordinances (*yuqātilūna fī sabīl allāh*) and so constitutes a core element in developing a notion of (Khārijite) *shirāʾ* that "clearly possessed strong associations with fighting injustice as well as following a life of piety (*taqwa*)".[9] The poetry and pious sayings ascribed to the early Khawārij abound with references to *shirāʾ*[10] – regardless of the historicity of the accounts, such narratives serve to associate Khārijism with a particular form of religious devotion in a way that underlines their extraordinary orientation towards the Hereafter. The combination of godliness and militance apparent here will shortly be addressed in more detail.

The piety of the Khārijites is not only demonstrated by their words and deeds, but also signalled by their physical appearance. They bear the signs of their devotion for all to see: their faces are said to have been black, their foreheads marked from prostration due to incessant prayer;[11] their leader at Nahrawān, ʿAbdallāh b. Wahb al-Rāsibī, had calluses on his face, knees and hands from his fervent prostrations and is therefore called *dhū al-thafināt*, 'he with the calluses'.[12] ʿAlī's murderer Ibn Muljam is likewise characterised as an ascetic through his outward appearance.[13] Khārijite bodies, beliefs and acts are thus presented as a holistic expression of absolute submission to God:

> We are the sons of Islam and God is One / and the most righteous among God's servants (*awlā ʿibād allāh bi-l-ḥaqq*) is he who gives thanks [to God].[14]

This feature of the characterisation of literary Khārijism is ubiquitous in accounts of Khārijite history. The abundant Qurʾānic quotations and other pious references in the sources' rendition of Khārijite rhetoric are one indication of this. A few examples will suffice.

A report in al-Balādhurī's *Ansāb* details an assembly in the house of ʿAbdallāh b. Wahb al-Rāsibī before the Khawārij swear allegiance to him in preparation for the battle at Nahrawān. During this meeting, Ibn Wahb summons his fellow rebels to "commanding right and forbidding wrong",[15] urges them to leave "this town whose people are oppressors [Q 4:75]" and condemns the arbitration, this "abominable innovation".[16] The rebels assembled around Ibn Wahb and Ḥurqūṣ b. Zuhayr, a Companion and veteran of the conquests, then discuss their "censure of the world (*dhamm al-dunyā*), the need to renounce it (*al-daʿāʾ ilā rafḍihā*), the striving for truth (*al-jidd fī ṭalab al-ḥaqq*) and the disapproval of innovation and injustice (*inkār al-bidaʿ wa-l-ẓulm*)".[17]

References to the Qurʾān are a stock ingredient of Khārijite discourse. When the Khārijite leader al-Mustawrid, who rebelled in the reign of Muʿāwiya, learns that the caliphal governor of al-Madāʾin refuses to acknowledge him, he quotes Q 2:6–7 ('It matters not to unbelievers whether you warn them or not. They will not believe. God has sealed their hearts and their hearing, and a veil conceals their sight. An awful punishment will be theirs').[18]

The day Shurayḥ b. Awfā al-ʿAbsī joins the Khārijites on the way to Nahrawān, he recites Q 4:75. The connection between violence and piety, which will be discussed below, is particularly apparent in the context of this verse: "[4:74] Let those fight in the cause of God who sell the life of this world for the Hereafter. And he who fights in the cause of God and is killed or victorious, We will grant him a great reward. [4:75] And why do you not fight in the cause of God and for the weak men, women and children who say: 'Our Lord, take us out of this town whose people are oppressors.'"[19]

Similarly, another Khārijite is said to have recited Q 28:20–1 when he left his home to rebel. These verses are part of the story of Moses and his flight following the killing of an adversary: '[28:20] Leave [the town]! I am a sincere advisor to you [Moses]! [28:21] So he left, fearful and in anticipation. He said 'My Lord, save me from the oppressors'. According to the report, upon crossing the Euphrates the Khārijite followed up with Q 28:22: 'And when he [Moses] turned towards Midian, he said 'Perhaps my Lord will guide me on the right path'.[20]

The Khawārij are thus depicted as God-fearing believers. The inclusion of quotations from the Qur'ān – the "rhetorical use of the Qur'an as a literary weapon"[21] – or of other forms of religious argument is of course not at all unusual in Islamic historiography or the Islamic literary tradition more generally.[22] Most protagonists, and certainly those who (are shown to have) participated in religio-political disputes, are credited with references to the Qur'ān or *sunna* (however defined) to substantiate their claims and underline their piety.[23] In the case of the Khawārij, however, it is difficult to find accounts without such references. As a result, they appear as believers whose devotion to God is their most prominent attribute, but this is a double-edged sword: while usually a praiseworthy quality, piety as interpreted by the Khawārij is so extreme that it causes them to transgress the boundaries of acceptable behaviour. This is the concern of the second theme.

Marrying Piety to Violence: Khārijite *Jihād*

The pious disdain for this world that the Khawārij exhibit in the sources is closely connected to the *topos* of their desire for *jihād*, which is presented as a natural corollary to their focus on living a godly life. The conviction that death *fī sabīl allāh* is preferable to a meaningless existence in this fleeting world is by no means exclusive to the Khārijites, but as in the case of their piety, the longing for *jihād* is so prevalent in the narratives of Khārijite origins that it emerges as the second defining characteristic of the Khawārij. The following examples highlight the ubiquity of this particular *topos* and explore Khārijism's marriage of piety and *jihād*. They also demonstrate the stylised nature of the accounts transmitted and thus emphasise the decidedly literary character of Khārijism as remembered by the early historical tradition.

The connection between Khārijite piety and their commitment to *jihād* is expressed in a multitude of speeches, discussions, exhortations, poetry and the like. Their prowess in battle is notorious: there are dozens of references to Khārijite groups fighting off caliphal troops many times their number.[24] The Khārijites' willingness to risk life and limb and their preoccupation with combatting their opponents are the stuff of legends:

> Tell the transgressors (*al-muḥillīn*) Ṣāliḥ[25] is upon you / and in war Ṣāliḥ is a battering ram (*kabsh nāṭiḥ*)[26]; and in clandestine slaughter Ṣāliḥ is a snarling lion (*layth kāliḥ*) . . .[27]

> People die in the morning and in the evening, and I cannot be sure that fate will not cut me off before I can strive against the evildoers – what a cheat that would be, and what benefit lost![28]

> [Nāfiʿ] died without compromising his faith / and when he was mentioned people feared him like lightning strike;
> Death – without question – is a set matter / to whom it does not come in the morning, it will come to later (*yuṭraq;* lit. "knock").[29]

Likewise, the Jazīran rebel Shabīb b. Yazīd was apparently so calm in the face of impending battle (and perhaps dismissive of his enemy) that he quietly finished his meal although the Umayyad forces had already arrived at his door, so to speak. In the same vein, he is shown to be so indifferent to enemy pursuit as to fall asleep in the saddle, to the mystification of his companions.[30] Indeed, not only do the Khārijites not care about the risk of dying, they purposefully seek out death in battle as a way of securing their place in Paradise. Consider the following accounts.

In al-Ṭabarī's version of the rebellion of Ṣāliḥ b. Musarriḥ in 76 H/695–6 CE,[31] the Khārijite is portrayed as a "humble and pious man" who "taught the Qurʾān and *tafsīr* and delivered sermons".[32] The report goes on to transmit one of Ṣāliḥ's sermons at length. As the selected passage illustrates, it serves to display the Khārijite emphasis on piety and *jihād* and makes explicit their connection in the Khārijite mindset:

> Prepare, then – God's mercy upon you – to strive against these fractious parties and unjust leaders of error,[33] and to go out from the abode of transience to the abode of eternity and join our believing, convinced brethren, who sold the present world for the afterworld and expended their wealth in quest of God's good pleasure in the final reckoning. Be not anxious about being killed for God's sake, for being killed is easier than dying naturally. Natural death comes upon you unexpectedly, separating you from your fathers, sons, wives, and this world; if your anxiety and aversion to this is too strong, then, indeed, sell your souls to God obediently, and your wealth, and you will enter Paradise in security and embrace the black-eyed houris. May God make you and us among the grateful and mindful 'who are guided by the truth and by it act justly' [Q 7:159] . . .[34]

Another example that showcases the militant piety espoused by Khārijism is a speech attributed to the Azraqite leader ʿAbd Rabbih before one of the faction's many battles against al-Muhallab.[35] He addresses his men as *muhājirūn* (Emigrants), thereby likening the Khawārij to Muḥammad's earliest and most faithful followers. This comparison both claims the highest Islamic credentials for his Khārijites and connects them to the original *muhājirūn*, who embody the combination of piety and combat readiness that characterises literary Khārijism. As Muḥammad and his early supporters had once been a minority, so are ʿAbd Rabbih's followers outnumbered by al-Muhallab's army, but the Khārijite exhorts his men to fight regardless: "Even if they overpower you in life, they will not be superior to you in death (*fa-in ghalabūkum ʿalā al-ḥayāt fa-lā yaghlubūkum ʿalā al-mawt*)." He admonishes them to ensure "that the spear's only destination are the chests [of the enemy] and the sword's targets the [enemies'] faces" and tells them to "turn your souls to God in this world" in anticipation of reward in the Hereafter. Despite the odds, the Khawārij should not "despair of victory, for you are 'the small group (*fiʾa qalīla*) that defeated the large group (*fiʾa kathīra*) by the will of God, and God is with those who endure (*al-ṣābirīn*)' [Q 2:249]".[36]

While imprisoned by al-Mughīra in Kufa, the Khārijite leader Muʿādh b. Juwayn composes a poem to his fellow Khawārij, whom the townspeople plan to expel from the city. Muʿādh bemoans the fact that he is forced to remain inactive and cannot join the battle against the Kufans:

> If only I were with you opposing your enemy / for I am given first the cup of fate to drink . . .;
> It is hard for me that you are wronged and decrease / and I become sorrowful as a prisoner in chains;
> If I were with you while they headed for you / then I would stir up dust between the two factions;
> For many a group have I broken up, and many an attack / have I experienced and many an opponent have I left dead on the ground.[37]

Just before the decisive battle between al-Mustawrid's rebels and al-Mughīra's troops in the course of which Maʿqil b. Qays and al-Mustawrid kill each other, al-Mustawrid calls upon his men to stand firm against the enemy: "By God, besides whom there is no god save He, Paradise belongs to whomever is killed with the genuine intention of *jihād* against those oppressors and their expression of enmity."[38]

When the Khārijite rebel Ḥayyān b. Ẓabyān, who had been imprisoned in Kufa as well, is finally set free after the death of al-Mughīra in

50–1 H/670–1 CE, he gathers his remaining companions to rise against the new governor of Kufa. His exhortations stress the importance of active resistance for securing a place in Paradise:

> God, almighty and great, decreed the *jihād* for us. Whoever among you desires God and His reward, let him follow the way of his companions and his brothers. God will grant him the reward of this world and the better reward of the other world . . .[39]

The Khawārij are convinced but then argue about where best to stage their revolt. Ḥayyān, however, maintains that it makes no difference.

> [W]hen God knows that you exert yourselves in *jihād* against His enemy and yours, you will have His reward and escape from sin . . . By God, there are not enough of you to expect victory in the world against the aggressive oppressors thereby. Rebel beside this city of yours [i.e., Kufa] and fight according to the command of God against whoever violates obedience to Him. Don't wait, and don't bide your time. Thus, you will hurry to Paradise and get yourself out of the discord thereby.[40]

The examples cited are representative of the general structure of reports concerning Khārijite *jihād*. The rebels are shown to rationalise their violent actions by pointing out the obligation to oppose unjust rule. The reprehensibility of their enemies, frequently referred to as unbelievers, is the justificatory basis on which they carry out their interpretation of God's will. Indeed, literary Khārijism across the entire period under study considers *jihād* the only certain way to attain God's reward in the Hereafter. Furthermore, there is not much variation at all in the *jihād* statements attributed to Khārijite rebels, no development of Khārijite thought regarding this issue. Khārijite calls to *jihād* thus appear as interchangeable phrases that can be employed regardless of specific contexts. The same applies to the expressions of Khārijite piety discussed above. The result is a loss of specificity that has serious consequences for the historicity and reliability of the accounts that render Khārijite history. A tangible Khārijite identity or 'substance' beyond such phrases remains elusive.[41]

This insubstantial, *topos*-laden depiction of Khārijism does serve a distinct purpose: it associates the Khawārij with certain characteristics and ideas that are immediately recognisable to the audience, turning stories of Khārijism into a type of "exemplary anecdote" that "permits the construction of a series of tales featuring the same [here: collective] protagonist".[42] While many of these ideas might not be uncommon or problematic as such, their specifically Khārijite interpretation leads to acts irreconcilable with accepted norms of Islamic behaviour: fighting against infidels is laudable, but not if a flawed definition of infidel directs the fighting inward. The Khawārij are presented as guilty of subverting Islamic ideals, and the early historical tradition denounces them for their excessive use of force and the 'excommunication' (*takfīr*) of non-Khārijite Muslims.

"A Word of Truth with an Evil Intention" – Censuring Khārijism

As we have seen, militant piety is the primary characteristic associated with literary Khārijism. Early Islamic historiography censures this Khārijite piety as a disruptive force by calling into question both the intentions of the Khawārij and the sincerity of their beliefs. Various tools, sources and strategies are utilised for this purpose, among them the Qurʾān, *ḥadīth* and the juxtaposition of Khārijite word and deed. Much of the criticism is expressly directed against habits and actions that violate religious as well as common social codes of conduct: Khārijites are portrayed as excessive in their use of violence, even against women, children and praying Muslims – in their mindless desire to attain God's favour, they infringe His laws and thus drop out of the very community of Muslims they aspire to purify.[43] Their conduct appears in sharp contrast to evolving notions of communal togetherness, embodied in the many *ḥadīth*s that have ʿAlī refuse to denounce his enemies as unbelievers, for instance.[44] The fact that the Khārijites' opponents are sometimes referred to as *ahl al-qibla*, perhaps the broadest umbrella term for the community of believers, underlines this further.[45] Some Khawārij are also accused of rebelling for material gain rather than out of true religious conviction,[46] which casts them in the role of hypocrites who do not act in line with their own ideals.[47] But it is the condemnation of Khārijism as a transgression of Islamic norms and precepts[48] that is most pervasive in the historical tradition and thus takes up much of the remainder of this chapter.

Once more, a good starting point is the Khārijite maxim *lā ḥukma illā li-llāh*. In itself, this dictum is not offensive or heretical; al-Ṭabarī preserves a report according to which ʿAlī, upon being confronted by Khārijite critics, responds by confirming that judgement indeed belongs to God.[49] However, ʿAlī follows up by declaring that the Khārijite interpretation of this notion is a distortion of its truth, asserting that the rebels use "a word of truth with an evil intention (*kalimatu ḥaqqin yurādu bihā bāṭilun*)".[50] Khārijite claims of defending God's rights and accusations of unbelief against non-Khārijites are thereby discredited. The account has ʿAlī expound that the use of the *lā ḥukma* watchword is a deliberate ploy to conceal the Khārijites' true intentions:

> This is so [i.e., judgement does belong only to God], but they [actually] mean 'no rule', and no necessity for the people to have a ruler, whether

> righteous or unrighteous, under whose [i.e., the latter's] command the believer toils and the unbeliever profits (*innahu kadhālika wa-lakinnahum yaqūlūna: innahu lā imrata, wa-lā budda li-l-nās min amīrin barrin aw fājirin yaʿmalu fī imratihi al-muʾmin wa-yastamtiʿu al-kāfir*).[51]

Khārijite piety is exposed as dishonest. Indeed, such charges of insincerity are rather common. The work of Ibn Aʿtham, for instance, preserves a heated argument between al-Ashtar, a fervent supporter of ʿAlī, and the *qurrāʾ*/future Khārijites at Ṣiffīn, when al-Ashtar is told about the arbitration agreement. His reaction is a damning indictment of the *qurrāʾ*:

> O people of the black foreheads! We used to think that your prayers mean abstinence from this world and a desire for the Hereafter; by God, you are only running towards this world. May you meet an evil end and perish like the oppressors perished (*fa-qubḥan lakum wa-buʿdan kamā baʿida al-qawm al-ẓālimūn*).[52]

Along these lines, the Khawārij are variously labelled "transgressors", "enemies of God", "unbelievers", "dogs of hell", "heretics", and the like.[53] Ibn Aʿtham in particular is rather fond of calling the Khārijites all manner of names associated with the root *k-l-b*, likening them to dogs and wild beasts.[54] Of course, such name-calling is nothing unusual and certainly not limited to conflicts involving Khārijites, who are also quite happy to insult their opponents with such epithets. The following exchange between the Azraqī leader ʿUbayda b. Hilāl and one of al-Muhallab's soldiers is a good example.

The scene is an unsuccessful Azraqī attack on al-Muhallab's camp. When the Khārijites retreat, one of al-Muhallab's soldiers calls out after them: "O People of Hell! Verily, hurry towards it quickly, for it is your place of rest and your abode!" The Khārijite reply is short and to the point: hell is in fact prepared for unbelievers and al-Muhallab's man is one of them. The soldier in question responds, "I would manumit every slave I own if you entered Paradise while there remained between Safawān and the furthest land of Khurāsān any Magian, who marries his mother, daughter and sister, who would not enter it also!" ʿUbayda answers him: "Shut up, O wicked one! You are merely a slave of the truculent tyrant and a helper (*wazīr*) of the iniquitous unbeliever," to which his opponent replies: "O wicked one, you are the enemy of the God-fearing believer and the helper of the accursed Devil."[55] A Khārijite retort is not forthcoming, so al-Muhallab's men congratulate their companion on having bested ʿUbayda.[56]

Accusations of Khārijites deliberately and unscrupulously violating the sacred ordinances of Islam go far beyond name-calling, however. Both Ibn Aʿtham and al-Dīnawarī transmit an episode that is set against the backdrop of the drawn-out confrontation between al-Muhallab and the Azāriqa. Al-Muhallab has just returned to Sābūr after yet another victory against the Khārijites and is in the process of celebrating *yawm al-naḥr* ('Day of Sacrifice', the third day of the *ḥajj*) when he is informed of an imminent Khārijite threat. He is outraged at this blatant breach of the inviolability of the feast day, "a noble day with God the Exalted, on which He does not allow the shedding of blood", and quotes Q 2:194 ('the holy month for the holy month and retribution for all violations [in it], and whoever assaults you, assault him in the manner in which he assaulted you').[57] As foreshadowed by this verse, the rebels are utterly destroyed by al-Muhallab.[58] Their abominable conduct justifies the violence against them and so from a literary perspective, their ignominious end is inevitable.

The analysis of such accounts reveals several different methods with which our authors pursue their censure of Khārijism. The following sections look at a selection of the most important ones: discussion of intra-Khārijite strife; recourse to the Qur'ān; utilisation of *ḥadīth*; and juxtaposition of Khārijite claims with their deeds.

Pitting Khawārij against Khawārij

One technique employed in early Islamic historiography to point out the iniquity of the Khawārij consists of letting one of their factions castigate another. A good example of this is an account that brings accusations of innovation (*bid'a*) against the Khārijites and specifically Nāfi' b. al-Azraq, which is all the more interesting because this is usually an offence that the rebels charge their opponents with. Here, Nāfi' is blamed for inventing the *miḥna* of non-Khārijites, meaning the alleged habit among some Khārijite groups of interrogating everyone they came across and executing those who did not agree with them (*isti'rāḍ*), although they usually spared *dhimmīs*.[59] Reproach comes primarily from fellow Khārijites who state that this was not common practice "among their forebears of the *ahl al-Nahrawān* and the *ahl al-qibla*" and therefore split from Nāfi'.[60]

This account and others like it primarily serve to illustrate the volatility of Khārijism, which will be discussed in greater detail in Chapter Six. It is possible that the reports in question reflect real doctrinal debates, at least to the extent that the ideas attributed to the various Khārijite groups constituted fertile soil for theoretical debates among scholars or perhaps arose out of such discussions. By the eighth century, creeds and epistles, intended to define different confessional communities and engage in scholarly discourse, had become common features of Islamic intellectual production.[61] But this method of critique also betrays decidedly heresiographical concerns, and the often rather mature doctrines attributed to first/seventh-century Khārijites should make us somewhat suspicious about the historicity of such accounts. For now, though, suffice it to say that depictions of internal strife among the Khawārij are a frequent occurrence in almost all of the sources studied here. For instance, both Najda b. ʿĀmir and the alleged founder of the Ṣufriyya apparently considered indiscriminate murder (*istiʿrāḍ*) and the killing of children as practiced by some Khārijite factions to be unlawful and unacceptable innovations.[62] In another report, Qaṭarī b. al-Fujāʾa is reprimanded for his excessive use of violence and warned that he will lose his followers if he persists.[63]

Perhaps the most explicit example of a Khārijite using religious sentiment to admonish another occurs in al-Ṭabarī's work. His *Taʾrīkh* preserves an account on the authority of Abū Mikhnaf (d. 157 H/774 CE) that relates a disagreement between Ṣāliḥ b. Musarriḥ, the pious rebel *par excellence*, and his more daring colleague Shabīb b. Yazīd regarding the treatment of non-Khārijites. While Shabīb is in favour of *istiʿrāḍ*, Ṣāliḥ strongly disagrees and warns his companions against intemperance:

> Fear God, you servants of God, and be not overhasty to fight any one of the people, unless they be hostile people who intend you harm. You are rebelling only out of wrath for God,[64] because His ordinances have been flouted, the earth filled with disobedience, blood spilled unjustly, and property taken wrongfully. Do not reproach people for deeds and then do them yourselves; for you are yourselves responsible for all that you do.[65]

Despite Ṣāliḥ's status as a rebel, he is portrayed as an embodiment of righteous piety that functions as a foil to Shabīb's propensity for violence. Ṣāliḥ is shown to follow proper procedure by insisting that only those who oppose the Khawārij should be fought. He allows the taking of spoils but argues that relinquishing this right would incur favour with God.[66] His readiness to fight other Muslims is deplorable, but as he considers them polytheists, his approach is technically correct and reflects both the Qurʾān and later Islamic law. Shabīb's opinion, on the other hand, is meant to be judged reprehensible and his exchange with Ṣāliḥ foreshadows the massacres committed by his men.[67]

Qurʾānic Condemnations

Utilising the Qurʾān to attack Khārijism is another method to censure the Khawārij on religious grounds and call out their erroneous understanding of what it means to be a Muslim. This is a common technique, of course: the Qurʾān makes for good ammunition against opponents of all sorts. The

Khawārij make frequent use of it especially when internal divisions require each faction to justify their opinions.[68] Nevertheless, Qur'ānic verses are overall mainly put into service against Khārijism.

It is important to note here that the cited verses "are no mere ornament or illustration". Rather, they "provide the logic and vocabulary" determining how a particular account is perceived and interpreted.[69] Their role is to draw parallels between a Qur'ānic event or statement and the situation at hand. This "context equivalence"[70] between a Qur'ānic quotation and the particular context to which it is applied differs from the techniques of *iqtibās* (quoting or 'borrowing' from the Qur'ān) and *talmīḥ* (alluding to the Qur'ān).[71] It evokes an emotional response on the part of the audience and can sometimes serve to 'sacralise' a speech or sermon.[72] *Iqtibās*, *talmīḥ* and context equivalence are common features of classical Arabic literature irrespective of the particular religio-political affiliations of the protagonists in question. They serve specific functions, here the invocation of divine authority against the Khārijites' misdeeds. Let us look at some instructive examples.[73]

Al-Dīnawarī's *Akhbār* contains a depiction of the conflict between al-Muhallab and the Azāriqa. On the second day of battle, when fighting is at fever pitch, the Khārijite commander exhorts his comrades to persevere in their struggle against the enemy. In response, al-Muhallab quotes Q 2:193: 'And fight them until there is no more *fitna* and the religion is God's,' which links the rebels with the opponents of Islam referred to in the verse. As usual, al-Muhallab proves triumphant, while only a few of the weakest Khārijites survive, presumably by avoiding the thick of battle.[74] The victorious general celebrates his success by praising God "who returned us to security and freed us from the burden of war (*wa-kafānā ma'ūnat al-ḥarb*) and repelled the affair of this enemy".[75] The Khārijites' defeat is thereby presented as God's will, an end to the *fitna* as demanded in the verse cited by al-Muhallab, the outcome of the battle having thus been aptly foretold. The envoy al-Muhallab sends to al-Ḥajjāj to inform the governor of their victory furthers this impression of the Khawārij as enemies of God by likening them to a notorious group of Qur'ānic evildoers:

> We have stopped the disease of the Azāriqa for ever / and they disappeared as one like the people of Thamūd . . .[76]

Another example of the Qur'ān as a tool of intellectual warfare against Khārijism consists of accounts detailing the conflict between al-Mustawrid and the governor of al-Madā'in, Simāk b. 'Ubayd. In one episode, Simāk prevents the Khārijites from crossing the Tigris and forces them to relocate to Bahurasīr, whereupon al-Mustawrid orders his nephew to write a letter to the governor. In this letter, al-Mustawrid calls himself "servant of God" and *amīr al-muʾminīn* (both caliphal titles),[77] then accuses the authorities of tyranny, failure to impose the *ḥudūd* and monopolisation of the *fayʾ*.[78] He summons Simāk to the Qurʾān, the *sunna* of Muḥammad and the rule of the first two caliphs, whereas he should disavow ʿUthmān and ʿAlī "for their innovation in religion [*iḥdāth fī l-dīn*] and their abandonment of the judgement of the Qurʾān".[79] If Simāk refuses, then al-Mustawrid considers battle against him to be lawful.

This highly stylised letter reflects the tenor and formulae typical of early Islamic rebels (Khārijite or other) as they are portrayed in the Islamic tradition, in particular the vague reference to the Qurʾān and the (variously defined) *sunna*.[80] The repetitiveness of these motifs, which appear in 'Khārijite' letters and speeches from the first confrontation with ʿAlī[81] to later ʿAbbāsid-era Khārijites such as Ḥamza al-Sīstānī,[82] underlines the sense of insubstantiality that is discussed in the next chapter.

When the letter is delivered to Simāk by al-Mustawrid's nephew, the governor is not amused. He refuses to heed al-Mustawrid's summons and declares that

> al-Mustawrid would not be my choice for caliph because of what I have seen of his hypocrisy and baseness in drawing his sword against the Muslims. Al-Mustawrid presents me with the denunciation of ʿAlī and ʿUthmān and calls me to acknowledge his rule. By God, what a wretched shaykh I would be then.[83]

Simāk nevertheless offers to petition for amnesty on behalf of the Khārijites if they "return to the community". But his proposal is rejected and al-Mustawrid's nephew insists on commitment to *jihād* as the means of securing God's favour. Outraged, Simāk denounces the Khawārij:

> They abandoned right guidance by what they did. They began to recite the Qurʾān to him [al-Mustawrid's nephew], they pretended to humble themselves and to weep. Thus he thought that they had something of the truth. 'Verily, they are just like cattle, nay, they have strayed further from the way' [Q 25:44]. By God! I never saw people who were in more manifest error nor a more obvious calamity than those whom you see![84]

The vilification of Khārijism reaches its peak in al-Ṭabarī's *Taʾrīkh*, in a detailed description of Shabīb's rebellion in the mid-690s. One of the commanders sent to fight the rebels, ʿAttāb b. Warqāʾ, tears down the Khārijites' rationalisation of their violent acts in a sermon to his soldiers before his battle with Shabīb:

> O people of Islam! Those who have the best lot in Paradise are the martyrs. God praises none of His creatures more than the steadfast; hear how He

says, 'Be ye steadfast; God is with the steadfast.' [Q 8:46] He whose deeds God praises, how great is his status! But God despises no one more than those who commit outrages. See how this enemy of yours slaughters the Muslims with his sword, and they insist that they thereby win God's favor. *They are the most wicked people on earth, the dogs of the people of Hell!*[85]

Excessive Piety in *Ḥadīth*

Khārijite zealotry is the subject of a number of *ḥadīth*s. In some reports of the murder of a Companion's son by a group of Khārijites,[86] we find two famous traditions that at least implicitly refer to the Khawārij. Both are quoted on the authority of the Prophet through the victim's father and both of them address the subject of *fitna*. The first version of the victim's encounter with the Khārijites has him volunteer a *ḥadīth* when faced with the rebels:

> My father told me on the authority of the Prophet (ṣ): 'There will be a *fitna* during which a man's heart dies [in the sense of his ability to distinguish between right and wrong being confounded?]. He will be a believer in the morning and have become an unbeliever by the evening, and he will be a believer in the evening and have become an unbeliever in the morning.'[87]

In the second version, the Khārijites specifically ask the victim, ʿAbdallāh b. Khabbāb, for a *ḥadīth* that his father had related to him from the Prophet. Ibn Khabbāb states:

> I heard him say: "The Messenger of God (ṣ) said: 'There will be a *fitna* during which the one sitting down is better than the one standing up, and the one who walks better than the one who runs. And if you live to see it, be ʿAbdallāh the slain and not ʿAbdallāh the slayer.'"[88]

Both *ḥadīth*s urge believers not to get involved in *fitna* because such periods of turmoil cloud one's ability to determine right from wrong. The Khawārij are not explicitly named, but the context clearly implicates them and their habit of "running" to slay those they accuse of unbelief. They are shown to violate the Prophetic exhortation to "be the slain, not the slayers" and so the error of their ways is proven beyond doubt.

Another example of this mechanism occurs in al-Balādhurī's *Ansāb* as part of the portrayal of the Battle of Nahrawān. In this episode, which comes in two versions, ʿAlī relates a well-known *ḥadīth* on the authority of the Prophet.[89] Once again, the Khārijites are not explicitly named, but in both versions of the story the *ḥadīth* includes the physical description of a man who belongs to the faction that is the focus of this tradition.[90] The account in the *Ansāb* (as well as the other works of historiography that preserve a variant of this *ḥadīth*[91]) creates a connection to the Khawārij by emphasising that this man was among the dead rebels at Nahrawān. The framing of the *ḥadīth* thus serves to confirm the validity of ʿAlī's treatment of the Khārijites.

There are slight differences between the two versions. The *ḥadīth* in the first report is longer and provides information on how to deal with the Khawārij:

> The Prophet (ṣ) said: '[There will be] a people who recite the Qurʾān, [but] it does not pass beyond their collarbones, they pass through religion like the arrow passes through the game (*yamruqūna min al-dīn kamā yamruqu al-sahm min al-ramiyya*). God's blessing and a good final state shall be for him who kills them and is killed by them (*ṭūbā li-man qatalahum wa-qatalūhu*).'[92]

The second report transmits a shorter variant of this *ḥadīth*. Here, ʿAlī relates a tradition from the Prophet in which he foresaw the emergence of a people who "speak the truth, [but] it does not pass beyond their throats, they go out from truth like an arrow shot".[93]

This *ḥadīth* reiterates ʿAlī's criticism that the Khawārij are misguided and insincere despite their professions of piety. By referring to the Prophet himself, ʿAlī can essentially declare their status as Muslims forfeit: they "pass through religion", free from any residual traces of Islam, due to their over-zealous religiosity – they overshoot the mark.[94] The *ḥadīth* also provides a justification for killing them and thus for the massacre at Nahrawān, which seems to have been a controversial issue.[95] The reference to "God's blessing and a good final state" being promised to him who kills them[96] *and is killed by them* not only legitimises ʿAlī's conduct towards the Khawārij, however. It also foreshadows his death at the hand of a Khārijite and thereby casts him in the role of a martyr.[97]

Beyond the condemnation of Khārijism, these *ḥadīth*s serve to decry piety in its extreme forms more generally.[98] Excessiveness in religious matters leads to imprudent decisions, which in turn results in the transgression of Islamic social norms. Ironically, zealotry thus entails the risk of engendering impiety. What we have here, then, is "eine Art Fundamentalismuskritik *avant la lettre*".[99] In al-Balādhurī's *Ansāb*, the *ḥadīth*s quoted by ʿAlī are embedded in the account of his denunciation of the *lā ḥukma* maxim as a rejection of all forms of rule, quoted above in full. These reports conclude al-Balādhurī's discussion of the conflict between ʿAlī and the Khawārij. He refers to some insignificant Khārijite rebellions after Nahrawān and devotes several pages to ʿAlī's assassination, but he no longer deals with the Khārijites as a group throughout the remainder of ʿAlī's reign. ʿAlī's condemnation of their intentions and deeds is therefore the last impression of the Khawārij as such that the audience is left with for this period. The effect thereby created effectively conveys the fallacies of Khārijism.

Contrasting Khārijite Words and Deeds

The final method of reproach discussed here involves the juxtaposition of what the Khārijites proclaim and how they act. Literary Khārijism is a movement of God-fearing believers concerned with following the provisions of the Qurʾān to the letter. They constantly assert their obedience to God and commitment to 'commanding right and forbidding wrong'. However, their actions are shown to contradict their claims to righteousness. This is best illustrated by the story of the murder of ʿAbdallāh b. Khabbāb alluded to above. All selected sources mention his death at the hands of the Khawārij,[100] which indicates the significance of this incident for the construction of literary Khārijism.

The two most elaborate accounts of this episode are preserved by al-Balādhurī and were briefly addressed above. The first version is set in the hometown of ʿAbdallāh b. Khabbāb, which is one day beset by Khārijites. Upon entering the village, the rebels encounter ʿAbdallāh b. Khabbāb, whose fear of them adumbrates his unfortunate end. They know who he is and also that his father was a Companion as they ask Ibn Khabbāb whether his father transmitted *ḥādīth*s from the Prophet to him. He confirms this and then relates the traditions about the *fitna* during which the one sitting down is better than the one standing up. The Khawārij inquire whether this is really the *ḥādīth* Ibn Khabbāb heard from his father; when he confirms this, they set upon and kill both him and his heavily pregnant *umm walad*, the latter by ripping open her womb.[101]

The main point of this account is the embedded *ḥadīth*, which both the Khārijites in the account and the audience of the story understand to pertain to the rebels. The tradition indicates the castigation of Khārijite conduct by the Prophet himself, which the Khārijites unsurprisingly do not take kindly to. The very action of killing Ibn Khabbāb nevertheless confirms that the *ḥadīth* indeed refers to them; through their overreaction they exemplify the "running slayers" of the Prophetic tradition. Their killing of Ibn Khabbāb's *umm walad* also represents a gross violation of social norms. The slaughter of a pregnant woman is a Biblical motif and very common especially in reports of rebel violence across many cultures and traditions. In (the literature of) medieval Europe, for instance, it represented the worst imaginable crime and was considered sacrilege.[102] The historicity of such repugnant deeds is indisputable, but it is important here to bear in mind that in many cases, "the sources' charge of rebel violence against women may have had more to do with their literary efforts to portray rebels as aliens to normal social practice than with the realities of revolt".[103] The sometimes gleeful disgust with which the Islamic tradition talks about Khārijite factions advocating the killing of women and children may represent an example of this exact dynamic.

The second version of this episode is rather different and itself extant in two variants. The longer version states that a group of Basran Khārijites led by Misʿar b. Fadakī came across ʿAbdallāh b. Khabbāb and his pregnant *umm walad* on their wanderings. They asked him about his identity and when he revealed that his father was a Companion, they initially refrained from attacking him. The encounter takes a bad turn when they eventually ask his opinion of ʿAlī. Ibn Khabbāb responds that ʿAlī is "the *amīr al-muʾminīn* and the *imām* of the Muslims", then goes on to relate the *ḥadīth* on the *fitna* during which a man's status as a believer can change overnight. The Khawārij are outraged: "By God, we will kill you in a fashion that no one ever endured." They take him and his *umm walad* captive and force them to come along. At some point, the Khārijites pass by a palm tree from which some dates have fallen to the ground. One of the rebels picks them up and puts them in his mouth, but he is immediately rebuked for having taken them unlawfully, without payment, and so he spits them out. A while later, the same Khārijite begins to play with his sword, and when a pig happens to walk past the group, he kills it. He is again at once reprimanded for this by his fellow Khārijites, so he looks for the owner in order to compensate him. All this leads Ibn Khabbāb to the – unfortunately erroneous – conclusion that "if you are [truly] sincere in what I see and hear, then I am surely safe from your wickedness". The Khawārij beg to differ. They thrust him onto the pig carcass by the side of a river and slaughter him. Then they rip open the belly of his *umm walad*, who exclaims in shock: "Do you not fear God?" They also kill three previously unmentioned women accompanying her.[104]

The shorter version does not mention Ibn Khabbāb's *umm walad*, the other women or the *ḥadīth*. Ibn Khabbāb's response upon witnessing the Khārijites' strict abidance by the law also differs somewhat from the longer variant: he surmises that surely they would not kill someone more inviolable (*aʿẓam ḥurmatan*) than a pig. Alas, his captors disagree in this rendering as well and Ibn Khabbāb is killed, this time without involving the dead pig.[105]

This story, in particular its longer version, is set up in a way that exposes Khārijite piety as thoroughly misconceived. Like Ibn Khabbāb, the audience is presented with their punctilious adherence to the letter of the law that prohibits the consumption even of fallen fruit because it is not their property. Like Ibn Khabbāb, the audience is led to believe that such deep-set propriety will prevent wrongdoing in general and transgressions as egregious as the murder of Muslims in particular. But the Khārijites' overzealousness clouds their reasoning, stops them from recognising the error of their ways and thus leads them to violate their own stated aim of living a godly life. Their excessive piety is mirrored by their extreme violence: they not only kill a Muslim of substantial religious credentials, but in the longer version also resort to truly reprehensible measures by slaughtering Ibn Khabbāb prone on a pig carcass. This violation of Islamic norms is only surpassed by the murder of his pregnant *umm walad*.

That there is an inherent contradiction to literary Khārijism in word and deed is manifest also in the figure of Ibn Muljam. He is portrayed as a deeply religious man of ascetic tendencies, who would loudly call out what he deemed to be improper conduct by his fellow Muslims.[106] His self-appointment as supervisor of public morality already bears the kernel of excess, however, which is demonstrated when he sees a mixed Muslim-Christian funeral procession and is so enraged that he can barely stop himself from attacking the group.[107] His superior piety is finally discredited utterly by his murder of ʿAlī, whose final words to Ibn Muljam in al-Balādhurī's narrative contain a Qurʾānic warning of the coming Judgement Day: [Q 99:7–8] 'So whoever does an atom's weight of good shall see it, and whoever does an atom's weight of evil shall see it [when the world ends]'.[108]

The reader is thereby left with one main conclusion: in their endeavours to adhere to the letter of the Qurʾān, the Khawārij subvert its spirit. Their claim to righteousness is false, their interpretation of belief perverted – the result can only be "random violence or absurd legalism".[109] From a narrative perspective one thus cannot help but follow ʿAlī's succinct summary of Khārijism: "From unbelief they fled, yet therein they dwelt (*min al-kufr harabū wa-fīhi waqaʿū*)."[110]

Conclusions

The reputation of the Khawārij in early Islamic historical writing is on the whole decidedly negative. The accounts discussed above abound with rhetorical features, but this highlights the essence of literary Khārijism all the better. The evaluation and consequent condemnation of Khārijism is based mostly on the rebels' (mis)understanding of religion and transgression of its precepts, which causes the sort of violent behaviour that defies all social, moral or religious codes of conduct incumbent upon every member of the *umma* and of society in general. Khārijism as depicted in the selected sources is a mentality of mindless zealotry that is inherently dangerous because it allows its proponents to cast the majority of the *umma* as unbelievers who can and should be fought at every stage in order to safeguard the purity of *dīn allāh*. The actions resulting from this mindset lead to bloodshed and strife within the Muslim community, which, apart from causing serious moral and ethical problems, also goes against the Islamic (tradition's) idea of social cohesion and communal togetherness. A famous *ḥadīth* has the Prophet declare three groups to die a pagan death, the first two – those who leave the community (*jamāʿa*) and those who rebel and kill indiscriminately – explicitly pertaining to the Khārijites.[111] This is echoed in the portrayal of the historical tradition, which constantly repeats the accusation that the rebels have 'left the community' and furnishes almost all debates between the Khārijites and their opponents with exhortations to 'return to the community'. This has the effect of showing Khārijism to stand in violation of the very norms and principles it purports to preserve; the logical conclusion is to reject it in its entirety: "I have disavowed the religion of the *Muḥakkimūn*; in respect to religion, that is the worst among us."[112]

The Khawārij also function as stand-ins for proponents of militant piety in general. The connection between them and the *qurrāʾ* already represents a fundamental tool of criticism against excessive piety. The sources blame the *qurrāʾ* for forcing ʿAlī to accept the arbitration: religious zealotry led them to ignore ʿAlī's words of caution against Muʿāwiya's ruse, only to later discover that the arbitration in fact relegated the Qurʾān to one source among several and that ʿAmr b. al-ʿĀṣ had outwitted the arbiter of their choice. The link between violence and misguided piety can therefore be shown to have existed from the start; that a group like the Khawārij could arise from the *qurrāʾ* is in itself a symbol of the danger of immoderate piety.

Reports of Khārijite violence (real or not) were certainly a convenient tool in that they gave the early historical tradition a vehicle for dismissing forms of piety that threatened the safety of the Muslim community. If we take this to be the primary concern of accounts dealing with Khārijite excess, this would also explain the relative monotony and homogeneity of the episodes in question – while the stories differ to some extent, the statements and conduct associated with the Khawārij are more or less the same because the point is not primarily to tell Khārijite history 'as it really was'. Rather, the rebels' narrative role is to provide negative archetypes chiefly aimed at reproaching the bloodshed that follows from intemperate piety.[113] The focus is on Khārijism as an expression of collective, rather than individual, action.

The typecasting and resulting reduction of Khārijism to a set of standardised characteristics highlight one of the functions of history-writing in both the medieval Islamic and European traditions, i.e. supplying a forum for edification, for moral and political discussion,[114] which led to "a willingness to reduce the complexity of human experience into stereotypes that could be utilized easily to make a moral point".[115] It is this approach to history and historiography that is at least partly responsible for the formation of the Khārijite *topoi* addressed in this study.

The tendency to declare other Muslims unbelievers whose lives and property could lawfully be taken is one of the consequences of excessive militant piety that the early Muslim scholars sought to discredit. The issue of communal togetherness and a correspondent aversion to factionalism seem to have been major concerns by the period that witnessed the compilation of the sources under study at the latest; in fact, we find such concerns already in extant early sources like the *Kitāb al-Taḥrīsh* of Ḍirār b. ʿAmr (wr. late eighth century), which does not dwell much on the violence associated with Khārijism but nevertheless reproaches overly exclusivist definitions of faith – Ḍirār "mahnt zur Toleranz nach innen".[116] Van Ess has argued that it was the memory of the Khārijites' incessant use of *takfīr* that restrained the *odium theologicum* among early Muslim intellectuals,[117] but perhaps it worked the other way round (as well): faced with heated theological debates that could lead to violence against people and property, as between Ḥanbalites and 'rationalists' in Baghdad, [118] and the accelerating fragmentation of the Islamic Empire,[119] narratives of the dire consequences of an overly narrow definition of the *umma* were (re-)purposed as cautionary tales intended to keep together an increasingly diverse Muslim community and state, not least by "preserving the memory of a unified caliphate".[120] The crystallisation of Sunnism in a form recognisable today over the course of the tenth to thirteenth century[121] could perhaps be considered the culmination of this process.

Notes

1. Gaddis, *There Is No Crime*, esp. 151–250 (on monks); Sizgorich, *Violence and Belief*; Morony, *Iraq*, 475.
2. Gaddis, *There Is No Crime* is perhaps the fullest study of the discourse of religious violence in early Christianity, covering the period from the persecution of Christians under the pagan emperor Diocletian at the beginning of the fourth century until the council of Chalcedon in 451 and its aftermath.
3. For the *qurrāʾ*, see also 42–3 and ns. 9 and 10 thereto.
4. Al-Dīnawarī, *Akhbār*, 204 [my emphasis].
5. For example, Ibn Muzāḥim, *Waqʿat Ṣiffīn*, 560; al-Balādhurī, *Ansāb*, II, 298; al-Ṭabarī, *Taʾrīkh*, I, 3330, 3333; al-Masʿūdī, *Murūj*, I–II, 391; Ibn Aʿtham, *Futūḥ*, III, 312.
6. Ibn Muzāhim, *Waqʿat Ṣiffīn*, 589. See also al-Balādhurī, *Ansāb*, II, 308, 312,

319, 325–6, 328, 330; al-Dīnawarī, *Akhbār*, 220, 222; al-Ṭabarī, *Taʾrīkh*, I, 3360–1, 3369, 3378.

7. EI[3], "Khārijīs" (A. Gaiser); Higgins, "Faces of Exchangers" and *Qurʾānic Exchange*; Gaiser, *Shurāt Legends*, 48–9. How the various terms for the Khawārij relate to each other is a difficult matter. Gaiser, *Shurāt Legends* uses '*shurāt*' to refer to the original movement that was later termed 'Khārijite', while he considers 'Khārijite' a reference to the militants of the second *fitna* and beyond. The sources are of little help here: al-Masʿūdī's *Murūj* (III–IV, 138), for example, refers in his summary of Khārijite doctrine to "*al-khawārij min al-shurāt wa-l-ḥarūriyya*".
8. The translations are taken from Khalidi, *Qurʾan*, 27 and 157, respectively. Other relevant verses are Q 9:46 and 9:83. Marsham, *Rituals of Islamic Monarchy*, 44–9, 56, 101; Gaiser, *Shurāt Legends*, 48–9; Van Ess, "*Kitāb at-Taḥrīš*", 2483 n. 135 and "Bild der Ḫāriǧiten", 2553 and n. 125.
9. Gaiser, *Shurāt Legends*, 50.
10. For a convenient overview including a brief discussion of late antique conceptual parallels, see Gaiser, *Shurāt Legends*, 47–70.
11. Ibn Muzāḥim, *Waqʿat Ṣiffīn*, 560; al-Balādhurī, *Ansāb*, II, 446; al-Ṭabarī, *Taʾrīkh*, I, 3332; Ibn Aʿtham, *Futūḥ*, III, 315. In the translation of this part of al-Ṭabarī's *History*, Hawting remarks that Caetani in *Annali dell'Islam* (Milan 1905–26) understood the reference to their black faces as an accusation of cowardice. Hawting himself does not offer an explanation of this passage: Hawting, *First Civil War*, 81 n. 327. Based on my understanding of the relevant line in *Waqʿat Ṣiffīn*, I rather consider this reference a part of the *topos* of Khārijite piety: their faces were dusty ('black') due to their constant prostrations in prayer.
12. Al-Balādhurī, *Ansāb*, II, 317, 318, 319.
13. Al-Balādhurī, *Ansāb*, II, 446. Typical features of an ascetic physique are calluses, emaciation, a yellow or pale complexion.
14. This is the last line of a poem ascribed to the quietist Khārijite ʿImrān b. Ḥiṭṭān. He reportedly composed this poem after he had finally succeeded in escaping al-Ḥajjāj's clutches and settled with a group of Azdī tribesmen in ʿUmān. Ibn Aʿtham, *Futūḥ*, VII, 105.
15. The seminal work on this core concept of Islamic doctrine is Cook, *Commanding Right*.
16. Al-Balādhurī, *Ansāb*, II, 320–1.
17. Ibid., 321.
18. Al-Ṭabarī, *Taʾrīkh*, II, 43.
19. See also above, 70–1, and the following note.
20. Al-Balādhurī, *Ansāb*, II, 322. See al-Ṭabarī, *Taʾrīkh*, I, 3365–6 for Shurayḥ b. Awfā citing these verses [Q 28:21–23] when the Khawārij leave Kufa for Nahrawān. This variance is another good example of a motif ('piety') being stable while its narrative content is mutable and prone to 'wandering' or, in Noth's parlance, 'drifting'.

21. Gruendler, "Abbasid Poets", 156.
22. For an excellent recent overview of the Qur'ān's influence on the types of literature commonly subsumed under *adab*, for instance, see the contributions in Alshaar, ed., *Qur'an and Adab*. The influence of religious texts (Qur'ān and *ḥadīth*) on pre-modern Arabic literature more generally is discussed in Zubaidi, "Impact of the Qur'an".
23. Al-Jomaih, *Use of the Qur'ān*; Donner, "Qur'ānicization"; Qutbuddin, "Qur'an Citation"; Zubaidi, "Impact of the Qur'ān", esp. 323–7. Al-Qāḍī has shown that the utilisation of Qur'anic language and themes in the letters of the Umayyad secretary 'Abd al-Ḥamīd b. Yaḥyā (d. 132 H/750 CE) is particularly pronounced in pieces of an ideological thrust, increasing noticeably over time as civil discord and resistance to the last Umayyad caliph Marwān escalated in the late 740s. Al-Qāḍī, "Impact of the Qur'an", 360–9, 374–5.
24. For example, al-Balādhurī, *Ansāb*, IV/2, 407; al-Dīnawarī, *Akhbār*, 279; Ibn Khayyāṭ, *Ta'rīkh*, I, 251; al-Mas'ūdī, *Murūj*, III–IV, 126; al-Ṭabarī, *Ta'rīkh*, II, 887–9; Ibn A'tham, *Futūḥ*, VII, 85–6.
25. Ṣāliḥ b. Mukhrāq, an Azraqī Khārijite during the second *fitna*.
26. *Kabsh* can also mean 'chief, army leader, hero'; *nāṭiḥ* can also be translated as 'distress, calamity'. In any case, it is clear that the poet wanted to convey Ṣāliḥ's valour in battle.
27. Ibn A'tham, *Futūḥ*, VII, 54.
28. Shabīb in a letter to Ṣāliḥ b. Musarriḥ explaining why he wants to join the latter's revolt. Al-Ṭabarī, *Ta'rīkh*, II, 884–5; Rowson, *Marwānid Restoration*, 36.
29. A Khārijite poet on the death of Nāfi' b. al-Azraq in battle against al-Muhallab. Al-Dīnawarī, *Akhbār*, 284.
30. For the meal, see al-Ṭabarī, *Ta'rīkh*, II, 909, 912 (a variant of the first report); for the saddle nap, al-Ṭabarī, *Ta'rīkh*, II, 961.
31. Ibid., 881–91.
32. Ibid., 881–2.
33. This appears to be one of the Khārijites' favourite accusations against their opponents. See, for example, al-Balādhurī, *Ansāb*, IV/2, 416 for a report on Nāfi' b. al-Azraq's justification of revolt against "those who kill the *sunna* and those who give life to *bid'a*".
34. Al-Ṭabarī, *Ta'rīkh*, II, 883–4; Rowson, *Marwānid Restoration*, 35. The sermon is also quoted at length in Chapter Three, 125.
35. On which, see Chapter Six.
36. Ibn A'tham, *Futūḥ*, VII, 67. The reference to the "small group" and the "large group" is a standard phrase in Islamic rhetoric. The Khārijites are shown to utilise this stock image (for instance, in al-Dīnawarī, *Akhbār*, 279), but so does everyone else. See, for example, Paret, "Futūḥ-Literatur", 742. For the argument that early Islamic historiography operates within a Qur'ānic framework, see Humphreys, "Qur'ānic Myth".
37. Al-Ṭabarī, *Ta'rīkh*, II, 36; Morony, *Mu'āwiyah*, 41–2.

38. Al-Ṭabarī, *Ta ʾrīkh*, II, 64.
39. Ibid., 181–2; Morony, *Mu ʿāwiyah*, 193.
40. Al-Ṭabarī, *Ta ʾrīkh*, II, 183–4; Morony, *Mu ʿāwiyah*, 193–5. See also al-Ṭabarī, *Ta ʾrīkh*, II, 182.
41. This is explored in more detail in Chapter Three.
42. Kilito, *Author and His Doubles*, 60.
43. The sources provide countless reports of Khārijites murdering people. For them killing women and people praying in the mosque, see, for example, Ibn Aʿtham, *Futūḥ*, VII, 87; al-Ṭabarī, *Ta ʾrīkh*, I, 3373–4 and II, 755–6, 918; al-Balādhurī, *Ansāb*, II, 328 and IV/2, 434; al-Yaʿqūbī, *Ta ʾrīkh*, II, 274. See also Sizgorich, *Violence and Belief*, 206; Morony, *Iraq*, 473.
44. See the remarks in Abou el Fadl, *Rebellion and Violence*, 125 and the notes thereto.
45. Al-Ṭabarī, *Ta ʾrīkh*, II, 1376.
46. Al-Ṭabarī, *Ta ʾrīkh*, I, 3352–3 and II, 941.
47. Al-Balādhurī, *Ansāb*, IV/2, 462, where Najdī Khārijites seek to elect a new leader after deposing Najda b. ʿĀmir. Instead of appointing Thābit al-Tammār, a *mawlā*, they decide on Abū Fudayk because "only an Arab could rule them", unconcerned by the fact that everyone agreed that Thābit was the most excellent in religion among them and hence technically the only possible choice from a properly Khārijite point of view. For another accusation of hypocrisy, see al-Ṭabarī, *Ta ʾrīkh*, II, 42.
48. See also Sizgorich, *Violence and Belief*, 195.
49. Al-Ṭabarī, *Ta ʾrīkh*, I, 3361–2.
50. Al-Balādhurī, *Ansāb*, II, 311. See also al-Yaʿqūbī, *Ta ʾrīkh*, II, 191; al-Ṭabarī, *Ta ʾrīkh*, I, 3361, 3362.
51. Al-Balādhurī, *Ansāb*, II, 336. See also ibid., 311, where the reference to the "righteous or unrighteous" ruler is missing, which renders the passage confusing as ʿAlī appears to confirm the negative image of rulers.
52. Ibn Aʿtham, *Futūḥ*, III, 315. The association of the appellation "people of the black foreheads" with praying in this account also supports the interpretation of "black faces" as referring to piety rather than cowardice, as argued above, 106 (n. 11).
53. For example, al-Ṭabarī, *Ta ʾrīkh*, II, 589, 762, 897, 902, 933; Ibn Aʿtham, *Futūḥ*, VII, 29, 30; al-Balādhurī, *Ansāb*, IV/2, 395, 401, 409, 438; al-Dīnawarī, *Akhbār*, 281, 285, 287. 'Dogs of hell' (*kilāb al-nār*) is also used in reference to the Khawārij in the late eighth(?)-century *Kitāb al-Taḥrīsh* attributed to Ḍirār b. ʿAmr. See Van Ess, "*Kitāb at-Taḥrīš*", 2481 and "Bild der Ḫāriǧiten", 2577.
54. Ibn Aʿtham, *Futūḥ*, VI, 29, 310 and VII, 27, 32, 44 (the phrase used at VII, 44 is *al-sibāʿ al-ḍāriyya*, 'rabid beasts', not 'dogs', but *ḍār* is often used to refer to dogs. Lane, *Arabic-English Lexicon*, "*ḍ-r-w* and *ḍ-r-yā*").
55. See also a report in Ibn Aʿtham, *Futūḥ*, VII, 64, where al-Muhallab likens five particular Khārijite leaders to "five companions of the devil".

56. Al-Ṭabarī, *Taʾrīkh*, II, 585–6; Hawting, *Collapse*, 169–70.
57. Ibn Aʿtham, *Futūḥ*, VII, 29. For a slightly shorter version, see al-Dīnawarī, *Akhbār*, 285.
58. Ibn Aʿtham, *Futūḥ*, VII, 30; al-Dīnawarī, *Akhbār*, 286.
59. EI², "Khāridjites" (G. Levi della Vida); Morony, *Iraq*, 471; Robinson, *Empire and Elites*, 120. Elizabeth Savage, "Iraqi Christian Links" has suggested that the name of the Khārijite subdivision al-Ibāḍiyya refers to the inclusion of Arab Christian elements (the *ʿibād* of al-Ḥīra and elsewhere in Iraq) among this group in Baṣra because it was more moderate and accepting of them than other forms of Islam in the late seventh century. She emphasised that the adoption of Ibāḍism on the part of Christian North African Berbers occurred for similar reasons, which also explains the centuries-long close connections between Ibāḍīs and Christians in that region. If one accepts her arguments, this may be another explanation for the leniency towards Christians shown by moderate Khārijites at least. However, even militant Khawārij are said to have left *dhimmīs* in peace (for Shabīb b. Yazīd al-Shaybānī, see below), as stipulated by the Qurʾān, and overall Savage's reading of the evidence (some of it *in absentia*) is not persuasive.
60. Al-Balādhurī, *Ansāb*, IV/2, 400–1. This account is unique to the *Ansāb* among the selected sources. Note that the reference to the *ahl al-qibla* implies the acceptability of the customs and norms of non-Khārijites. The term here may exclusively denote the *umma* under Abū Bakr and ʿUmar (the only two caliphs accepted by the Khawārij); in any case, quietist or at least non-Azraqite Khārijites are shown here to have had a more moderate approach to non-Khārijite Muslims.
61. See, for example, Crone and Zimmermann, *Epistle*; Cook, *Early Muslim Dogma*; Van Ess, "*Kitāb at-Taḥrīš*".
62. Al-Balādhurī, *Ansāb*, IV/2, 403–4.
63. Ibn Aʿtham, *Futūḥ*, VII, 57.
64. 'Wrath for God' was a common rhetorical feature in political speeches of the Umayyad period and not limited to Khārijites. Van Ess, "Bild der Ḫāriǧiten", 2538 n. 27. This expression is one of several examples of Khārijites and non-Khārijites sharing language and sentiments, which underlines the intangible essence of literary Khārijism to be discussed in Chapter Three. Beyond the early Islamic case, 'zeal' or 'wrath' for God is a frequent motif in late antique/early Christian rhetoric. See Gaddis, *There Is No Crime*, esp. 179–91, but *passim*.
65. Al-Ṭabarī, *Taʾrīkh*, II, 886–7; Rowson, *Marwānid Restoration*, 37–8.
66. Al-Ṭabarī, *Taʾrīkh*, II, 886.
67. For example, ibid., 895, 899, 918, 955–6; Ibn Khayyāṭ, *Taʾrīkh*, I, 272; al-Yaʿqūbī, *Taʾrīkh*, II, 274; Ibn Aʿtham, *Futūḥ*, VII, 87.
68. See, for example, the debates between Nāfiʿ and Najda regarding *istiʿrāḍ* and the status of the *quʿūd* in al-Balādhurī, *Ansāb*, IV/2, 402–4. Khārijite use of

the Qur'ān will be addressed throughout Chapters Four to Six; intra-Khārijite strife is discussed in Chapter Six.

69. Humphreys, "Qur'ānic Myth", 276 with reference to 'Uthmān's letter to Ibn 'Abbās while the caliph was besieged by rebels in his own house.
70. Dähne, "Context Equivalence". For the mechanism see also al-Qāḍī, "Impact of the Qur'an", esp. 363.
71. On which, see Hawting, "Two Citations", 260–8; Alshaar, "Introduction", 21–2, 24–7; Orfali and Pomerantz, "I See a Distant Fire"; al-Qāḍī and Mir, "Literature", 213–21 (on the Qur'ān's use in Arabic literature more generally).
72. Dähne, "Context Equivalence", 13. Qur'ān citations were considered by many early scholars to be indispensable to oration, certainly not only for aesthetic reasons: "artistic prose tacitly persuades". Qutbuddin, "Qur'an Citation", 323–4 (quote on 324).
73. See also the discussion in Chapter Three.
74. On the depiction of al-Muhallab, see Chapter Six.
75. Al-Dīnawarī, *Akhbār*, 288.
76. Ibid. A variant of this poem in Ibn A'tham mentions both 'Ād and Thamūd together, as is more common: Ibn A'tham, *Futūḥ*, VII, 74. On Thamūd and their divine punishment for disobeying the prophet Ṣāliḥ, see Chapter Seven, 265 and n. 47 thereto. An implicit parallel between the Khārijites and 'Ād/Thamūd is also drawn in some *ḥādīth*s; see, for example, Muslim, *Ṣaḥīḥ*, III, 741–3 (nos. 143–6).
77. This seems to be the earliest attestation of the Khārijite use of this title. Compare with Crone, "Caliphal Title", 88, who had argued that the Azāriqa were the first to call their leaders *amīr al-mu'minīn*.
78. On the *fay'* and the common accusation of its misappropriation by the government, see EI[3], "Fay'" (A. Marsham).
79. Al-Ṭabarī, *Ta'rīkh*, II, 40–1.
80. Abou el Fadl, *Rebellion and Violence*, 129; Crone and Hinds, *God's Caliph*, 58–96.
81. See the references in Chapter Four, section on 'Apologia for 'Alī'.
82. Crone and Hinds, *God's Caliph*, 89. On Ḥamza al-Sīstānī, see Meisami, *Persian Historiography*, 113–15, 133, 241; Bosworth, *Sīstān*, 91–104; Scarcia, "Scambio di lettere"; Van Ess, *Theologie und Gesellschaft*, II, 585–8.
83. Al-Ṭabarī, *Ta'rīkh*, II, 42; Morony, *Mu'āwiyah*, 48.
84. Al-Ṭabarī, *Ta'rīkh*, II, 42.
85. Ibid., 950–1; Rowson, *Marwānid Restoration*, 101–2 [my emphasis].
86. Al-Mas'ūdī, *Murūj*, I–II, 404 is the only one who does not present the victim, Ibn Khabbāb, as the son of a Companion but as 'Alī's governor of al-Madā'in. This episode is discussed in the following section.
87. Al-Balādhurī, *Ansāb*, II, 326. See al-Ṭabarī, *Ta'rīkh*, I, 3374–5 for a variant of this story.
88. Al-Balādhurī, *Ansāb*, II, 328. See also Ibn A'tham, *Futūḥ*, IV, 98; al-Ṭabarī,

Taʾrīkh, I, 3373–4. Al-Ṭabarī preserves a slightly different version according to which the Khārijites quote this *ḥadīth* to Ibn Khabbāb and then ask him whether he had heard it from his father on the authority of the Prophet. Another version of the *ḥadīth* that ends with the same line occurs in Ḍirār b. ʿAmr's *Kitāb al-Taḥrīsh*, quoted in Van Ess, "Bild der Ḫāriǧiten", 2578.

89. Al-Balādhurī, *Ansāb*, II, 334, 335.
90. On the many variants of the identity and description of this man, see Van Ess, "Unfertige Studien I", 1401–3, 1410, 1416.
91. See, for example, al-Ṭabarī, *Taʾrīkh*, I, 3383, 3384, 3388, 3389; Ibn Aʿtham, *Futūḥ*, IV, 97, 130. Ibn Aʿtham's account does not include the description of the man's physical appearance, but it is clear from the context that he belongs to the Khārijites.
92. Al-Balādhurī, *Ansāb*, II, 334. See also al-Ṭabarī, *Taʾrīkh*, I, 3388; Ibn Aʿtham, *Futūḥ*, IV, 128. Ibn Aʿtham also preserves references to the Khawārij as those who "turn away from guidance" [*māriqīn ʿan al-hudā*, IV, 105; first hemistich of the third verse of the reproduced poem] or "pass through the religion of Islam" [IV, 106]. The poem in the first reference is attributed to ʿAdī b. Ḥātim, a close confidant of ʿAlī. Van Ess, "Unfertige Studien I", 1414–15 offers a German translation of the poem as quoted by al-Baghdādī (d. 429 H/1037 CE) in his *Farq bayn al-Firaq*, stating that it was unclear where al-Baghdādī got it and drawing particular attention to the somewhat unusual combination of *maraqa* + *ʿan*. Ibn Aʿtham most likely died in the first half of the tenth century (see Chapter Seven) and so, while not very early, at least predates the only other occurrence of *maraqa ʿan* found by Van Ess (in a poem by Sharīf al-Murtaḍā (d. 436 H/1044 CE)) as well as al-Baghdādī by about a century.
93. Al-Balādhurī, *Ansāb*, II, 335.
94. On the term *al-māriqa*, which is based on the 'arrow/game' *ḥadīth*, in its application to the Khārijites including connected issues of provenance and referents, see Van Ess, "Unfertige Studien I".
95. See the relevant section in Chapter Four.
96. Such exhortations are common in *ḥadīth* literature. Muslim's chapter on *zakāt*, for instance, has an entire sub-section on killing Khārijites (*bāb al-taḥrīḍ ʿalā qatl al-Khawārij*). Another example is al-Shaybānī, *Sunna*, 419–47, esp. 424, 427.
97. Versions of the cited traditions and others associated with Khārijism abound in the *ḥadīth* collections. See, for example, Ibn Abī Shayba, *al-Muṣannaf*, VIII, 729–43, nos. 2, 3, 38–40, 48; Ibn Ḥanbal, *Musnad*, IV, 482; al-Bukhārī, *Ṣaḥīḥ*, IV, 298–9, nos. 6930–4; Abū Dāwūd, *Sunan*, IV, 91–4, 96–9; Muslim, *Ṣaḥīḥ*, III, 740–50, nos. 142–160 (*Kitāb al-zakāt*, *bāb*s 47–9). For a modern study by an Omani Ibāḍī author concerned with separating Ibāḍism from Khārijism, see al-Sābiʿī, *al-Khawārij*, who collected and analysed with the tools of classical *ḥadīth* criticism all eight *ḥadīth*s connected with the Khārijites (section 2, 182–394). The author concludes that all of these traditions were forged

in the process of establishing a Sunnī 'orthodoxy'. See also the remarks in Abou el Fadl, *Rebellion and Violence*, 117–18. Prophetic *ḥadīth* on the Khārijites is anachronistic, of course, which might be why Ḍirār's rather early (late eighth-century) *Taḥrīsh* does not really mention such traditions and so generally keeps its criticism of Khārijism limited, especially compared with the section that addresses their merits. Van Ess, "Bild der Ḫāriǧiten", 2536, 2576, 2580.

98. See Van Ess, "Unfertige Studien I", 1392–3.
99. Van Ess, "Unfertige Studien I", 1393 n. 16.
100. Al-Balādhurī, *Ansāb*, II, 325, 326–7, 328; al-Ṭabarī, *Taʾrīkh*, I, 3373–4, 3374–5; al-Dīnawarī, *Akhbār*, 220; al-Yaʿqūbī, *Taʾrīkh*, II, 191; Ibn Khayyāṭ, *Taʾrīkh*, I, 225; al-Masʿūdī, *Murūj*, I–II, 404, 405; Ibn Aʿtham, *Futūḥ*, IV, 98, 107, 119. Ibn Saʿd, *Ṭabaqāt*, III, 32 and Ibn Qutayba, *Maʿārif*, 317 also transmit this episode.
101. Al-Balādhurī, *Ansāb*, II, 328. See also al-Ṭabarī, *Taʾrīkh*, I, 3373–4.
102. Challet, "Violence", 282.
103. Firnhaber-Baker, "Introduction", 7.
104. Al-Balādhurī, *Ansāb*, II, 326–7. See also al-Ṭabarī, *Taʾrīkh*, I, 3374–5. Al-Ṭabarī's version is longer and emphasises Ibn Khabbāb's fear at encountering the Khārijites. Initially, they assure him that he does not need to be frightened. Ibn Khabbāb refers to this assurance later on, stating "you gave me security when you said 'There is no need to be frightened'". The Khawārij nevertheless kill him and his pregnant *umm walad*, which underlines their disregard for any social or moral code apart from their own fastidious but/therefore misguided understanding of the divine law.
105. Al-Balādhurī, *Ansāb*, II, 325.
106. Al-Balādhurī, *Ansāb*, II, 436, 446.
107. Al-Ṭabarī, *Taʾrīkh*, I, 3460. See also the brief remarks in Sizgorich, *Violence and Belief*, 224–5; Gaiser, *Shurāt Legends*, 97–8 (who raises some doubts about Sizgorich's interpretation of this episode).
108. Al-Balādhurī, *Ansāb*, II, 441.
109. Gaiser, "*Takfīr* Re-Examined", 32.
110. Ibn Aʿtham, *Futūḥ*, IV, 128.
111. Abou el Fadl, *Rebellion and Violence*, 124.
112. Al-Ṭabarī, *Taʾrīkh*, II, 647; Fishbein, *Victory*, 8.
113. See also Sizgorich, *Violence and Belief*, 206, 214, 215.
114. "No matter how attenuated the literary form of the medieval [European] chronicle, it takes its point of departure from the essentially rhetorical conception of history as a means to persuade men to imitate good and avoid evil. The basic purpose of historical writing, then, is edification; at least in theory, it is more concerned with the propagation of moral idealism than with a concrete analysis of reality." Spiegel, "Political Utility", 89.
115. Spiegel, "Political Utility", 89–90. For the Islamic tradition, see Hoyland, "History, Fiction and Authorship", 32; Mattock, "History and Fiction", 96.

116. Van Ess, "*Kitāb at-Taḥrīš*", 2566.
117. Van Ess, *Flowering of Muslim Theology*, 30, 32.
118. See, for example, Cook, *Commanding Right*, 115–18; Hurvitz, "Early Hanbalism"; Sabari, *Mouvements populaires*; Heilman, *Popular Protest*.
119. This process accelerated over the ninth century and continued well into the tenth century, manifesting in phenomena like the increasing autonomy of regional ruling families and governors, lower tax revenues reaching Iraq from the provinces and the changing power dynamics between the caliphs and their armies. For a discussion of these developments and their impact on al-Balādhurī's writerly output in particular, see Lynch, *Arab Conquests*, 35–64, esp. 43–55.
120. Lynch, *Arab Conquests*, 55. The quote refers to al-Balādhurī's *Futūḥ*, but the notion is applicable to early Islamic historiography more generally, for which see briefly Haider, *Rebel and Imām*, 253.
121. Zaman, *Religion and Politics*, 49–59; Andersson, *Early Sunnī Historiography*, 4–5.

3

Composing Khārijism

The previous two chapters have thrown into relief the problematic nature of the accounts that tell Khārijite history. We have seen that the structural components of a report – dates, locations, names or sequences of events – cannot easily be used to reconstruct Khārijite history: they are full of contradictions and bear signs of rhetorical (re)arrangement in the form of *topoi* and *schemata*. Turning to the narrative content of these accounts similarly comes with its own challenges. Chapter Two illustrated the characterisation of Khārijism on the basis of certain motifs and literary patterns. As Noth observed, such *Erzählmotive* lack any relation to a specific context and can thus be re-employed wherever necessary.[1] Overall, much of the material on the Khawārij appears repetitive and devoid of substance.

This chapter will argue along the same lines, but its focus will not be on the portrayal of Khārijites as such. Rather, it will take a closer look at how this impression of repetitiveness and insubstantiality is effected. Various textual strategies can be observed, such as the repetition of certain expressions, the replication of events and situations (and so the creation of Khārijite-specific *schemata* and *topoi*) and the mobility of particular statements. One result of these strategies is the construction of stock phrases and events intended to imbue accounts of Khārijite activities with verisimilitude, i.e. to create an illusion of actuality, of something that *could* have been.[2] This is a key function of historiography[3] and particularly chronicles,[4] served further by the incorporation of names, dates and numbers that "add texture to narrative",[5] which is one reason for the often conflicting data in structural components.

The following analysis will focus on two case studies: (1) the use of 'Khārijite' language and sentiment by non-Khārijites and (2) the replication of events and narrative content. Their effect, I will argue, is to contribute to the standardisation and thus dehistoricisation of Khārijite history, calling into question literary Khārijism as a discrete phenomenon. As in Chapter Two, the observations made here indicate that stories about the Khawārij had a didactic purpose aimed at problematising issues beyond Khārijism. These findings have serious implications not just for the study of literary Khārijism, but also and especially for the question of how much we can learn about Khārijite history 'as it really was'.

'Khārijite Language' among Non-Khārijites

A detailed examination of statements attributed to various opponents of the Khawārij reveals a striking resemblance to Khārijite utterances and sentiments. This use of 'Khārijite language' by other protagonists, most notably ʿAbdallāh b. al-Zubayr and al-Muhallab b. Abī Ṣufra, is somewhat unexpected at first. It is also a prime example of the insubstantiality of the Khārijite self in the early Islamic historical tradition.

Consider the following report contained in al-Ṭabarī's *Taʾrīkh*, which involves al-Muhallab and a decidedly Khārijite-sounding letter he reportedly wrote to the governor of Basra following another victory over the Azāriqa. The account as related on the authority of Abū Mikhnaf has al-Muhallab begin his report with a rather dramatic opening: "God . . . had vanquished the transgressors, sent down His punishment upon them, slaughtered them in every way and drove them away completely". The letter continues with a description of the battle and finally turns to the subject of al-Muhallab's men, those who, after initial hesitation, had heeded his summons to combat the threat posed by the Khārijites: "A number of groups *willing to sell themselves in their desire for the favor of God*, men of religion, fortitude and patience in the face of hardship, uprightness and fidelity, rejoined me."[6]

The description of al-Muhallab's soldiers as those "willing to sell themselves" draws a direct semantic line from them to their Khārijite enemies. The report is perhaps the most prominent example of this phenomenon. As we saw in the previous chapter, the idea of selling or 'exchanging' oneself is deeply associated with Khārijism and finds expression in one of their names, *al-shurāt*. Non-Khārijite reference to it is not unusual *per se* – it is a Qurʾānic concept and thus universally employable by all believers.[7] A scholar as revered as al-Ḥasan al-Baṣrī is credited with similar teachings.[8] Because of its close association with Khārijism, however, it is striking to find it here attributed to non-Khārijites in a context of direct confrontation with Khārijites. The negative connotations of Khārijite 'exchange' are thereby juxtaposed with righteous, Qurʾānic practice while simultaneously thinning out the substance of literary Khārijism.

Another remarkable example, also transmitted in al-Ṭabarī's *Taʾrīkh* but on the authority of ʿUmar b. Shabba (d. c. 262 H/878 CE), is found in a sermon of Ibn al-Zubayr. When his brother Muṣʿab was killed by ʿAbd al-Malik's troops in 691, Ibn al-Zubayr mourned him "like he mourned his father and ʿUthmān", cursing the Iraqis for selling him out to ʿAbd al-Malik. His eulogy on Muṣʿab is remarkable for its use of belligerently pious language:

> If he [Muṣʿab] has been slain, we, by God, do not die in our beds like the sons of Abū al-ʿĀṣ, none of whom died in war either in pre-Islamic times or in Islam. We die a sudden death by spears or under the shadow of swords. The present world is but a loan from the Supreme King, whose authority does not pass away, and whose dominion does not perish. If it turns its face toward me, I do not take it like a man whose head is turned and who exults immoderately; if it turns its back, I do not weep over it like an abject man confounded by fear.[9]

This combination of disdain for the present world and longing for death in battle is Khārijite sentiment at its finest.[10] It also echoes a poem that the Khārijite quietist ʿImrān b. Ḥiṭṭān is said to have composed upon the death of the famous Khārijite leader Abū Bilāl.[11] ʿImrān's elegy embodies the Khārijite fear of dying a peaceful death, despite there being no reports at all of him participating in armed conflict himself; his reputation was for learning and poetic penmanship.[12] The idiomatic similarities between Ibn al-Zubayr's sermon and ʿImrān's poem are noteworthy. Compare Ibn al-Zubayr's statements above to verses 3–5 of ʿImrān's composition, which read:

> I guard against dying in my bed / and strive for death under the spearheads;
> If I knew that my death / was like the death of Abū Bilāl, I would not worry;
> Whoever cares for this world / by God, the Lord of the Kaʿba, I am averse to it.[13]

There is little difference here between the words of a Khārijite and that of a revered Companion. The historiography of Ibn al-Zubayr's relationship with the Khawārij will be discussed later; what is of significance at this point is that such 'Khārijite' sentiments are in fact not at all specific to literary Khārijism. Al-Muhallab and Ibn al-Zubayr are significant figures in early Islamic history and so it is noteworthy that in both cases the resemblance between Khārijite and non-Khārijite parlance goes beyond a general thematic overlap. This similarity is due to context: al-Muhallab and Ibn al-Zubayr both react to the aftermath of battle, when recourse to such language is expected. There was obviously a shared 'nexus of ideas' concerning martyrdom and dying for God among the members of the early Islamic polity,[14] and we shall see more of this in the discussion of early Islamic ascetic poetry below. The (perhaps unintended) literary effect of such similarities is to largely efface Khārijite specificity.

Occasions on which non-Khārijite protagonists use Khārijite language are plentiful. For instance, Ibn Khayyāṭ remarks briefly on a Baḥraynī rebel who was killed by troops dispatched by the Basran governor al-Ḥakam b.

Ayyūb in 75 H/694–5 CE. This rebel is not explicitly called a Khārijite, but he apparently expressed himself in Khārijite sentiment:

> Remember Dāwūd! He sold himself / and gave of himself generously, seeking Paradise through noble deeds.[15]

In the same vein, Ibn Aʿtham's material on al-Muhallab's conflict with the Azāriqa includes an account in which one of al-Muhallab's men encourages his fellow soldiers to enter a covenant with him to fight the enemy until death (*yubāyiʿunī ʿalā al-mawt*).[16] This reflects Khārijite bellicosity and battlefield habits, but more importantly, the verb used here is synonymous with *sharā/ishtarā* from which the term *al-shurāt* is derived. The *bayʿa* as the 'oath of allegiance' also has strong connections with the concept of selling oneself to/for God.[17] And pre- or mid-battle pledges of this kind and phrased in this language were commonplace in the (literature of the) late antique and early Islamic Near East,[18] peculiar neither to the Khawārij nor to their opponents.

A more general echo of notions of ascetic piety expressed by literary Khārijism also resonates in ʿAbd al-Malik's musings upon Muṣʿab b. al-Zubayr's death, which he celebrates with a feast. On several occasions during the meal and ensuing tour of the palace in Kufa, he comments on the ephemerality of life:

> All that is new . . . turns toward decline, and some day every man will become a has-been.
> Work with deliberation for you are [only] mortal, and toil [only] for yourself, O man. What was, now that it is gone, seems as if it had never existed; and what is appears as if it had already passed away.[19]

These contemplations directly follow Ibn al-Zubayr's sermon for his slain brother Muṣʿab, cited above. Both of them are characterised by a renunciant tenor that recalls Khārijite disdain for the material world and they further underline the cross-confessional significance of concepts and terminology associated with literary Khārijism. This is not to say that early Islamic forms of piety and ascetism originated with the Khawārij (literary or historical), of course, or that the use of pious language is in any way unusual among non-Khārijites. The point is rather that if we go looking for something specifically Khārijite that enables us to understand the historical phenomenon better, we do not necessarily find it here. These are interchangeable motifs that say something about the historiographical idea and memory of Khārijism, but they are less helpful in discerning its historical features. It is telling that a sermon attributed to the Azraqī leader Qaṭarī b. al-Fujāʾa could elsewhere be ascribed to ʿAlī b. Abī Ṭālib.[20]

The final example provides a telling instance of moving 'Khārijite' phrases. In this particular instance, a certain statement passes between Khārijite and Zubayrid contexts. The setting is an argument between the (by then) quietist Khārijite ʿUrwa b. Udayya and Muʿāwiya's governor of Iraq, ʿUbaydallāh b. Ziyād. As a result of their confrontation, ʿUbaydallāh sentences ʿUrwa to death and proceeds to have his extremities cut off. Just before ʿUrwa dies, Ibn Ziyād asks for his thoughts on the whole affair and ʿUrwa responds: "I think that you ruined this world for me and that you ruined the Hereafter for yourself".[21]

We encounter his exact dying words again in a very different context. Al-Balādhurī's *Ansāb* contains a detailed discussion of Ibn al-Zubayr's conflict with al-Ḥajjāj and ʿAbd al-Malik. Towards the end of that section, the text offers a series of reports that pit Ibn al-Zubayr's mother Asmāʾ bt. Abī Bakr against al-Ḥajjāj. Asmāʾ shows open contempt towards al-Ḥajjāj, but one particular statement stands out. Following Ibn al-Zubayr's death, al-Ḥajjāj and Asmāʾ exchange letters and finally personal visits. In one such personal confrontation Asmāʾ condemns al-Ḥajjāj's actions against her son and declares that "you ruined this world for him, but you ruined the Hereafter for yourself!"[22]

The settings in which this phrase is used are rather different, but there is one constant: the censure of an Umayyad governor, first ʿUbaydallāh b. Ziyād and then al-Ḥajjāj. We seem to be dealing here with an expression that has little to do with the Khawārij specifically – certainly no one would accuse Asmāʾ of Khārijism – but rather belongs to a set of standard pious phrases associated with a context of martyrdom and/or unjust killing. This transferability of narrative content stems at least partially from the predominant core unit of early Islamic historiography, the *khabar*: "the fact that each *khabar* was (or could be) a freestanding textual unit meant that the sense of cause and effect between two events or episodes was often left unarticulated, which weakened the sense of larger historical relationships".[23] Al-Balādhurī must have been aware of this statement occurring in different frameworks as he also incorporated two versions of ʿUrwa's execution into his *Ansāb* that include it.[24] Scholars had no qualms about recycling material and the case here suggests that narrative content was not so much fixed by a specific historical incident but rather by a specific narrative purpose or setting.[25]

The impression that there is little distinct about literary Khārijism increases further when we turn to (early) Islamic ascetic poetry, perhaps the best indication that the core Khārijite concerns – piety coupled with longing for *jihād* and death on the battlefield – are by no means a specialty of the Khawārij. The (admittedly ill-defined) genre of ascetic poetry (*zuhdiyyāt*) has a long history and can perhaps even be traced back to pre-Islamic times.[26] By the early ninth century, "the poetry of *zuhd* was recognized as a distinct literary activity",[27] resulting in the establishment of poetic conventions around the same time. "On the whole, *zuhdīyāt* tend to be extremely conventional in theme and simple in language"; this did not change much as time went on.[28] The repetitiveness of Khārijite language with its focus on pious devotion and renunciation probably owes something to this particular feature of the genre.

Zuhd poetry is rooted predominantly in the Qur'ān and related to homiletics and advice literature, with which it shares a number of themes.[29] The most important of these are renunciation, which gave the genre its name and is a "major feature of early Islamic piety",[30] and repentance,[31] which is a staple of Khārijite exhortative language. There are similarities with the Christian tradition of renunciation, and it is very likely that early forms of Muslim *zuhd* were based on or at least related to Christian and other late antique forms of asceticism.[32] Books of renunciant sayings abound in Islamic literature, among the most famous being the works attributed to Ibn al-Mubārak (d. 181 H/797 CE) and Aḥmad b. Ḥanbal (d. 241 H/855 CE).[33] Other motifs include contemplation of the vanity of human endeavours and the frailty of human life.[34] These themes permeate several genres of the Islamic literary tradition: many works of *adab*, for example, contain *kuttāb al-zuhd*, such as al-Jāḥiẓ's *Bayān* or Ibn Qutayba's *'Uyūn*.[35] The same is true for Ṣūfī literature.[36] In *ḥadīth*, Muḥammad is credited with the following definition of a true renunciant: "He who is ever mindful of decay in the tomb, who prizes the enduring above the transitory, and who numbers himself among the dead."[37]

All of this should sound familiar by now: Khārijite piety clearly does not differ much from general early Islamic pious sentiment.[38] Echoes of their concerns abound in ascetic poetry and sayings that are in fact almost indistinguishable from 'Khārijite' rhetoric:

> You rejoice in what passes away and delight in wishes, as a dreamer is fooled by the pleasures he dreams.[39]

> Many a man goes to bed and gets up in the morning thinking himself safe when his shroud has already been woven.[40]

> Every living man is mortal, the son of a mortal. Every last one is descended from a long line of purebred mortals.[41]

Chapter Two mentioned the Khārijite poet 'Imrān b. Ḥiṭṭān. Let us take another look at his notion of kinship ties based on Islam rather than tribalism, cited above:

> We are the sons of Islam and God is One / and the most righteous among God's servants (*awlā ʿibād allāh bi-l-ḥaqq*) is he who gives thanks [to God].[42]

His verse finds correspondence in lines composed by Ibn Abī Ḥāzim:

> Be humble towards God, not your fellow men. Be content with giving up worldly hope – that is where nobility lies /
> Learn to do without kin and connections – he is wealthy who can do without others.[43]

It was not just the 'Khārijite' devotion to God that was shared by the early Islamic community at large: the connection between piety and *jihād* appears to have been a very early feature, as indicated by the memory of the Companion ʿAbdallāh b. Rawwāḥa, for instance. While accompanying the Prophet on a campaign, he is said to have proclaimed his longing for death in battle:

> I beseech the Merciful for forgiveness / and a gaping slash that sprays my bubbling blood;
> Or the thrust of a spinning spear from a zealot's hand / running through my entrails and liver;
> So that he who passes my grave one day cries out:
> God guided him as warrior to the right path / and on it he walked.[44]

The combination of piety and militance is perhaps most pronounced in warrior-ascetics like Ibn al-Mubārak, whose commitment to militant piety is demonstrated by the attribution to him of both a *Kitāb al-Jihād* and a *Kitāb al-Zuhd*. His well-known statement that "the sword wipes [away] sins"[45] but not hypocrisy is reminiscent of the Khārijites' repeated calls for repentance for perceived transgressions against God – transgressions that serve both as the cause and the justification of the violence enacted by the Khawārij. Ibn al-Mubārak and his companions are credited with the belief that the soul needed to be purged from all worldly temptations, which would be achieved by 'going out' from the Muslim community to avoid the temptations mankind falls prey to so easily.[46]

The practice of frontier combat as pursued by Ibn al-Mubārak and large numbers of volunteers in the eighth and ninth centuries did not necessarily serve a direct political aim; rather, these frontier warriors (*ghāzīs*) acted at least partially out of pious conviction:

> Death as a proof of piety was the fruit of an extremely idiomatic appropriation of revelation and its reproduction as military exploit . . . Pious action, according to the logic of the frontier, went hand-in-hand with martyrdom, since it was only by a readiness to offer one's life for the Islamic cause that

> one could be certain of the purity of one's Islamic intention and thereby the redemptive worth of one's acts.[47]

This particular form of frontier warfare is thus a close relative of Khārijite militant piety as the historical tradition describes it.

In fact, fighting as a principal expression of piety was a perfectly acceptable practice well beyond the eighth century and may have represented a "reaction to and reflection of the continuing vitality of the Qurʾānic vision of *jihād*".[48] Based on a study by Maher Jarrar, Angelika Neuwirth has argued that "the image of the warrior martyr as an exemplary hero did not . . . develop in sectarian circles":[49] while the Khawārij are associated with a yearning for death in battle, the notion of bellicosity as religiously commendable in fact seems to have emerged in eighth-century Iraq among ascetics and other particularly devout groups.[50]

Early Ṣūfism also emphasised the importance of pious combat.[51] Probably the most famous of these ascetics was the proto-Ṣūfī martyr Ibrāhīm b. Adham (d. c. 161 H/778 CE), who despised worldly affairs and embraced poverty. He reportedly died in battle against a Byzantine army.[52] Many of these frontier warriors were regularly credited with a pious lifestyle away from the battlefield as well – dedicated to fasting, praying and giving alms in excess, they were sometimes compared to monks.[53]

Early Muslim and thus Khārijite militant piety was probably heavily influenced by, or at least ran parallel to, similar notions among Christian communities (not just) in Syria, whose traditions "frequently figure Christian ascetics as zealous and violent warriors".[54] Such stories of pious warriors were indeed shared by all communities of the late antique and early Islamic Near East,[55] just as the states in that region and period (and beyond) shared an uneasy stance on actualised militant piety.[56] In the early Islamic period, boundaries were fluid enough that sometimes Christian monks converted to Islam and joined the frontier combat, while former Muslim soldiers occasionally joined a monastery upon conversion to Christianity.[57]

Militant Khārijite piety as rendered by the sources is distinguished from its non-Khārijite Muslim counterpart by the fact that its focus is inward looking: rather than combatting external opponents, the Khawārij seek to eliminate the *umma*'s internal enemies. It is here that we finally arrive at a feature of literary Khārijism that stands out: while the attempt to root out and neutralise 'heretics' was apparently pursued by early Islamic authorities as a matter of course,[58] the scale on which the sources have the Khārijites demand the eradication of unbelievers from the Muslim community is unmatched; the violence they are portrayed as employing in the pursuit of religious purity unparalleled; and the resulting upheaval profoundly unacceptable. The potential ramifications of such an uncompromising outlook – whatever its precise correspondence with actual seventh-century events – may over time have contributed to the formation of a theory of *jihād* that distinguished between an individual and a communal duty of warfare (*farḍ ʿayn* and *farḍ kifāya*, respectively), restricting the former to an extent that it essentially made it legally impossible except in case of foreign invasion.[59]

Replication and Repetition

The second case study deals with the replication of particular events and narrative content. The appointment of Khārijite leaders, for instance, displays a particular pattern both at the structural and the content level. The 'appointment' *schema* comprises several features, most of which are present in reports of Khārijite elections, although not necessarily in the same order.[60] The checklist includes the following items: Khārijites gather to appoint a leader; leadership is offered to a prominent member of the group; the prospective leader declines and suggests other candidates; the candidates in turn defer to the former as being more worthy of the post; the first Khārijite to be nominated eventually accepts, but stresses that he is not interested in worldly power but merely strives to achieve favour with God; finally, the newly chosen leader delivers a declamation of the Khārijites' pious intentions and his own desire for *jihād*, underlined by any number of Qurʾānic verses. The two last stages also provide ample occasion for the deployment of Khārijite topical sentiment. Consider the following two examples:

ʿAbdallāh b. Wahb al-Rāsibī is remembered as the first Khārijite *imām* and the one who led the rebel troops against ʿAlī at Nahrawān. He was offered the position of commander by his fellow Khawārij in 38 H/658 CE, but only accepted after two others had refused out of deference to his superiority in all things. The address he gives following his election belongs to the final stage of the 'appointment' *schema*:

> I do not accept it [i.e., leadership] desiring worldly gains or eluding death, but I accept it hoping for [God's] great reward therein. God accepted our covenant on the condition to command right and forbid wrong, to speak the truth and pursue *jihād* for His cause, for 'Verily, those who stray from God's path will suffer great punishment' [Q 38:26]. And God said: 'Those who do not judge by what God has sent down, they are the transgressors' [Q 5:47] . . .[61]

The story of the election of al-Mustawrid b. ʿUllafa al-Taymī in 42 H/662–3 CE in Kufa as leader of the largest Khārijite revolt during the caliphate of

Muʿāwiya closely resembles the election of Ibn Wahb. In al-Ṭabarī's rendering, the Khārijites of Kufa assembled at the house of one of their leaders, Ḥayyān b. Ẓabyān al-Sulamī, to decide whom to put in charge of an impending Khārijite rebellion.[62] Apart from Ḥayyān, two other Khārijites were considered for leadership: al-Mustawrid and Muʿādh b. Juwayn. Muʿādh and Ḥayyān had both been wounded at Nahrawān and were later pardoned by ʿAlī; Muʿādh's uncle Zayd b. Ḥusayn had been killed at Nahrawān as one of the Khārijite commanders. Thereafter, neither Muʿādh nor Ḥayyān appear in the accounts of Khārijite uprisings during ʿAlī's reign.

As in the case of Ibn Wahb's election, all three prospective leaders are eager to declare their contempt for the temporal world and their desire for God's favour. Al-Mustawrid emphasises that he is not interested in attaining power for its own sake:

> Appoint whomever you like over you . . . I do not mind which one of you governs me. We do not seek the glory of this world and there is no way to remain in it. We only desire immortality in the realm of everlasting life.[63]

Ḥayyān also humbly insists that he is not motivated by the lust for power: "I have no need to rule and I am satisfied with every one of my brothers."[64] While Muʿādh points out that not everyone is "virtuous enough for that command", he does not put himself forward either but suggests al-Mustawrid or Ḥayyān instead, who in turn offer to pledge allegiance to him because he is "perfect in your religion and your opinions".[65] Finally, because they all appear to share the same impeccable religious virtues, they turn to the principle of seniority: al-Mustawrid as the oldest is chosen as *imām*, despite his protest.[66]

The parallels to Ibn Wahb's election are clear. In each case, there are three potential nominees for Khārijite *imām*; the candidates initially refuse to accept the position of leadership offered by their comrades because they defer to their fellow nominees; and throughout the election process all candidates declare their utter disinterest in worldly power despite their assumption of leadership.

There are several other examples of this particular *schema* in the source material, even if the episodes are often described in much less detail and hence lack one or more of the identified components.[67] Such schematised accounts of the appointment of Khārijite leaders suggest that we are dealing with literary conventions rather than genuine descriptions of 'what happened'. This is not to say that such depictions are not based on real events, but identifying which specific depiction reflects historical occurrences is difficult. This material therefore cannot easily be used for writing positivist history but lends itself more readily to a literary analysis. In fact, the replication of events and narrative content conceals, rather than reveals, meaningful information about the Khawārij. The standardisation of certain settings and sentiments turns the individual components of a report into building blocks that are assigned to specific sets of narrative situations and thus dehistoricise the events they purport to describe. Individual circumstances appear less important than the depiction of Khārijism as a specific movement with certain characteristics, supporting the impression that scholars were at least as invested in portraying Khārijism as a set of ideas as they were interested in the historical phenomenon.

This is particularly obvious in the case of two other types of replicated narrative, Khārijite death scenes and expressions of Khārijite 'doctrine'. Like the 'appointment' *schema*, execution accounts of Khārijite rebels mostly follow a clear pattern that depicts their impressive pious fortitude during the ordeal and usually culminates in a dire warning of punishment in the Hereafter for the executioners. We will encounter such scenes at a later stage,[68] so let us focus here on Khārijite doctrine as presented in speeches, sermons, letters and poems, the majority of which are replicated in content to such an extent that there hardly remains a trace of specificity. A good point of departure for the investigation of such harmonisations is the sermon attributed to the Jazīran Khārijite Ṣāliḥ b. Musarriḥ, who rebelled in 695. The most detailed account is transmitted in al-Ṭabarī, which will serve as our template and most of which I therefore quote here at length:

> 'Praise be to God, who created the heavens and the earth, and made the darkness and the light. Yet those who have disbelieved ascribe rivals to their Lord.' [Q 6:1] O God! We ascribe no rivals to You, we serve none but You, and none but You do we worship . . . We testify that Muḥammad is Your servant, whom You chose, and Your messenger, whom You selected and approved to convey Your messages and Your counsel for Your servants. We testify that he conveyed the message and counseled the community, summoned to the truth and acted equitably, supported religion and strove against the polytheists, until God took him. I commend to you the fear of God, austerity in this world, desire for the afterlife, frequent recollection of death, avoidance of the sinners, and love for the believers . . . Love for the believers is recommended because it is in this way that one obtains God's grace and mercy and His Paradise – may God cause us and you to be among the sincere and patient! Indeed, it is a blessing from God on the believers that He sent to them a messenger from among themselves, who taught them the Book and the wisdom, purified and sanctified them, and led them aright in their religion; he was kind and merciful to the believers until God took him away, God's blessings be upon him! Then, after him, authority was taken by the God-fearing Veracious One [*al-Ṣiddīq*; epithet of Abū

> Bakr], with the approval of the Muslims. He followed the right guidance of the messenger and continued in his way [*sunna*] until he joined God, God's mercy be upon him. He designated ʿUmar as his successor, and God entrusted him with the authority over this flock. ʿUmar acted in accordance with the Book of God and kept to the way [*aḥyā sunna*] of the messenger of God. He begrudged his flock none of their rights and feared the reproach of no one before God, until he joined Him, God's mercy be upon him. After him, the Muslims were ruled by ʿUthmān. He expropriated the spoils, failed to enforce the Qurʾānic punishments, rendered unjust judgments, and treated the believer with contempt and the evildoer with esteem. The Muslims went to him and killed him, and God, His messenger and the upright among the believers were quit of him. After him, the people were governed by ʿAlī b. Abī Ṭālib. He did not hesitate to give men authority to judge in the affairs of God; he vacillated with regard to the people of error, and appeased and blandished them. We are quit of ʿAlī and his supporters. Prepare, then – God's mercy upon you – to strive against these fractious parties and unjust leaders of error, and to go out from the abode of transience to the abode of eternity and join our believing, convinced brethren, who sold the present world for the afterworld and expended their wealth in quest of God's good pleasure in the final reckoning. Be not anxious about being killed for God's sake, for being killed is easier than dying naturally. Natural death comes upon you unexpectedly, separating you from your fathers, sons, wives, and this world; if your anxiety and aversion to this is too strong, then, indeed, sell your souls to God obediently, and your wealth, and you will enter Paradise in security and embrace the black-eyed houris. May God make you and us among the grateful and mindful 'who are guided by the truth and by it act justly'[Q 7:159].[69]

Khārijite discourse repeats these same motifs over and over again regardless of the setting. Literary Khārijism is thereby turned into a reservoir of standard formulae that are applied to the phenomenon as a whole. Speech after speech and sermon after sermon follow the same well-established pattern: praise of God, Muḥammad and the first two *rāshidūn* caliphs – one half of the "mission *topos*" of early Islamic epistles identified by Michael Cook[70] – is followed by a severe castigation of ʿUthmān and ʿAlī, finishing with a condemnation of the state of the *umma* under Umayyad (and later ʿAbbāsid) leadership and an exhortation to do battle against the tyrants in power. This structure is rounded out with a display of Khārijite pious sentiment and a discussion of the merits of *jihād* against an unjust ruler, death generally being the desired outcome of such endeavours. The length and detail of Khārijite speeches and sermons may vary, but the structure is the same and likewise Khārijite grievances and accusations are expressed in the same terms[71]:

> Then the Muslims appointed ʿUthmān as caliph, but he created reserved areas, favored kinship, appointed youths to positions of authority, abolished the lash and laid aside the whip, destroyed the Book, shed the blood of the Muslim . . . Not content with that, he seized the spoils [*fay*ʾ] which God had given to them and shared it out among the godless ones of Quraysh and the shameless ones of the Arabs.[72]

> You [ʿAlī] have fallen short in the affair of God and you appointed judges over His Book and you have broken with the community [*al-jamāʿa*].[73]

> What we advocate is the Book of God and the *sunnah* of Muḥammad, God bless him. What we object to for our people is the expropriation of the spoils, the failure to enforce the Qurʾānic punishments, and the autocratic nature of the regime.[74]

> Verily, the people of our *daʿwa* have given human beings authority over the affair of God and did not judge by the Book of God and neither the *sunna* of the Prophet of God. They committed *kufr* through this and turned away from the right way, and have dissolved the league between us. 'God does not love the treacherous' [Q 4:107].[75]

> We take revenge on behalf of our folk for tyranny in judgment, failure to enforce prescriptions, and the monopolization of the *fay*ʾ. I summon you to the Book of God, Almighty and Great, and the example [*sunnah*] of His Prophet, and the rule [*wilāyah*] of Abū Bakr and ʿUmar. I also call upon you to disavow ʿUthmān and ʿAlī for their innovation in religion . . . and their abandonment of the judgment of the Book.[76]

This unchanging nature of Khārijite rhetoric is a good indicator of the narrative role and function of Khārijism in the early historical tradition. Looking at Khārijite discourse from later periods not covered here confirms this further. The rebel al-Ḍaḥḥāk b. Qays, who led a large revolt against the last Umayyad caliph from 127–8 H/744–6 CE, is oratorically indistinguishable from his predecessors. When his companions encourage him to stay safely behind instead of engaging directly with the caliphal army, he responds:

> By God, I require nothing in this world of yours. I seek only this tyrant (*al-ṭārīya)* [i.e., Marwān]! I have made it incumbent on me before God that if I see him [Marwān], I will charge him until God decides between us.[77]

Consider also the famous sermon of Abū Ḥamza, another Khārijite active at the very end of the Umayyad era. While the exact details and circumstances of his preaching are contested,[78] the speech puts him firmly within the framework of literary Khārijism, as the following passage demonstrates:

> Then ʿUthmān took charge. For six years he proceeded in a way which fell short of the mode of conduct of his two companions [i.e., Abū Bakr and ʿUmar – H-L H.]. Then he [acted in a manner which] annulled what he had done earlier, and passed on his way. Then ʿAlī b. Abī Ṭālib took charge. He acted in a proper manner until he established arbitration concerning the book of God and had doubts about His religion. [Thereafter] he did not achieve any goal in respect of what was right, nor did he erect any beacon for that.[79]

It is not at all impossible that these allegations reflect contemporary concerns and conflicts, and we know that certain individuals like Qaṭarī b. al-Fujāʾa and al-Ḍaḥḥāk b. Qays were historical figures because of the numismatic evidence they left behind.[80] But to what extent do the literary and the historical figure align? The problem is that such stylisation and harmonisation make it a challenge to work out in which instances rhetoric of that kind refers to historical events and encounters. Above, we categorised stories of Khārijism as a type of 'exemplary anecdote'. A main characteristic of this kind of narrative is its "transcendence of time and place";[81] in our case, this means that where we do not have external evidence like coins, determining whether we are dealing with a literary stock figure or a historical person can be very problematic. Morony argued regarding the late seventh-century Khārijite bandit-rebel Shabīb that "his program was still essentially political and rooted in grievances that went back to the reign of ʿUthmān", precisely on the basis of yet another such enumeration of caliphal failures.[82] This appears perfectly plausible considering the individual context, but if we line up Shabīb's complaints with those of the Khārijites before and after him, the individuality of the image begins to blur. Refocusing it requires prior recognition of the rhetorical elements and narrative strategies that constitute its frame.

Conclusions

The chapters of Part II have shown that Khārijite history, as depicted in the selected sources, is more immediately suited to literary than historical study. The wealth of structural components transmitted in accounts of Khārijism seems at first glance to convey an impressive amount of data on the Khawārij and their revolts. A second look, however, reveals that much of this information corresponds to a set of *topoi* and *schemata.* The profusion of detail also often disguises a lack of narrative substance. We can identify various contributing factors, such as the use of 'Khārijite language' by non-Khārijite actors or the creation of Khārijite-specific motifs and *schemata.* 'Specific' here does not mean 'exclusive', but signals core characteristics associated with literary Khārijism.

I have argued – and will continue to argue – that the historians' major concern was not primarily the depiction of Khārijite history 'as it was', but rather the portrayal of Khārijism as a set of specific ideas. This book suggests that there existed a broad consensus in the early historical tradition on how Khārijites were to be understood and delineated. Accordingly, Khārijism was shown to remain essentially unchanged regardless of the particular circumstances of a revolt; a mid-eighth-century Khārijite rebel consequently sounds almost identical to his companions from nearly a century earlier or later. In other words, Khārijite identity is presented as static and thus manifestly ahistorical, which raises serious issues for positivist reconstructions of Khārijite history.

Notes

1. Noth, "Iṣfahān-Nihāwand", 278–9.
2. Verisimilitude "presupposes things, concepts, or sign systems against which [a] text may be tested for accuracy and evaluated in the light of their authority". Riffaterre, *Fictional Truth*, 84.
3. See Cubitt, "Memory and Narrative", 47; Spiegel, introduction to *Past as Text*, xiii; White, *Tropics of Discourse*, 98, 99, 122. According to Luce, verisimilitude in ancient Greek historiography "was equivalent to veracity". Luce, *Greek Historians*, 3. For mechanisms of verisimilitude, or *mimesis*, in early Islamic historical writing, see Shoshan, *Poetics*, 3–60.
4. Melve, "Conceptions of Authorship", 143.
5. Robinson, "Heilsgeschichte".
6. Al-Ṭabarī, *Taʾrīkh*, II, 589; Hawting, *Collapse*, 172–3 [my emphasis].
7. On Umayyad and Khārijite poetry sharing the same "nexus of ideas" of selling oneself to God, see Marsham, *Rituals of Islamic Monarchy*, 102; al-Jomaih, *Use of the Qurʾān*, 364–5.
8. Al-Jāḥiẓ, *al-Bayān*, III, 132, quoted in Van Ess, "Bild der Ḫāriǧiten", 2553 n. 125.
9. Al-Ṭabarī, *Taʾrīkh*, II, 818–19; Fishbein, *Victory*, 194–5.
10. This is not to say that it was exclusive to the Khawārij, of course. As mentioned already, militant piety was an integral part of early Islamic society. For more on this, see the discussion below.
11. He was the brother of ʿUrwa b. Udayya, whom we encountered in Chapter One in the discussion of Khārijite *awāʾil.* On Abū Bilāl, see Chapter Five.
12. On ʿImrān, see the references on 56 (n. 86).
13. Al-Balādhurī, *Ansāb*, IV/1, 388.
14. See also n. 7.
15. Ibn Khayyāṭ, *Taʾrīkh*, I, 270.
16. Ibn Aʿtham, *Futūḥ*, VII, 66.
17. See Marsham, *Rituals of Islamic Monarchy*, 44–9, 100–2 (on Khārijites spe-

cifically) and the poem ascribed to a late Umayyad Khārijite rebel, quoted in Higgins, "Faces of Exchangers", 29.

18. Marsham, *Rituals of Islamic Monarchy*, 67–8.
19. Al-Ṭabarī, *Taʾrīkh*, II, 820–1; Fishbein, *Victory*, 195–6, with slight changes.
20. Qutbuddin, "Qur'an Citation", 336 n. 34.
21. For a detailed discussion of this episode, see Chapter Five (section on 'The Basran Quietists').
22. Al-Balādhurī, *Ansāb*, IV/2, 386. All of this will be addressed in more detail in Chapter Six.
23. Donner, *Narratives*, 262.
24. Al-Balādhurī, *Ansāb*, IV/1, 386–7, 387–8.
25. See above, 68, 73-4; Hoyland, "Arabic, Syriac and Greek", 220–2. For another example of such transferable motifs, see Leder, *Korpus*, 170.
26. Hamori, "Ascetic Poetry", 265.
27. Ibid., 268.
28. Ibid., 269.
29. Ibid., 267–8.
30. Melchert, "Aḥmad b. Ḥanbal", 345.
31. Hamori, "Ascetic Poetry", 265.
32. D. Cook, *Martyrdom*, 63. See also Livne-Kafri, "Early Muslim Ascetics"; Sizgorich, *Violence and Belief*, 13, 150, 170; Sahner, "Monasticism", 165–6 and *passim*; Donner, *Narratives*, 70; Morony, *Iraq*, 475–7, esp. 476 for the connection between death and asceticism in Christian monasticism and Jewish piety.
33. Melchert, "Aḥmad b. Ḥanbal", 349.
34. Hamori, "Ascetic Poetry", 265; Melchert, "Aḥmad b. Ḥanbal", 358.
35. Melchert, "Aḥmad b. Ḥanbal", 357.
36. Ibid.
37. Hamori, "Ascetic Poetry", 266.
38. On *zuhd* as "an entire way of conduct . . . destined for the Islamic community as a whole", see Kinberg, "What Is Meant by Zuhd" (quote on 29).
39. Attributed to ʿUmar II, quoted in Hamori, "Ascetic Poetry", 272.
40. Anonymous, cited ibid.
41. Abū Nuwās, cited ibid., 270. See also the examples quoted from Ibn al-Mubārak's *Kitāb al-Zuhd* in F. Salem, *ʿAbd Allāh b. al-Mubārak*, 209–11 and the remarks in Kinberg, "What Is Meant by Zuhd", 36–41.
42. Ibn Aʿtham, *Futūḥ*, VII, 105.
43. Cited in Hamori, "Ascetic Poetry", 271.
44. Quoted in Neuwirth, "Sacrilege to Sacrifice", 262.
45. Ibn al-Mubārak, *Kitāb al-Jihād*, quoted in D. Cook, *Martyrdom*, 36.
46. Sizgorich, *Violence and Belief*, 210.
47. Heck, "Jihād Revisited", 100–1. See also F. Salem, *ʿAbd Allāh b. al-Mubārak*, 131–85, esp. 136–43; Sizgorich, *Violence and Belief*, 208; M. Bonner, *Aristocratic Violence*, esp. chapter four and appendix.

48. Robinson, "Reconstructing", 127.
49. Neuwirth, "Sacrilege to Sacrifice", 263.
50. Ibid., 263–4.
51. D. Cook, *Martyrdom*, 64.
52. Ibid., 64–5.
53. Noth, *Heiliger Krieg*, 25–32, 47–61.
54. Sizgorich, *Violence and Belief*, 109. On this and other commonalities between the portrayal of the Khawārij and contemporary religious communities in Iraq aimed at circumscribing group boundaries and striving for a deeply pious way of life through excommunication, ostracisation and execution of apostates, see Morony, *Iraq*, 475–7. Pannewick has pointed out parallels between Khārijite piety and the doctrine of the (much earlier) Christian sect of the Montanists, who championed renunciation and actively sought out persecution. Her call for a comparative study of both phenomena remains a *desideratum*. Pannewick, "Introduction", 4 and notes 15 and 17 thereto. A similar case could be made for North African Donatism – especially its militant wing, the Circumcellions – which likewise emphasised separation from a sinful environment, demanded faultlessness from its leadership and advocated both spiritual and military combat against 'heretics'. For Donatist discourse and its reception in non-Donatist circles, see Gaddis, *There Is No Crime*, 103–30. For potential connections between Donatists and Khārijites, see Prevost, "Dernières communautés", 467–8 and note 28; Fiaccadori, "Kharidjites", for the need to establish an actual historical connection between North African Donatist and Khārijite communities beyond a similarity of spirit (our understanding of which in both cases is predominantly informed by hostile sources).
55. Sizgorich, *Violence and Belief*, 150. On shared late antique notions of asceticism, (militant) piety and martyrdom, see also Gaiser, *Shurāt Legends*, *passim* but esp. chapters 1 and 2; Robinson, *Empire and Elites*, 116–17; Marsham, "Attitudes", 119–21.
56. Robinson, "Reconstructing", 127–8; Gaddis, *There Is No Crime*.
57. Sahner, "Monasticism", 178–82.
58. See, for example, Judd, "Muslim Persecution"; Tucker, *Mahdis and Millenarians*. It should be noted that many of the discussed 'heretics' resorted to violence and openly opposed the ruling authorities, which seems to have had a strong influence on whether or not they were persecuted. The distinction between 'heretic' and 'rebel' (not to mention the definition of what exactly 'heretic' meant in the absence of a clearly defined orthodoxy) can thus be very problematic. In the case of the 'Zindīqs' it has been argued that the persecution under the early ʿAbbāsid caliph al-Mahdī was not so much motivated by religious reasons but rather related to the transition to a new socio-political system. For a discussion of these issues, see, for example, Hawting, "Jaʿd b. Dirham"; Fierro, "Heresy", esp. 900–3; Ibrahim, "Religious Inquisition".
59. Lahoud, "Early Kharijites", 302–3. Needless to say, I am more sceptical than

Lahoud as regards the historicity of the events she recounts, but the contention that scholarly engagement with social strife and intra-communal bloodshed led to a restriction of legitimate use of violence within the *umma* is certainly plausible.

60. See for a different example of this Noth, "Iṣfahān-Nihāwand", 282.
61. Al-Dīnawarī, *Akhbār*, 215–16. See also al-Ṭabarī, *Taʾrīkh*, I, 3363–5; al-Balādhurī, *Ansāb*, II, 300, 318, 320–1.
62. For this episode, see al-Ṭabarī, *Taʾrīkh*, II, 17–21.
63. Ibid., 20.
64. Ibid., 21.
65. Ibid.
66. See also the discussion on 189–90.
67. See, for example, al-Balādhurī, *Ansāb*, IV/2, 441, 446; al-Ṭabarī, *Taʾrīkh*, II, 184, 517, 985.
68. See below, 199, 264 and the notes thereto.
69. Al-Ṭabarī, *Taʾrīkh*, II, 882–4; Rowson, *Marwānid Restoration*, 33–5.
70. Cook, *Early Muslim Dogma*, 7. On the related 'caliph theme' in Khārijite discourse, see Dähne, "Abū Ḥamza aš-Šārī", 32–5. For the use of the 'mission topos' by the Khārijites' opponents, see, for example, ʿAlī's reaction to the murder of a Companion by a group of Khawārij in Ibn Aʿtham, *Futūḥ*, IV, 99–100; ʿAlī's discussion with Muʿāwiya's envoys at Ṣiffīn in al-Ṭabarī, Taʾrīkh, I, 3278–9.
71. In addition to the following quotes, see also al-Masʿūdī, *Murūj*, I–II, 395 and III–IV, 138; Ibn Aʿtham, *Futūḥ*, VI, 122–3, 126 and VII, 92, 93–4; al-Ṭabarī, *Taʾrīkh*, II, 329–30, 900; al-Dīnawarī, *Akhbār*, 202, 216, 217, 279; al-Yaʿqūbī, *Taʾrīkh*, II, 192; al-Balādhurī, *Ansāb*, II, 312, 313, 320–1, 329, 330 and IV/1, 178; Ibn Saʿd, *Ṭabaqāt*, III, 32, 37. See also the references in Chapter Four (section on 'Apologia for ʿAlī').
72. Al-Ṭabarī, *Taʾrīkh*, II, 516 (the future Azraqī ʿUbayda b. Hilāl); Hawting, *Collapse*, 99–100.
73. Al-Balādhurī, *Ansāb*, II, 300 ("the" Khārijites on their return from Ṣiffīn).
74. Al-Ṭabarī, *Taʾrīkh*, II, 984 (Suwayd, one of Shabīb's companions); Rowson, *Marwānid Restoration*, 132.
75. Al-Dīnawarī, *Akhbār*, 217 (Ibn Wahb and Shurayḥ b. Abī Awfā in a letter to Basran Khārijites).
76. Al-Ṭabarī, *Taʾrīkh*, II, 40–1 (al-Mustawrid in a letter to the governor of al-Madāʾin); Morony, *Between Civil Wars*, 46.
77. Ibn Khayyāṭ, *Taʾrīkh* (ed. ʿUmarī), 379. The end of the last sentence echoes the Qurʾān, e.g. Q 7:87, which reassures the believer that God will judge between those who have believed and those who have not. Both the verb for 'judge' (*yaḥkuma*) and the description of God as 'the best of judges' (*khayru al-ḥākimīna*) as well as the tenor of the verse allude to the Khārijite watchword *lā ḥukma illā li-llāh*.
78. Crone and Hinds, *God's Caliph*, 129.

79. Translation ibid., 130.
80. For Qaṭarī, see 55 (n. 76); for al-Ḍaḥḥāk, see Gaiser, "What Do We Learn", 181–3.
81. Kilito, *Author and His Doubles*, 61.
82. Morony, *Iraq*, 477.

PART III

THE PORTRAYAL OF KHĀRIJITE HISTORY FROM ṢIFFĪN TO THE DEATH OF ʿABD AL-MALIK

4

Narratives of Khārijite Origins

So far, this book has looked at the general portrayal of literary Khārijism independent of time and place. By contrast, the chapters of Part III will focus on specific periods in early Khārijite history. The present chapter examines the narrative function of Khārijism in the depiction of ʿAlī b. Abī Ṭālib's reign, from the arbitration at Ṣiffīn until his assassination by a Khārijite in 40 H/661 CE.[1] Here we can again observe that discussion of the Khawārij was not an end in itself but served to highlight, illustrate, criticise or vindicate other actors and points of contention. This accords with the findings of the proceeding chapters.

The analysis of ʿAlī's confrontations with the Khawārij reveals three main concerns. First, our historians discuss at great length the various allegations levelled against ʿAlī and take care to refute them one by one. This theme, or rather group of themes, recurs in nearly all relevant accounts, which indicates that ʿAlī's status and conduct at Ṣiffīn and afterwards was a controversial issue and therefore an important concern of the early (historical) tradition. ʿAlī's significance for the later development of Islamic law and doctrine as well as the formation of early Shīʿism in opposition to (as well as alongside) what later became Sunnī Islam was certainly an important factor here, as can generally be seen in much of the largely retrospective historiography of the *rāshidūn* period.

A secondary theme in the material for this period is the relationship between ʿAlī and Ibn ʿAbbās. The (actual or perceived) ties between the fourth caliph and his cousin were an important aspect in the negotiation of ʿAbbāsid–ʿAlid relations following the former's takeover in 132 H/749–50 CE. It is important to keep in mind here that our sources for early Islamic history were compiled in the early ʿAbbāsid period and shaped by this negotiation process as much as other factors.[2] It is thus telling that the historians present Ibn ʿAbbās as a close confidant of ʿAlī, particularly regarding the debates between ʿAlī/his agents and Khārijite rebels. The selected sources are unanimous in their portrayal of this relationship; the tensions between ʿAlids and ʿAbbāsids do not seem to have prompted the ʿAlid-leaning authors to depict Ibn ʿAbbās in a negative fashion vis-à-vis ʿAlī, for instance. In turn, the clearest indication of ʿAlī's superiority to Ibn ʿAbbās is found not in the works of Ibn Aʿtham or al-Yaʿqūbī, but in the *Taʾrīkh* of al-Ṭabarī, who, despite contemporary accusations to the contrary,[3] is not known for his strong Shīʿī tendencies.

The last theme is that of militant piety, which as noted is not limited to a particular period but is rather a constant in the depiction of literary Khārijism across time and space. The same pattern thus applies: the sources not only criticise the Khārijite interpretation of religious devotion, but also pass judgement on the pitfalls of excessive piety more generally. Because this motif was discussed at length in the preceding chapters, particularly Chapter Two, it will only occasionally feature in what follows.

Apologia for ʿAlī b. Abī Ṭālib

The main purpose of the reports that depict the disputes between ʿAlī and the Khawārij is to vindicate ʿAlī's acceptance of the arbitration, which in retrospect was considered to have caused his downfall. This is done by means of three different lines of argument. First, it is argued that ʿAlī initially refused to accept the call for arbitration because he saw through Muʿāwiya's ploy and that it was his own followers who coerced him into agreeing to the *taḥkīm* by threatening to desert him. Second, and somewhat at odds with the preceding argumentation, the legitimacy of arbitration in general is asserted on the basis of Qurʾānic evidence and Prophetic precedence. Third, the point is made that the caliph could not renege on his word and resume battle against his enemies after he had agreed to settle the conflict by arbitration. Furthermore, the Khārijite demand that he repent towards God for his sinful agreement to the arbitration is rejected with reference to ʿAlī's excellence in religion. In short, ʿAlī is portrayed as a victim of his own followers as well as the Syrians and subsequently excused from all allegations levelled against him.

Accusing the Caliph

In order to understand the justifications of ʿAlī's conduct, we must first briefly examine the accusations they were supposed to counter. In total, five Khārijite allegations against ʿAlī, which cover a wide spectrum of religious and socio-political issues, can be identified.

With the exception of Ibn Khayyāṭ's *Taʾrīkh*, the core sources examined for this chapter present ʿAlī's agreement to the arbitration as the chief Khārijite accusation against him because he thereby "gave men authority over the religion of God (*ḥakkama al-rijāl fī dīn allāh*)".[4] This issue is portrayed as the 'original sin' that gave rise to the Khawārij, encapsulated in their watchword *lā ḥukma illā li-llāh*. We shall see that this is also by far the most frequently cited reason for their opposition to ʿAlī, as well as to later Umayyad and ʿAbbāsid opponents. Accordingly, justifications for ʿAlī's agreement to the appointment of arbiters "over the religion of God" predominate, mostly in ʿAlī's debates with the Khawārij but also in the discussions with his often-hesitant followers in Kufa and elsewhere.

The second Khārijite accusation levelled against ʿAlī is his acceptance of the erasure of his title, *amīr al-muʾminīn*, from the arbitration document written at Ṣiffīn. Some of Muʿāwiya's followers had objected to ʿAlī's use of the epithet 'Commander of the Believers', maintaining that if they accepted him as such they would not fight him. ʿAlī's supporters presciently warn him not to drop the title lest he will never be able to assume it again, but he eventually agrees to have it struck from the arbitration agreement under pressure from Muʿāwiya and the Syrians.[5] This particular allegation must be considered in light of a corollary accusation, namely that ʿAlī gave in to the arbitration – and by extension agreed to have his title erased – because he doubted himself and his case. This the Khawārij interpret as doubting God and His provisions, which in turn is tantamount to unbelief (*kufr*).[6]

These two charges are the main arguments that the Khawārij are shown to employ in their confrontations with ʿAlī. Three further allegations are only preserved by individual author-compilers. To begin with, Ibn Aʿtham and al-Balādhurī preserve an account in which ʿAlī is accused of not taking prisoners or booty after the Battle of the Camel (which preceded Ṣiffīn), thereby depriving his supporters of their rightful share of the spoils.[7] Al-Yaʿqūbī's *Taʾrīkh* contains another two accusations: first, that ʿAlī failed to "strike us [the nascent Khārijites] with his sword until we return[ed] to God (*fa-lam yaḍribnā bi-sayfihi ḥatta nafiʾa ilā allāh*)"[8] when the future Khawārij initially agreed to the arbitration at Ṣiffīn. The second is decidedly Shīʿī: ʿAlī's status as *waṣī* ('legatee, inheritor') of the Prophet, so the Khārijites apparently argued, was forfeit when he agreed to the arbitration.[9]

Excusing the Caliph

Let us now turn to the counterarguments offered by ʿAlī and by Ibn ʿAbbās as caliphal envoy. The sources differ concerning the time and place of the first extended dispute between the Khārijites and these two main characters. It occurred, variously, when ʿAlī and his troops returned from Ṣiffīn; when the Khawārij had gone to Ḥarūrāʾ; when they had gone to Nahrawān; or at some point between going to Ḥarūrāʾ and leaving for Nahrawān. Three different categories of argument are utilised to legitimise ʿAlī's acceptance of the arbitration: religious, pragmatic and moral justifications.

Religious Justifications

The first category is specifically religious and based on (1) a selection of Qur'ān verses according to which God enjoined the believers to appoint judges from among themselves to settle an issue; and (2) on Prophetic precedence. In response to the first Khārijite accusation of granting authority over God's affairs to mere human beings, three verses are most commonly cited. These are Q 4:35 ('And if you fear dissension between them, appoint an arbiter from his people and an arbiter from her people'),[10] Q 5:95 ('judging in this two just men from among you')[11] and Q 3:23 ('Have you not seen those who were given a portion of the Scripture called to the Book of God, that it may judge between them?').[12]

Al-Balādhurī and Ibn Aʿtham also preserve accounts in which a combination of these verses is quoted. Al-Balādhurī's *Ansāb* contains three reports that address this line of argumentation; two display shared features. The third report paints quite a different picture and will be considered in more detail later. In the two that concern us here, Ibn ʿAbbās refers to Q 4:35 and 5:95 in order to justify ʿAlī's agreement to the arbitration.[13] He invokes these verses to prove the legitimacy of settling a conflict through arbitration and argues that if God allowed men to judge over comparatively petty issues like dissension between spouses or the unlawful killing of wild game, then adjudication in a serious matter like at Ṣiffīn, which was intended to avoid the shedding of Muslim blood, must surely be legitimate as well. His reasoning elegantly exculpates ʿAlī.[14]

In Ibn Aʿtham's account, Ibn ʿAbbās cites the same two verses at the end of a long discussion with an otherwise unknown Khārijite at Ḥarūrāʾ.[15] The exact details of this debate, or rather this monologue on the part of Ibn ʿAbbās, will be discussed below. For now, it is important to note that this time round the Khawārij are not wholly convinced by his argumentation and challenge him by asking whether he considers ʿAmr b. al-ʿĀṣ, Muʿāwiya's arbiter, a just man in the sense of Q 5:95. Ibn ʿAbbās counters by pointing out that ʿAmr was not appointed by ʿAlī but by Muʿāwiya. We can observe here a merging of two different justificatory categories. This is unusual and we will return to this issue in the following subsection on pragmatic justifications.

Recourse to the example of Muḥammad is another means by which ʿAlī is cleared from wrongdoing. For instance, Ibn Aʿtham's *Futūḥ* contains a rather long passage describing a debate between ʿAlī and the Khārijites at Nahrawān.[16] Here, ʿAlī does not refer to the Qur'ān in order to defend his acceptance of the arbitration. Instead, he argues that the Prophet had also appointed an arbiter to judge in a certain matter.[17] ʿAlī's conduct is hereby made legitimate, the Khārijite protest rendered void.

Another example of Muḥammad being used as a model for ʿAlī is found in response to the second Khārijite accusation against ʿAlī, the erasure of his title from the Ṣiffīn arbitration document. In this episode, the caliph is vindicated with reference to Muḥammad's conduct on the day of al-Ḥudaybiyya.[18] Specifically, the Khawārij are reminded that when the Muslims and the Meccans drew up the treaty of al-Ḥudaybiyya, Muḥammad's title 'Messenger of God' was dropped from the document.[19] In al-Balādhurī's versions, it is Ibn ʿAbbās who calls this incident to mind:

> The unbelievers (*al-mushrikūn*) said to the Messenger of God (ṣ) on the day of al-Ḥudaybiyya: 'If we knew that you are the Messenger of God we would not fight you.' The Messenger of God (ṣ) said: 'Erase [the title 'Messenger of God'], O ʿAlī, and write Muḥammad b. ʿAbdallāh.' And the Messenger of God is more excellent than ʿAlī.[20]

Ibn Aʿtham's *Futūḥ* refers to this incident in two different contexts: in his account of the composition of the arbitration agreement and then again during ʿAlī's discussions with the Khārijites at Nahrawān.[21] His rendering of this episode is the longest and most complex of the selected sources. It also emphasises most strongly the close connection between ʿAlī and the Prophet while underlining the wickedness of their opponents (Abū Sufyān at al-Ḥudaybiyya, his son Muʿāwiya and ʿAmr b. al-ʿĀṣ at Ṣiffīn). This was probably owing to Ibn Aʿtham's pro-ʿAlid stance, which is noticeable throughout his work.[22]

In recounting the Ḥudaybiyya episode during the process of writing the arbitration document, ʿAlī is shown to draw a direct line from the Prophet to himself. It is thereby implied that the believers – ʿAlī and his supporters – still confront the same opponents: enemies of God, of the Prophet and the Prophet's family.[23] By comparing Muʿāwiya and his followers to the Meccan unbelievers of Muḥammad's time, Ibn Aʿtham's work stresses the righteousness of ʿAlī as against the sinfulness of his opponents. In his rendering, ʿAlī informs those present that Muḥammad foresaw the caliph having to face "a day like this [al-Ḥudaybiyya]".[24] ʿAlī is thus acquitted of his conduct; because the Prophet had predicted it, it was fate, unalterable. Moreover, if the Prophet himself had had to give in to the Meccans and omit the title 'Messenger of God', what could ʿAlī possibly have done to prevent history from repeating itself?

This rationalisation of ʿAlī's agreement to erase his title is shown to persuade many of his opponents.[25] By adducing examples from the life of the

Prophet – here indeed a perfect template for ʿAlī's situation at Ṣiffīn – the legitimacy of ʿAlī's conduct appears unquestionable. Far from introducing an innovation or infringing God's divine provisions, it is instead demonstrated that he followed Prophetic precedence, which provides a "good example" (*uswa ḥasana*)[26] and sanctions his actions. Ibn Aʿtham in particular is keen to highlight this: in his version of ʿAlī's debate with the Khārijites at Nahrawān, the caliph relies exclusively on Muḥammad's *sunna* to illustrate the lawfulness of his conduct, and not once on the Qurʾān.[27]

Both al-Yaʿqūbī and Ibn Aʿtham also transmit reports that relate the hostility towards the Prophet and ʿAlī to hostility against pre-Islamic prophets.[28] Muḥammad and by association ʿAlī are here portrayed as links in a long chain of righteous and God-fearing men who were wronged by their opponents. Following this reading, resistance to ʿAlī can only have resulted from lack of judgement or from wickedness. Accordingly, those who were only misguided are shown to return to ʿAlī and the (religious, political, social) safety of the community, whereas the malevolent insist on their error and are consequently obliterated in battle.

Al-Yaʿqūbī's work is the only source that does not mention Ibn ʿAbbās in the confrontation with the Khawārij at all but ascribes the whole range of arguments to ʿAlī himself.[29] As alluded to above, he also preserves two Khārijite charges against ʿAlī that are not found in any of the other sources. The first of these is that ʿAlī should have used force to compel the Khārijites to reject the arbitration; the second articulates the concern that ʿAlī may have lost his status as *waṣī* when he accepted the adjudication.[30]

The caliph in al-Yaʿqūbī's narrative counters the first of these allegations with reference to the Qurʾān. He cites Q 2:195 ('and do not be cast into destruction by your own hands') to make the point that the Khārijites *in spe* were many at Ṣiffīn, whereas he and his house were only a few.[31] Along the lines of that specific verse, ʿAlī is shown to have been out of options, meaning that he gave in to their demands instead of risking himself and his small group of loyal followers.

The allegation that ʿAlī lost his status as *waṣī* betrays a distinctly Shīʿī concern and may well have been the result of proto-Shīʿī/pro-ʿAlid debates in the 'real world'. In consequence, ʿAlī is shown to refute this particular criticism with a seminally Shīʿī line of argument. He calls to mind Q 3:97 – 'And incumbent upon mankind unto God is the pilgrimage to the House, for whoever can find his way to it' – and then identifies himself as this 'House'.[32] It follows from this that whoever fails to perform the 'pilgrimage to ʿAlī' despite their ability to do so should be considered as falling short of the divine commandments. The Khārijites are guilty of this as well because of their abandonment of ʿAlī.[33] This accusation has a strong confessional tenor; it is unlikely to have been a concern contemporary with the early Khawārij. Nevertheless, it provides another piece of evidence for the proposition that stories of Khārijism serve a distinct narrative function beyond the surface account.

Pragmatic Justifications

The second category advances pragmatic arguments against Khārijite accusations. These are invoked almost exclusively by ʿAlī himself, not by Ibn ʿAbbās (except in Ibn Aʿtham's *Futūḥ*). The categories of argument identified in the material thus represent intersecting but distinct levels of discourse with a clear division of labour.

In this category, ʿAlī counters Khārijite protest against the arbitration with three main arguments. First, he maintains that he had to accept the adjudication because his own followers, among them the future Khārijites, forced him to agree. The accounts that detail this confrontation have the Khawārij literally threaten ʿAlī to kill him like they killed ʿUthmān. This accomplishes two things: it illustrates ʿAlī's blamelessness regarding the arbitration and it shifts responsibility for the murder of ʿUthmān away from ʿAlī to the Khawārij, who are thereby presented as rebels against legitimate rule at large. ʿUthmān's killers might have initially joined ʿAlī, but rather than acting as their leader he is shown to be at their mercy. This also explains why he was unable (as opposed to unwilling) to punish ʿUthmān's killers as Muʿāwiya had apparently demanded. Unlike in the case of the Khārijite demand, included in al-Yaʿqūbī's work, that ʿAlī should have forced them to repent and reject the suggested arbitration, there is no reference to Qurʾānic material here – ʿAlī appeals to common sense and pragmatic reasoning.

Second, ʿAlī repeatedly reminds the Khawārij that he had warned them of the treachery behind the call for arbitration.[34] In one of his discussions with them at Ḥarūrāʾ, ʿAlī says to their *imām* ʿAbdallāh b. al-Kawwāʾ: "Woe unto you, O Ibn al-Kawwāʾ! Did I not tell you that day when the *maṣāḥif* were raised how the Syrians intend to deceive you with them?"[35] Moreover, ʿAlī rebukes his critics for changing their minds concerning the *taḥkīm*: "You have let yourselves be enticed into the abandonment of this arbitration process that you yourselves initiated and asked for, while I abhorred it".[36]

The final argument responds to Khārijite objections to the conduct and decision of the arbiters. ʿAlī insists that he is not to blame for their transgressions. He reminds his opponents that he ordered the arbiters to judge by "what is in the Book of God" and to only "uphold what the Qurʾān has brought into being and prohibit what the Qurʾān put an end to".[37] He cannot be held responsible for them acting "in disagreement with the Book of God and follow[ing] their evil inclinations without guidance from God".[38]

This last point is discussed in more detail in an account preserved by al-Dīnawarī which details the debate between ʿAlī and ʿAbdallāh b. al-Kawwāʾ at Nahrawān. ʿAlī here overcomes his opponent by rational argument: when the Khārijite accuses the caliph of having chosen an unbeliever (*kāfir*) as arbiter, ʿAlī asks him at what point Abū Mūsā became an unbeliever – when ʿAlī sent him to the arbitration or when he made his ruling? Ibn al-Kawwāʾ confirms that Abū Mūsā became an unbeliever when he issued his judgement. ʿAlī then asks:

> Do you not think that I was a Muslim when I sent him out and that he became an unbeliever, according to what you say [yourself], after I sent him off? If the Prophet of God (ṣ) sent out one of the Muslims to some of the unbelievers in order to summon them to God, but he instead summoned them to something different, would you think that the Prophet of God is to be blamed for this?

When Ibn al-Kawwāʾ expectedly replies in the negative, ʿAlī concludes: "And I am not responsible for Abū Mūsā going astray."[39]

This account is noteworthy also in that the Khārijite *imām* does not seem to object to the arbitration itself but only to the choice of arbiter – the implication here being that ʿAlī chose Abū Mūsā himself! – and to ʿAlī's conduct after the decision had been announced. Contrary to this, most sources – including al-Dīnawarī's *Akhbār*[40] – claim that the Khārijite protest first occurred when the document stipulating the conditions of the adjudication had been drawn up and was read out to ʿAlī's followers. A few reports that similarly indicate a different chronology are scattered throughout the sources. Although insignificant at first glance, the question of when the protest occurred has consequences for the interpretation of why it occurred. Protest against the arbiters being allowed to make their decision based on sources other than the Qurʾān betrays religious concerns, whereas criticism of ʿAlī's choice of arbiter after the fact may indicate rather more pragmatic reasons for Khārijite objections. Deciding on one or the other is not a concern here, of course, but such issues of chronology are another reminder of why the positivist reconstruction of Khārijite history is a sensitive matter indeed.

The only example of Ibn ʿAbbās engaging in a disputation of a similar kind rather than invoking the Qurʾān or Prophetic *sunna* is found in Ibn Aʿtham's *Kitāb al-Futūḥ*. This discussion (really a monologue by Ibn ʿAbbās) is also the only example of Ibn ʿAbbās engaging in a detailed and eloquent verbal confrontation with the Khārijites – in all other reports, he is shown to defend ʿAlī against the rebels' accusations, but in a brief and stylised manner. Ibn Aʿtham's account is set at the time of the first Khārijite withdrawal to Ḥarūrāʾ.[41] ʿAlī sends Ibn ʿAbbās to the rebels to enquire about their concerns and intentions; Ibn ʿAbbās listens quietly to what their representative has to say[42] and then proceeds to ask him a number of questions designed to convince him of the truth of Ibn ʿAbbās' argument.

The length and detail of this particular debate are unique to Ibn Aʿtham. The form of this disputation resembles the conventions of *kalām* (dialectical reasoning),[43] elements of which can also be discerned in the above discussion between ʿAlī and Ibn al-Kawwāʾ as preserved by al-Dīnawarī, but which are much more noticeable in the following account. While *kalām* conventions are very varied and have undergone significant change over time, certain basic ingredients make up an early template roughly contemporaneous with the material studied here. For instance, these formalised debates rely on the construction of an opponent who has to be convinced of the truth of one's argument. In that sense, *kalām* can be understood as

> the resort to the adversarial employment of sophisticated dialectical techniques constellated around forms of dialogue in which an opponent's premises were critiqued through the process of drawing attention to perceived flaws and logical inconsistencies perceived inherent in them.[44]

This process, which is probably rooted in Syriac and Greek Christian theological disputation styles,[45] usually follows certain patterns that "invariably begin with a disjunctive question ('Do you believe X, yes or no?' or 'Do you believe X or Y?')" and then systematically refute the opponent or demonstrate that their opposition was based on a misunderstanding because their opinion actually agrees with what the questioner holds true.[46] Proofs are retroactive, meaning that if an argument is put forward as proof and subsequently falsified, the very thing it was intended to prove is also nullified. These features, but above all the "function of defensive apologia" that characterises *kalām*,[47] are clearly observable in the following debate.

Ibn ʿAbbās begins by asking his opponent whom the *dār al-Islām* belongs to and who created it. The Khārijite responds that it belongs to God and that He created it through His prophets and the believers. Ibn ʿAbbās confirms this and then inquires whether Muḥammad had ordered the affairs of the *umma*, taught the right beliefs and generally acted like the prophets before him when he established the *dār al-Islām*. The Khārijite affirms that Muḥammad succeeded in this, whereupon Ibn ʿAbbās asks whether Muḥammad has died. The rebel confirms again. Ibn ʿAbbās follows up with the question of whether the Prophet had left the *dār al-Islām* in perfect condition when he died, which the

Khārijite asserts he did. The next question addresses the issue of Muḥammad's successors: was there anyone after him who looked after the *dār al-Islām*? The rebel answers that, indeed, the Companions, the *ahl al-bayt*, the *waṣī*[48] and the Successors tended the *umma* after Muḥammad. Finally, Ibn ʿAbbās asks whether the *dār al-Islām* is still in the complete condition that the Prophet left it in, which the Khārijite denies. When asked whether the Prophet's successors or his *umma* were responsible for this, the rebel names the *umma*.

At this point, the direction of Ibn ʿAbbās' questioning becomes clear. He wants to know whether the Khārijite belongs to the successors or the *umma*, and when the rebel says he belongs to the *umma*, Ibn ʿAbbās rejoins: "Tell me now, how do you hope to escape the Fire as long as you belong to a community that destroyed the realm of God and the realm of His Prophet?"[49] The Khārijite's mind is boggled. He asks Ibn ʿAbbās what to do to escape hell, whereupon he is told to help rebuild what the *umma* has destroyed. The (now former?) Khārijite must first learn who destroyed the *dār al-Islām*, however, and declare himself their enemy while associating with those who want it to thrive. The rebel responds that he does not know anyone who could maintain the *umma* except ʿAlī, if only he had not appointed Abū Mūsā.

Ibn ʿAbbās now points to examples of arbitration in the Qurʾān, specifically the verses referred to above, Q 4:35 ('appoint an arbiter from his people and an arbiter from her people') and Q 5:95 ('judging in this two just men from among you'). There is thus a merging of categories and lines of argument here that is noteworthy because it does not happen often in the material examined. It does, however, represent a classic feature of *kalām*-style debates, which follow up rational arguments with those "from authority", i.e. the Qurʾān or *ḥadīth*, as confirmation of the former.[50] It is also possible that Ibn ʿAbbās' reference to the Qurʾān at this point is an interpolation – as noted, he is usually shown to rely on the Qurʾān and Muḥammad's *sunna* in his discussions with the Khārijites, but the narrative would actually flow more smoothly if this particular section was omitted.

In response to Ibn ʿAbbās' Qurʾānic quotes, the Khawārij (now as a collective, no longer as a single dialogue 'partner') challenge his choice of verses, particularly the latter one, arguing that ʿAmr b. al-ʿĀṣ cannot be called just as he had fought the Prophet and brought affliction upon the *umma* after Muḥammad's death. Ibn ʿAbbās' reply to this realigns with the narrative before the Qurʾānic interjection: he points out that ʿAmr was Muʿāwiya's arbiter, not ʿAlī's, and that ʿAlī had actually wanted to send Ibn ʿAbbās. The Khawārij, however, had rejected this choice in favour of Abū Mūsā, who was subsequently deceived by ʿAmr. Ibn ʿAbbās concludes: "So fear your Lord and return to your former obedience to the *amīr al-muʾminīn*".[51]

None of the other sources except al-Dīnawarī preserves an account even remotely similar in content. It serves to illustrate several points: ʿAlī's trust in Ibn ʿAbbās; Ibn ʿAbbās' rhetorical brilliance; the rebels' responsibility for the outcome of the arbitration meeting; their involvement in the 'destruction' of the *umma* and thus their flawed argumentation – it is in fact them who are to be blamed for the whole arbitration affair and its ramifications, not ʿAlī. What also becomes apparent again is that the narratives of Khārijite origins are not primarily concerned with the rebels themselves. Ibn Aʿtham's account does not discuss Khārijite counterarguments at all but devotes five pages to Ibn ʿAbbās' reasoning. The Khārijite representative is reduced to single-sentence replies and eventually embraces Ibn ʿAbbās' viewpoint without further ado. In fact, the narrative substance of Ibn ʿAbbās' opponent is so feeble that he may as well not be present at all – neither Ibn ʿAbbās nor the reader would notice. The 'debate' is essentially a soliloquy. Here as elsewhere, the Khawārij serve as mouthpieces designed to voice (potential) accusations against ʿAlī so that they can be refuted. It is very rare indeed that we come across a report that has the Khārijites challenge the justifications of ʿAlī's conduct and also allows them to have the final word.[52]

Before continuing with the third category of argument, let us briefly address the tension between the first two categories (religious and pragmatic justifications). There appears to be a rough distinction between the exonerations of ʿAlī attributed to Ibn ʿAbbās and those associated with the caliph himself. Ibn ʿAbbās usually argues on the basis of the Qurʾān and other religious and moral considerations. ʿAlī, on the other hand, is predominantly shown to dispute with his opponents on the basis of pragmatic arguments – he was forced to accept the arbitration, and the arbiters did not obey his command to judge by the Qurʾān. In Ibn Aʿtham's work, he is also shown to rely heavily on Prophetic precedence.

These two lines of argument do not contradict each other, but they indicate a multi-tiered debate. Maintaining that ʿAlī was forced to accept the arbitration is quite different from stressing the religious legitimacy of the adjudication. Accordingly, the two are almost never encountered in the same justificatory passage. Exceptions are few. Al-Yaʿqūbī's *Taʾrīkh* attributes all refutations of Khārijite accusations to ʿAlī himself, thereby relegating Ibn ʿAbbās to the status of a mere mouthpiece and stripping him of the rhetorical skills that most sources credit him with.[53] Al-Dīnawarī does not mention Ibn ʿAbbās in the context of debates with the Khawārij, not even as ʿAlī's mouthpiece. Instead, his work has ʿAlī himself negotiate with the Khawārij at Ḥarūrāʾ and Nahrawān. The legitimisation of ʿAlī's conduct in al-Dīnawarī's *Akhbār* is thus squarely based on pragmatism and analogy, as we saw above in the discussion between ʿAlī and Ibn al-Kawwāʾ. ʿAlī does refer to certain verses from the Qurʾān in that particular episode (though not elsewhere in the *Akhbār*'s depiction of his conflict with the Khawārij), but they do not serve to directly defend the lawfulness of arbitration,[54] unlike the verses invoked by Ibn ʿAbbās in other sources. The exclusion of Ibn ʿAbbās and thus of the religious category of justification from al-Dīnawarī's material suggests that these were pre-formed thematic units belonging to different, though at times overlapping, tiers in the overall discursive structure of ʿAlī's apologia. That al-Dīnawarī chose the pragmatic category fits the tenor of his work, which appears to be "free from overtly religious sentiment".[55]

This division of arguments is further supported by the 'odd' account in al-Balādhurī's *Ansāb* referred to above in the section on religious justifications.[56] The report contains the Qurʾān verses usually invoked by Ibn ʿAbbās to sanction arbitration in general and the adjudication at Ṣiffīn in particular; it is also the only one to include Q 3:23 ('Have you not seen those who were given a portion of the Scripture called to the Book of God, that it may judge between them?') in the list. However, here ʿAlī himself argues in a twist of the usual pattern that if he had refused to consent to the arbitration, those who urged him to accept it might have employed these very verses *against* him.[57] Furthermore, Ibn ʿAbbās is shown to argue elsewhere that if arbitration is allowed in petty affairs, then it is also allowed in important matters to avoid bloodshed among Muslims.[58] By contrast, the 'odd' report preserved by al-Balādhurī classifies this particular rationalisation as a potential Khārijite argument *against* ʿAlī's initial rejection of the arbitration.[59]

We may have two originally distinct lines of reasoning here that were combined at some point. The account transmitted in al-Balādhurī's *Ansāb* belongs to the pragmatic category due to its emphasis on ʿAlī being forced into agreement to the arbitration. The included verses may represent a secondary stage, but it is also possible that this is an earlier, not yet systematised account. The 'original' context is uncertain, in any case – the verses clearly support arbitration as a mediation mechanism, but which side they were originally supposed to sustain is near impossible to work out. What this does illustrate is the already-mentioned mobility of narrative content as well as the complexities of the transmission and compilation/composition process, which combine into a vexing problem for the historian of early Islam.

Moral Justifications

The third category of argument is based on moral considerations and can be dealt with rather briefly. It is not directly connected to the legitimation of the arbitration, but rather addresses ʿAlī's refusal to recommence fighting while the arbiters were still deliberating. The early historical tradition preserves several reports in which (mostly anonymous) Khārijites call on ʿAlī to resume hostilities against the common Syrian enemy. ʿAlī rejects their summons because he cannot break his word: "I have granted them [the Syrians] a contract for a [certain] period, and fighting them is not lawful until this period comes to an end."[60] Two verses from the Qurʾān are quoted to legitimise this decision (Q 5:1 and 16:91), both of which urge the believers to fulfil the covenants they agree to.[61] These accounts thus portray ʿAlī as following God's law while also asserting his superior morals against opponents who do not care to honour the accord they themselves insisted on.

Along similar lines, we saw above that ʿAlī is accused of failing to take prisoners and spoils after the Battle of the Camel.[62] Al-Balādhurī and Ibn Aʿtham present rather different versions of this episode. In al-Balādhurī's account, Ibn ʿAbbās offers a poignant counterargument: he asks the Khārijites whether they had seriously intended to take prisoner "your mother ʿĀʾisha bt. Abī Bakr al-Ṣiddīq",[63] wife of Muḥammad and daughter of the revered first caliph. Ibn ʿAbbās' phrasing underlines the enormity of this prospect and puts the rebels on the spot, so it is not surprising that the Khawārij quickly backpedal and agree with him.

In Ibn Aʿtham's rendering, it is ʿAlī himself who argues with the Khārijites. He justifies his decision to prohibit the taking of prisoners from among the Basran women and children by arguing that the women had not fought him, while the children had been born into Islam and hence could not be enslaved. He then adduces Prophetic *sunna* to further validate his actions, reminding the Khawārij of Muḥammad's conquest of Mecca. The Prophet also had not taken the Meccan women and children prisoner but had shown mercy: "So if the Prophet bestowed his favour on the polytheists, do not be surprised that I bestowed my favour on the believers."[64]

Opposition to ʿAlī is thus again shown to be unreasonable; the caliph himself is portrayed as an image of steadfast morality even in times of conflict. The reference to the *sunna* of the Prophet further bolsters ʿAlī's claim to righteous conduct, while the respect Ibn ʿAbbās and by implication ʿAlī show for ʿĀʾisha contradicts the unfavourable accounts of outright enmity between them.[65]

Such deliberations also seek to underline ʿAlī's religious eminence. The Khārijite demand to recommence fighting is most often accompanied by requests that the caliph repent for his sins, i.e. his agreement to the arbitration. Only then would the Khārijites be willing to reconcile. They give the same ultimatum at Nahrawān when ʿAlī informs them of his decision to fight the Syrians once more following the verdict of the arbiters. Instead of joining him right away, the Khawārij require the caliph to repent first. Each time, ʿAlī refuses to heed them:

> After my *jihād* with the Messenger of God and my faith should I confess unbelief against myself? 'Then I should go astray and not be of the rightly guided' (Q 6:56, *ḍalaltu idhan wa-mā ana min al-muhtadīn*).[66]

ʿAlī's religious credentials elevate him above the insolent Khārijites. As ʿAlī is one of the earliest converts to Islam, as well as son-in-law, cousin and close confidant of the Prophet, the rebels' demands for his repentance appear ludicrous.

Such narratives contribute to the depiction of the Khawārij as transgressors who have been led astray by "the devil and their evil inclinations".[67] ʿAlī likens them to sheep without a shepherd who have lost their way, which echoes Q 21:78 ('And David and Solomon, when they gave judgement concerning the field, when the people's sheep had strayed and browsed therein by night'). And further: "You separated from me after you pledged allegiance to me . . ., you broke your oaths and exhausted your faith."[68] In light of such severe offences, the Khārijite claim that ʿAlī is a sinner can easily be dismissed as unfounded ramblings. Ibn Aʿtham's rendering of Khārijite origins in particular goes to great lengths to assert ʿAlī's superiority in faith and character. More than any other author-compiler, he accentuates the caliph's impeccable faith, closeness with the Prophet and prudence in political and religious matters. Let us look at two examples.

Ibn Aʿtham's section on the composition of the arbitration agreement at Ṣiffīn is frequently interrupted by speeches that praise ʿAlī's excellence, harshly condemn the Syrians and on one occasion mention a Prophetic prediction according to which ʿAlī would have to experience his own "day of al-Ḥudaybiyya".[69] Even the rebels themselves are portrayed as conceding ʿAlī's superiority, as during their dispute with the caliph at Ḥarūrāʾ. When ʿAlī and the Khārijite *imām* Ibn al-Kawwāʾ finally meet, one of ʿAlī's men tells the rebel to let the more truthful of the two speak first. According to the logic of the narrative, Ibn al-Kawwāʾ remains silent and yields to ʿAlī.[70]

In the second example, ʿAlī is depicted as the recipient of divine knowledge. On several occasions, he is shown to utter predictions such as the exact number of Khārijites that would escape the massacre at Nahrawān,[71] how many of his own supporters would be killed in the course of this battle[72] and his own death by the hands of a man from the tribe of Murād (i.e., Ibn Muljam al-Murādī).[73] Needless to say, everything he foretells comes to pass exactly as predicted.

That it is the Khārijites who have gone astray is further emphasised in an account included in al-Balādhurī's *Ansāb*. The setting is one of ʿAlī's disputes with the Khawārij at Nahrawān, where he is confronted with their call to repentance. His response draws not only on his own religious eminence, but also on the divine guidance his community enjoys:

> God forbid that I should have doubted in matters of religion (*irtabtu*) since I became a Muslim or erred since I was rightly guided. Rather, *through us God guided you on the right path* away from error and saved you from unbelief and protected you from ignorance (*bal bi-nā hadākum allāh min al-ḍalāla wa-instanqadhakum min al-kufr wa-ʿaṣamakum min al-jahāla*).[74]

Rebellion against ʿAlī is thereby cast as rebellion against God. By abandoning ʿAlī, the Khawārij abandon their only hope of right guidance and so ultimately their chance for salvation. This is a bold claim, but it is left undisputed by the Khārijites we encounter in these stories. This is unexpected seeing as they were also remembered as insisting on the necessity of physically separating from ʿAlī – to perform a *hijra* – rather than adopting a quietist stance. We can best make sense of this silence by regarding the main purpose of literary Khārijism as lying outside of itself. As the focus here is on ʿAlī, any response on their part is extraneous.

The Battle of Nahrawān

Now that the legitimacy of ʿAlī's conduct at Ṣiffīn as well as his religious and moral eminence have been established, the sources turn to the massacre at Nahrawān. Almost all Khārijite fighters were slain by ʿAlī's troops on that occasion, to the extent that, of the 3,000–4,000 rebels, not more than ten survived unharmed. ʿAlī, on the other hand, is said to have lost no more than approximately ten men,[75] this presumably another example of "the obvious pleasure which the early tradents took in the construction of parallels".[76] This event appears to have weighed heavily on the early community and so required justification,[77] not least because both Companions and known ascetics were said to have perished on the Khārijite side. ʿAlī may have proved superior in terms of military strength, but the outcome seems to have been a "pyrrhic victory" in some ways.[78] Significant space is dedicated to ʿAlī's treatment of the Khawārij and particular attention is paid to his reconciliation efforts, which the Khawārij lamentably rejected to their own detriment. ʿAlī is so exculpated from the ensuing carnage.

As we have seen already, the caliph goes to great lengths to persuade the Khārijites of the error of their ways. The same applies to the confrontation at Nahrawān: there are numerous accounts of such debates featuring ʿAlī, either in person or through the medium of letters and messengers. The content largely follows familiar patterns. ʿAlī reminds the rebels of their oath to him; he admonishes them with recourse to the Qurʾān (e.g., Q 3:105: 'And do not be like those who separated and disputed after clear proofs had come to them') and summons them to "fear of God, goodness (*al-birr*) and the return to what is right".[79] The selected sources are generally keen to convey that ʿAlī is highly reluctant to use force against the rebels. Al-Balādhurī's *Ansāb* in particular contains many accounts according to which ʿAlī was initially prepared to leave the Khārijites to their own devices. Already at Ḥarūrāʾ, he told his followers that he would send the dissidents on their merry way and leave them be as long as they did not behave unlawfully:

> We do not deny them [their share of] the tribute and we do not prevent them from entering the mosques and we do not provoke them *as long as* they do not shed blood and do not pursue what is prohibited.[80]

He also prohibited violence against the Khārijites "until they originate an innovation".[81]

Despite his aversion to armed conflict, however, ʿAlī is eventually forced to take action against them. The sources locate the reason for this in the rebels' vicious assaults on non-Khārijites, especially the cruel killing of ʿAbdallāh b. Khabbāb discussed in Chapter Two. Even here, ʿAlī is shown to react with restraint by requesting that only the murderers of Ibn Khabbāb be handed over to him.[82] His supporters, however, incensed by the atrocities committed by the dissidents, insist that he engage all of the Khārijites first before going to Syria to fight Muʿāwiya.[83] His commensurate approach is thus shown to be doomed to fail due to Khārijite barbarity and his men's obstinacy alike: "He [ʿAlī] did not cease to warn and summon them [the Khārijites], but when he saw no signs of submission in them . . . he prepared the people for war."[84]

Having resigned himself to battle, ʿAlī nevertheless orders his troops not to commence fighting but to wait for the Khārijites to attack first.[85] He appoints commanders over the various units of his army – another example of the ubiquity of the 'battle order' *topos* discussed in Chapter One – and then makes a last attempt to prevent Muslim bloodshed by offering the rebels refuge under his banner of safe-conduct (*ghāyat al-amn*).[86] Some of them finally repent and return to ʿAlī. The remaining Khārijites chant their battle cry, "*lā ḥukma illā li-llāh,* 'even though the polytheists may detest it!' [Q 9:33]", then charge against ʿAlī's troops and thereby bury his hopes for a peaceful resolution.[87]

As in the case of Ṣiffīn, ʿAlī's conduct is explained, legitimised and thus vindicated by shifting responsibility for the events in question from him to the Khawārij, whose evil deeds require him to take action, as well as to his supporters, whose refusal to fight Muʿāwiya until the Khārijite threat has been dealt with forces his hand. ʿAlī's reputation thus emerges largely unscathed from the sources' portrayal of this messy conflict. The reports of his conduct and decisions at Ṣiffīn and at Nahrawān became the basis for the Islamic law of war and rebellion as it developed over the course of the first three centuries, just as he developed into a pivotal figure for Islamic law and doctrine more generally.[88] The shape of these reports, the different levels of argument identified, the focus on ʿAlī vis-à-vis the near silencing of his opponents – all this indicates the simultaneous formation and mutual influence of the legal discourse and the early historical tradition regarding these issues. We thus learn much about early Islamic scholarly discourse, but little about historical Khārijism.

ʿAlids and ʿAbbāsids

The first section of this chapter focused on the narrative role of Khārijism in relation to ʿAlī and concluded that it serves an apologetic purpose. The second most prominent actor in the confrontation between ʿAlī and the Khawārij is ʿAbdallāh b. ʿAbbās, cousin to both the Prophet and ʿAlī and an important ʿAbbāsid ancestor. That he plays a part in the accounts of Khārijite origins may not be surprising, but the details and specific function of his appearance in these reports deserve a closer examination, not least because the familial and political ties between Ibn ʿAbbās and ʿAlī mattered in terms of later ʿAlid-ʿAbbāsid relations, both actual and literary.[89] Due to their familial connection, Ibn ʿAbbās may well have picked ʿAlī's side, but there is also no denying that Ibn ʿAbbās serves a particular role in early Islamic historiography that is difficult to reconcile with his historical figure: his involvement appears "disproportionate relative to the more likely involvement of other leaders in the early period".[90] The many debates and question-answer-sessions attributed to Ibn ʿAbbās[91] further underline that he (and Muʿāwiya) functioned "not just as real actors in Islamic history, but as detached observers who assess the course of this history and debate its future".[92]

Overall, Ibn ʿAbbās is cast as ʿAlī's adviser, confidant and loyal agent, although this role does not extend to the battlefield.[93] He first enters the stage at an early point of ʿAlī's confrontation with the future Khārijites. Al-Ashʿath b. Qays and his companions have just forced ʿAlī to accept the armistice requested by Muʿāwiya and agree to arbitration. Now the difficult task of choosing an arbiter for ʿAlī's side arises. The sources are divided as to whether al-Ashʿath and the *qurrāʾ* had already decided upon Abū Mūsā before ʿAlī made his wishes known or whether "they"[94] insisted on Abū Mūsā in reaction to ʿAlī's choice of arbiter, but they are unanimous in their assertion that ʿAlī wanted Ibn ʿAbbās to represent him.[95]

Much seems to have been at stake for ʿAlī in this confrontation with Muʿāwiya, even if the sources do not provide detailed information on the precise subject matter of the arbitration. His choice of Ibn ʿAbbās as arbiter therefore emphasises the close ties of kinship and trust between the cousins while attesting to Ibn ʿAbbās' aptitude for such a difficult task. This in turn underlines the latter's standing as a scholar and religious authority. Ibn Aʿtham's *Futūḥ* in particular has ʿAlī offer high praise for his relative and his incorruptible character, which is entirely uninterested in earthly pleasures.[96] When ʿAlī's opponents within his own camp protest against his choice of Ibn ʿAbbās, they do so not because they think him incapable, but because of his closeness with ʿAlī: "By God, we do not distinguish between you and Ibn ʿAbbās".[97] Ibn ʿAbbās' complete loyalty to the caliph is established to the extent that ʿAlī's supporters/opponents accuse him of trying to "be the judge yourself".[98]

We next encounter Ibn ʿAbbās as part of Abū Mūsā's entourage, deployed by ʿAlī to accompany the arbitrator to the agreed meeting place. ʿAlī sent Ibn ʿAbbās to lead the men in prayer and see to their affairs.[99] This was a prestigious assignment; these accounts hence reinforce the high regard in which ʿAlī held Ibn ʿAbbās. Indeed, the arbitration would have had a more favourable outcome for ʿAlī if Ibn ʿAbbās had been in charge of the negotiations:

> Ibn ʿAbbās said, 'God damn the decision [*raʾy*] of Abū Mūsā! I warned him and told him to be circumspect, but he took no heed.' And Abū Mūsā used to say about ʿAmr b. al-ʿĀṣ: 'Ibn ʿAbbās warned me of the treachery of the evildoer [*fāsiq*], but I trusted him and did not imagine that he would put anything above sincere advice to his community.'[100]

The most pronounced part of Ibn ʿAbbās' role in the conflict between ʿAlī and the Khārijites is that of emissary to the rebels. Some reports feature envoys other than Ibn ʿAbbās, but these hardly have a speaking part – here it is mostly ʿAlī who debates with the Khawārij. These envoys also fail in their efforts to reconcile the dissidents.[101] The only exception here is ʿAlī's emissary Ṣaʿṣaʿa b. Ṣūḥān, but he is shown to have shared the task with Ibn ʿAbbās and they are only successful after ʿAlī himself gets involved.[102]

As discussed, Ibn ʿAbbās is the main proponent of the religious justifications employed to justify ʿAlī's acceptance of the fateful arbitration, utilising those verses of the Qurʾān that provide precedence for God's transfer of His prerogative of judgement to human beings. Apart from ʿAlī himself, he is the only protagonist capable of persuading some Khawārij to return to the caliph. The early historical tradition here emphasises the close relationship between Ibn ʿAbbās and ʿAlī by casting the former in the role of the caliph's most committed and effective confidant. At the same time, it stresses Ibn ʿAbbās' eloquence and persuasiveness, characteristics that fit his reputation as a master of oratory and religious learning. A similar tendency can be observed regarding Ibn ʿAbbās' father – his good relationship with ʿAlī is "a well-known theme" in Islamic historiography.[103]

However, there is a clear hierarchy in the relationship between the caliph and his cousin. ʿAlī's superiority is asserted in all of his interactions with Ibn ʿAbbās in the context of their dealings with the Khārijites. This is done by contrasting Ibn ʿAbbās' failure to reconcile the rebels with ʿAlī's success in doing so[104] or by having ʿAlī rebuke Ibn ʿAbbās.[105] The second, explicit form of confirming ʿAlī's supremacy over Ibn ʿAbbās is rare, however, and found exclusively in a report transmitted in al-Ṭabarī's *Taʾrīkh* on the authority of Abū Mikhnaf, who had strong ʿAlid sympathies.[106] The setting is ʿAlī's return to Kufa from Ṣiffīn, whereupon the Khārijites abandon him. Ibn ʿAbbās is sent to them but told to wait for ʿAlī's arrival at Ḥarūrāʾ before engaging the Khārijites in debate. Ibn ʿAbbās disobeys ʿAlī's command and consequently fails to convince the dissidents to return. ʿAlī (mildly) reprimands him for defying his orders and then proceeds to debate them himself. As the logic of this story again dictates, his own efforts are crowned with success.

Otherwise, however, there is no serious disagreement between the two. On the contrary, the report asserts that Ibn ʿAbbās only disobeyed ʿAlī because he was so eager to counter the rebels' arguments and clear ʿAlī of their allegations.[107] Even this report therefore affirms that ʿAlī and Ibn ʿAbbās were intimate friends and allies. Their relationship as portrayed here thus qualifies Lassner's observation that ʿAbbāsid-era historiography generally reflects the dynasty's desire to legitimise their claims to power by underlining their superiority over the ʿAlids.[108] While this pattern can be observed with regard to some later ʿAlids and ʿAbbāsids,[109] in their ancestors' case the picture is more complex.

Conclusions

The present chapter discussed narratives of Khārijism during ʿAlī's reign. Little could be discerned regarding the Khawārij themselves, however. The analysis suggests that this is due to the fact that the sources were mainly concerned with Khārijites as a narrative backdrop against which to discuss other actors and issues, while Khārijism as a historical phenomenon appears as of minor interest.

Several factors contribute to the impalpability of literary Khārijism and support the notion that it was chiefly used as a discussion device. For instance, as Chapter One showed, there is some confusion over who actually belonged to the Khārijites, who repented and rejoined ʿAlī at Ḥarūrāʾ, who reconciled with the caliph before the Battle of Nahrawān, and so forth. The same applies to information concerning the precise sequence of events, the dates, places or battle positions featured in the accounts of Khārijite origins. Moreover, the reports abound with *topoi* and *schemata*, which call into question the historicity of the information thus conveyed. Khārijite militant piety is a prime example.

Another contributing factor is the very limited space that the sources concede to Khārijite arguments, responses and motives in comparison with the much more extensive and detailed narratives depicting the thought and conduct of their opponents. Ibn ʿAbbās' *kalām*-style debate with Khārijites at Ḥarūrāʾ is a perfect example of this tendency – his discussion partner is essentially rendered mute, which, while in this particular case not an unusual feature because of the conventions of *kalām*, is nevertheless representative of the overall picture. That this is a deliberate technique is thrown into even sharper relief when we look at Ibāḍī depictions of the debates before the Battle of Nahrawān: here, the Khārijites do argue back, eloquently so, to the extent that some narratives have ʿAlī concede all of their points.[110]

The analysis uncovered three major recurring themes in the narratives of Khārijite origins, two of which were discussed in detail while the third – piety – was the subject of Chapter Two and thus considered only peripherally.

This chapter has argued that ʿAlī's conduct from Ṣiffīn to Nahrawān represents the major concern of the relevant accounts. The narrative function of Khārijism in the disputes between ʿAlī/Ibn ʿAbbās and the dissidents is to provide an apologia for ʿAlī through the invocation, discussion and subsequent dismissal of potential accusations. Three categories of argument were identified:

i. ʿAlī's eventual acceptance of the adjudication is justified on religious grounds, especially with recourse to those Qurʾān verses that call on the believers to appoint judges to settle disputes. The accusation of having forgone his title of *amīr al-muʾminīn* in the arbitration document is countered with reference to Prophetic precedence at al-Ḥudaybiyya, when the Prophet had his title erased from the peace agreement between Muslims and Meccans. Religious argumentation based on the Qurʾān is almost exclusively evoked by Ibn ʿAbbās; ʿAlī himself argues on the basis of pragmatic considerations and Prophetic precedence.
ii. Complementary to religious vindication, ʿAlī is relieved of all responsibility for the arbitration itself on the basis of pragmatic reasoning.

Various different actors (al-Ashʿath b. Qays, the *qurrāʾ*, 'the people', the future Khārijites) are blamed for forcing both the adjudication and the particular arbiter (Abū Mūsā) on him despite his warnings against Syrian treachery. The sources also point to the general disunity in his camp and his followers' recalcitrance to explain the caliph's actions.

iii. Our historians also emphasise ʿAlī's moral excellence and Islamic credentials in order to repudiate Khārijite accusations that he committed a sin when he agreed to the arbitration. His probity and righteousness, it is argued, would have prevented him from engaging in sinful conduct. These laudable aspects of his character are then contrasted with the rebels' own lack of morality.

A similarly vindicatory tenor resounds in the reports of the Battle of Nahrawān. The sources affirm that ʿAlī cannot be blamed for the slaughter of his former followers at Nahrawān. He tried valiantly to bring about a peaceful solution, but the Khārijites' murderous conduct towards non-Khārijite Muslims and the pressure his own supporters exerted on him to take action against the rebels left him no choice.

The sources present ʿAlī and Ibn ʿAbbās as very convincing negotiators. As noted, they hardly ever record Khārijite responses to their opponents during these verbal confrontations. Instead, tacit (dis)approval is communicated through their reactions. Khārijite recognition of the validity of ʿAlī's/Ibn ʿAbbās' arguments, for example, is expressed in their return to ʿAlī's camp.[111] Indeed, with three exceptions,[112] the Khawārij do not argue their point at all beyond the reiteration of their accusations against ʿAlī and their demand for his repentance. A passage in Ibn Aʿtham's *Futūḥ* even states that some Khawārij acknowledged ʿAlī's power of persuasion and therefore refused to listen to his arguments at Nahrawān, worried that he would be able to confound them the way he had shaken the faith of the rebels at Ḥarūrāʾ.[113] This further supports the storytelling aspect of these accounts, as does a closer look at the allegations ʿAlī is confronted with.

Khārijite rhetoric (as well as ʿAlī's response to it) is not particular to this specific conflict. In al-Balādhurī's rendition of the murder of ʿUthmān, for instance, the rebels demand that he repent and ask God for forgiveness for his sins. ʿUthmān in turn orders them to fear God and return to the truth and His Book.[114] We saw above that this is standard early Islamic religio-political language.[115] Similarly, al-Ḥasan b. ʿAlī faces severe criticism from his own *shīʿa* for his decision to surrender to Muʿāwiya. His supporters here take up the role previously held by the Khārijites and question his decisions and intentions.[116] This conflict is presented in analogous terms to ʿAlī's troubles with the Khawārij, from accusations down to justificatory speeches and Qur ʾān citations intended to legitimise the peace agreement between al-Ḥasan and Mu ʿāwiya.[117] The parallels between al-Ḥasan and his father are pointed out by the Khārijites themselves, who accuse al-Ḥasan of having become "an unbeliever like your father".[118]

In short, Khārijite accusations appear as stock motifs that can be made to fit various contexts. This is evident particularly when contrasted with the portrayal of other opponents of ʿAlī. The confrontations between ʿAlī's messengers and Mu ʿāwiya at Ṣiffīn, for instance, are markedly different. Mu ʿāwiya defends his opposition to ʿAlī eloquently and responds at length to the charges brought against him by the envoys; he is also not persuaded by their argumentation.[119] On the other hand, ʿAlī or Ibn ʿAbbās almost always have the last word in their debates with the Khārijites.[120] The Khawārij are thus reduced to the role of supporting actors whose purpose consists in cueing the lead actor to deliver his performance. ʿAlī's supporters sometimes serve a similar function: by asking about the Khārijites, they operate as triggers for ʿAlī to expound on the evils of Khārijism and militant piety more generally.[121]

The relationship between ʿAlī and ʿAbdallāh b. ʿAbbās is a secondary concern of the historians. With the exception of Ibn Khayyāṭ, all authors depict Ibn ʿAbbās as ʿAlī's closest confidant, his most important envoy and the only one apart from ʿAlī himself who successfully argues with the rebels. Nevertheless, a clear hierarchy is established between them; al-Ya ʿqūbī's work most clearly relegates Ibn ʿAbbās to a supporting character as only ʿAlī is cast as an active agent in the debates with the Khawārij. Overall, however, the sources are intent on underlining the close relationship between the caliph and Ibn ʿAbbās.

Much has been said on the characterisation and narrative function of literary Khārijism. In closing, let us turn to the main protagonist of this chapter, ʿAlī. Despite the concerted effort that has gone into justifying his actions, it is difficult to avoid the impression that he lacked strength and assertiveness. From the call to arbitration onward, he appears strangely cut off from the centre of action – he reacts rather than acts. His own followers are able to force him to do their bidding, and the quick and unanimous decision for ʿAmr b. al-ʿĀṣ as arbiter on Mu ʿāwiya's side only serves to stress the disunity in the caliph's camp. Later on, when ʿAlī intends to engage the Syrians, he is shown to be held back both by his followers, who are unwilling to fight, and by the Khārijites, whose activities lead the Iraqis to insist on ʿAlī engaging them first. While this frees him from all responsibility for the arbitration itself as well as its ramifications, this depiction also gives the appearance of weakness.

As already noted by El-Hibri,[122] there is also a certain irony[123] in the reports that describe ʿAlī's demand for the murderers of ʿAbdallāh b. Khabbāb to be handed over to him. The Khārijites refuse to reveal and deliver the murderers, stating that "we all killed him".[124] This episode bears a strong resemblance to the exchange between ʿAlī and envoys sent by Muʿāwiya to demand that the killers of ʿUthmān be held responsible for their crime and/or handed over to Muʿāwiya.[125] ʿAlī's failure to avenge the death of his predecessor is thus turned back on him and the parallel drawn between these situations further enhances the impression of ineffectuality.

El-Hibri understands the irony in these reports to be an expression of the historians' disapproval of ʿAlī's overly pious stance prior to becoming caliph. The excessive piety of the Khārijites thus represents a reflection of his own.[126] His theory is intriguing, but caution is in order, not just regarding his reading of these episodes but especially concerning his macro-perspective on early Islamic history-writing. El-Hibri contends that the historical tradition originally constituted a cohesive narrative[127] that was not made up of different layers but displayed "unity in scheme and plot line".[128] This seems to me to underestimate the complexity of early Muslim storytelling and of the transmission/compilation process. None of the works under study speak with a single voice internally, not to mention the differences between them.[129] Depictions of early Islamic history are too contradictory and multi-faceted to allow for the idea of a unified narrative. El-Hibri is certainly right to detect critical notes in the portrayal of ʿAlī, but the fact that these are woven into a largely favourable portrait contradicts his notion of a cohesive early Islamic narrative.

Notes

1. For a detailed retelling of the events from the supposed raising of the Qurʾān leaves by the Syrians to the meetings of the arbitrators and the Battle of Nahrawān, see Madelung, *Succession*, 238–61. His narrative is very close to the sources (almost exclusively al-Ṭabarī's *Taʾrīkh* and al-Balādhurī's *Ansāb*), however, and strongly coloured by sympathy for ʿAlī. See on this also the critical comments by Shoshan, *Poetics*, 209 n. 3, 211 n. 14.
2. See, for example, Lassner, *Islamic Revolution*; El-Hibri, *Reinterpreting Islamic History*.
3. EI^2, "al-Ṭabarī" (C. E. Bosworth).
4. Al-Ṭabarī, *Taʾrīkh*, I, 3341, 3351, 3361; al-Balādhurī, *Ansāb*, II, 300, 311, 312, 318, 329, 434; al-Dīnawarī, *Akhbār*, 210, 217, 220, 222; al-Yaʿqūbī, *Taʾrīkh*, II, 192; Ibn Muzāḥim, *Waqʿat Ṣiffīn*, 588, 589, 594. See also al-Masʿūdī, *Murūj*, I–II, 393, 395; Ibn Saʿd, *Ṭabaqāt*, III, 32, 37; Ibn Aʿtham, *Futūḥ*, IV, 89, 93, 125, 126.

5. Al-Ṭabarī, *Ta'rīkh*, I, 3334–5; al-Dīnawarī, *Akhbār*, 206–7; Ibn A'tham, *Futūḥ*, IV, 8–9, 14, 123–4.
6. Al-Balādhurī, *Ansāb*, II, 297, 311, 312; Ibn A'tham, *Futūḥ*, IV, 124, 125.
7. Al-Balādhurī, *Ansāb*, II, 318; Ibn A'tham, *Futūḥ*, IV, 122.
8. Al-Ya'qūbī, *Ta'rīkh*, II, 192. The expression "until we return to God" is a slight rephrasing of Q 49:9, which refers to conflict among the believers: 'If two parties of the believers fight [each other], make peace between them. If one of them wrongs the other, fight those who do wrong until they return to the ordinance of God (*ḥatta tafi'a ilā amr allāh*)'.
9. Al-Ya'qūbī, *Ta'rīkh*, II, 192. For the term *waṣī* in Shī'ī theology, see EI², "Waṣī (Ar., pl. awṣiyā, wāsiyyūn)" (E. Kohlberg). On the use of this term in al-Ya'qūbī's chronicle as evidence for his alleged *rāfiḍī* Shī'ī tendencies, see Anthony, "Ibn Wāḍiḥ", 30–3.
10. This verse refers to dissension between husband and wife and how to solve it.
11. The context here is the prohibition to kill wild game during the pilgrimage and the appropriate compensation for its violation.
12. Al-Balādhurī, *Ansāb*, II, 307, 312, 318; al-Ya'qūbī, *Ta'rīkh*, II, 192.
13. Al-Balādhurī, *Ansāb*, II, 307, 318. The first transmitted from Abū Mikhnaf and 'Awāna b. al-Ḥakam (d. 764 or 770) through 'Abbās b. Hishām, the second from al-Sha'bī (d. 721–8) through Yaḥya b. Ādam (d. 818) and 'Abdallāh b. Ṣāliḥ.
14. Al-Balādhurī, *Ansāb*, II, 318.
15. Ibn A'tham, *Futūḥ*, IV, 94.
16. Ibid., 122–5.
17. Ibid., 125.
18. On al-Ḥudaybiyya, see Görke, "Frühislamische Geschichtsüberlieferung".
19. Al-Ya'qūbī, *Ta'rīkh*, II, 192; al-Balādhurī, *Ansāb*, II, 319; Ibn A'tham, *Futūḥ*, IV, 123–4. See al-Ṭabarī, *Ta'rīkh*, I, 3334–5; Ibn A'tham, *Futūḥ*, IV, 8–9; and al-Dīnawarī, *Akhbār*, 207 for an account of 'Alī remembering the Day of al-Ḥudaybiyya while erasing his title of *amīr al-mu'minīn* from the Ṣiffīn arbitration document.
20. Al-Balādhurī, *Ansāb*, II, 319.
21. Ibn A'tham, *Futūḥ*, IV, 8–10, 14 (first episode) and 123–4 (second episode).
22. This is discussed briefly in Chapter Seven.
23. Ibn A'tham, *Futūḥ*, IV, 8–9, 10.
24. Ibid., 9.
25. Al-Balādhurī, *Ansāb*, II, 319; Ibn A'tham, *Futūḥ*, IV, 125.
26. Al-Ya'qūbī, *Ta'rīkh*, II, 192.
27. Ibn A'tham, *Futūḥ*, IV, 122–5.
28. Al-Ya'qūbī, *Ta'rīkh*, II, 192; Ibn A'tham, *Futūḥ*, IV, 9.
29. Al-Ya'qūbī, *Ta'rīkh*, 192.
30. Ibid.
31. Ibid.

32. Sharon has argued that the idea of *ahl al-bayt* as the Prophet's family, variously extended to include different clans, was prominent under both Umayyads and ʿAbbāsids and that it appears rooted in pre-Islamic Arabian conceptions of rulership. In the context of al-Yaʿqūbī's depiction of ʿAlī's specific defence against the Khārijites' accusations, however, I would argue for a (proto-)Shīʿī flavour in the caliph's argument. Sharon, "The Umayyads as *Ahl al-Bayt*", esp. 135–43, as well as "*Ahl al-Bayt*" and "Development of the Debate".
33. Al-Yaʿqūbī, *Taʾrīkh*, 192–3.
34. Al-Balādhurī, *Ansāb*, II, 312, 314, 324; al-Dīnawarī, *Akhbār*, 221–2; al-Ṭabarī, *Taʾrīkh*, I, 3377–8; al-Masʿūdī, *Murūj*, I–II, 390–1; Ibn Aʿtham, *Futūḥ*, III, 307, 312–13, 314, 319 and IV, 96. It is also implied in al-Yaʿqūbī, *Taʾrīkh*, II, 192, when ʿAlī points out that those of his followers who agreed to the arbitration far outnumbered himself and the "people of my house" (*ahl baytī*).
35. Ibn Aʿtham, *Futūḥ*, IV, 96.
36. Al-Ṭabarī, *Taʾrīkh*, I, 3378–9; Hawting, *First Civil War*, 129.
37. Al-Dīnawarī, *Akhbār*, 221. See also al-Balādhurī, *Ansāb*, II, 313; Ibn Aʿtham, *Futūḥ*, III, 317 and IV, 96; al-Masʿūdī, *Murūj*, I–II, 392
38. Al-Dīnawarī, *Akhbār*, 219.
39. Ibid., 223.
40. Ibid., 210.
41. Ibn Aʿtham, *Futūḥ*, IV, 90–5.
42. Ibn Aʿtham's account of the disputation does not include this part, which – assuming the omission is not due to the vagaries of the transmission process – is another mechanism to silence the Khārijites and amplify their opponents.
43. *Kalām* refers both to a particular argumentative style (dialectic reasoning) and the form of Islamic theology that utilises this style. Treiger, "Origins of *Kalām*", 28–9. In what follows, reference is to the first, more technical meaning
44. Shah, "Kalām".
45. Treiger, "Origins of *Kalām*", 30–4.
46. Ibid., 30.
47. EI[2], " ʿIlm al-kalām" (L. Gardet).
48. The use of this term further highlights the pro-ʿAlid/proto-Shīʿī background to Ibn Aʿtham's work.
49. Ibn Aʿtham, *Futūḥ*, IV, 93.
50. EI[2], " ʿIlm al-kalām" (L. Gardet).
51. Ibn Aʿtham, *Futūḥ*, IV, 94.
52. See, for example, al-Balādhurī, *Ansāb*, II, 307; al-Ṭabarī, *Taʾrīkh*, I, 3351–2 (where the rebels only best Ibn ʿAbbās in debate because he acted specifically against ʿAlī's instructions).
53. For Ibn ʿAbbās' role as agent of ʿAlī, see below. This might imply a less favourable attitude towards the ʿAbbāsids on the part of al-Yaʿqūbī compared

to the other sources studied here, but in light of his portrayal of ʿAlī and the ʿAlids more generally this may also be just one more example of their reverent treatment in his *Taʾrīkh* rather than an explicit slight against Ibn ʿAbbās/the ʿAbbāsids.

54. Al-Dīnawarī, *Akhbār*, 221–3.
55. M. R. J. Bonner, *Historiographical Study*, 50. Bonner's work is the most recent and to date most comprehensive study of al-Dīnawarī and his *Akhbār*.
56. Above, 138.
57. Al-Balādhurī, *Ansāb*, II, 312.
58. See above, 138.
59. Al-Balādhurī, *Ansāb*, II, 312.
60. Ibid., 316, also 296. See further al-Ṭabarī, *Taʾrīkh*, I, 3344, 3360–1; Ibn Aʿtham, *Futūḥ*, IV, 94, 97.
61. Ibn Muzāḥim, *Waqʿat Ṣiffīn*, 589. This passage is reproduced almost identically on 593–4.
62. See above, 137.
63. Al-Balādhurī, *Ansāb*, II, 319. This term echoes the title 'Mother of the Believers' given to the Prophet's wives.
64. Ibn Aʿtham, *Futūḥ*, IV, 123.
65. For approaches to the problem of reconciling the Companions in light of the many intra-communal conflicts of the early Islamic period, see Tayob, "Ṭabarī on the Companions"; Khalek, "Medieval Biographical Literature". More generally, Hoyland, "History, Fiction, and Authorship", 29–30.
66. Al-Balādhurī, *Ansāb*, II, 328. See also al-Ṭabarī, *Taʾrīkh*, I, 3378; Ibn Muzāḥim, *Waqʿat Ṣiffīn*, 561; al-Dīnawarī, *Akhbār*, 222; al-Masʿūdī, *Murūj*, I–II, 405; Ibn Aʿtham, *Futūḥ*, IV, 89, 97.
67. Al-Masʿūdī, *Murūj*, I–II, 407.
68. Ibn Aʿtham, *Futūḥ*, IV, 107.
69. Ibid., 8–14.
70. Ibid., 95.
71. Ibid., 120. The accuracy of his prediction is confirmed on 132.
72. Ibid., 120. The accuracy of his prediction is confirmed on 128.
73. Ibid., 136. For a discussion of Ibn Muljam's tribal affiliation and connected narrative functions, see Leube, *Kinda*, 125 and n. 376, 180–2.
74. Al-Balādhurī, *Ansāb*, II, 312–13 (emphasis added); see also al-Ṭabarī, *Taʾrīkh*, I, 3351: "[ʿAlī] follows the truth and right guidance, and those who oppose him are [both] lost and misleading."
75. See Ibn Khayyāṭ, *Taʾrīkh*, I, 225; al-Ṭabarī, *Taʾrīkh*, I, 3385; al-Yaʿqūbī, *Taʾrīkh*, II, 193; al-Balādhurī, *Ansāb*, II, 333; al-Dīnawarī, *Akhbār*, 224.
76. Noth, *Early Arabic Historical Tradition*, 201.
77. Van Ess, "Unfertige Studien I", 1423–4; Madelung, *Succession*, 261–2.
78. Donner, *Muhammad*, 164.
79. Al-Balādhurī, *Ansāb*, II, 329.

80. Al-Balādhurī, *Ansāb*, II, 317 (emphasis added). See also ibid., 325; al-Ṭabarī, *Taʾrīkh*, I, 3362, 3363.
81. Al-Balādhurī, *Ansāb*, II, 325.
82. Al-Ṭabarī, *Taʾrīkh*, I, 3376; al-Balādhurī, *Ansāb*, II, 320, 328; Ibn Aʿtham, *Futūḥ*, IV, 107; al-Masʿūdī, *Murūj*, I–II, 405.
83. Al-Dīnawarī, *Akhbār*, 220; al-Ṭabarī, *Taʾrīkh*, I, 3375; al-Balādhurī, *Ansāb*, II, 325, 237, 328; al-Masʿūdī, *Murūj*, I–II, 405. Ibn Aʿtham, *Futūḥ*, IV, 98–105 ascribes the initiative to confront the Khawārij to ʿAlī himself. In his depiction, ʿAlī had to deliver three sermons in order to rouse his supporters to march against the Khārijites.
84. Al-Balādhurī, *Ansāb*, II, 330.
85. Al-Dīnawarī, *Akhbār*, 224; al-Balādhurī, *Ansāb*, II, 331; al-Masʿūdī, *Murūj*, I–II, 405. Ibn Aʿtham, *Futūḥ*, IV, 127–8 presents a different picture by having ʿAlī's men strike first. In general, Ibn Aʿtham's portrayal of ʿAlī is more activist and martial compared with the other selected sources.
86. Al-Balādhurī, *Ansāb*, 330; al-Dīnawarī, *Akhbār*, 223; al-Ṭabarī, *Taʾrīkh*, I, 3380–1.
87. Al-Dīnawarī, *Akhbār*, 224. ʿAlī is shown to have taken a similarly conciliatory approach to Muʿāwiya and the Syrians at Ṣiffīn. See the discussion in Shoshan, *Poetics*, 219–21. We can see here the beginning evolution of the 'lawgiver' ʿAlī.
88. On the importance of ʿAlī for the treatment of rebellion in Islamic law, see Kraemer, "Apostates", 50–1, 55–7; Abou el Fadl, *Rebellion and Violence*, 34–61 and *passim*.
89. For a largely antagonistic view of their relations, see Lassner, *Islamic Revolution*, 11–71. See also El-Hibri, "Redemption", who argues that favourable depictions of the Umayyads could sometimes serve to assert ʿAbbāsid superiority over the ʿAlids (who unlike the Umayyads posed a real threat to ʿAbbāsid legitimacy); Haider, *Rebel and Imām*, 130–1, 132.
90. El-Hibri, "Redemption", 245.
91. In addition to his debates with the Khārijites, see, for example, the 'Questions' posed to Ibn ʿAbbās by one or another Khārijite leader over difficult or obscure Qurʾānic terminology (Neuwirth, "Die *Masāʾil*", discusses the textual tradition, philological milieu and variants of the version that names Nāfiʿ b. al-Azraq as questioner) and his dialogues with Muʿāwiya as portrayed in the anonymous *Akhbār al-Dawla al-ʿAbbāsiyya* and al-Balādhurī's *Ansāb* (discussed in El-Hibri, "Redemption", 247–50, 257–65).
92. El-Hibri, "Redemption", 246.
93. On Ibn ʿAbbās as adviser to the caliph, see EI^2, "ʿAbd Allāh b. al-ʿAbbās" (L. Veccia Vaglieri). There are two (partial) exceptions to the portrayal of Ibn ʿAbbās in relation to the ʿAlī–Khawārij conflict: al-Yaʿqūbī mentions him as ʿAlī's envoy, but the lines of arguments usually attributed to Ibn ʿAbbās are ascribed to ʿAlī himself. Ibn Khayyāṭ's *Taʾrīkh*, on the other hand, does not mention Ibn ʿAbbās in connection with the Khārijites at all.

94. At this stage, ʿAlī's opponents are always presented as a unified group, regardless of social, political, economic, religious or tribal background.
95. Al-Balādhurī, *Ansāb*, II, 293; al-Dīnawarī, *Akhbār*, 205; Ibn Muzāḥim, *Waqʿat Ṣiffīn*, 572–3; al-Yaʿqūbī, *Taʾrīkh*, II, 189; al-Ṭabarī, *Taʾrīkh*, I, 3333; al-Masʿūdī, *Murūj*, I–II, 391; Ibn Aʿtham, *Futūḥ*, IV, 2, 96. This is in sharp contrast to the depiction of Abū Ḥayyān al-Tawḥīdī (d. 414 H/1023 CE) in his *Baṣāʾir wa-l-Dhakhāʾir*, for instance, where ʿAlī is shown to foolishly reject Ibn ʿAbbās' offer of negotiating on his behalf instead of Abū Mūsā. Overall, al-Tawḥīdī's work is strongly proto-Sunnī and the portrayal of ʿAlī more critical than in the chronicles and histories examined here. See al-Qāḍī, "Abū Ḥayyān al-Tawḥīdī", 138–40 (for Ibn ʿAbbās), *passim* (for al-Tawḥīdī's proto-Sunnī inclinations and ambivalent stance on ʿAlī).
96. Ibn Aʿtham, *Futūḥ*, IV, 96.
97. Al-Dīnawarī, *Akhbār*, 205. See also al-Yaʿqūbī, *Taʾrīkh*, II, 189; al-Ṭabarī, *Taʾrīkh*, I, 3333; al-Balādhurī, *Ansāb*, II, 293; Ibn Muzāḥim, *Waqʿat Ṣiffīn*, 572; Ibn Aʿtham, *Futūḥ*, IV, 2. Similar reservations against ʿAlī's choice of al-Ashtar as arbiter are ascribed to al-Ashʿath/'the people'/the *qurrāʾ*, but here the argument rests not so much on the closeness of ʿAlī and al-Ashtar but rather on the latter's involvement in the war. See, for example, al-Dīnawarī, *Akhbār*, 205; Ibn Aʿtham, *Futūḥ*, IV, 2–3.
98. Al-Dīnawarī, *Akhbār*, 205.
99. Ibn Khayyāṭ, *Taʾrīkh*, I, 216; al-Dīnawarī, *Akhbār*, 211; al-Ṭabarī, *Taʾrīkh*, I, 3354; al-Masʿūdī, *Murūj*, I–II, 395.
100. Al-Ṭabarī, *Taʾrīkh*, I, 3359; Hawting, *First Civil War*, 110. See also Ibn Aʿtham, *Futūḥ*, IV, 96.
101. Al-Dīnawarī, *Akhbār*, 221–2; al-Balādhurī, *Ansāb*, II, 311, 327, 330; al-Ṭabarī, *Taʾrīkh*, I, 3375.
102. Al-Balādhurī, *Ansāb*, II, 311–13, 314.
103. Leder, "Composite Form", 131. See also Petersen, *ʿAlī and Muʿāwiya*, 108, 147. For Ibn ʿAbbās as a figure of myth and legend in the Islamic tradition, see Gilliot, "Portrait".
104. Al-Ṭabarī, *Taʾrīkh*, I, 3352–3, 3363; al-Balādhurī, *Ansāb*, II, 307, 311, 317; al-Yaʿqūbī, *Taʾrīkh*, II, 192; Ibn Aʿtham, *Futūḥ*, IV, 95–7, 122–5.
105. Al-Ṭabarī, *Taʾrīkh*, I, 3352.
106. Ibid., 3351–3.
107. Ibid., 3351.
108. Lassner, *Islamic Revolution*, 4–5, 8. Similarly Petersen, *ʿAlī and Muʿāwiya*, 71, 77; El-Hibri, "Redemption", although El-Hibri's discussion is more nuanced, arguing that there are also reports in which ʿAlids and ʿAbbāsids present a united Hāshimite front against the Umayyads (and sometimes the Zubayrids).
109. Madelung, "Abū ʿUbayda", 50, 52–3.

110. Gaiser, "Ibāḍī Accounts". It must be noted, however, that while the Ibāḍī sources Gaiser used purport to contain much early material, these sources themselves date from the thirteenth to eighteenth century. For a brief discussion of this issue, the reader is referred back to Part I, section on 'Sources, Genre, Authorship'.
111. For example, al-Yaʿqūbī, *Taʾrīkh*, II, 193.
112. Al-Balādhurī, *Ansāb*, II, 307; al-Ṭabarī, *Taʾrīkh*, I, 3351–2; Ibn Aʿtham, *Futūḥ*, IV, 94. In each of these accounts, it is Ibn ʿAbbās who initially fails to persuade the rebels to return, not ʿAlī. In al-Ṭabarī's report, Ibn ʿAbbās' failure is connected to his disobedience towards ʿAlī (see above).
113. Ibn Aʿtham, *Futūḥ*, IV, 106.
114. Keaney, "Confronting the Caliph", 62.
115. See 98, as well as below, 198 and n. 174 thereto.
116. Al-Balādhurī, *Ansāb*, II, 474–80.
117. Ibid., 475, 476.
118. Ibid., 470.
119. See, for example, al-Ṭabarī, *Taʾrīkh*, I, 3271–2, 3274–6.
120. For example, ibid., 3353; al-Yaʿqūbī, *Taʾrīkh*, II, 192; al-Balādhurī, *Ansāb*, II, 311–13, 319; al-Dīnawarī, *Akhbār*, 221–3; al-Masʿūdī, *Murūj*, I–II, 395; Ibn Aʿtham, *Futūḥ*, IV, 94, 97, 125, 127.
121. See, for example, al-Balādhurī, *Ansāb*, II, 313, 314; al-Ṭabarī, *Taʾrīkh*, I, 3362, 3363; Ibn Aʿtham, *Futūḥ*, IV, 128.
122. El-Hibri, *Parable and Politics*, 248–9.
123. Shoshan, *Poetics*, 209–31 also considers the Ṣiffīn narrative as it is presented in al-Ṭabarī's *History* (based almost exclusively on Abū Mikhnaf) an ironic story, but he sees the irony in the matter of the *ḥukm*, or recourse to God's judgement, which the involved parties understand in very different ways and which has results very different from what one might have expected. He observes a role reversal of ʿAlī's and Muʿāwiya's side halfway through Abū Mikhnaf's account that questions ʿAlī's moral superiority a little. Unfortunately, Shoshan does not elaborate on why the Ṣiffīn story took on elements of irony, what this says about the memory of ʿAlī and the *fitna*, or for what reason al-Ṭabarī chose Abū Mikhnaf's version over other available sources.
124. See, for example, al-Ṭabarī, *Taʾrīkh*, I, 3376; al-Masʿūdī, *Murūj*, I–II, 405; Ibn Aʿtham, *Futūḥ*, IV, 119.
125. El-Hibri, *Parable and Politics*, 249.
126. Ibid., 248.
127. Ibid., ix.
128. Ibid., 23. See also his *Reinterpreting Islamic Historiography*, 15.
129. On the multi-voiced character of early Islamic historiography, see Leder, "Composite Form", 126; Donner, "ʿUthmān and the Rāshidūn Caliphs", 46–7. Shoshan, *Poetics*, 124–40 analyses al-Ṭabarī's inclusion of several contradictory versions of an event. Robinson, *Historiography*, 144: "for every

historian who suppresses a fact or point of view, one can usually find another who provides it; and for every historian with a taste for the miraculous and the legendary, one can usually find another with a nose for documentary materials (or another who embraces both)."

5

Khārijism during the Reign of Muʿāwiya b. Abī Sufyān

The portrayal of Khārijism in relation to the reign of Muʿāwiya (r. 41–60 H/661–80 CE) is markedly different from its representation under ʿAlī, both in terms of volume and of content.[1] Most of our historians do not mention the Khārijites much or at all during Muʿāwiya's rule. Only four of them provide any information: the *Taʾrīkh* works by Ibn Khayyāṭ, al-Yaʿqūbī and al-Ṭabarī, and al-Balādhurī's *Ansāb*. Of these, al-Balādhurī and al-Ṭabarī alone preserve the kind of material that allows us to analyse the narrative function of Khārijites, i.e. letters, speeches or poetry. Ibn Khayyāṭ and al-Yaʿqūbī, on the other hand, impart only scarce and often contradictory details – some names, a few locations and occasionally dates of Khārijite uprisings.[2] There is no discernible pattern to these references and Ibn Khayyāṭ's work in particular also provides no comprehensive narrative. Many of the rebels mentioned are not even clearly identified as Khārijite – it is only with reference to al-Balādhurī and al-Ṭabarī that the connection can be made.[3] The largest Khārijite rebellion of that time, the one led by al-Mustawrid, is omitted entirely by Ibn Khayyāṭ. Both his and al-Yaʿqūbī's work will thus be largely absent from the discussion.

Second, whereas the stories of the confrontation between ʿAlī and the Khārijites served as a means of engaging in discussions of certain religio-political issues, the accounts of Khārijism under Muʿāwiya do not immediately appear to fulfil a similar purpose. While the odd comment on Umayyad or Syrian rule can be found, there is no discussion of Muʿāwiya's policies and decisions even remotely resembling the occupation with ʿAlī's policies discussed in the preceding chapter. In fact, Muʿāwiya hardly features at all. The main protagonists who have to deal with the Khawārij are his governors of Iraq, first al-Mughīra b. Shuʿba and ʿAbdallāh b. ʿĀmir, then Ziyād b. Abīhi and his son ʿUbaydallāh. There are few direct confrontations between these governors and the Khārijites, however; such contact is for the most part restricted to the inhabitants of the regions in which Khārijite activities occurred and the troops sent out to fight the rebels.

Third, the material on Khārijite revolts during the reign of Muʿāwiya, while voluminous in places, is rather thin. Not only are there fewer accounts, but what we do have is often restricted to structural components. This impedes the detection of underlying themes. The general tendency noticed in the preceding chapter is even more pronounced here: despite preserving several names and locations, the sources do not provide us with much substantial information on Khārijism. No new narrative themes or motifs are introduced for this period, for example. The fundamental theme of piety is the only topic to be fleshed out in more detail, such accounts containing more narrative substance than much of the rest. This indicates the importance of piety as a 'nexus of ideas' not only for the characterisation of literary Khārijism, but also for the formation and negotiation of Islamic doctrine and socio-political praxis. The following exploration will focus on this subject as the major motif arising from the delineation of Khārijite history in this period, but will avoid overlap with the discussion in Chapter Two as far as possible. It will show that Khārijite devotion gains a new dimension here, a twist in its understanding and assessment that provides intriguing insight into the complex narrative function of Khārijism.

The analysis is divided into two main parts. The first section will focus on al-Balādhurī, the second will investigate al-Ṭabarī. There are notable disparities in how the two works present Khārijism in this period. Al-Balādhurī's *Ansāb* addresses various Khārijite rebels that are not mentioned by al-Ṭabarī. While the two often transmit much the same material, they arrive at rather different conclusions: al-Ṭabarī mostly continues the tendency to discredit Khārijite piety for its socially disruptive effects, although it is necessary to distinguish between his treatment of activist Khārijites and their quietist counterparts. His censure of the former is evident, but there is some quiet approval in his portrayal of the latter. Al-Balādhurī is more straightforward and includes accounts in his *Ansāb* that explicitly utilise Khārijite piety as a foil for Umayyad corruption. This variance in how al-Balādhurī and al-Ṭabarī approach early Umayyad-era Khārijism is more distinct than was the case for the preceding period.

This disparity supports the conclusions Steven Judd arrived at in a comparative study on characterisation in the works of al-Ṭabarī and al-Balādhurī.[4] Using their material on late Umayyad-era figures and events as a case study, Judd observed that they offer opposing views regarding the decline of Umayyad power: al-Ṭabarī is foremost concerned with matters relating to the maintenance of social order by pointing out the dangers of personal greed and tribal strife.[5] Accordingly, he omits or downplays religious and moral sentiments and motivations wherever possible.[6] Al-Balādhurī, on the other hand, focuses on the moral corruption and heretical inclinations of late

Umayyad personalities.[7] Both manipulate their material in similar ways, but create very different overall themes.[8] The pattern Judd identified reappears in this chapter. However, tribal strife is a concern for al-Balādhurī elsewhere, which will be shown in Chapter Six. This highlights the polyphony of Islamic historiography.

Al-Balādhurī on Early Umayyad-era Khārijism

Al-Balādhurī's *Ansāb* contains by far the largest amount of material on Khārijism under Muʿāwiya; his accounts also display greater variety and depth compared to al-Ṭabarī's *Taʾrīkh*. Al-Balādhurī differs from the latter in two significant ways: first, his material has a great deal more narrative substance and for the most part clearly identifies the various rebels and revolts it addresses as Khārijite. As a result, his depiction of Khārijism in this period appears more tangible than al-Ṭabarī's. The Khārijite 'essence' thus discerned is nevertheless still explicitly literary: al-Balādhurī's material is infused with *topoi* and rhetorical devices that make it difficult to get a sense of the real actors and events behind the stories, even though his particular concerns – and perhaps the scope of his work – resulted in a focus on Khārijite thought and doctrine unmatched by the other sources.

Second, al-Balādhurī presents an image of the Khawārij that is markedly more positive than al-Ṭabarī's. Along the same lines, his criticism of the Umayyads is more explicit than al-Ṭabarī's. One reason for this contrast can be tied to different interests: al-Balādhurī was apparently concerned with questions of moral and ethical significance, not primarily the ramifications of social unrest or – as in his *Futūḥ* – the creation of an administrator's handbook; his intent in the *Ansāb* was to entertain and edify his audience as well. He could thus be more candid in his criticism of the Umayyads than someone like al-Ṭabarī, whose work betrays a serious concern for communal togetherness and social stability. It must be stressed, however, that these two voluminous works do not display a single intent or speak with a single voice. The assessment of their depictions of Khārijism should therefore not be taken as indicative of a single agenda underlying the entire compilation, but as components of a larger whole.

Forms and Functions

Al-Balādhurī's comparatively well-developed portrayal of Khārijism is the result of certain narrative techniques. For instance, he reverses the tendency to limit Khārijite statements to a minimum and focus on their opponents. Many of the longer speeches and dialogues and all but one of the poems[9] transmitted in his reports of Khārijite confrontations with government agents and pro-ʿAlid protagonists give the dissidents ample opportunity to argue their position. This applies in particular to the Khārijite revolts directed against Ziyād and ʿUbaydallāh b. Ziyād. Conversely, opponents of the Khawārij are frequently restricted to short statements and repetitive stock phrases, which diverges from the pattern identified in the preceding chapter as well as al-Ṭabarī's approach discussed below. Consider the following two examples.

In his position as governor of Basra, ʿUbaydallāh b. Ziyād reportedly arrested a Khārijite by the name of Khālid b. ʿAbbād (or ʿUbbād). He interrogated him, but Khālid refused to give ʿUbaydallāh the location of his fellow Khārijites. The governor next ordered Khālid to curse "the people of Nahrawān", to which Khālid responded rather cleverly: "If they were enemies of God, then God [already] cursed them".[10] The Khārijite also side-stepped Ibn Ziyād's demand that he declare his loyalty to Muʿāwiya: "If he [Muʿāwiya] is a believer, then he is a friend of God and I am his friend".[11] Frustrated, ʿUbaydallāh finally ordered Khālid's execution.[12]

The second example is set during the revolt of the famous Khārijite leader Abū Bilāl against ʿUbaydallāh b. Ziyād. During their confrontation, one of the governor's soldiers tells the Khārijites to "fear God and return [to the community]".[13] As discussed in the preceding chapter, ʿAlī or one of his representatives frequently uses this particular demand as well to urge the rebels to rejoin the *umma*. The Khārijites usually do not reply and leave the last word to ʿAlī. Here, the situation is very different. The soldier's request to return to the community and thus accept Umayyad authority provokes an angry reply on the part of Abū Bilāl and his Khārijites: "You would have us return to Ibn Ziyād the transgressor [*al-fāsiq*]?"[14] The soldier does not reply; no attempt is made to argue with the rebels or defend ʿUbaydallāh. Essentially, the Umayyad troops take over the role of mouthpiece hitherto associated with the Khawārij. This role reversal stresses further that just as ʿAlī's opponents were in the wrong and therefore could not counter his righteous claims, so the Umayyad troops are now struck speechless by the Khārijites.

That some major Khārijite protagonists appear more fleshed out in al-Balādhurī's work than their opponents, both Umayyads and pro-ʿAlids, is also due to the level of detail provided. The story of Abū Bilāl and his rebellion is generally a good case in point. Many of his opponents remain lifeless, indistinct and interchangeable from a narrative perspective, while he himself is described in great detail. We learn about his family background, his religious and political thought, daily habits, personal virtues and concerns.[15] Most of these details can easily be assigned to a particular *topos* or storytelling technique, but they contribute to creating verisimilitude. Moreover, this is the first successful attempt at crafting a comprehensive image of a Khārijite rebel so far, which underlines the particular significance of Abū Bilāl in the Islamic tradition.[16]

The narrative wealth of al-Balādhurī's work therefore lets us discern what at first seems to be a more specific Khārijite identity. This is not to say that we can determine with any degree of certainty how the events described actually came to pass – the essence of Khārijism we detect is still fundamentally literary. Because al-Balādhurī was interested in discussing the Khārijites beyond the implications of rebellion for the cohesion of the community, he had to fill out the otherwise rather skeletal portrayal of Khārijism in this period. This allows us to make some observations regarding the political, religious and social issues pertinent to his time; the comparison with al-Ṭabarī in particular will facilitate this.

Opposing Tyranny with Piety

Al-Balādhurī's approach to Khārijism during the reign of Muʿāwiya is significantly more positive than anything we have seen thus far. He does criticise Khārijite violence against other Muslims, but his censure of the Umayyads is similarly pronounced and so leads to a more balanced image. Unlike opposition to ʿAlī, whose superior standing in Muslim tradition allowed for clear-cut divisions between good (ʿAlī) and bad (the Khawārij), opposition to the Umayyads was not as readily classified as reproachable. Al-Balādhurī's interest in questions of morality and his position at the ʿAbbāsid court, at a time when Khārijite rebellions were no longer a serious problem, accommodated some cautious praise of the Khawārij as pious rebels against a reprehensible regime. His work here departs from the tenor of his *Futūḥ*, which was intended for a different audience (state secretaries and administrators)[17] and had a 'unifying agenda' that subordinated the partisan inclinations of the ʿAbbāsid courtier al-Balādhurī to the portrayal of a strong and efficient Islamic caliphate as having existed from the very beginning.[18] The *Ansāb* fulfilled different purposes – its edificatory tone is much stronger, for instance – and so could be more outspoken in its censure of the Umayyads.[19]

The careful approval of Khārijite resistance to the Umayyads in the *Ansāb* is expressed in a variety of ways, ranging from explicit statements to subtle literary techniques. The connections and correlations between narrative content (statements, poems, speeches, and such) and techniques (placement, omission, emphasis, interjection, among others) in al-Balādhurī's accounts can tell us quite a bit about his composition of literary Khārijism concerning this period.[20]

As is common for the early historical tradition, al-Balādhurī's work is suffused with the motifs of Khārijite piety, longing for *jihād*, ferocity in battle and bravery in the face of overwhelming opposition.[21] It is here that the clearest indications of al-Balādhurī's comparatively favourable depiction of the Khārijites can be found. The accounts that address the Khārijite concern for piety in personal and communal matters in the period of Muʿāwiya's rule are largely similar to the material examined in Chapter Two and so again will not be dealt with in full here. One example, which already alludes to the fundamental difference between al-Balādhurī and al-Ṭabarī's approach to Khārijite piety as discussed below, should suffice.

The report tells the story of a Khārijite called Abū al-Wāziʿ, who summons his companions to take up arms after the execution of Abū Bilāl's brother ʿUrwa b. Udayya by ʿUbaydallāh b. Ziyād.[22] He accuses his fellow Khārijites of having neglected to deal with the "people of injustice (*ahl al-baghy*)" who would take advantage of this inaction and "kill you in your beds like dogs in their kennels (*yaqtalūnakum fī maḍājiʿikum qatl al-kilāb fī marābiḍihā*)".[23] He specifically calls on a certain Nāfiʿ b. al-Azraq al-Ḥanafī to abandon his restraint:

> You were given a sharp tongue (*lisānan ṣāriman*) and a faint heart (*qalban kalīlan*). Would that the faintness of your heart was in your tongue and the strength of your tongue in your heart (*fa-layta kalāl qalbika li-lisānika wa-ṣalābat lisānika li-qalbika*)! I fear that love of this impermanent world (*al-dunyā al-fāmiyya*) conquered your heart and you turned towards it and observed piety in it with your tongue (*fa-milta ilayhā wa-aẓharta bi-lisānika al-zuhd fīhā*).[24]

This speech contains all of the core components of Khārijism: piety, a focus on *jihād* and disdain for the material world, which in turn fuels the Khārijite desire to find favour with God through armed struggle. At the same time, however, the account also emphasises those elements that feature prominently throughout al-Balādhurī's presentation of Khārijite rebellions in this period: the injustice of their opponents and a pressing sense of impending doom, having failed to take action.

Let us continue our investigation into Khārijite militant piety as a double-edged sword with the story of Abū Bilāl's revolt against ʿUbaydallāh b. Ziyād. This is a tale of righteous resistance to tyranny *par excellence*. Al-Balādhurī's accounts are much longer and more developed than al-Ṭabarī's material on Abū Bilāl, focusing in particular on the events after Abū Bilāl's decision to rebel, which al-Ṭabarī merely touches on.

In al-Balādhurī's rendering, Abū Bilāl was driven to revolt by ʿUbaydallāh b. Ziyād's merciless persecution of the Khawārij in Basra, specifically the suffering of a Khārijite woman named al-Thabjāʾ. Al-Thabjāʾ constantly pointed out ʿUbaydallāh's misdeeds so that eventually the governor decided to arrest her. Abū Bilāl, having learned this, warned her, but because she did not want to cause harm to others she refused to hide. When she was finally caught, her hands and feet were cut off before she was killed. Abū Bilāl walked past the execution site in the market and thus witnessed her ordeal, which after ʿUbaydallāh's mistreatment of the Khawārij proved to be the last straw. No longer able to remain inactive, Abū Bilāl decided on rebellion as the only course of action available to him now. Having summoned his comrades, he accused the authorities (*al-wulāt*) of "oppressing the righteous (*ahl al-ḥaqq*)" through "treachery and unbelief". He argued that it was a sin to stay behind: drawing one's sword and killing people was certainly distressing, but the Khārijites had not begun this conflict – indeed, they were the wronged party. The account has Abū Bilāl highlight that provocation was not their stated aim, but that they would protect themselves from oppression.[25]

Abū Bilāl reportedly left Basra with a small number of companions and settled in al-Ahwāz. ʿUbaydallāh first sent an army of 2,000 men against them; Abū Bilāl's reaction was calm: "God is the Helper (*al-mustaʿān*), and they [the government troops] are the helpers of the oppressors (*aʿwān al-ẓalama*)".[26] The narrative follows the familiar pattern: the Khārijites are called upon to return to the community and obey ʿUbaydallāh; the rebels on their part dismiss the request and point out the governor's iniquity; following some initial quarrelling, the Khārijites attack the Umayyad army and put it to flight. ʿUbaydallāh was furious that such a small group of rebels had managed to defeat his troops and sent out another army twice the size of the previous one, under the command of ʿAbbād b. Akhḍar al-Māzanī.

The two factions met at Darābjird on a Friday. ʿAbbād called on Abū Bilāl to obey the authorities (*al-sulṭān*), but the Khārijite declined sharply: "Do you call us to obedience towards him who sheds blood and violates the sacred ordinances of God, and to return to the hypocrite Ibn Ziyād who kills on suspicion and arrests on confusion?"[27] His men then charged ʿAbbād's troops and fought until prayer time. Abū Bilāl asked for and was granted a ceasefire for the duration of the prayer, but the Umayyad troops hastened the prayer and then attacked the Khawārij, who were still prostrated on the ground. Not one of them turned away from his prayer position until the enemy was directly upon them. They were all slain and Abū Bilāl's head cut off.[28]

This story is largely self-explanatory. Abū Bilāl is the reluctant but nevertheless unequivocal hero of the story, pitted against ignoble villains represented by ʿUbaydallāh and his agents. This is a common mechanism not just in al-Balādhurī's *Ansāb* but also in his *Futūḥ*, where the comparatively limited criticism of the Umayyads is expressed almost exclusively through criticism of their agents.[29] The *Ansāb* is overall much more outspoken about the Umayyads and contains direct censure of individual caliphs as well,[30] likely owing to the work's different audience and purpose, and so here we see both techniques side-by-side.

In the Abū Bilāl episode, the Khawārij are portrayed as pious and conscientious: they struggle with their choice to rebel against the authorities, but feel they have no option but to oppose Umayyad tyranny. An independent, very short report of Abū Bilāl's rebellion is anxious to emphasise that he only fought those who fought him and that he did not misappropriate any money,[31] which stands in sharp contrast to Khārijite accusations against the caliphs. The longer first account gives expression to the wickedness of ʿUbaydallāh (and by extension the Umayyads) through Abū Bilāl's accusations and the accompanying actions of the government agents, in particular ʿAbbād's breach of the ceasefire. The army's haste in finishing the prayer – on a Friday, no less – in order to gain an advantage over the otherwise seemingly invincible Khārijites highlights the troops' malevolence and cowardice, contrasting with the fervent devotion of the rebels whose immersion in prayer will not be broken even under imminent threat. The rebels' iron comportment impresses even their enemies: the commander of the first army sent out against Abū Bilāl tells ʿUbaydallāh that he would rather be cursed and alive than praised and dead on account of the Khawārij, "a people unlike any other (lit. 'not like people')".[32]

Three elegiac poems in al-Balādhurī's accounts of Abū Bilāl mourn his passing and praise his virtues as a pious Muslim at the same time. A fourth one is rather oddly placed at the end of a report that describes the death of Abū Bilāl's brother ʿUrwa and ʿUrwa's daughter at the hands of ʿUbaydallāh. It is said to have been written either by the Khārijite poet ʿImrān b. Ḥiṭṭān or by another Khārijite called Saʿīd b. Masjūj, although it is firmly attributed to ʿImrān elsewhere.[33] This poem was reportedly composed upon Abū Bilāl's death and is one of ʿImrān's (if the attribution is correct) most well-known pieces. While verses 3–5 were quoted already in Chapter Three, they bear repeating:

> Abū Bilāl has increased my disdain for this life / and strengthened my love for the *khurūj*;
> . . .
> I guard against dying in my bed / and strive for death under the spearheads;
> If I knew that my death / was like the death of Abū Bilāl, I would not worry;
> Whoever cares for this world / by God, the Lord of the Kaʿba, I am averse to it.[34]

This poem gives a good indication of the malleability of 'Khārijite' material and its potential to be turned into a celebration of righteous Khārijite rebellions like Abū Bilāl's. There is not a hint of criticism regarding his use of force in the *Ansāb*; instead, the rebels are quietly lauded for their opposition to the Umayyads. The two reports al-Balādhurī provides combine to set Abū Bilāl apart both from corrupt authorities, who were indeed frequently accused of stealing tax money, and from his extremist fellow Khārijites, who had no compunction whatsoever about killing non-Khārijite Muslims.[35] The inclusion of ʿImrān's poem fits into this framework as well, as do the others we shall turn to shortly. This poetry, and indeed the entire Abū Bilāl narrative, also conveys an impression of the type of stories a courtly audience would have found rewarding.

Of the three elegies contained within the account of Abū Bilāl's revolt, the first one is attributed to ʿImrān as well. The second one is ascribed to a Khārijite woman, a certain Umm al-Jarrāḥ. Both these poems survive in the *Ansāb* only in fragments. The third elegy is credited to Kaʿb b. ʿUmayr al-Sumnī, a companion of Abū Bilāl. It is located at the end of al-Balādhurī's account of Abū Bilāl and thus the last impression of his rebellion that the audience (of the text in the present edition at least) is left with. (As to when Kaʿb would have had an opportunity to compose it and who would have passed it on, considering that the account tells us that Abū Bilāl's entire party was killed, is another question.) If the poem's placement reflects contemporary arrangement of the material, it may indeed perhaps be read as al-Balādhurī's final summary of this particular expression of Khārijism:

> Ibn Ḥudayr [Abū Bilāl] sold his soul to God and gained / Gardens of Paradise whose blessings are many;
> A people assisted him whose faces are like / stars of overcast skies whose clouds are dispersed;
> They advanced with Indian swords and lances / on horses who are prone to running [lit. 'whose lean backs are protruding'].[36]

The rebellion of Abū Bilāl is perhaps the most prominent Khārijite endeavour in al-Balādhurī's work for this period, but there are plenty of other accounts in the *Ansāb* that similarly position Khārijite piety in opposition to Umayyad injustice. One such instance is the story of the Khārijite *mujtahid* Khālid b. ʿAbbād, whom we have already encountered. Khālid had been held captive by ʿUbaydallāh b. Ziyād while the latter was governor of Basra, hoping that the Khārijite might disclose the location of his comrades. When Khālid remained steadfast, ʿUbaydallāh ordered him to be executed publicly in the market square. Al-Balādhurī's account depicts the Khārijite as emaciated from his continuous fasting. As a result, no one was willing to come forward and kill Khālid until a member of ʿUbaydallāh's *shurṭa* walked past and killed the Khārijite.[37]

The point of this episode is clearly literary in the main. Why would ʿUbaydallāh have to wait for an ordinary citizen or a passer-by to kill Khālid? As governor, he could have just ordered his executioner or one of his soldiers to carry out the sentence. How did the people know that Khālid was emaciated from fasting rather than having been starved, for instance? The report mentions no other tell-tale signs of piety like prostration marks, a yellow complexion or a reputation for asceticism. Similarly, while public executions were commonplace at the time, the choice of marketplace as killing site also suggests an ulterior narrative motive: the purpose of this report is to establish Khālid – and perhaps by extension his fellow Khārijites – as a pious believer who is easily recognised as such by the people. Khālid's emaciation serves to achieve exactly that, both with regard to the hypothetical spectators on the Basran marketplace and the later audience of this story. Fasting and other ascetic practices like night vigils are trademarks of literary Khārijism and so the figure of Khālid is immediately familiar. Even if the reason for his gauntness was not instantly apparent to said hypothetical spectators, the later audience would have made the connection at once. The Basran citizens in the story hesitate to kill Khālid, and this account may have been intended to elicit a similar reaction among al-Balādhurī's and/or his source's contemporaries. The message is clear – while decent people shy away from executing an ascetic, representatives of Umayyad authority have no qualms about disregarding his standing and putting him to death. The market was probably the most crowded and public place in an early Islamic town – that so many refused to kill a devout man like Khālid emphasises the particular malevolence of the Umayyads and their agents.

This malevolence also explains and partly legitimises the rebels' use of force in their struggle against the Umayyads. While al-Balādhurī's work does contain reports that criticise Khārijite violence, some of his material suggests that the Khawārij had no choice but to take up arms in their mission to combat injustice and oppression. An eloquent example of this is Abū al-Wāziʿ's exhortation to fight after the killing of Abū Bilāl's brother ʿUrwa. A similar tendency is present already in the *Kitāb al-Taḥrīsh* attributed to Ḍirār b. ʿAmr, which pre-dates the *Ansāb* by at least half a century (likely more). The Khārijites are here depicted as defenders of the truth[38] who should not be opposed when they take up arms against unjust rulers.[39] The section of the *Taḥrīsh* that illustrates Khārijite beliefs accordingly keeps the enumeration of their negative aspects much shorter than the list of their positive characteristics.[40] Despite their rebellious nature and exclusivist definition of faith, the *Taḥrīsh* considered them good Muslims.[41]

That we find this reflected in al-Balādhurī's Khārijite material indicates that the discourse on Khārijism, especially before the ninth century, was more nuanced that is often acknowledged. It also shows that while literary Khārijism in the *Ansāb* is more elaborate than has so far been the case, it still serves a rhetorical purpose in acting as a foil for the despotism of the Umayyads and their representatives. This is particularly evident when we turn to reports that deal with the Khawārij without pitting them against any Umayyad agents directly – the tenor of these accounts is noticeably more critical of Khārijite violence and intransigence. Additionally, whereas both Ziyād and ʿUbaydallāh are portrayed as cruel despots, their predecessor al-Mughīra b. Shuʿba fares a lot better. He is not cast as the hero in the reports that delineate the several Khārijite rebellions during his governorship of Kufa, but neither is he portrayed as the villain in the same way as the later governors of Iraq, and the reports do not explicitly emphasise Khārijite piety or bravery either. Al-Mughīra was not considered a steadfast supporter of the Umayyads,[42] which seems to have influenced the depiction of the Khārijites.

Clearly, then, it is the Umayyads and their agents whom al-Balādhurī, his sources and his audience (are supposed to) find fault with. As noted above, Ziyād and ʿUbaydallāh bear the brunt of the disapproval. Ziyād, for example, was charged with cruelty towards Khārijite women. There are numerous reports according to which he persecuted female Khārijites just as fiercely as male rebels and subjected them to the same punishments of cross-amputation, death and crucifixion.[43] On one occasion, Ziyād reportedly gave the 'women' of two Khārijite leaders – presumably their wives and/or concubines – to their opponents after the rebellion in question had been quelled successfully. Only one of the two recipients returned his 'gifts' to the tribe the women belonged to.[44] In another case, Ziyād threatened to exile and withhold the stipends from any tribe that would not follow his example and crucify any woman who intended to participate in a revolt.[45] Other reports draw attention to Ziyād's threat of collective punishment as articulated in his inaugural speech in Basra, which drew Abū Bilāl's censure on the grounds that God had abolished this particular form of punishment.[46]

Popular opinion of Ziyād's son ʿUbaydallāh is just as bad. Several reports portray ʿUbaydallāh as a faithless tyrant who pays no heed to the provisions of Islam or even basic human decency. One such account tells the story of ʿUbaydallāh's imprisonment of a group of Khārijites under the command of Ṭawwāf b. ʿAllāq. He tells the rebels that their release is contingent upon one half of them killing the other half. Twelve Khārijites give in and kill their companions, whereupon they are released from prison. When their fellow Khawārij curse them for their actions, they reply: "We were made to do this against our will (*ukrihnā*). Man is forced into unbelief, and he rests easy in belief (*muṭma'in bi-l-īmān*)."[47]

The surviving Khārijites eventually regret their actions deeply and seek redemption. Finding support in Q 16:110 ('Verily, your Lord, to those who emigrated after they had been compelled [to renounce their religion] and thereafter fought [for the cause of God] and were patient, verily, your Lord, after that, is forgiving and merciful'), they pledge the *bay'a* to Ṭawwāf and set out to kill 'Ubaydallāh as a means of asking God's forgiveness. The Khārijites are killed in the course of their undertaking and Ṭawwāf is crucified,[48] but in the eyes of their fellow Khawārij at least they have attempted to atone for their transgression, which cannot be said for 'Ubaydallāh.

It is interesting to note that, in language, subject matter and result, this episode resembles portrayals of the campaign of the proto-Shī'ī *tawwābūn* ('penitents') a few years later, which we are told was caused by intense regret over having stood aside when Muḥammad's grandson al-Ḥusayn was beleaguered and eventually slain at Karbalā'. The penitents, too, were killed in battle by Umayyad troops that far exceeded them in number, but from a narrative perspective their quest for expiation through personal sacrifice was ultimately successful.[49]

The *Ansāb* section dealing with 'Ubaydallāh in the context of Khārijite uprisings concludes with a damning judgement. The final report tells the story of the Khārijite 'Īsā (b. 'Ātik) al-Khaṭṭī, whose utter disgust with 'Ubaydallāh led him to seek the *khurūj*. He had daughters, however, and worried about their welfare were he to rise in armed revolt. His fellow Khawārij admonished him for his hesitation and reminded him of 'Ubaydallāh's misdeeds. Thus chastened, and anxious about his fate in the Hereafter, 'Īsā decided to take up arms physically and poetically:

> I fear God's punishment if I died satisfied / with the rule of 'Ubaydallāh, tyrant and evildoer.[50]

Again, the placement of this episode is as important as its content. Such strong condemnation of 'Ubaydallāh is certain to have left an impression on the audience of this story, all the more so because there is no complementary narrative telling 'Ubaydallāh's side of things. His conflict with the Khārijites culminates in 'Īsā's line of verse, which thereby functions essentially as the summary lesson to be taken from the *Ansāb*'s portrayal of Khārijite resistance against the governor.

This brief episode is also interesting because it draws attention to another feature of Khārijite piety: the Khawārij are so committed to their cause that – notwithstanding the occasional second thought – having to leave their families behind does not deter them from their course of action.[51] As with everything related to Khārijite piety, however, there are two sides to the coin. Commitment to one's cause is laudable, but the disruptive effect on the rebels' families, clans and tribes is a recurrent concern and adds to the problematisation of Khārijism.

It is not only the Umayyads' notorious governors, however, who suffer censure. The *Ansāb*'s (admittedly limited) portrayal of Muʿāwiya in relation to Khārijism in this period is similarly unfavourable. Consider, for instance, the reports of Farwa b. Nawfal's revolt at al-Nukhayla in c. 41 H/661–2 CE. According to the account as transmitted by al-Balādhurī, Farwa and about 500 of his companions had not engaged in combat at Nahrawān because they had had doubts about the correctness of fighting ʿAlī. When Farwa heard about al-Ḥasan's surrender to Muʿāwiya and the latter's arrival at Kufa, however, he summoned his fellow Khārijites and told them that "someone has come about whom we had no doubt, and we do not doubt that killing him is lawful".[52] His companions agreed and they marched towards al-Nukhayla, where Muʿāwiya had set up camp. When Muʿāwiya heard of Farwa's approach, he wrote to al-Ḥasan in Medina and requested that al-Ḥasan fight the Khārijites on his behalf. Unsurprisingly, al-Ḥasan had no intention of doing so. He also made it very clear to Muʿāwiya that he should not mistake him for an ally: "Indeed, if I intended to kill anyone from the *ahl al-qibla*, I would begin by killing you [Muʿāwiya]."[53] The only reason he had not opposed Muʿāwiya, he concluded, was his concern for the "(moral) wellbeing and cohesion of the *umma*".[54] This also serves an apologetic function in indicating why al-Ḥasan chose to renounce his claim to the caliphate.

Thus rebuffed, Muʿāwiya sent a group of Syrian soldiers against the Khawārij, but his men were routed. This fits the narrative pattern: only rarely are Khārijites shown to be defeated at first try. Muʿāwiya thereupon turned to the Kufans and forced them to engage the Khārijites under threat of withholding the *amān* he had held out in prospect to the very pro-ʿAlid town. The Kufans grudgingly obliged and killed the Khārijites under Farwa's command. A second revolt instigated by Farwa's successor was also swiftly quelled by the Kufan troops.[55]

This episode's main objective is to vilify Muʿāwiya, whereas al-Ḥasan as ʿAlī's son is painted in a favourable light and exonerated from his relinquishment of the caliphate. That he reportedly subordinated his own interests to those of the Muslim community also impresses upon the audience that he would have made a better leader than Muʿāwiya. Of note, al-Ṭabarī's version of this incident is identical to the first part of al-Balādhurī's account, with the exception that the interaction between Muʿāwiya and al-Ḥasan is altogether absent.[56] This further supports the impression that al-Balādhurī was more critical in his treatment of the Umayyads.

Muʿāwiya's villainous status is also upheld by virtue of the doubts that Farwa's Khārijites displayed regarding the righteousness of their opposition to ʿAlī, but which are entirely absent in the case of the Umayyad. Their unwillingness to participate at Nahrawān or otherwise oppose ʿAlī with violence is a forceful contrast to their reaction to Muʿāwiya. That al-Ḥasan seems to rank the Khārijites among the believers, the *ahl al-qibla*, further increases the validity of their criticism. The Kufans also do not fight the Khārijites voluntarily, as we have seen, which demonstrates Muʿāwiya's political shrewdness but also indicates that the Kufans (and the audience?) knew quite well that the Umayyads were the true enemies here, not the Khawārij.[57]

The examples discussed so far are all rather explicit in their approval of the Khārijites and censure of the Umayyads. But al-Balādhurī also employed more subtle methods of presenting a somewhat more positive image of the rebels. Four distinct narrative techniques can be observed: first, as already mentioned, the accounts preserved by al-Balādhurī transmit many longer Khārijite statements, speeches and exhortations. The Khawārij are thus not restricted to short, often repetitive stock phrases. On many occasions it is the rebels who have the last word (or poem) and thereby pronounce a report's concluding judgement of a person or issue. This pertains especially to accounts that portray the Khārijites as victims of Umayyad agents.[58]

Second, the employment of certain arguments within a specific report reveals much about how it might have been intended to come across. By way of example, let us take another look at a specific narrative building block of literary Khārijism. We saw in the preceding chapter that ʿAlī frequently urges the Khārijites to 'fear God and return to the community', a summons that is later repeated by representatives of the Umayyads.[59] While the request is the same, its narrative purpose is markedly different. When uttered by ʿAlī, this demand serves as a means of disparaging Khārijite conduct. Consequently, there is no need for the rebels to respond; their view of the matter is irrelevant. In the case of the Umayyad agents, however, the same demand elicits angry and often eloquent replies from the Khawārij.[60] In the *Ansāb*, the rebels of this period thus resemble ʿAlī more closely than their own predecessors, especially in the case of Abū Bilāl: both are depicted in confrontation with deeply flawed opponents whose understanding of religion and politics is misguided, which leads them to transgress Islamic norms. While the identity of both the offending and the injured party differ, the dynamics of the victim–perpetrator relationship remain the same. This might imply that such accounts follow a general narrative pattern into which specific actors and issues are inserted and which is only loosely connected to particular contexts.

A third technique pertains to the use of Qurʾānic quotations. Al-Balādhurī's work contains more such citations than al-Ṭabarī's material, but more importantly, in the *Ansāb* it is now exclusively the Khārijites who resort to referencing the Qurʾān.[61] There does not appear to be a single account in the section on Khārijism in this period in which an Umayyad representative cites the Qurʾān when confronted with the Khārijites, not even in response to their quotations of Scripture. The result is that the piety of the Khawārij appears enhanced in juxtaposition to the lack of proper religious devotion associated with the Umayyads and their agents.

Finally, the use of omission as a storytelling technique also contributes to the *Ansāb*'s relatively positive approach to Khārijism. A comparison of the work's depiction of the revolt of al-Mustawrid[62] with al-Ṭabarī's rendering of the same episode[63] reveals that al-Balādhurī's account is not only significantly shorter; as we shall see, it also omits all longer speeches and dialogues of the main actors. Al-Ṭabarī's rendering of al-Mustawrid's letter to the governor of al-Madāʾin[64] or his nephew's confrontation with the latter[65] is absent from al-Balādhurī's account, for instance. More importantly, al-Balādhurī preserves none of the speeches that in al-Ṭabarī's version censure Khārijism.[66] Apart from two short remarks,[67] there is also no indication of the deep-rooted enmity between the Khārijites and ʿAlid supporters that is so pronounced in al-Ṭabarī's work, as we will see. Al-Balādhurī's portrayal of al-Mustawrid's uprising thus contains no particular criticism of the Khārijites and their motives. Al-Ṭabarī's concern with the consequences of rebellion for the social fabric of the *umma*, which will be discussed below, is not discernible here. As already noted, this supports Judd's conclusions regarding al-Ṭabarī and al-Balādhurī's particular historiographical approaches and socio-political concerns.[68]

Perhaps al-Balādhurī did not know the longer reports which contain the condemnatory speeches, or perhaps the longer, embellished accounts did not yet exist when he was composing the *Ansāb*. Option one is not entirely convincing, for two reasons. First, the extraordinary length of his *Ansāb* does not imply a shortage of accessible material. Al-Balādhurī frequently preserves more variants of a particular report and provides more details than any other contemporary source, including al-Ṭabarī. Second, even though his *isnāds* often differ substantially from al-Ṭabarī's, the reports of al-Mustawrid's uprising are very similar in both works. The sequence of events, the main actors and the locations as well as the wording in many places are the same; it is only the speeches and the episodes pertaining to them that are missing from al-Balādhurī's account. It seems unlikely, therefore, that al-Balādhurī received his information from a different source or accessed a very different pool of material.

Maybe the reports containing the critical speeches had not yet come into being. After all, al-Balādhurī presumably died about 40 years before al-Ṭabarī. If this is the case, then either al-Ṭabarī or one of his more immediate informants must be considered the author of these speeches, which were subsequently inserted into the story. Alternatively, al-Balādhurī was aware of these story elements but cut them to better make his point. Either would have required major interference with the narrative, which is difficult to assess: it has been argued that "straightforward editing" of this kind is unlikely,[69] but then how are we to explain such significant differences in the delineation of certain events? As we have seen, others have argued for considerable editorial/authorial freedom, and in general I would lean that way as well.[70]

It is possible, of course, that several versions of this episode were in circulation and that each author made a deliberate choice which one to include. Khalīfa b. Khayyāṭ and al-Yaʿqūbī are no help here, unfortunately. If we do not accept the premise that al-Balādhurī actively omitted these story elements in his rendering or that al-Ṭabarī invented them, then we will have to leave open the question of who was responsible for the transformation of the account in the transmission process, a phenomenon Leder termed "stillschweigende autorenlose Gestaltung überlieferter Erzählungen",[71] or "unavowed authorship".[72] This is not an argument against editorial freedom, of course – it just demonstrates that the agency of the authors of the sources extant today extends to their predecessors and even later editors or copyists of their works. And none of this changes the fact that al-Balādhurī and al-Ṭabarī's texts as we have them today display fundamentally different approaches to Khārijism.

Reproaching Khārijite Piety

We have seen that al-Balādhurī is overall at least as critical of the Umayyads as he is of the Khawārij. In fact, the preceding discussion has mostly focused on the ways in which Umayyad conduct is reproached. This section will thus conclude with a brief survey of accounts that are more clearly condemning of Khārijite activities. This pertains especially to Khārijites who rejected ʿAlī and those who are not shown in direct conflict with the Umayyads or their representatives. Perhaps due to his focus on moral and ethical questions, al-Balādhurī here addresses the actions and ideas of individuals and their impact on other human beings rather more than the institutions of the state, as the following examples demonstrate.

Al-Balādhurī's account of Shabīb b. Bajara al-Ashjāʿī's uprising early in Muʿāwiya's reign introduces the Khārijite as one of Ibn Muljam's companions and thus associates him with the murder of ʿAlī.[73] The account emphasises that the rebel "killed every child, man and woman" he came across until he was killed by al-Mughīra's soldiers. Shabīb is cast as a violent criminal who needs to be stopped to prevent further bloodshed, which is certainly a castigation of this particular Khārijite rebel. But his revolt as depicted in the *Ansāb* is essentially a closed system. Larger issues such as the threat of rebellion for the cohesion of the *umma* do not come into play.

Al-Balādhurī's report of Hawthara b. Wadāʿ al-Asadī's revolt exhibits similar features. It begins by stating that Hawthara disapproved of Farwa b. Nawfal's hesitation to fight ʿAlī and acknowledge the legitimacy of his assassination.[74] Like Shabīb, Hawthara is thus presented as an evildoer and his opposition to ʿAlī a result of bad judgement. When he decided to rebel, Muʿāwiya asked Hawthara's father to plead with him, but to no avail. Hawthara's determination to win Paradise through martyrdom led his father to conclude that Hawthara was "excessively proud and disobedient" (*ʿātin*; the adjective can also mean 'revolting, corrupt, unbelieving').[75] Muʿāwiya sent an army under the command of ʿAbdallāh b. ʿAwf and accompanied by Hawthara's father to fight the Khārijites; the rebels were utterly defeated and almost all of them killed.[76] Again, the condemnation of Khārijite actions is clear here. Hawthara is presented as an obstinate, foolish young man whose zealotry precipitates him into ruin, but this is primarily a personal disaster. The threat he poses is fixed to a particular space and time; once eliminated, the *umma* at large is no longer affected.

Nevertheless, the account displays a certain ambiguity regarding Hawthara. ʿAbdallāh b. ʿAwf is shown to regret his killing because Hawthara had been a devout Muslim with *sujūd* marks on his face. Four lines of poetry on ʿAbdallāh's remorse and Hawthara's piety conclude the report.[77] Unlike the previous example, ʿAbdallāh's conflict – having to kill a pious man who nevertheless threatened the lives of other Muslims – may well be read as a reflection of a larger personal, but also social dilemma: does the end (opposing unjust rulers) justify the means (rebellion and bloodshed)? What were people supposed to do in this situation, which side were they supposed to choose? Such contemplations had certainly lost nothing of their relevance and difficulty by al-Balādhurī's time, on the contrary: the issue of whether and under what circumstances rebellion constituted a legitimate means of opposition was subject to fierce debates especially among legal scholars throughout the period in which the works of the early historical tradition were being compiled. We will return to this in the following section on al-Ṭabarī.

A much less ambivalent example of Khārijism as an objectionable phenomenon is al-Balādhurī's material on the uprising of Sahm b. Ghālib and Yazīd b. Mālik (al-Khaṭīm al-Bāhilī).[78] Sahm and al-Khaṭīm rebelled in Basra in 44 H/664–5 CE during the governorship of ʿAbdallāh b. ʿĀmir.[79] Al-Balādhurī's version has it that Sahm was the first to accuse other Muslims of unbelief. One day, when he led the morning prayer among his group of Khārijites, a man by the name of ʿUbāda b. Qurṣ al-Laythī walked by along with his son and nephew. The rebels stopped and asked them who they were, to which they replied that they were Muslims. The Khārijites accused them of lying, but ʿUbāda insisted, saying that he had opposed the Prophet at first but then came to follow him. The Prophet accepted him after his (ʿUbāda's) profession of the *shahāda*. When he asked the Khārijites to grant them the same and let them go, however, the rebels called him an unbeliever (*kāfir*) and killed his and his relatives. In a rare display of direct involvement, the governor of Basra went into battle against Sahm and al-Khaṭīm himself; many Khārijites were killed, but both leaders survived and were given an *amān* by Ibn ʿĀmir.[80] During the governorship of Ziyād or ʿUbaydallāh, both of them were eventually killed and crucified.[81]

The story of ʿUbāda's murder casts the Khawārij as cold-blooded killers and thus as transgressors of the Islamic norms they claim to uphold. It recalls the slaughter of ʿAbdallāh b. Khabbāb by Khārijites under the command of Misʿar b. Fadakī just before the Battle of Nahrawān.[82] In both cases, the Khawārij kill Companions and/or the sons of a Companion without scruples; they deny other Muslims their status as believers and declare them fit for slaughter. The victims in both cases are astonished by this behaviour: ʿAbdallāh b. Khabbāb struggles to believe that people who outwardly display such piety have no compunction about homicide; ʿUbāda is utterly perplexed that the Khārijites refuse to acknowledge him as a Muslim when the Prophet himself had accepted him into the community. This last point in particular stresses how far these Khārijites have gone astray: what was acceptable to the Prophet is no longer good enough for them. Their incessant religiosity overshoots the mark – as *ḥadīth* forewarns – and thus places them firmly outwith the *umma*.

The similarities between the two episodes are striking, which might again imply the formation of a story prototype that could be employed in various settings, much like the other rhetorical devices and stock phrases that make up literary Khārijism. The murder of Companions and other eminent Muslims might be seen as a sub-motif of Khārijite piety that contributes further to the impression of Khārijism as a narrative tool and once again brings to mind Noth's description of the blank formulae found in conquest accounts.

Al-Balādhurī also uses a 'good' Khārijite, namely Abū Bilāl, to criticise the actions not only of the Umayyads and their supporters, but also of 'bad' Khawārij. For example, Abū Bilāl is shown to oppose the allegedly Khārijite practice of *istiʿrāḍ*, the investigation of others regarding their religio-political beliefs, and he is said to have been the first to do so – another example of the *awāʾil* schema.[83] He apparently disapproved of the unbridled use of force on the part of militant Khawārij, as in the report dealing with the uprising of a certain Qarīb (or Qurayb) and Zuḥḥāf (or Zaḥḥāf): "Abū Bilāl said about them: 'Qarīb [or Qurayb], God did not draw him near, and Zuḥḥāf [or Zaḥḥāf], God did not efface his sins (*lā ʿafā allāh ʿanhu*).' "[84]

Finally, the *Ansāb* also betrays a curious fascination with the participation of women in rebellion as a point of Khārijite practice and doctrine. Other doctrinal concerns, including the treatment of *dhimmīs*,[85] the practice of *istiʿrāḍ*[86] and the position of the *imām*,[87] are briefly referred to as well, but these are minor compared to the issue of female rebels, which appears to have hit a nerve with al-Balādhurī and his audience: his work transmits more material dealing with Khārijite women than any of the other sources under examination.[88] Like the preceding examples, female Khawārij primarily represent a tool for censuring Khārijism.

The question of whether women actually fought on the battlefield in pre-Islamic and early Islamic times, rather than just accompanying the fighters to care for the wounded or manage supplies, is extremely difficult to assess. It has been argued that women did in fact engage in fighting, but that the Iraqi *ʿulamāʾ* of the eighth to tenth century erased their active participation in the process of articulating properly Islamic models of behaviour,[89] signalling a transition from the ʿĀʾisha model of female activism to the quietist Fāṭima model.[90] Such research is sometimes influenced by feminist scholarship on early Islam, which frequently postulates that there was more space in the early period for women to take part in the public sphere, including in warfare.[91] Certain tribes or minorities in particular are said to have been more accepting of women engaging in such activities,[92] which might then also pertain to the Khawārij as an early Islamic minority. In fact, they are known in the sources for their acceptance of women on the battlefield.[93] But overall there is very little evidence to go on; accounts are anecdotal and, even in pre-Islamic Arabia, female warriors were not the norm. Khārijite women have nonetheless drawn much increased attention recently, not just as poets but specifically as fighters.[94] On the whole, such research focuses on female Khawārij as historical phenomena and seeks to study them as "women revolutionaries"[95] or uphold them as exemplars of female agency in early Islam. Questions of representation, of narrative purpose and rhetorical effect, are usually set aside, despite much of the argument resting on poetry, for instance.[96] By contrast, the following remarks may serve as a preliminary engagement with the literary function of rebel women on the early Islamic battlefield.

Chronologically, the *Ansāb*'s first mention of female participation in a Khārijite rebellion in the period covered here occurs in the account of the rebel Abū Maryam, a *mawlā* of Banū al-Ḥārith b. Kaʿb. Abū Maryam is said to have been the first to allow women to accompany him during his uprising. All of them were killed by the troops al-Mughīra sent against them.[97] This is a general pattern in al-Balādhurī's material: whenever a woman is mentioned as participating in a Khārijite rebellion, her fate is almost always certain death. This applies even to those who are not involved in armed resistance to the Umayyads, as the cases of ʿUrwa b. Udayya's daughter[98] and Abū Bilāl's acquaintance al- Thabjāʾ[99] show. Moreover, female Khārijism is closely associated with Ziyād or ʿUbaydallāh's cruelty: the unfortunate victims are variously mutilated, crucified, drowned, occasionally simply "killed" or "given" to allies of the Umayyads.[100] One account explicitly says that Ziyād stripped and crucified a Khārijite woman while threatening to do the same to any other who decided to take up arms. Consequently, "the women held back from the *khurūj* for fear of being exposed".[101]

These reports are evidently meant as a warning to both male and female believers. They emphasise the dire consequences of a woman's involvement in rebellion for her life and – perhaps more importantly – her honour. Regardless of the account's historicity, Ziyād's public exposure of a woman accomplishes several goals: it depicts Ziyād as a transgressor of social norms while at the same time providing a cautionary tale of women presuming to get involved in the public sphere in what is supposed to be men's business. At the same time, the very fact that the Khārijites allow women in their ranks underlines how far they have strayed from the community.[102] Apart from such edifying effects, this episode also makes for some scandalous and thus entertaining storytelling – these were tales suited to evening entertainment (*asmār*).[103] This facet of al-Balādhurī's *Ansāb* is quite noticeable here and might in turn have influenced the selection of such material, which also appears in works like al-Jāḥiẓ's *Kitāb al-Ḥayawān* and al-Mubarrad's *Kāmil*[104] but not in the chronicles. The complexity of a massive work like the *Ansāb* and the fluid boundaries of genre in early Islamic literature come to the fore here.[105] That the idea of women taking up arms was frowned upon is further indicated by the reappearance of Abū Bilāl as a critic of fellow Khawārij – three times on two separate occasions, he is shown to strongly disapprove of women fighting alongside men;[106] he is also said to have been the first to condemn the *khurūj* of women.[107] Al-Balādhurī's use of Abū Bilāl here again stresses the exceptional position he occupies in the early Islamic (historical) tradition.

On the whole, however, al-Balādhurī's criticism of Khārijism is mild compared to al-Ṭabarī. For the most part, the material for this period that denounces Khārijism includes some form of reproach of the Umayyads or their agents as well.[108] This does not detract from the condemnation of Khārijite violence, against ordinary Muslims in particular, but it does mitigate the severity of the rebuke and create a more balanced picture.

"No Folk are Worse Enemies of God": Al-Ṭabarī on Khārijism during the Reign of Mu'āwiya

Al-Ṭabarī's *Ta'rīkh* is the other work that contains enough material on Khārijite revolts during the reign of Mu'āwiya, much of it transmitted on the authority of Abū Mikhnaf,[109] to allow for a more sustained analysis. Nevertheless, the difference to al-Balādhurī's treatment of the same topic is immediately obvious. Al-Ṭabarī does preserve information on a number of small-scale Khārijite rebellions in this period, but much of this material remains sketchy: we are given names, dates and some locations, but no specific reasons are mentioned for the revolts and we learn next to nothing about the rebels' personal backgrounds. Apart from Abū Bilāl, the only exception here is the detailed portrayal of the period's largest Khārijite revolt led by al-Mustawrid b. 'Ullafa.[110] Al-Ṭabarī's rendering of this uprising is largely made up of battle descriptions, strategy discussions in both camps and deliberations among al-Mustawrid's enemies about how to deal with the Khawārij, but it best showcases al-Ṭabarī's storytelling techniques regarding Khārijism. Beyond these particular episodes, however, the Khārijites remain decidedly indistinct. The *lā ḥukma* maxim all but disappears from al-Ṭabarī's accounts[111] and there is only one reference to the supposed point of origin of the Khārijite protest, 'Alī's "abandonment of the judgement of the Book".[112]

Similarly, the use of Qur'ānic references has also decreased significantly in comparison with the accounts of Khārijite origins. Al-Ṭabarī includes only four instances of Khārijites citing the Qur'ān, two of whom (Abū Bilāl and his brother 'Urwa) are (largely) quietists. There is only one instance of an Umayyad governor quoting the Qur'ān in response to a Khārijite envoy. This change in the frequency with which the Khārijites' opponents resort to the Qur'ān to best the rebels might be intended to reflect on their character, especially when contrasted with 'Alī. Regarding the Khārijite case, we saw in the preceding chapter that many of the verses they quote deal with the subject of arbitration and thus function as prompts for 'Alī or his envoys to challenge the Khārijites' flawed interpretation; the remaining verses underline their extreme piety. As al-Ṭabarī transmits significantly fewer of such debates and confrontations for Muʿāwiya's reign, there are hence also fewer occasions on which the Qurʾān might be cited. However, the comparison with al-Balādhurī also highlights the importance of editorial choice in what to include. That the Khawārij now also faced very different opponents compared with an authority figure like ʿAlī will have influenced al-Ṭabarī's portrayal as well, just as it did al-Balādhurī's. We will return to this issue below.

Overall, the period of Muʿāwiya's reign constitutes something of an anomaly in relation to the representation of Khārijite history. This is evident not just in comparison with the preceding chapter, but especially with the following, which deals with the first main period of development of Khārijite thought as portrayed in the historical tradition. There, we have at least as much material as for the reign of ʿAlī, spread across all sources under study and including an abundance of Qurʾān references in both Khārijite and non-Khārijite rhetoric.

Al-Ṭabarī's accounts of Khārijism under Muʿāwiya do not engage with most of the main themes identified in the reports of Khārijite origins. As ʿAlī no longer features as the main protagonist, the allegations against him do not require detailed discussion. The piety theme prevails, of course; al-Ṭabarī's material abounds with such phrases ascribed to the Khawārij.[113] Their prime distinguishing feature, a singular focus on God's will and the Hereafter, thus continues here. In al-Ṭabarī's *Taʾrīkh*, however, Khārijite piety is rarely a cause for celebration because of its immediate connection with violence. The dangers of Khārijite piety are a prominent theme in the *Taʾrīkh* because its intemperance disrupts the social order and threatens to plunge the *umma* into more bloodshed and strife. In consequence, excessive piety needs to be rejected at all turns. This is a different approach to what we saw above regarding al-Balādhurī's *Ansāb*, one that is reflected in the divergent forms and structures of the accounts they both preserve.

Although al-Ṭabarī occasionally transmits some longer descriptions of Khārijite activities, there are no counterparts to the extensive and elaborate debates between the first Khawārij and ʿAlī/his envoys in the case of Muʿāwiya or his governors. It is possible that al-Ṭabarī saw no need to include material of this kind because of the diminished stature of Khārijite opponents and a lack of the urgency that infuses the vindications of ʿAlī. However, such material is not altogether absent and what he does include is often provided in lengthy versions. A comparison with the accounts contained in al-Balādhurī's *Ansāb* also reveals that there certainly was no dearth of substantial reports on Khārijism during this period, which might otherwise have explained the relative scarcity of information in al-Ṭabarī's work and the almost complete silence in the other historiographical sources.

Al-Ṭabarī may have faced a dilemma here: he could not depict the Khawārij as righteous warriors fighting the good fight without compromising the developing broad (proto-Sunnī) consensus that rebellion was on the whole illegitimate regardless of a ruler's tyranny.[114] This position is expressed most clearly in legal and tradition literature, especially in the *ḥadīth* collections such as that of al-Bukhārī (d. 256 H/870 CE): his chapter on *fitna* fiercely condemns violence among Muslims, explicitly also when directed against a seemingly impious ruler.[115] As a jurist and religious scholar, such notions likely had a great influence on al-Ṭabarī's approach to revolt as well. At the same time, however, he appears to have struggled with a favourable portrayal of the Umayyad authorities, as was fairly common among ʿAbbāsid-era scholars,[116] although the caliphs also functioned as upholders of law and order.[117] As a result, the delineation of ideological debates between Khawārij and Umayyads posed a fundamental difficulty: neither side could claim unequivocal moral superiority, as ʿAlī had been able to, and so there were not really any good lessons to be learned. Perhaps as a consequence, al-Ṭabarī's accounts of Khārijite revolts in this period are more concerned with tactics than ideology. Moreover, the discussion of quietist Khārijites, and Abū Bilāl in particular, turns more sympathetic to them, or rather more hostile toward Umayyad representatives. Al-Ṭabarī might have felt that he had more room for manoeuvre here.

Nonetheless, it is clear that al-Ṭabarī is not particularly fond of either side. A report of how Khārijites rejoice after ʿAlī's death at the hand of Ibn Muljam concludes with, "May God be satisfied with him [ʿAlī] and not be satisfied with them [the Khārijites]".[118] On the other hand, another report has Muʿāwiya's own governor of Kufa, al-Mughīra b. Shuʿba, denounce the Umayyads as unjust and tyrannical. The setting is a conversation between al-Mughīra and one of ʿAlī's fiercest supporters, Ṣaʿṣaʿa b. Ṣūḥān, who had served the caliph as envoy to the Khawārij before the Battle of Nahrawān. When Ṣaʿṣaʿa insists on praising ʿAlī and criticising ʿUthmān in public, al-Mughīra urges him to desist because "this regime [*al-sulṭān*; i.e., the Umayyads] has appeared, and we have been ordered to announce ʿAlī's faults to the people". He warns Ṣaʿṣaʿa to comply with Muʿāwiya's orders "to protect ourselves from these folks by means of dissimulation [*taqiyya*]".[119]

There is thus plenty of censure to go around. In fact, let us here take another look at the above account of a group of Khawārij cheering upon the murder of ʿAlī. The Khārijite rebel Ḥayyān b. Ẓabyān al-Sulamī had fought at the Battle of Nahrawān and was among those who had been wounded and later pardoned by ʿAlī. After his recovery, Ḥayyān left his family and went to al-Rayy in northern Iran with a small group of like-minded companions, among them a certain Sālim b. Rabīʿa al-ʿAbsī. They stayed there until they heard about the assassination of ʿAlī. Summoning his comrades to impart the news to them, Ḥayyān gives them a highly detailed account of the deed of "your brother" Ibn Muljam.[120] Sālim is delighted: "May God not cut off the right hand of whoever struck his [ʿAlī's] skull with the sword!"[121] This section of the account then concludes with the line quoted above: "May God be satisfied with him [ʿAlī] and not be satisfied with them [the Khārijites]". Ḥayyān next turns to Khārijite stock topics like the transient nature of the material world and the need to engage in *jihād*. Just before, however, a short passage on Sālim b. Rabīʿa is interpolated in which it is claimed that he later abandoned Khārijism and regretted his erstwhile involvement deeply.[122]

This episode as presented by al-Ṭabarī accomplishes two things primarily: first, reproaching the Khārijites puts their actions into perspective for the audience; their celebration of ʿAlī's death especially should suffice to demonstrate their wickedness. While ʿAlī is shown to have been merciful even towards his sworn enemies (he pardoned the wounded Khawārij at Nahrawān, after all), Ḥayyān as a representative of Khārijism does not shy away from openly displaying his joy at the murder of the man who had spared him. By referring to Ibn Muljam as their brother, Ḥayyān irrevocably associates the Khawārij with the actions of this reviled individual and simultaneously demolishes Khārijite claims to true piety and righteousness.

Second, Sālim's regret further underscores the sinfulness of the Khārijites' actions and beliefs, but it also serves to establish his reputation as a transmitter. As a former Khārijite, Sālim had at one point been (considered) a rebel and presumably a heretic; using his testimony in the chain of authorities may have required some justification.[123] In mentioning Sālim's remorse, al-Ṭabarī enhances his trustworthiness as an informant. The same technique can also be observed with regard to al-Mustawrid's nephew ʿAbdallāh b. ʿUqba al-Ghanawī, the youngest and sole surviving member of the rebel party, who is the main eyewitness source of the reports from within that particular Khārijite camp.[124] Throughout the rendering of al-Mustawrid's rebellion, ʿAbdallāh is described as an immature and inexperienced young man,[125] which excuses his mistakes, while his presence in the Khārijite camp simultaneously establishes him as a knowledgeable informant.

It was argued above that al-Ṭabarī's material for this period does not refer back to most of the themes identified in the preceding chapter. The one consistent theme is piety and, as a corollary, the Khārijite understanding of *jihād*. This twin motif features prominently and is mostly employed to censure Khārijism. The placement and phrasing of many of these accounts indicate that their primary purpose is literary. In other words, while Khārijite statements on *jihād* and its importance for a devout Muslim life are incorporated into reports of their activities, these statements do not necessarily move the story along but rather endeavour to illuminate particular aspects of Khārijite doctrine. To illustrate this, let us take a look at the rebellions of al-Mustawrid b. ʿUllafa in 42–3 H/662–4 CE[126] and Ḥayyān b. Ẓabyān in Kufa in 58 H/677–8 CE,[127] specifically the election process that led to al-Mustawrid and Ḥayyān being acknowledged as leaders of their rebel groups. Both episodes are examples of the 'appointment *schema*' discussed in Chapter Three.[128]

The narrative of the election of Ḥayyān b. Ẓabyān dives directly into the representation of *jihād* as the core element of Khārijism by underlining that the Khawārij are terrified of divine punishment if they show leniency and that they cling to the certainty of a heavenly reward for pursuing *jihād*.[129] This commitment to doing battle for God is reinforced by Ḥayyān when the Khārijites discuss suitable locations for a revolt: even though he is convinced that his group does not stand a chance because they are seriously outnumbered, he rests assured in the knowledge that "God knows that you exert yourselves in *jihād* against His enemy and yours". Regardless of the outcome, he and his companions will thus have attained "His reward and escape from sin".[130]

Despite being relatively long and containing many such sermons, al-Ṭabarī's account of Ḥayyān's revolt is less substantial than it first appears. The speeches and interactions between the Khawārij serve to convey the importance of *jihād*, but they do not do much else. Overall, we learn very little about Ḥayyān's revolt and the discussion of where to rebel is perhaps the best indicator that the precise details do not matter all that much. The point of such reports is to illustrate Khārijite thought and then demonstrate its flaws, which requires textual signifiers of Khārijite ideology but no elaborate framework or backdrop. This observation is substantiated by the fact that Ḥayyān's final speech,[131] for instance, closely resembles that of Ibn Wahb before the Battle of Nahrawān in both wording and tenor.[132] This uniformity of Khārijite rhetoric has already been addressed, but it bears repeating that much if not most of what we read about early Khārijism consists of standardised phrases, situations and ideas that were variously combined and recombined regardless of the particular circumstances of a specific revolt.

The election of al-Mustawrid in 42 H/662–3 CE follows a similar, but more complex pattern. The account does not address *jihād* as the focal point of Khārijite life as such but rather discusses their approach to the question of leadership. We are told that the prominent Kufan Khawārij at the time, among them Ḥayyān and Muʿādh b. Juwayn, assemble and deliberate whom to elect as their leader. The first two statements by al-Mustawrid and Ḥayyān establish the 'Khārijite' doctrine of egalitarianism – neither of them is concerned about "which of you would govern me",[133] stressing that they are "satisfied with every one of my brothers".[134] The immediately following declaration by Muʿādh qualifies this stance by pointing out that not all of them are "virtuous enough for that command". When all members of a group do happen to be equal in virtue, then the most accomplished in war and religion must take charge. The idea of the leader as *primus inter pares* is thus introduced to the doctrinal melange. Upon hearing Muʿādh's argument, both al-Mustawrid and Ḥayyān declare their willingness to follow him in good egalitarian fashion, but he refuses because they are older than him. The principle of seniority thus plays a role, too; the Khawārij eventually agree on al-Mustawrid, as the oldest among them, as leader.

While the passages that deal with the later developments of al-Mustawrid's revolt are overwhelmingly 'structural' in nature in that they focus mostly on the locations, dates and participants of the various battles with al-Mughīra's troops, the account of how his rebellion started is markedly different in nature. The section on al-Mustawrid's appointment as leader here serves to establish Khārijite doctrine and render it recognisable to the audience. As noted, it thus follows the same pattern as the elections of Ibn Wahb and Ḥayyān, which supports the notion of a basic *schema* for Khārijite elections being discernible in the historiographical material. The presence of such *schemata* alongside other rhetorical devices bears the danger of dehistoricisation – we may get a good impression of literary Khārijism, but the historical phenomenon remains blurred.

The examples adduced so far also highlight that Khārijism serves several functions in al-Ṭabarī's material that have little to do with a sober reconstruction of early Khārijite history. His *Taʾrīkh* shares this feature with al-Balādhurī's *Ansāb*, but their approaches and concerns differ. Where al-Balādhurī fleshes out Khārijism to make his points, the accounts in the *Taʾrīkh* resemble the material investigated in the preceding chapter in that while they use the Khawārij as a negative foil, Khārijism itself remains skeletal. The issue of militant piety continues to define literary Khārijism in both works. It bears repeating, however, that while these traits are portrayed as distinctly Khārijite, they do not necessarily tell us much about Khārijism. The following section, which draws particular attention to al-Ṭabarī's different treatment of activist and quietist Khawārij, will illustrate this.

Al-Ṭabarī's Criticism of Activist Khārijism

Al-Ṭabarī uses his discussion of Khārijite activities to condemn violent piety and armed conflict in general. He employs different techniques to convey this disapproval. Explicit direct interventions in a narrative are not very common because they run counter to the widespread scholarly convention of (claiming to be) faithfully transmitting material from authorities considered more distinguished than oneself,[135] a notion that was shared by other traditions from Antiquity to the Renaissance.[136] Authors may on occasion even have purposefully concealed their authorship in order to give their works the appearance of being 'traditional' in the sense of having a long history, of having been passed on through the generations and therefore commanding authority. Anonymity emphasises the appearance of impersonal, factual re-telling of an authoritative custom or story that belongs (or is made out to belong) to a body of traditions and thereby creates legitimacy.[137] Among the most important techniques that allowed scholars to weigh in on the matters they described were thus *condemnation by proxy* and *characterisation*, which shall be given pride of place in what follows. The section concludes with a brief discussion of more subtle forms in which al-Ṭabarī expresses censure.

Condemnation by Proxy

A common technique in framing one's selection of narratives consists in letting one's characters express approval or reprimand of certain groups or issues.[138] The various utterances of al-Mughīra regarding Khārijite activities in and around Kufa are a prime example of this. When first informed of an impending Khārijite revolt, al-Mughīra warns his subjects to "restrain the impudent among you" before the entire community is afflicted with misfortune. He tells them that he will crush any rebellion and set a warning example for those thinking about upsetting public order.[139] The Kufan clan leaders are obviously impressed by his words and implore their people "by God and Islam" to inform the tribal notables about those who might intend "to incite discord or withdraw from the *umma*".[140]

Similarly, when al-Mughīra sends Maʿqil b. Qays against al-Mustawrid, he describes the Khārijite rebels as a "renegade group (*al-māriqa*) who withdrew from our community and accused it of unbelief".[141] Like ʿAlī at Nahrawān, however, al-Mughīra does not give Maʿqil *carte blanche* to do with the Khārijites as he sees fit, but instructs him on proper procedure: first, the rebels have to be called on to repent and return to the *umma*. Only once they have refused this offer is Maʿqil allowed to confront them on the battlefield;[142] al-Mughīra is here shown to emulate ʿAlī's practice at Nahrawān, when he had given his Khārijite opponents ample opportunity to abandon their endeavour and rejoin him.[143] Following 'proper procedure' distinguishes both of them from the Khawārij and their propensity to kill indiscriminately, which underlines that the rebels are on the wrong side of history. Al-Mughīra then tells Maʿqil where to look for the Khārijites and emphasises that quelling their revolt quickly is important because of their bad influence on those around them: "they do not stay in a territory for two days without corrupting anyone associating with them".[144] These first two accounts in particular underline al-Ṭabarī's focus on the socio-political ramifications of rebellion, and specifically Khārijism.

A final example is the conflict between al-Mustawrid's group and the governor of al-Madāʾin, Simāk b. ʿUbayd. To revisit briefly: al-Mustawrid had ordered his nephew ʿAbdallāh to deliver a letter to Simāk in which the rebel summoned the governor to fear God, heed the Qurʾān and reject the "innovators", both ʿAlī and ʿUthmān. This provoked an angry retort from Simāk, who condemns them in a most candid fashion:

> They abandoned right guidance by what they did. They began to recite the Qurʾān to him [al-Mustawrid's nephew], they pretended to humble themselves and to weep. Thus, he thought that they had something of the truth. 'Verily, they are just like cattle, nay, they have strayed further from the way' [Q 25:44]. By God! I never saw people who were in more manifest error nor a more obvious calamity than those whom you see![145]

This characterisation of the Khawārij as hypocritical evildoers who pose a threat to the community because of their violent behaviour and secessionist tendencies is a clear enough castigation of Khārijism, but it is made all the more severe through al-Ṭabarī's particular selection of personalities said to be thus opposed to the rebels.

Characterisation

Al-Mughīra is only one in a series of high-profile Companions and well-regarded early Muslims who are shown to object to Khārijite actions and beliefs. He is presented as a fair, honourable and honest man who does not persecute people merely for holding Khārijite beliefs:

> He [al-Mughīra] treated people well and did not ask about their factions . . . He would say, 'God decided that you will continue to disagree. God will settle between you anything over which you might disagree [Q 42:10].' Thus, the people felt safe with him.[146]

When al-Mughīra does condemn Khārijism, his judgement therefore carries weight. The same applies to the other characters who are shown to censure the Khawārij, especially because none of them are depicted as devoted supporters of the Umayyads.

Simāk b. ʿUbayd's refusal to wash his hands of either ʿUthmān or ʿAlī is a clear indication of this. His attitude of acknowledging both caliphs alongside Abū Bakr and ʿUmar is instead characteristic of the *'jamāʿī'* view that was well under way to acquiring majority status within the Muslim (scholarly) communities by al-Ṭabarī's time.[147] Connected to this is the development of the 'four-caliph thesis', which holds Muḥammad's four successors (Abū Bakr, ʿUmar, ʿUthmān and ʿAlī) to be 'rightly guided' (*rāshidūn*) in equal measure. The development of this idea is probably linked at least in part to the many conflicts that ravaged early Muslim society, necessitating the creation of an umbrella under which as many believers as possible could place themselves. The four-caliph thesis has become a core tenet of Sunnī Islam; it has long been credited to figures like Ibn Ḥanbal (d. 241 H/855 CE) and al-Shāfiʿī (d. 204 H/820 CE). Recent scholarship has traced the idea back to the second half of the eighth century, however, and shown that it enjoyed support among varied groups (Murjiʾīs, proto-Shīʿis, proto-Sunnīs) in Basra and Kufa before it became prominent in Baghdad.[148] Indeed, the focus on community, on keeping together a complex and fractious structure like the *umma*, is an old concern that may harken back to the Umayyad period,[149] meaning that the catholic outlook of much of the material compiled in the works examined in this study was, to an extent, already present.[150] The socio-political and religious developments of the ninth and tenth century may then have led some of them, notably al-Ṭabarī, to accentuate this outlook further.

Returning to the episode in question, Simāk is portrayed as representative of the wider *umma* and communal consensus rather than a specifically Umayyad worldview. We can also discern a further pattern: many of the Khārijites' opponents in this period are not only early converts, but pro-ʿAlids as well. In fact, al-Ṭabarī makes a point of underlining the particular enmity between ʿAlī's supporters and the Khawārij. His portrayal of Khārijite activities at this time consequently reads like a continuation of the ʿAlid–Khārijite conflict, albeit without a similarly exalted protagonist. This is evident in the ways in which well-known champions of the ʿAlid cause are shown to engage with the Khawārij. That those who promoted ʿAlī and his family are especially ill-disposed towards the Khārijites does not appear far-fetched, but this inveterate antagonism is a particular feature of al-Ṭabarī's work and highlights the importance of this strategy for his representation of Khārijism. Consider the following examples.

When the Khārijite leader al-Mustawrid arrives in Kufa, he seeks refuge with a relative from the ʿAbd al-Qays. Ṣaʿṣaʿa b. Ṣūḥān, another member of this tribe, arrives in Kufa at some point and discovers al-Mustawrid's presence there. Ṣaʿṣaʿa does not want to endanger his people by alerting the authorities and thus remains quiet about the rebels in hiding, but his opinion of them – and thus of al-Mustawrid's stay in Kufa – is clarified in a speech to his fellow tribesmen. He begins by calling the ʿAbd al-Qays the "most favoured by God" because they stood firmly on the side of righteousness (i.e., ʿAlī's side) throughout the succession conflicts. During the first *fitna*, they chose to follow the "People of the House (*ahl al-bayt*) [the term here references ʿAlī and his family], through whom God first gave us glory". The ʿAbd al-Qays were God's instrument in destroying "the faithless at the Battle of the Camel and the renegades at the Battle of Nahrawān".[151]

Ṣaʿṣaʿa is thereby cast as an avid pro-ʿAlid with proto-Shīʿī undertones, as the particular use of the term *ahl al-bayt* implies. The narrative of Ṣaʿṣaʿa's address is interrupted at this point by a brief statement that Ṣaʿṣaʿa did not mention the Syrians in his speech because they were in power at that time.[152] Not only does this emphasise the hostility between ʿAlī's faction and the Syrians/Umayyads, it is also an opportunity to voice disaffection with the Umayyad authorities by implying that they did not take kindly to criticism. Towards the end of his speech, Ṣaʿṣaʿa again urges caution because the authorities are aware of the political leanings of the ʿAbd al-Qays.[153] This clarifies the position of the pro-ʿAlids vis-à-vis the Umayyads, but also prepares the ground for al-Ṭabarī's more sympathetic portrayal of quietist Khārijism in opposition to Umayyad injustice.

Ṣaʿṣaʿa's speech continues with an explicit condemnation of Khārijism: "No folk are worse enemies of God, you, the family of your Prophet and the community of Muslims than these mistaken renegades".[154] He warns his people not to give shelter to the Khawārij or hold back information about them, arguing that they should not give the (Syrian) authorities grounds for punishing them. He concludes with a promise to kill every Khārijite he finds in Kufa, an act that would bestow God's favour on him.[155] This final remark supports the lawfulness of killing the Khārijite rebels – a concern we already encountered in the reports of Nahrawān – and even claims explicit divine sanction for this act.

Ṣaʿṣaʿa's speech is well received; the tribespeople curse the Khawārij and swear to turn them in if discovered. This appears to contradict Ṣaʿṣaʿa's intention of keeping his tribe out of trouble by not disclosing publicly that some of its members harbour Khārijite dissidents, but al-Ṭabarī does not seem too concerned about resolving this particular inconsistency.

Another of ʿAlī's fervent followers who is described as resolutely hostile towards Khārijism is ʿAdī b. Ḥātim, whose son Ḥujr was executed for his stalwart support of ʿAlī's family in 672 and is counted among the great Shīʿī heroes.[156] ʿAdī was a member of Kinda, the same tribe as al-Ashʿath b. Qays, who serves the role of villain in ʿAlī's troubles with the future Khārijites at Ṣiffīn. The families of ʿAdī and Ḥujr represent a counterpoint to that of al-Ashʿath, 'good Kindīs', as it were, to be juxtaposed with the general mass of Kinda tribesmen who are accused of malice and disloyalty. The contrast between the two families is further sharpened by the betrayal of Ḥujr b. ʿAdī by al-Ashʿath's son, who delivered him to the Umayyads for execution.[157] Beyond this, ʿAdī's family also embodies the fragmentation of the early *umma*: while his son Ḥujr remained faithful to the ʿAlids until death, another of his sons joined Muʿāwiya,[158] while a third son appears to have died at Nahrawān on the side of the Khawārij after ʿAdī had tried in vain to deter him,[159] which might further explain his enmity towards the Khārijites. At the same time, this very even distribution of his sons among the factions available at the time should rouse our suspicion – while its historicity is possible, its symbolism implies a literary purpose as well.

We encounter ʿAdī in the story of al-Mustawrid's rebellion, in the aftermath of Ṣaʿṣaʿa's speech. Al-Mustawrid has since learned that his presence among the ʿAbd al-Qays endangers his host, so he decides to leave Kufa. It is unclear how or by whom, but the governor al-Mughīra is told about al-Mustawrid's departure and sends for the tribal leaders to discuss who should follow the rebels. ʿAdī is present as well and tells al-Mughīra that he would be happy to go after the Khārijites; in fact, he states that al-Mughīra does not have to worry about volunteers for this particular endeavour: "We are all their enemy and consider their opinion foolish".[160] As it happens, ʿAdī's words prove to be true: Ṣaʿṣaʿa b. Ṣūḥān and Maʿqil b. Qays, both supporters of the ʿAlids, vie with each other to be given command over the troops. Al-Mughīra eventually chooses Maʿqil, both because of friction between himself and Ṣaʿṣaʿa and because Maʿqil is said to be the greatest enemy of the Khawārij.[161]

The way in which al-Ṭabarī points out the hostility between ʿAlī's followers and the Khārijites is straightforward: on various occasions, the authorities are shown to choose pro-ʿAlids to do battle against the rebels deliberately because they were "the strongest in allowing the blood of these renegades to be shed, and [they] were more courageous against them [the Khārijites] than others, as they had fought them previously".[162] It is for this reason that al-Mughīra sends "the best of the Shīʿa and their cavalry"[163] with Maʿqil to fight against al-Mustawrid.

This pattern continues in the hunt for al-Mustawrid. When he crosses over into Basran territory on his flight from Maʿqil, the governor of Basra, ʿAbdallāh b. ʿĀmir, enquires about the situation and is told that a Kufan army is in pursuit. Upon learning that Maʿqil and other supporters of ʿAlī were chosen to fight the Khawārij because of their hostility towards them, ʿAbdallāh sees the wisdom of this decision and sends for a Basran sympathiser of the ʿAlids, Sharīk b. al-Aʿwar al-Ḥārithī, who is ordered to put together an army to engage the rebels and drive them out of Basran territory. The governor privately tells Sharīk to select those who consider lawful the killing of God's enemies, meaning the Khārijites. Sharīk, who detests the "evil folk" of the Khawārij,[164] ultimately decides to draft the cavalry of the Basran Rabīʿa, who hold 'Shīʿī' views.[165]

Al-Ṭabarī's characterisation of the Khārijites' adversaries offers another means of circumventing the problem of depicting either the rebels or the Umayyad agents as righteous. Neither al-Mughīra nor Simāk b. ʿUbayd are presented as hard and fast supporters of the Umayyad regime; al-Mughīra even seems (moderately) critical of the ruling house. It is thus possible to depict these particular government agents at least in a favourable light and censure the Khawārij without praising the Umayyads. In the same vein, by pitting the Kufan Khārijites against prominent pro-ʿAlid protagonists, al-Ṭabarī manages to portray the hostilities as a continuation of the conflict between ʿAlī and the Khārijites, in which the allocation of roles is unambiguous: ʿAlī is right, the Khārijites are wrong. In short, not putting the rebels in direct opposition to the Umayyads has the undeniable advantage of not having to side with either faction.

The narrative techniques outlined so far enable explicit forms of reproach of Khārijism. Beyond these, al-Ṭabarī also uses subtler editing and storytelling techniques to convey disaffection with the Khawārij. There is a continuity of 'personnel' from the rebels at Nahrawān to many of the Khārijites of Muʿāwiya's reign, such as Muʿādh b. Juwayn and Ḥayyān b. Ẓabyān, for instance. This might well be historical information, of course, but there is also a clear rhetorical effect: as those who fought at Nahrawān on the Khārijite side are mostly depicted as violent criminals, this continuity casts aspersions on their own later activities and those of their rebel 'offspring'.

Moreover, virtually every account of a Khārijite revolt in this period ends with a dry remark to the effect that all rebels were killed.[166] This is the case even with the insurgency of al-Mustawrid, which is otherwise discussed at considerable length.[167] The final paragraph on al-Mustawrid can be paraphrased as follows: the Khārijites and Maʿqil's troops valiantly fight each other until al-Mustawrid challenges Maʿqil to a duel. Maʿqil's men implore their commander not to fight "this dog of whose soul God has despaired",[168] but Maʿqil accepts the challenge. The two leaders kill each other, but because Maʿqil had appointed his successor before his death,[169] the Kufans immediately rally under their new commander and slay the remaining Khawārij. This is the first and final major rebellion by an activist, militant Khārijite of this period in al-Ṭabarī's work. The last impression is thus one of utter defeat, which in itself can be understood as indicative of the failure of Khārijism as a whole.

The Basran Quietists

We have seen that al-Ṭabarī uses both explicit and indirect ways of criticising Khārijism. However, this condemnation is primarily directed at its violent modes of expression. It appears that it is not Khārijite ideas *per se* that are objectionable, but rather the exceedingly violent, socially disruptive forms that (certain strands of) Khārijism can take. 'Divergent' beliefs could be ignored as long as these did not turn openly political and inspire rebellion, thereby threatening the stability of the community.[170] This important distinction lies at the core of al-Ṭabarī's treatment of the Khārijite quietists of Basra.

With the failure of al-Mustawrid's revolt, al-Ṭabarī's focus shifts from Kufa to Basra and the conflict between the Basran governors and the town's Khārijites. The single exception is the rebellion of Muʿādh b. Juwayn and Ḥayyān b. Ẓabyān in Kufa in 58 H/677–8 CE, but the main point of the reports on their uprising is not to delineate their interactions with non-Khārijites – as a matter of fact, there are none – but to discuss *jihād* as a Khārijite core belief. The account does not even disclose the location of their eventual revolt; at the end of the entry, it just states that an army was sent out against them and that they were all killed.[171]

The stories of Khārijism in Basra are different from the accounts of Kufan Khārijism. Basran Khārijism has more narrative substance and there is little condemnation of the Khārijite protagonists in these stories. There are two main reasons for this: first, some of the Basran Khawārij mentioned by al-Ṭabarī are quietists, meaning that their opposition to the Umayyads is on the whole restricted to socially more acceptable forms of opposition. This is further underlined by a crucial difference between militants and quietists: while we have seen that the former frequently condemn the caliphs ʿUthmān and ʿAlī,[172] the latter refrain from doing so entirely in al-Ṭabarī's material. One of the major points of contention between Khārijite doctrine and the proto-Sunnī four-caliph consensus is thereby removed. Second, the Basran Khārijites of this time are opposed to, and by, two notorious governors, Ziyād b. Abīhi and his son ʿUbaydallāh. Al-Ṭabarī's work portrays them as cruel and unjust, which corresponds with their loyalty to the equally despotic Umayyads.

Al-Ṭabarī's approach to Basran Khārijism is thus considerably more sympathetic compared with how the activist Kufan Khārijites are pictured.

Importantly, the quietists are depicted as dissenters, not as criminals who shed blood, which accords them a different status in Islamic law as it developed over time.[173] They fulfil a distinct narrative purpose at variance with their militant counterparts, but the accounts are just as stylised. Regardless of the identity of a particular Khārijite, quietist or activist, and independent from the circumstances of any specific revolt or confrontation, they all express themselves in the same manner and repeat the same statements over and over again.[174] This observation was discussed in more detail in Chapter Three, but it warrants repeated mention because of its consequences for the reconstruction of Khārijite history. In terms of narrative effect, this appearance of sameness has obvious advantages: otherwise obscure literary Khārijism can be utilised as a general discussion tool irrespective of individual contexts and be moulded into a recognisable narrative signal. It is at this stage that we encounter the tentative beginnings of the pious martyrdom stories associated with Marwānid-era Khārijism.[175]

Al-Ṭabarī's accounts of the Basran Khārijites focus chiefly on two Khārijite brothers whom we have already met, Abū Bilāl Mirdās b. Udayya and ʿUrwa b. Udayya. Both of them appear as critics of Umayyad injustice and are eventually put to death at ʿUbaydallāh's behest. The story begins in the year 45 H/665–6 CE with Muʿāwiya's appointment of Ziyād as governor of Basra, Khurāsān and Sīstān, which occasioned Ziyād's famous inaugural speech in Basra.[176] This is the first instance in which Ziyād is confronted with Khārijite criticism. At the end of Ziyād's speech, Abū Bilāl reprimands him for threatening his subjects with collective punishment.[177] He quotes Q 53:37–8 ('[Or was he not informed of what is in the scrolls of Moses,] and of Abraham, who fulfilled his obligations? That no soul burdened shall bear the burden of another; that man shall gain only what he endeavours'[178]) and concludes that "God promised us better than you, O Ziyād".[179] While Ziyād has the last word in this confrontation, it is Abū Bilāl who appears as the voice of righteousness.

That Ziyād and ʿUbaydallāh's policies transgress the boundaries of acceptable behaviour is reiterated throughout al-Ṭabarī's discussion of their dealings with the Khārijites. Ziyād is repeatedly shown to threaten the Basrans with dire consequences should they fail to take action against the Khārijites: "By God, take care of these for me or I shall certainly start with you"; "by God, if a single man of them escapes, you won't get one dirham of your stipends".[180] Ziyād and his deputy Samura also killed many Khārijites, particularly in the aftermath of one of the rare revolts of Basran Khawārij in 46 H/666–7 CE.[181]

ʿUbaydallāh is depicted as even harsher than his father and almost obsessed with persecuting the Khārijites, particularly from 58 H/677–8 CE onward.[182] He reportedly killed groups of Khārijite prisoners, among them Abū Bilāl's brother ʿUrwa b. Udayya, whom we first encountered in the reports of the origins of Khārijism at Ṣiffīn.[183] Both ʿUrwa and Abū Bilāl are said to have participated in the battle of Nahrawān,[184] where they were wounded in the fighting and carried off the battlefield. Thereafter and until their confrontations with ʿUbaydallāh b. Ziyād, both apparently lived in Basra as quietists. As Abū Bilāl occupies an important position in Khārijite/Ibāḍī as well as (to a lesser extent) the Sunnī and Shīʿī tradition, let us examine the account of his brother's execution by ʿUbaydallāh in greater detail.[185]

As the story goes, ʿUrwa approaches ʿUbaydallāh one day and criticises the state of the *umma*, quoting Q 26:128–30 ('Do you build on every height a marvellous mansion for your delight? And erect palaces so that you may live eternally? When you strike, you strike like tyrants.'). ʿUbaydallāh assumes that ʿUrwa only addresses him so boldly because his companions are close by, so the governor leaves without reply. ʿUrwa is told that he should be cautious and hide from ʿUbaydallāh, who would surely want to kill him for his words. ʿUrwa heeds the warning but for some undisclosed reason decides to go to Kufa, which results in his prompt arrest. He is brought to ʿUbaydallāh, who has ʿUrwa's hands and feet cut off. The governor then demands to know what the Khārijite thinks of his punishment. ʿUrwa responds, "I think that you ruined this world for me and that you ruined the Hereafter for yourself".[186] ʿUbaydallāh is outraged, kills him and sends for ʿUrwa's daughter, whom he executes as well.

Such heroically pious dying statements are a staple of Khārijite death scenes. Ibn Muljam, al-Thabjāʾ,[187] ʿUrwa, Umm ʿAlqama[188] – the list is long. We will return to this point a little later, but it is clear that this is a *topos* of Khārijite martyrdom narratives. In ʿUrwa's death scene, ʿUbaydallāh is without doubt the villain. He is portrayed as a coward who does not dare respond to ʿUrwa for fear of being outnumbered by Khārijites. Apart from this physical weakness, ʿUbaydallāh's mental prowess is equally in doubt: his reactions to ʿUrwa's verbal challenges, especially at the end, show that violence is his only means of defence and communication – a feature often associated with Khārijism, in fact. ʿUrwa's verdict on ʿUbaydallāh's fate in the Hereafter is a stark final judgement, and the execution of ʿUrwa's daughter only serves to reinforce it. This killing of a woman who as far as we know has done nothing wrong exemplifies injustice and brutality as embodied in the person of a faithful Umayyad servant. Conversely, ʿUrwa's concern for the *umma*, his all but reckless honesty in the face of a stronger adversary and his stoicism throughout an excruciating ordeal turn him into a shining example of pious fortitude reminiscent of Christian martyrdom narratives.[189] While the delineation of the Basran quietists contains the now familiar association of Khārijism and piety, there is thus no condemnation of this piety as dishonest, misguided or socially disruptive here. On the contrary, Khārijite piety and bravery are what make them stand out against the Umayyads.

This is epitomised in the story of Abū Bilāl's imprisonment by ʿUbaydallāh. In comparison with al-Balādhurī,[190] al-Ṭabarī transmits a rather short version of this episode,[191] but this makes it all the more interesting to look at which details were included. Al-Ṭabarī begins with the endpoint of Abū Bilāl's tale, his rebellion in al-Ahwāz in 58 H/677–8 CE.[192] The account then immediately explains that he had previously been imprisoned by ʿUbaydallāh along with a number of other Khārijites. The jailer was so impressed with Abū Bilāl's religious zeal, however, that he let him leave the prison at night to return to his family; every morning without fail, the Khārijite would be back by dawn. One day, ʿUbaydallāh decided to kill the imprisoned Khārijites and news of this reached Abū Bilāl at home. The jailer was worried that his charge would not return, but found to his utter surprise that he was back in the morning as usual. When asked why he returned despite the threat to his life, Abū Bilāl told the jailer that "you would not be rewarded for your kindness if you were punished because of me".[193] Thereupon the jailer, who just so happened to be ʿUbaydallāh's milk brother, interceded on Abū Bilāl's behalf, told ʿUbaydallāh the story of the Khārijite's return to prison and asked him to spare Abū Bilāl. ʿUbaydallāh agreed and gave the Khārijite to the jailer, who released Abū Bilāl. The Khārijite's later revolt against ʿUbaydallāh is not discussed in detail by al-Ṭabarī, in particular contrast to al-Balādhurī's version, although the blame for his rebellion is placed on ʿUbaydallāh here as well.

A key point of Abū Bilāl's pre-rebellion story as told by al-Ṭabarī is to emphasise his exceptional piety, honesty and integrity – virtues that are more important to him than his own life and which seem to have interested al-Ṭabarī a lot more than Abū Bilāl's ill-fated rebellion, which appears almost as an afterthought and so puts the quietist phase of Abū Bilāl's tale centre stage. This stands in sharp contrast to the many accounts of misguided, violent godliness in much of his material on Khārijism. As the militant aspect fades from the story, it is apparently not an issue to portray some Khārijites as pious martyrs slaughtered for their beliefs by Umayyad tyrants. As suggested above, this might indicate that al-Ṭabarī was not so much concerned about Khārijism as a specific set of religious ideas or doctrines, but rather took issue with its potential for upsetting law and order and causing bloodshed among Muslims.

This is further supported by al-Ṭabarī's discussion of the two violent revolts carried out by Basran Khārijites, which serve a very different narrative purpose than Abū Bilāl's rebellion. Regarding the latter, Khārijite violence is almost completely absent from the reports and only mentioned in the context of Abū Bilāl's battle against Umayyad troops. The focus is on Abū Bilāl's piety and righteous conduct, and the fierce determination of his companions against impossible odds: they were defeated only by an army almost 100 times the size of their own small group.[194] Al-Ṭabarī's portrayal of the Basran militants, by contrast, highlights Khārijite violence to the exclusion of almost everything else. The first case is that of al-Khaṭīm, also known by his proper name Yazīd b. Mālik al-Bāhilī, and Sahm b. Ghālib al-Ḥujaymī, both of whom we have met already. They rebelled in 46 H/666–7 CE. Sahm left for al-Ahwāz, but later returned to Basra and asked the governor Ziyād for a guarantee of safe-conduct (*amān*), which was denied, and he was crucified. Al-Khaṭīm was exiled to Baḥrayn, but later allowed to return under certain conditions. When he violated his curfew, Ziyād ordered his execution.[195] Al-Ṭabarī's *Taʾrīkh* also includes a variant account that places their rebellion much earlier, in 41 H/661–2 CE, during the governorship of ʿAbdallāh b. ʿĀmir.[196]

Both versions of Sahm and al-Khaṭīm's revolt are short and do not impart much detail beyond the structural components. If it were not for mention of the *lā ḥukma* watchword, their identity would be difficult to determine. In fact, al-Ṭabarī's second report does not mention it or any other Khārijite identifier; it is only with recourse to the first account as well as reports transmitted in other sources[197] that their affiliation can be ascertained. As sparse as al-Ṭabarī's depiction is, however, it clearly reverts to the established pattern of censuring Khārijism. The variant report states that the rebels killed a Companion while he performed his prayers. This repulsive act contradicts Khārijite claims to righteousness; as in al-Balādhurī's narrative, it is also reminiscent of ʿAbdallāh b. al-Khabbāb's murder before Nahrawān. Sahm and al-Khaṭīm thus fit into a Khārijite tradition of murdering eminent Muslims.[198]

The fate both Khārijites eventually meet reflects the general censure of Khārijism. In the Qurʾān [Q 5:33], crucifixion and exile are punishments for those who rebel against God and his Messenger:

> In truth, the punishment of those who make war against God and His Messenger, and roam the earth corrupting it, is that they be killed, or crucified, or have their hands and feet amputated, alternately, or be exiled from the land. This would be their shame in the present life, and in the next a terrible torment awaits them.[199]

The sources describe crucifixion and amputation as standard punishments for Khārijite rebels; the exegetical tradition even names Khārijism as one of several possible *asbāb al-nuzūl* ('occasions for revelation') for this verse.[200] This is an anachronistic ascription, of course, but one that reflects the discourse on Khārijism in the early period. That Islamic law turned crucifixion and amputation into the penalties for brigandage (*ḥirāba*) in explicit contradistinction to rebellion[201] may be another strike against the Khawārij. It is unlikely that this distinction reflects actual practice in the Umayyad era,[202] but the later evolution of this legal discourse is an undercurrent of the stories that tell such punishment and execution tales and thus a narrative guide for the 'correct' evaluation of Khārijite actions on the part of the audience of these texts. At the same time, however, this is not a straightforward mechanism: it is not uncommon for such scenes to convey reproach of the Khārijite and his/her executioner simultaneously,[203] and in the case of ʿUrwa b. Udayya, for instance, the story of his conflict with ʿUbaydallāh and eventual execution diverges so substantially in content and narrative technique that it implies a different reading altogether of this particular Khārijite martyr narrative.

The second instance of armed revolt by Basran Khārijites is preserved in an even shorter report. It states that Qarīb (or Qurayb) of the Iyād tribe and Zuḥḥāf (or Zaḥḥāf) of the Ṭayyiʾ were the first to rebel after the Khārijites at Nahrawān.[204] Al-Ṭabarī's version does not offer much additional information regarding this revolt and is almost identical to al-Balādhurī's report;[205] its reproach of these Khārijites is straightforward: "God did not draw Qarīb close. I swear by God that I would rather fall from the sky than do what he did [i.e., rebel and cause conflict and bloodshed]."[206] This censure of Qarīb and Zuḥḥāf's actions is all the more compelling because it is attributed to a fellow Khārijite, Abū Bilāl. The account is thus a good example of characterisation as a vehicle of criticism: Abū Bilāl has been established as a righteous and 'correctly' pious man, whereby he serves as a foil to Qarīb and Zuḥḥāf. The story of this particular Basran Khārijite revolt therefore asserts that al-Ṭabarī is critical of unrestrainedly militant, but not necessarily quietist Khārijism; it further demonstrates that Abū Bilāl came to be considered authoritative not just among his peers, but by the Islamic tradition more broadly.

Conclusions

This chapter looked at the representation of Khārijism during the reign of Muʿāwiya (r. 40–60 H/661–80 CE). The discussion centred on al-Balādhurī and al-Ṭabarī as the only authors to provide accounts with the narrative substance necessary for an analysis of literary Khārijism. The investigation of their approaches to Khārijism revealed an interesting dichotomy: while they present much the same material and focus on Khārijite militant piety, their assessments of this issue vary greatly, especially with regard to the complex relationship between piety and violence. In this, their approaches almost represent mirror images of one another.

Al-Balādhurī's portrayal of the Khawārij is considerably more favourable. Instead of using his material to discredit Khārijite piety and condemn their commitment to *jihād* wholesale, he contrasts these characteristics with the iniquity of the Umayyads and their representatives. His portrayal suggests that the Khawārij were frequently forced to take up arms in order to defend themselves against the authorities or because they could no longer ignore the rulers' wrongdoing. Many of the accounts transmitted in the *Ansāb* therefore depict the rebels as morally superior to their opponents. Al-Balādhurī's work also contains some criticism of Khārijite violence, but it is comparatively moderate and focuses on instances of extreme brutality as well as cases where the rebels confront Muslims who are not representatives of the ruling house.

Al-Ṭabarī offers a negative view of early Umayyad-era Khārijism that is based on the ramifications of excessive piety for the *umma*. His work condemns the Khawārij for causing mayhem and destruction, which threatens the cohesion of the Muslim community and potentially endangers the stability of the empire.[207] Khārijism here fulfils the narrative function of discussing legitimate and illegitimate forms of religious and political dissent, with the latter resulting in bloodshed and thus illustrating the dangers of excessive piety. This criticism of militant Khārijism is further elucidated by the more positive depiction of quietist Khārijites. As the immediate threat of violence drops from the narrative, al-Ṭabarī's portrayal appears more comfortable with addressing Umayyad misdeeds and delineating their opponents as righteous victims persecuted and martyred for challenging the rulers – here, the Khārijite pursuit of a godly life is cause for quiet approval.

The difference between al-Ṭabarī and al-Balādhurī's assessment of Khārijism is perhaps based on their particular concerns as scholars. Al-Ṭabarī cannot praise Khārijite piety because the violence it breeds poses a threat to community and state. Indeed, the perils of rebellion are such that it is discouraged regardless of a ruler's conduct – any ruler is better than anarchy. Al-Ṭabarī was a jurist first and the legal discourse of his day shines through here. This is not to say that his depiction is sympathetic to the Umayyads beyond their function as upholders of law and order. There is little laudatory concerning them or their agents in his material on their interactions with the Khawārij. The dilemma of depicting a conflict in which neither side is morally superior to the other is partly solved by the selection of prominent pro-ʿAlids and other respected members of the *umma* as opponents of the Khārijites. This way, neither the rebels nor the

Umayyads are proven right. Presenting Khārijite rebellions in this period as a continuation of their conflict with ʿAlī also enables al-Ṭabarī to delegitimise their accusations further.

Al-Balādhurī, on the other hand, appears more concerned with questions of ethics and morals, how they are relevant to and influence an individual's behaviour. The *Ansāb* also betrays *adab* components in its dual focus on edification and entertainment. This is exemplified in the accounts of Khārijite women on the battlefield, a topic equally suited for moral deliberations and diverting tales. As al-Balādhurī does not focus primarily on the ramifications of rebellion for state and empire, he is also freer to voice his criticism of the Umayyads. His status as boon companion to an ʿAbbāsid caliph may also have caused the tone of his material to be more disparaging of them here than al-Ṭabarī's. If known, external influences on a particular work, such as occupation or patronage, can thus be helpful in analysing how a specific event, group or individual is portrayed, even and especially if the pool of material is similar.

Al-Balādhurī and al-Ṭabarī's differences of approach are particularly well reflected in their assessment of Abū Bilāl. They both present rather favourable images of him, but while al-Ṭabarī's positive portrayal of Abū Bilāl's exemplary piety and integrity overshadows his eventual rebellion, al-Balādhurī focuses on his piety as the motivation behind his decision to take up arms and revolt when he could no longer stand Umayyad wrongdoing. Al-Ṭabarī acknowledges that Abū Bilāl was a righteous believer who was forced into rebellion, although this is a last and desperate resort that should be avoided almost at any cost. Al-Balādhurī celebrates – or at least approves of – Abū Bilāl's revolt as pious opposition to injustice. This might also explain why al-Balādhurī's account of Abū Bilāl's rebellion is significantly longer and much more detailed than al-Ṭabarī's.

As much as al-Ṭabarī and al-Balādhurī may differ in their delineations of Khārijism, however, they nevertheless pursue the same approach in utilising accounts of the rebels to discuss different matters. Much of the material contains elaborate Khārijite statements and debates, but as we saw already in the preceding chapters, the bulk of these are comprised of pious phrases that are employed time and again irrespective of the specific circumstances of an individual revolt. The Khārijite election process for their leaders is a prime example of this standardisation: the wording, tenor and course of action are essentially the same, illustrated here on the example of Ibn Wahb, al-Mustawrid and Ḥayyān b. Ẓabyān's appointments.

We also saw that al-Balādhurī and al-Ṭabarī include much the same material; its provenance, however, remains somewhat obscure. Al-Ṭabarī provides the *isnād* for most of his reports, but we cannot trace their evolution further back than approximately the mid- to late eighth century. He appears to have relied mainly on Iraqi transmitters from that period, most prominently Abū Mikhnaf, who provided the bulk of al-Ṭabarī's information on the early Khawārij in general. Other authorities referred to are ʿAwāna b. al-Ḥakam (d. 147–58 H/764–74 CE), Hishām b. Muḥammad al-Kalbī (d. 204–6 H/819–21 CE) and Wahb b. Jarīr (d. 206 H/822 CE), known transmitters of Khārijite material, but al-Ṭabarī only refers to them on a couple of occasions. His material attributed to Wahb b. Jarīr is basically identical to Ibn Khayyāṭ's sparse information on the Khārijites, also transmitted on Wahb's authority, though we do not know whether al-Ṭabarī accessed the material attributed to Ibn Khayyāṭ, a common source or Wahb's work directly.

Al-Balādhurī, on the other hand, only gives the *isnād* on two occasions. Both times, the two immediate authorities quoted are Zuhayr b. Ḥarb (d. 234 H/849 CE) and Wahb b. Jarīr. Almost all other accounts are introduced by a simple *qālū*. This is highly unusual when we compare this to al-Balādhurī's material on Khārijite origins in ʿAlī's caliphate, almost all of which has an *isnād*, although he otherwise uses *qālū*/*qāla* frequently throughout the *Ansāb*[208] and the *Futūḥ*, where this signifies the amalgamation or summarisation (*ikhtiṣār*) of disparate accounts.[209]

One of the reports that features an *isnād*, ʿUrwa's execution by ʿUbaydallāh, is almost identical to al-Ṭabarī's version of the same episode, both in *matn* and *isnād* (the other is not included in al-Ṭabarī's work). This does not mean that we can simply turn to al-Ṭabarī's work to identify the origin of al-Balādhurī's reports, however. While they often preserve almost identical accounts, these are mostly prefaced by entirely different chains of transmission. At least once, al-Balādhurī's account of a particular event is also closer to Khalīfa b. Khayyāṭ's version, with Ibn Khayyāṭ providing a different *isnād* from al-Ṭabarī's rendering.[210] Moreover, al-Balādhurī's more voluminous material on the Khārijites sometimes combines passages identical in al-Ṭabarī's work with sections not included there.[211] The reshaping of accounts as part of the usual redaction process of early Islamic historiography hampers the identification of the material's origins. Al-Yaʿqūbī's *Taʾrīkh* is not helpful here either, of course, as he provides virtually no *isnād*s at all throughout his work. While we can say with certainty that al-Balādhurī and al-Ṭabarī – and by extension other early Islamic scholars – received much of their material from the same source pool, we know much less about this material before it began the slow process of systematisation in mid- to late eighth-century Iraq.

Notes

1. A version of this chapter was published in *al-Masāq* in 2016 (Hagemann, "Challenging Authority"). The article was based on the relevant chapter of my 2015 PhD dissertation; the present chapter has been thoroughly revised, but the main findings still stand. My thanks to *al-Masāq*'s editorial board for granting permission to re-use the material.
2. For instance, Ibn Khayyāṭ, *Taʾrīkh*, I, 234 places the revolt against Muʿāwiya at al-Nukhayla in the year 41 H and under the command of ʿAbdallāh b. Abī al-Ḥawsāʾ. Al-Yaʿqūbī, *Taʾrīkh*, II, 217 states that this revolt took place in 40 H and was led by Farwa b. Nawfal al-Ashjāʿī.
3. See, for example, Ibn Khayyāṭ, *Taʾrīkh*, I, 234 (on Ibn Abī al-Ḥawsāʾ), 235 (on Saḥm b. Ghālib and al-Khaṭīm), 264 (on Abū Bilāl); al-Yaʿqūbī, *Taʾrīkh*, II, 221 (on al-Mustawrid).
4. Judd, "Narratives and Character Development".
5. Ibid., 210.
6. Ibid., *passim*.
7. Ibid., 210.
8. Ibid., 210; see also 222.
9. The exception is a poem ascribed to ʿAbdallāh b. ʿAwf b. Aḥmar, the commander of Muʿāwiya's troops during the confrontation with the Khārijites at al-Nukhayla. Al-Balādhurī, *Ansāb*, IV/1, 165.
10. Ibid., 389.
11. Ibid.
12. Ibid., 390.
13. Ibid., 182.
14. Ibid.
15. Ibid., 180–6.
16. On this, see Gaiser, "Tracing the Ascetic Life". See also the discussion of the Abū Bilāl story below.
17. Lynch, *Arab Conquests*, esp. 173–6. Lynch calls the *Futūḥ* "an administrator's reference handbook" (175).
18. Ibid., 123.
19. ʿAthamina ("Sources") argued in his study of the *Ansāb*'s sources that al-Balādhurī exhibited no particular partisanship, but this is not borne out by the analysis here or elsewhere (e.g., Haider, *Rebel and Imām*, 206 and "Community Divided", 462, 464).
20. On such storytelling techniques, see Donner, "ʿUthmān and the Rāshidūn Caliphs"; Keaney, "Confronting the Caliph". On al-Balādhurī employing these techniques in his *Futūḥ* and for observations about his authorial intentions, see Lynch, *Arab Conquests*, 103–51.
21. See, for example, al-Balādhurī, *Ansāb*, IV/1, 165 (for a government agent acknowledging the piety of his Khārijite opponent), 183 (for a small Khārijite

force putting to flight an Umayyad army fifty times its size), 392 (for a Khārijite exhorting a comrade to engage in *jihād*).

22. For which, see below.
23. Al-Balādhurī, *Ansāb*, IV/1, 392.
24. Ibid.
25. Ibid., 181–2.
26. Ibid., 182.
27. Ibid., 183.
28. Ibid., 183–4.
29. Lynch, *Arab Conquests*, 122–3.
30. For example, of al-Walīd: Judd, "Narratives and Character Development". See also below, on Muʿāwiya.
31. Al-Balādhurī, *Ansāb*, IV/1, 186.
32. Ibid., 183.
33. See ʿAbbās, *Shiʿr*, 142–3, nr. 154.
34. Al-Balādhurī, *Ansāb*, IV/1, 388.
35. Gaiser, "Tracing the Ascetic Life", 66 and *passim* argues that this is an echo of early Ibāḍī efforts to claim Abū Bilāl as one of their *imām*s and refute their rivals among the militant Khawārij, primarily the Azāriqa and Najdiyya, at the same time. Considering that Abū Bilāl is also claimed by the (proto-)Sunnī tradition, the portrayal of his character and eventual rebellion may well serve other purposes as well, like the continued censure of the Umayyads and a general hesitance to get involved in armed resistance unless absolutely necessary. Abū Bilāl as a critic of militant Khārijism and related issues will reappear below.
36. Al-Balādhurī, *Ansāb*, IV/1, 186.
37. Ibid., 389–90.
38. Van Ess, "Bild der Ḫāriǧiten", 2552–3.
39. Ibid., 2577.
40. Ibid., 2536.
41. Ibid., 2565.
42. This is particularly obvious in al-Ṭabarī's rendering of his governorship; see below.
43. Al-Balādhurī, *Ansāb*, IV/1, 173, 176, 177, 181, 388.
44. Ibid., 176.
45. Ibid.
46. Ibid., 180. Either the account, the manuscript or the edition mistakenly give Q 6:6 as the basis for Abū Bilāl's objection to Ziyād's threat of collective punishment. In al-Ṭabarī's version, Abū Bilāl quotes Q 53:37–8, which fits the context exactly. Al-Ṭabarī, *Taʾrīkh*, II, 76; his version will be discussed below.
47. Al-Balādhurī, *Ansāb*, IV/1, 178.
48. Ibid., 178–9. Immediately following this report, al-Balādhurī has an alternative account of this episode, which is lacking in detail.

49. See Hylén, "Date of the Story"; Hawting, "Tawwābūn".
50. Al-Balādhurī, *Ansāb*, IV/1, 393–4.
51. See, for example, ibid., 165; al-Ṭabarī, *Ta'rīkh*, II, 18.
52. Al-Balādhurī, *Ansāb*, IV/1, 163.
53. Ibid.
54. Ibid.
55. Ibid., 164.
56. See al-Ṭabarī, *Ta'rīkh*, II, 9–10. This report is much shorter than al-Balādhurī's version, which also includes the subsequent revolts led by Farwa's successors.
57. In al-Ṭabarī's account, the Khārijites tell the Kufans exactly that, but fail to convince them as the Kufans fear Muʿāwiya more than the rebels. Ibid., 10.
58. See, for example, al-Balādhurī, *Ansāb*, IV/1, 167, 170, 172, 186, 387.
59. See above and ibid., 183, 167, 389 (the last two for examples of a Khārijite refusing to accept Muʿāwiya as leader of the community).
60. See, for example, ibid., 182, 183.
61. Al-Balādhurī's section on the Khārijites during Muʿāwiya's caliphate covers pp. 163–86 and 386–93 (–96 when including Ibn Ziyād's persecution of the Khārijites beyond the death of Muʿāwiya) of the edition. For instances of the Khārijites quoting the Qur'ān, see, for example, ibid., 178, 180, 387, 388, 391.
62. Ibid., 168–71.
63. Al-Ṭabarī, *Ta'rīkh*, II, 20–64.
64. Ibid., 40–1.
65. Ibid., 41–3.
66. Ibid., 33, 34, 37, 39, 40, 42, 64. For a discussion of these speeches, see below.
67. Al-Balādhurī, *Ansāb*, IV/1, 169, 170.
68. Another example of this difference is provided in Leder's study of Khālid al-Qasrī's rise and fall: al-Balādhurī's version is much shorter and omits several of the story elements included in al-Ṭabarī's rendering of Khālid's fate. See Leder, "Features of the Novel", 88, 90.
69. Hoyland, "History, Fiction and Authorship", 31. His case study is the episode of Khālid al-Qasrī's downfall also discussed by Leder, which shows evidence of the same redaction process. See the previous note.
70. See above, 73–4, as well as Landau-Tasseron, "Processes of Redaction".
71. Leder, "Grenzen der Rekonstruktion", 27.
72. Leder, "Literary Use", 284–5, 291; see also his "Authorship and Transmission".
73. Al-Balādhurī, *Ansāb*, IV/1, 166. See also Ibn Saʿd (ed. ʿUmar), *Ṭabaqāt*, III, 35.
74. See above, 177.
75. Al-Balādhurī, *Ansāb*, IV/1, 165. It is also possible that Muʿāwiya pronounces this judgement of Hawthara; the Arabic simply says "*qāla*" without specifying the speaker.
76. Ibid.

77. Al-Balādhurī, *Ansāb*, IV/1, 165.
78. Ibid., 172–3.
79. For different dates, see the discussion on 201.
80. Al-Balādhurī, *Ansāb*, IV/1, 172–3.
81. Ibid., 173.
82. See above, 99, 101–3.
83. Al-Balādhurī, *Ansāb*, IV/1, 180.
84. Ibid., 175. The statement about Qarīb/Qurayb (*lā qarrabahu allāh*) is a pun on his name, which is derived from the same root (q-r-b) as the condemning verb. For al-Ṭabarī's version of Abū Bilāl's criticism of this particular revolt and the pun on Qarīb/Qurayb's name (though without the reference to Zuḥḥāf/Zaḥḥāf), see 202.
85. Al-Balādhurī, *Ansāb*, IV/1, 173. In this report, the Khārijites let a group of Jews go because as *dhimmī*s they are protected. See also al-Balādhurī, *Ansāb*, II, 325. Generally, Khārijites are said to have respected the life and property of *ahl al-kitāb*, in line with their reportedly strict observance of Qur'ānic provisions.
86. Al-Balādhurī, *Ansāb*, IV/1, 172 (implied by the Khārijites questioning ʿUbāda about his identity), 173 (implicit in the notion that the Khawārij let a group of people go because they claimed to be Jews), 175, 180.
87. Ibid., 175, where a group of Khārijite rebels is divided over the issue of whether an *imām* is necessary in order to do battle.
88. Ibid., 167, 173, 176, 177, 180, 181, 388, 391–2.
89. Del Río, "Combatientes jāriŷíes", 142–5 (esp. 143), 147.
90. Ibid.,146.
91. Del Río's approach, for instance, is informed by the work of Fatma Mernissi. Baugh, "Revolting Women", is another example of modern perspectives, here Gender and Women's Studies, influencing the reading of historical events, protagonists and sources. For instance, what she considers an allusion to "a debate over the use of gender-inclusive language" in al-Mubarrad's *Kāmil* (44) is perhaps better framed as a remark on Arabic grammar. Geissinger, *Gender and Muslim Constructions*, 57 maintains that the classical Islamic tradition misrepresents "the way that space was gendered in Muhammad's time". Ruth Roded is another prominent proponent of this view. See the collection of essays in her *Women in Islam*, esp. Part I, chapter 2 ("The Biography of the Prophet: Women in Battle").
92. Del Río, "Combatientes jāriŷíes", 143, 145, 152.
93. For instance, Najda b. ʿĀmir is said to have asked Ibn ʿAbbās about the permissibility of female participation in *jihād*. This – almost certainly ahistorical – exchange is not transmitted in the historiographical material but rather in legal compendia and *ḥadīth* collections. See Mikati, "Fighting for the Faith", 210 and the references in n. 79. The early Ibāḍī epistle of Sālim b. Dhakwān considers the *khurūj* of women and slaves legitimate (Crone and Zimmermann, *Epistle*, 140 ls. 917–23 (Arabic text), 141 §127 (English translation); a brief

discussion with further examples follows on 180–1). But there was also intra-Khārijite disagreement over this issue, which is discussed below.

94. In addition to Del Río's article, see Baugh, "Revolting Women" and Mikati, "Fighting for the Faith", 210–13.
95. Baugh, "Revolting Women", 36; see also 51.
96. For 'fictional' female fighters in Arabic literature, see Kruk, *Warrior Women.*
97. Al-Balādhurī, *Ansāb*, IV/1, 167–8.
98. See below, 199.
99. See above, 171.
100. See above, 175 and the notes thereto.
101. Al-Balādhurī, *Ansāb*, IV/1, 177.
102. See on this now also Mikati, "Fighting for the Faith", 212–13.
103. On such evening entertainment, see Leder, "Conventions".
104. Crone and Zimmermann, *Epistle*, 180.
105. See the discussion in Part I ('Sources, Genre, Authorship') and Chapter One.
106. Al-Balādhurī, *Ansāb*, IV/1, 167, 180 (where his disapproval is mentioned twice).
107. Ibid., 167. This criticism contradicts the espousal of women's participation in rebellion by the early Ibāḍī Sālim, as noted by Crone and Zimmermann (*Epistle*, 180–1). Abū Bilāl is claimed as an *imām* by the Ibāḍiyya so this is an interesting observation pertinent to the development of Ibāḍī doctrine, but here the main issue is that Abū Bilāl's authority was used to discredit the practice, which tells us something about how it was perceived in certain scholarly circles and about the authority Abū Bilāl enjoyed beyond the immediate Ibāḍī/Khārijite milieu.
108. In addition to the cases discussed here, see al-Balādhurī, *Ansāb*, IV/1, 178–80 (Ṭawwāf b. ʿAllāq).
109. Abū Mikhnaf is said to have taught extensively on the history of Khārijism. Ibn al-Nadīm, *Fihrist*, 105–6.
110. Conversely, al-Balādhurī only has a highly condensed account of al-Mustawrid's rebellion: al-Balādhurī, *Ansāb*, IV/1, 169–70.
111. The only mention occurs in the report of al-Khaṭīm and Sahm b. Ghālib's rebellion in Basra in 46 H/666–7 CE. Al-Ṭabarī, *Taʾrīkh*, II, 83–4. This episode will be discussed below.
112. Ibid., 40–1.
113. See, for example, ibid., 18, 20–1, 184.
114. Crone, *Medieval Islamic Political Thought*, 135–8, 229–32; Abou el Fadl, *Rebellion and Violence*, 98–9, 100–61, esp. 111–18, and *passim*; Lewis, "Quietist and Activist Traditions", 141–7; Kraemer, "Apostates", 72–3; Andersson, *Early Sunnī Historiography*, 82–3. This consensus was never absolute, of course. See, for example, Abou el Fadl, *Rebellion and Violence*, 118–31.
115. Al-Bukhārī, *Ṣaḥīḥ*, IV, 333–50.
116. Hawting, *First Dynasty*, 11–18; Borrut, "*Memoria* omeyyade"; El-Hibri,

"Redemption", 241–2. For modern views of the Umayyads, see Hawting, *First Dynasty*, 123–8; Judd, *Religious Scholars*, chapter one (but see the critical remarks in Borrut, "Review"). Ende, *Arabische Nation* demonstrates a change in the portrayal of the Umayyads among modern Arab historians related to, among other factors, the rise of nationalism.

117. The (presumably) contemporary poetry is more positively inclined towards the Umayyad caliphs compared with later portrayals, even allowing for – often standardised – criticism of traits like miserliness. See Nadler, *Umayyadenkalifen*; Eisener, *Faktum und Fiktion*, 144–62 (concerning the caliph Sulaymān; Eisener's approach to Umayyad-era poetry, its historical reliability and usefulness for reconstructing historical fact, is more circumspect overall than Nadler's). Against the notion of the Umayyads as godless tyrants, Judd argues in his *Religious Scholars* that the Marwānid caliphs in fact patronised and received support from renowned religious authorities and pious scholars. Anti-Umayyad sentiment was not universal in the ʿAbbāsid period, either: see Shahin, "In Defense of Muʿāwiya", esp. 184–94; Bellamy, "Pro-Umayyad Propaganda"; El-Hibri, "Redemption". Al-Qāḍī, "Abū Ḥayyān al-Tawḥīdī", 140: "Al-Tawḥīdī's attitude towards the Umayyads is generally favourable."

118. Al-Ṭabarī, *Taʾrīkh*, II, 18. It is not entirely clear whether this line was part of the account as transmitted by Hishām b. Muḥammad al-Kalbī and Abū Mikhnaf or whether it was added by al-Ṭabarī, but the '*qāla Abū Jaʿfar*', which usually introduces such interjections, is missing here. In any case, reproach of the Khawārij comes through loud and clear.

119. Al-Ṭabarī, *Taʾrīkh*, II, 38–9. See also ibid., 34 for an account in which Ṣaʿṣaʿa gives a speech about the first *fitna* but says "nothing [negative] about the Syrians because government was theirs at that time".

120. Ibid., 18.

121. Ibid.; Morony, *Muʿāwiyah*, 22. It is peculiar that Sālim does not seem to know the identity of ʿAlī's killer, even though Ḥayyān had just revealed it in the previous sentence. This might imply that the report was put together from different accounts; if that is the case, then Ḥayyān's statement and Sālim's exclamation might not have originally formed part of the same narrative. Donner, *Narratives*, 264–6 calls the result of such a process a "*combined* or *synthetic* account" rather than using the term 'collective *isnād*', which he argues draws attention away from the text(s) to the chain of transmitters.

122. Al-Ṭabarī, *Taʾrīkh*, II, 18.

123. Al-Ṭabarī himself declares in his foreword that it is his intention to discuss whose transmission is acceptable and who is considered unreliable: *Taʾrīkh*, I, 6. This refers to traditionists primarily, but nevertheless demonstrates his concern with such questions, which for a jurist is to be expected, of course. This tendency is also reflected in the repeated and formalised statements regarding transmitter reliability typical of *ḥadīth* literature as discussed in Stetter's *Topoi und Schemata*, for which see above, 65–7.

124. Al-Ṭabarī, *Taʾrīkh*, II, 40–61.
125. Ibid., 41.
126. Ibid., 20–64, here 20–1.
127. Ibid., 181–5.
128. See above, 122–4.
129. Thus Ḥayyān b. Ẓabyān and Muʿādh b. Juwayn. Al-Ṭabarī, *Taʾrīkh*, II, 181; see also 184.
130. Ibid., 183–4.
131. Ibid., 184.
132. See Chapter Three, 88.
133. Al-Ṭabarī, *Taʾrīkh*, II, 20.
134. Ibid., 21.
135. Hoyland, "History, Fiction and Authorship", 20–2. For Ibn Aʿtham flaunting such conventions, see Conrad, "Ibn Aʿtham", 99–100. For al-Ṭabarī claiming merely to convey what he himself was told, see his *Taʾrīkh*, I, 6–7; a brief discussion of this patently untrue claim is offered, with further references, by Peacock, *Medieval Islamic Historiography*, 75–6. For Balʿamī's active adaptation and alteration of al-Ṭabarī's *History* and unusual frankness about his interventions, see ibid., esp. 83–6; Daniel, "Balʿamī's Account".
136. Sonnesyn, "Obedient Creativity", 130–2; Wellendorf, "Scriptorial Scruples", 306 and *passim*; Woodmansee, "Genius", 426, 428, 429, 434; Schmitt, *Inszenierungen*, *passim* but esp. 53–5.
137. Lethbridge, "Authors and Anonymity", 347. Sometimes, authors also concealed themselves for more prosaic reasons, such as when al-Jāḥiẓ attributed some of his books to 'the ancients' to escape the rancour and scathing attacks of his contemporary critics. Kilito, *Author and His Doubles*, 67–70. This could backfire when one attempted to reclaim a work, not to mention the many problems such false attributions cause for the modern scholar. Ibid., 71–7. Al-Masʿūdī, on the other hand, rejected blind preference of the 'ancients' over the 'moderns' and condemned al-Jāḥiẓ having to obscure his authorship. Khalidi, *Islamic Historiography*, 11, 15–27 (reference to al-Jāḥiẓ on 16, n. 1). Al-Masʿūdī's stance was likely influenced by the new literary critics of the late ninth and tenth century (ibid.). He was also opposed to scholarship (and thus history-writing) purporting only to transmit older accounts and established authorities (ibid., 11, 31–2, 36–7, 54). Ibn ʿAbd Rabbih might have called for more nuance (see above, 30–1). Parallels to al-Jāḥiẓ' attempts at literary camouflage can be found – for very similar reasons – among medieval European scholars like the twelfth-century man of letters Adelard of Bath (quoted in LeGoff, *Die Intellektuellen*, 60) as well as (late) ancient Greek and Roman writers (Potter, *Literary Texts*, 38).
138. See on this briefly Meisami, "History as Literature", 21.
139. Al-Ṭabarī, *Taʾrīkh*, II, 32, 33.
140. Ibid., 33.

141. Ibid., 39. For a description of the Khārijites as 'renegades', see also ibid., 40, 46.
142. Ibid., 39.
143. Al-Ṭabarī, *Taʾrīkh*, I, 3376–81.
144. Al-Ṭabarī, *Taʾrīkh*, II, 40; see also ibid., 37.
145. Ibid., 42.
146. Ibid., 19–20; see also 112.
147. Crone, *Medieval Islamic Political Thought*, 28–9. Crone uses the term *sunnī-jamāʿī*, which goes back to Hodgson. I have dropped the '*sunnī*' to avoid confusion with the Sunnīs of later periods (post-tenth century). For a brief summary of early discussions regarding the suspension of judgement to avoid communal conflict (the Murjiʾī position) and commonalities with contemporary Christian notions of postponing judgement, see Morony, *Iraq*, 478–80.
148. Su, "Early Shiʿi".
149. Van Ess, "Unfertige Studien I", 1411.
150. An early reference to *ahl al-sunna wa-l-jamāʿa* appears to occur in the late eighth-century *Taḥrīsh* of Ḍirār b. ʿAmr, although elsewhere the work seems to apply the designation to a specific group rather than using it to refer to a collective. It is likely that the term initially had different meanings in different contexts. See Van Ess, "Bild der Ḫāriǧiten", 2593.
151. Al-Ṭabarī, *Taʾrīkh*, II, 34.
152. Ibid.
153. Ibid., 35.
154. Ibid., 34.
155. Ibid., 35.
156. EI[3], "Ḥujr b. ʿAdī l-Kindī" (W. Madelung).
157. See Leube, *Kinda*, 47–8, 118–23 (where he argues for a conflation of the stories of Ḥujr and al-Ḥusayn's cousin Muslim, both of whom are said to have been betrayed by al-Ashʿath's son), 131, 133–4.
158. The son was Zayd b. ʿAdī. EI[3], "ʿAdī b. Ḥātim" (E. Kohlberg).
159. Al-Balādhurī, *Ansāb*, II, 323 has Zayd, although Zayd is often said to have joined Muʿāwiya. Al-Ṭabarī, *Taʾrīkh*, I, 3366, 3384 has Ṭarafa b. ʿAdī.
160. Al-Ṭabarī, *Taʾrīkh*, II, 37.
161. Ibid.
162. Ibid.; Morony, *Muʿāwiyah*, 43.
163. Al-Ṭabarī, *Taʾrīkh*, II, 39.
164. Ibid., 54.
165. Ibid., 44–5.
166. See, for example, ibid., 13, 84, 184.
167. Ibid., 65.
168. Ibid.
169. This is one element in the 'order of battle' *topos* discussed in Chapter One.
170. Fierro, "Heresy", 900–3; Clarke, "'Most Treacherous'", 515–16.

171. Al-Ṭabarī, *Taʾrīkh*, II, 181–4.
172. See, for example, ibid., 40–1, 329–30, 516.
173. Abou el Fadl, *Rebellion and Violence*, 151–2.
174. See, for example, al-Ṭabarī, *Taʾrīkh*, II, 40–1, 329–30, 516, 882–4, 900, 984. The rather vague call to the Book of God and the *sunna* that is a frequent feature of Khārijite rhetoric seems to have been typical of rebels in the early Islamic period in general. Crone and Hinds, *God's Caliph*, 58–96; Abou el Fadl, *Rebellion*, 129. Quite tellingly, Abū Mikhnaf's account of Ṣiffīn as transmitted in al-Ṭabarī also has ʿAlī call Muʿāwiya to the Book of God and the *sunna* of His Prophet, and related phrases. See, for example, al-Ṭabarī, *Taʾrīkh*, I, 3279.
175. One could argue that the story of Ibn Muljam's execution is the earliest example of a Khārijite martyrdom 'cycle', but his crime of murdering a figure so beloved by later generations of Muslims did not easily allow for the account of his ordeal to be turned into narrative precedent. The term 'cycle' in relation to tales of martyrdom is Gaiser's in *Shurāt Legends*.
176. Ziyād's speech is quoted at length in al-Ṭabarī, *Taʾrīkh,* II, 73–6.
177. Ibid., 74.
178. My translation mostly follows Khalidi, *Qurʾan*, 436.
179. Al-Ṭabarī, *Taʾrīkh*, II, 76.
180. Ibid., 91; Morony, *Muʿāwiyah*, 101.
181. Al-Ṭabarī, *Taʾrīkh*, II, 83–4, 91. However, another report states that this revolt took place in 50 H/670–1 CE and that the rebels involved were the first to revolt after the "people of the canal" (*ahl al-nahr*), i.e. the Khārijites at Nahrawān in 658. This contradicts all other reports of Khārijite activities after Nahrawān, including al-Ṭabarī's own.
182. Ibid., 185.
183. See the section on *awāʾil* in Chapter One.
184. The standard accounts of Nahrawān in the historiographical sources do not mention their participation, however. It is only mentioned in the reports of ʿUrwa's execution and Abū Bilāl's rebellion.
185. For the following, see al-Ṭabarī, *Taʾrīkh*, II, 186.
186. Ibid.
187. See al-Jāḥiẓ, *al-Ḥayawān*, V, 588–90 for an account of her death that shows her stoicism and focus on the Hereafter throughout her ordeal down to her defiant last words to ʿUbaydallāh b. Ziyād. Note that al-Jāḥiẓ calls her al-Shajāʾ; there seems to have been much confusion regarding her name.
188. For whom, see below, 235.
189. On similarities between early Christian and Muslim martyr stories, see Sizogrich, *Violence and Belief*; Marsham, "Attitudes", esp. 114, 118–21; Gaiser, "Tracing" (regarding Ibāḍī renderings of the Abū Bilāl episode that echo Christian martyr narratives) and *Shurāt Legends*, esp. chapters one and two.

190. Al-Balādhurī, *Ansāb*, IV/1, 180–6.
191. Al-Ṭabarī, *Taʾrīkh*, II, 186–8.
192. There are issues with the dating of Abū Bilāl's revolt in al-Ṭabarī's work. It is placed in the entry on the year 58 H, but the report breaks off after only a couple of pages to then be resumed under the entry for the year 61 H. He claims that his first account of Abū Bilāl's revolt only included the events up to the Khārijite's victory over the first army sent against him, but the extension of the Abū Bilāl episode over three years contradicts the reports transmitted in the other sources. Al-Ṭabarī, *Taʾrīkh*, II, 390–1. For different dates, see al-Balādhurī, *Ansāb*, IV/1, 182 (60 H); Ibn Khayyāṭ, *Taʾrīkh*, I, 251 (the entry is placed under the year 64 H/683–4 CE, but the report also states that Abū Bilāl revolted during the governorship of ʿUbaydallāh b. Ziyād, which might imply an earlier date – ʿUbaydallāh had to flee Iraq around the death of the caliph Yazīd I, probably in 63 or 64 H).
193. Al-Ṭabarī, *Taʾrīkh*, II, 187.
194. Ibid., 186–8 (year 58), 391 (year 61).
195. Ibid., 83–4.
196. Ibid., 15–16.
197. Ibn Khayyāṭ, *Taʾrīkh*, I, 235, 241, 246; al-Balādhurī, *Ansāb*, IV/1, 172–3.
198. For al-Balādhurī's rendering of this episode, see above.
199. My translation follows Khalidi, *Qurʾan*. On this particular verse and its significance in the context of early Islamic rebellion and brigandage, see Marsham, "Those Who Make War". For a discussion of this verse in pre-modern and modern exegesis, see Sauer, *Rebellion und Widerstand.*
200. Marsham, "Public Execution", 107.
201. Abou el Fadl, *Rebellion and Violence*, 32–3, 131–5; Judd, "Muslim Persecution", 12; Marsham, "Public Execution", 104, 107, 119–20; Seidensticker, "Responses to Crucifixion". An exhaustive collection of poetry on the crucifixion motif is provided in Ullmann, *Motiv der Kreuzigung*; see also Hämeen-Anttila, "ʿAmr b. Hawbar". A comprehensive survey discussing references to crucifixions in early Islamic history is Anthony, *Crucifixion*. See also Reinfandt, "Kreuzigung", who discusses the exceedingly rare case of a seventh to early eighth-century papyrus fragment mentioning a group of highway robbers being crucified.
202. As argued by Hawting, "Jaʿd b. Dirham" and discussed by Marsham, "Public Execution".
203. One such instance is discussed in Marsham, "Attitudes", 119.
204. Al-Ṭabarī, *Taʾrīkh*, II, 91.
205. For al-Balādhurī's rendering, see the first part of this chapter.
206. Al-Ṭabarī, *Taʾrīkh*, II, 91. The idea of certain beings and people being drawn close to God (or a worldly ruler) is echoed in a number of Qurʾānic verses. See Hawting, "'Has God Sent a Mortal'", 378–9.
207. On this feature of al-Ṭabarī's work, see also Hodgson, "Pre-Modern Muslim Historians", 55, 58. For his "propensity for viewing local developments within

a regional political framework" and his depiction of al-Mukhtār's rebellion "as part of a broad upheaval within the Muslim world shaped by tribal politics and changing ethnic demographics", see Haider, *Rebel and Imām*, 104.

208. ʿAthamina, "Sources", 237–40.
209. Lynch, *Arab Conquests*, 109; see on *qālū* as introducing a particular type of material in the *Futūḥ* ibid., 72–80.
210. The episode in question is the revolt of Sahm and al-Khaṭīm. Al-Balādhurī, *Ansāb*, IV/1, 172 and Ibn Khayyāṭ, *Taʾrīkh*, I, 235 both mention the murder of the Companion ʿUbāda b. Qurṣ al-Laythī, whereas al-Ṭabarī, *Taʾrīkh*, II, 83–4 does not. Ibn Khayyāṭ transmits his version on the authority of Abū ʿUbayda and Abū al-Ḥasan, al-Ṭabarī quotes "ʿUmar from ʿAlī".
211. Compare, for example, al-Balādhurī's much more detailed version of Farwa b. Nawfal's revolt at al-Nukhayla (*Ansāb*, IV/1, 163–4) with al-Ṭabarī's report of only a few lines (*Taʾrīkh*, II, 10).

6

Khārijism from the Second Fitna until the Death of ʿAbd al-Malik

The final chronological chapter will look at the reigns of Yazīd b. Muʿāwiya (r. c. 60–4 H/c. 680–3 CE), ʿAbdallāh b. al-Zubayr (r. c. 63–73 H/c. 683–92 CE) and ʿAbd al-Malik b. Marwān (r. c. 73–86 H/c. 692–705 CE). This period was dominated by the second *fitna* that followed the death of Muʿāwiya in 680 and lasted until the defeat of Ibn al-Zubayr in 692. This tumultuous time witnessed a succession crisis within the Umayyad family that led to violent conflict among the Syrian factions, the transition of power from Damascus to the Ḥijāz and from the Umayyads to the Zubayrids, as well as widespread social unrest in Iraq, Iran and northern Arabia in the form of various (pro-)ʿAlid and Khārijite revolts. With the consolidation of ʿAbd al-Malik's rule in 692, one centre of Umayyad power returned to Syria; another moved to Iraq with the establishment of ʿAbd al-Malik's viceroy of the east, al-Ḥajjāj b. Yūsuf, in 694.

The chronicles and other historiographical sources preserve a wealth of material for this eventful period in Islamic history, including stories of Khārijite activities. In order to structure this abundance of reports and avoid repetition, I will focus mainly on aspects that are new to how the sources treat Khārijism. The conclusions arrived at over the preceding chapters still apply: we are confronted not with a straightforward, sober historiographical record of Khārijism 'as it really was' but with a literary construct that serves diverse narrative purposes and throws up roadblocks for positivist studies of early Khārijite history.

Two Khārijite revolts in particular attracted the attention of our authors: the insurgency of the Azāriqa and the rebellion of the most notorious Khārijite of the late seventh century, Shabīb b. Yazīd al-Shaybānī. The latter is particularly prominent in al-Ṭabarī's *Taʾrīkh*. His treatment of Shabīb's rebellion, including the (connected?) revolts of Ṣāliḥ b. Musarriḥ and Muṭarrif b. al-Mughīra b. Shuʿba,[1] covers 120 pages in the Leiden edition of the Arabic text.[2] While spread out over several years, Shabīb's story is told in one continuous narrative, which underlines its significance. The details, especially the sequence and exact dating of events, are still often confused or contradictory.[3]

I will gloss over most of these structural components as the purpose is not to reconstruct Shabīb's rebellion as a historical phenomenon but to illuminate its narrative significance.

It is worth noting here that the sources are almost exclusively concerned with violent forms of Khārijism in this period. Very little information is available on quietists like the Ibāḍiyya or Ṣufriyya,[4] who, if we believe the standard narrative, developed in Basra alongside the militant factions of the Azāriqa and Najdiyya. The more moderate Najdites in turn feature less than their Azraqī contemporaries. Evidently, extremists like the Azāriqa and successful rebels like Shabīb were more interesting – and more useful – from a narrative perspective. The lack of interest in the quietists of this period can perhaps also be explained with the changed nature of Khārijite revolts: for the first time, Khārijite groups are shown to be successful in establishing control over a significant territory (the Najdiyya) or in eluding the authorities for an extended time while wreaking havoc on an unprecedented scale (the Azāriqa, Shabīb). The actions (or lack thereof) of the quietists, in Basra and elsewhere, pale in comparison to the adventures of the militants.

The following analysis will investigate the main facets of literary Khārijism in this period. Only those groups and individuals whom the sources discuss at some length will be addressed here. The material is unruly and reveals a multitude of themes and concerns. As in the case of Khārijite beginnings discussed in Chapter Four, however, we can observe something of a consensus concerning the main events in Khārijite history: while there is a larger degree of variance between the individual sources compared to Chapter Four, they do provide a roughly coherent picture of the major revolts and interactions between the Khawārij and their opponents. This chapter will therefore revert to a thematic structure.

Predictably, the theme of Khārijite piety with its emphasis on *jihād* and the Khārijites' prowess in battle continues. Here as well, these by-now familiar motifs permeate the accounts of Khārijism irrespective of particular historical settings and support the conclusion that we are presented with standardised images. Khārijite piety will not be explored here again unless it is related to a new theme, but the mere fact that this motif is perpetuated points out two things: that this is a schematised portrayal of Khārijism which assigns specific attributes to the individuals and groups subsumed under this heading; and the corollary observation that the identity ascribed to the various Khārijite groups is in fact *collective* and thus has little explanatory value with regard to individual motivations or circumstances. This collective identity cannot easily be used for positivist purposes: what we see, first and foremost, is Khārijism as a literary construct, not as a historical phenomenon. Again, this does not mean that Khārijism is an invention, that actors and events are not rooted in a historical reality; it means that determining the exact relationship of actors and events with said reality is a challenge that cannot be undertaken without acknowledging the profound rhetorical *Überformung* of the available material.

The analysis to follow will lead us to the overarching conclusion we are already familiar with: Khārijism is not the primary concern of our sources. I will argue that they instead concentrate predominantly on five distinct subjects. These can be summarised as follows: (1) the political and military importance of al-Muhallab and his family; (2) the volatility of Khārijism as a direct counterpoint to the *jamāʿī* approach; (3) the censure of the Umayyad governors of Iraq; (4) the faults and merits of Ibn al-Zubayr; and lastly, (5) military strategy.

"He Has No Equal" – Eulogising al-Muhallab and the Muhallabids

The conflict between al-Muhallab and the Azāriqa is an important subject in the Khārijite material for this period. Al-Balādhurī, al-Ṭabarī and Ibn Aʿtham transmit comprehensive accounts of these wars that cover dozens of pages; all but one of the remaining author-compilers give at least a brief description of al-Muhallab's struggles against the Khawārij. Al-Masʿūdī states in his *Murūj* that he describes al-Muhallab's conflict with the Azāriqa at length in his *Akhbār al-Zamān*,[5] but as this work is not extant, we unfortunately only have his very brief overview of this episode to work with.[6] Ibn Khayyāṭ is the exception here: his material either skips this conflict or the relevant sections were not passed on. While the remaining sources sometimes preserve diverging reports of particular events in this drawn-out confrontation, they have one thing in common: their main focus rests not on the Azraqites, but on al-Muhallab and his sons. This applies in particular to Ibn Aʿtham, who preserves the most material on the Muhallabid–Azraqite battles and represents the strongest proponent of al-Muhallab's family among the works under study.

Irrespective of the level of detail or particular framing of their reports, our historians agree on al-Muhallab's courage and superior battle skills, and the enormous effort he put into fighting the Khārijites despite the cost to himself and his family. When the Azāriqa first begins to terrorise the people of Basra and the surrounding region, the Basran notables and common people alike "know" that the only person who can fight off the rebels successfully is al-Muhallab, the *shaykh al-nās* and *sayf al-ʿIrāq*.[7] The sources reiterate this point over and over.[8] It is 'proven' when the commanders sent out in pursuit of the Azāriqa before al-Muhallab all fail in their mission and in most cases lose the bulk of their troops to the ferocious Khawārij.[9] The situation is so dire that the Basrans insist on al-Muhallab despite his recent investiture over Khurāsān, pleading with Ibn al-Zubayr to send him after the Azraqites.[10] According to one of al-Ṭabarī's reports, the people are so desperate that they forge a letter from Ibn al-Zubayr to al-Muhallab in which he is ordered to fight the Azāriqa:

> . . . the renegade [*al-māriqa*] Azāriqah have smitten an army of the Muslims which was large and contained many of the notables, and [it is] reported that they have advanced on al-Baṣrah . . . I have decided that you will be in charge of the fight against them . . . The reward for that will be greater than for going to Khurāsān,[11] so go against them rightly guided, fight the enemies of God and of you, and protect your rights and those of the people of your garrison town.[12]

This account is striking particularly because fabricating the letter was apparently the idea of the very commander Ibn al-Zubayr had actually sent to Basra to take charge of affairs there. It highlights the panic inspired by Azraqī violence and emphasises the unique suitability of al-Muhallab for this task.

Once the Basrans agree to al-Muhallab's conditions for combatting the Khārijites and he takes over as commander-in-chief, the tide turns on the Azāriqa. Proving that the people's belief in him is well founded, al-Muhallab succeeds in defeating wave after wave of Azraqī fighters hurling themselves against him and his men. He is portrayed as a shrewd commander, well versed in battle tactics and strategy, courageous and pious. Accordingly, he is victorious in almost every encounter against the Khārijites, despite his enemy's famed valour.[13] On the rare occasion that he is defeated or at least fails to achieve a clear victory, the sources are quick to excuse him by blaming the cowardice of his (Basran) troops, for instance.[14] Al-Muhallab is so successful that he not only survives the regime change following the deaths of Muṣʿab and ʿAbdallāh b. al-Zubayr, but retains his exalted position under al-Ḥajjāj and ʿAbd al-Malik, the latter expressing his supreme confidence in al-Muhallab and rewarding his achievements handsomely.[15]

Consistent with this depiction of al-Muhallab, even the most committed Khārijites are shown to grow weary and despairing of their chances at defeating him. They lament their forced retreat to al-Ahwāz and then further into Iran to Kirmān and Sīstān, grudgingly acknowledging his superior battle skills and the bravery that leads him to fight relentlessly even after having "received seventeen wounds"[16]:

> If we are distressed by al-Muhallab, that is because he is / a man of war and the lion of the people of the east;

> Perhaps he causes us grief and perhaps we / cause him grief in everything we share;
>
> . . .
>
> He makes us taste war and we make him taste [war]; / everyone says to the other: taste![17]

That the Khawārij praise their opponent's skill is highly unusual, but it is even more remarkable that some Azraqites are shown to abandon their cause in favour of seeking protection with (and thus from) al-Muhallab.[18] These almost unheard-of events occur mainly after internal schisms, but they are nevertheless testament to al-Muhallab's reputation as a fearsome 'man of war', as exemplified by an exchange between the Azraqī leader Qaṭarī b. al-Fujāʾa and one of his critics: "If you truly seek God and the Hereafter, then persevere and die as we will die with you, but if not, then leave your companions so that they can enter al-Muhallab's protection."[19]

Along the same lines, there are reports of the Azāriqa – of all Khārijite groups! – turning their backs on the battlefield and fleeing before al-Muhallab.[20] This even includes Azraqite leaders like ʿUbayda b. Hilāl, "who had never withdrawn from battle until that day" but retreated from al-Muhallab's son Mudarrik "howling like a dog".[21] Similarly, the Azraqī commander Ṣāliḥ b. Mukhrāq tries to bolt when al-Muhallab's son al-Mufaḍḍal proves too formidable an enemy and is mocked by his enemy for this display of cowardice: "Where to, O Ibn Mukhrāq? If you are truthful [in what you believe], you will persist!"[22]

Virtually all such stories are related by Ibn Aʿtham. They stress his special interest in and endorsement of al-Muhallab and his family. This comes through particularly clearly in the depiction of al-Muhallab's sons. He is the only author who includes comprehensive information on their involvement in the Azraqī wars. Al-Muhallab apparently had ten sons, all of whom he summoned to join him in his pursuit of the Khawārij and all of whom answered his call.[23] They, too, are shown to be courageous and skilled fighters who are just as committed to wiping out the Khārijites as al-Muhallab himself and engage them in both verbal and physical battles.[24] During an Azraqī night attack, it is al-Muhallab's son Mudarrik who is the first to mount his horse and lead his men again the rebels. "Since that night, Mudarrik was beloved by his brothers and the people."[25] Even al-Muhallab's nephew Bishr is part of the company pursuing the Azāriqa and depicted as a valiant warrior.[26] Battling the Khārijites thus turns into a Muhallabid family endeavour.

Ibn Aʿtham's treatment of the Muhallabids stands out among the selected sources. His portrayal of al-Muhallab and the Muhallabid family has all the components of a heroic epic, or perhaps a hagiography. Al-Muhallab's continued success against the foe everyone else fails to overcome, coupled with his almost preternatural insight into Azraqī troop movements, could perhaps be construed as his own little miracle story, told in dramatic, gripping narrative. Chase Robinson ascribes this 'literary' quality of the *Kitāb al-Futūḥ* to it being part of the tradition of conquest monographs "where romantic heroism is as prominent as a careful chronology is absent" and contrasts Ibn Aʿtham's narrative style with "the sober and eirenic traditionalism exemplified by al-Ṭabarī or al-Balādhurī".[27] Robinson's assessment of al-Balādhurī as a "sober and eirenic" traditionalist does not hold up, I would argue, and the extent to which Ibn Aʿtham's work fits into a *futūḥ* category alongside al-Balādhurī's *Futūḥ al-Buldān* or al-Azdī's *Futūḥ al-Shām*, for instance, is uncertain, not least because his work was likely produced a good deal later than the latter two.[28] Ibn Aʿtham also includes many detailed accounts of early Islamic history that do not pertain to conquest history (the long chapters on the first civil war and Khārijite history being cases in point) and thus either not included at all or mentioned only briefly in other conquest monographs.[29] It is certainly true that Ibn Aʿtham's choice of narrative style and content single him out among the other sources, but instead of putting his work into another category, perhaps we should view this feature as an example of the fluidity and variety of genre in the early Islamic period, not to mention the titling issue discussed in Part I.

Ibn Aʿtham's portrayal of al-Muhallab also casts him as an exemplary Muslim of impeccable, correctly enacted piety. Chapter Two referred to the story of the Azraqī attack during the month of pilgrimage and al-Muhallab's outrage at their breach of the sanctity of the Day of Sacrifice. The Qurʾānic verses he draws on to counter Khārijite assertions of doing God's work have been discussed already.[30] This facet of al-Muhallab's characterisation is not peculiar to Ibn Aʿtham but a feature of other works as well. They present al-Muhallab as a steadfast believer, while the Azraqites are shown to have incurred God's wrath. After one of his first successful victories over the rebels, for instance, al-Muhallab sends a letter to the Basran governor to inform him of the Khārijite defeat. He describes the battle and concludes: "But then God sent down his aid to the Believers and smote the faces of the unbelievers. Their tyrant [*ṭāghiyah*] fell . . . and God killed them in the battle."[31] Throughout, al-Muhallab refers to his men as Muslims and to the Khārijites as unbelievers, reinforcing the image of the rebels as deviators against whom divine assistance is granted. At one of the final battles against a severely worn-down Azāriqa, al-Muhallab accordingly tells his soldiers: "Praise be to God who returned us to security and freed us from the burden of war and repelled the affair of this enemy."[32]

It is again Ibn Aʿtham, however, who preserves the most extensive depiction of al-Muhallab's piety. His work contains a letter to the Basrans in which al-Muhallab exhorts them to stay strong in the face of adversity. He accuses the Khawārij of hypocrisy, but assures the townspeople that the rebels cannot cause any permanent damage to God's religion:

> Islam is not weakened by those who leave it (*lā yūhinu al-Islām khurūj man kharaja minhu*), and those who deviate from it do not render it defective (*wa-lā yaʿībuhu ilḥād man alḥada fīhi*) . . . Those who plot against Islam are many and those who support it are few, and not everyone who fights in the name of Islam belongs to its people (*wa-laysa kull man yuqātil ʿan al-Islām min ahlihi*), but he who fights for the religion of Islam is one of its people (*wa-lakinna man yuqātil ʿan dīn al-Islām fa-huwa min ahlihi*).[33]

In the same way, when al-Muhallab exhorts his men before battle, he emphasises the religious dimension to the conflict with the Khawārij: his soldiers should speed the rebels in their "exit from life (*makhārij min al-ḥayāt*; a pun on 'Khawārij')" and remember always that

> these people [the Azāriqa] fight against your religion and your world, and if they overpower you, you will have no religion and no world. So fight them over what they fight you for![34]

In an account set just before another ultimately successful battle against the Khārijites, al-Muhallab reminds his sons of their mission in similar terms: "I fight for God and you fight for God and your father. You defend the religion of Islam; God has blessed everyone who fights with you with the intention for *jihād*".[35] This statement is reminiscent of Khārijite sentiment. At the same time, however, it is so general as to render it virtually meaningless and consequently employable regardless of context. We thus have here another example of how unspecific 'Khārijite' rhetoric can be.

Considering this glowing portrayal of al-Muhallab, it is not surprising to read that things begin to go wrong again as soon as he is removed from his position. This appears to have happened more frequently than one would expect given the many successful campaigns against the Azāriqa he is credited with. Nevertheless, apparently due mostly to politics and personal grudges held against him,[36] al-Muhallab is recalled several times. The sequence and chronology of events are confused, and it is possible that the sources present what was originally only one report of al-Muhallab being dismissed from office as several different, fragmentary accounts – a common feature of early Islamic historiography, which, under the influence of traditionalism, often adopted the *ḥadīth* format in the presentation of historical accounts.[37] Such fragmentation further facilitated the transferability of *topoi* for rhetorical or ideological embellishment.[38] The reports of al-Muhallab's endeavours under the Zubayrids and then during ʿAbd al-Malik's reign exhibit certain similarities that may indicate a replication process of the account narrating the episode in question. For instance, the stories of al-Muhallab's removal make a point both about his superiority as a warrior and the necessity of sound decision-making (or lack thereof) by the authorities. We will return to the latter issue in a moment; here it is important to note that the decision to recall al-Muhallab is shown to have dire consequences.[39]

The first time al-Muhallab is replaced as commander occurs under Zubayrid authority.[40] Muṣʿab himself removes him and puts ʿUmar b. ʿUbaydallāh b. Maʿmar in charge instead. As is common in Ibn Aʿtham's work, much of this story is told in verse, but the events can be summarised as follows: once dispatched, Ibn Maʿmar pursues the Azraqites who are at that point encamped at Sābūr. The Khārijites "know" that Ibn Maʿmar is approaching and thus decide to attack him at night. Qaṭarī provokes Ibn Maʿmar by boasting about Khārijite fierceness:

> Nightly fighting holds gains for the *shurāt* / but for the deviators it holds perdition;
> Participating in it is desirable [for the *shurāt*] / [but for the deviators] it means afflictions [bearing down on them] like torrents.[41]

Enraged, Ibn Maʿmar charges Qaṭarī, but the Khārijite strikes him and Ibn Maʿmar flees back to his companions. As the fighting intensifies, Ibn Maʿmar finally asks one of the soldiers who had served under al-Muhallab how the latter had managed to defeat the Khārijites. The man responds that al-Muhallab had been shrewd and patient, implying that Ibn Maʿmar had acted without the necessary circumspection. The two groups fight until morning; many of Ibn Maʿmar's men are killed and the remainder put to flight. The Khārijites raid Ibn Maʿmar's camp and then return to Sābūr. Ibn Maʿmar blames his Basran troops for this defeat, claiming that their lacklustre fighting was based on their mistrust of him as a Ḥijāzī, while al-Muhallab had been an Azdī from Basra and thus enjoyed their complete support. Muṣʿab b. al-Zubayr regrets his removal of al-Muhallab when he is apprised of the outcome, so decides to reinstate him: he is now convinced that al-Muhallab is the only one capable of combatting the Khawārij.

A very similar event is said to have taken place after ʿAbd al-Malik had secured the caliphate for himself by defeating the Zubayrids in 692.[42] The setting is ʿAbd al-Malik's appointment of his brother Bishr as governor of Kufa and of Khālid b. ʿAbdallāh as governor of Basra. When Khālid arrives, he puts al-Muhallab in charge of the taxes and special revenue of al-Ahwāz instead of letting him continue his fight against the Azāriqa. In his place, Khālid sends Muqātil b. Mismaʿ and his own brother, ʿAbd al-ʿAzīz b. ʿAbdallāh, after the Khawārij. By that point, Qaṭarī is in charge of the Azraqites. He engages the Basran troops in combat until Muqātil is killed and ʿAbd al-ʿAzīz is forced to flee. Al-Muhallab sends a messenger to ʿAbd al-ʿAzīz to console him for his flight and remind him that others had fled from the Khārijites as well, which either highlights al-Muhallab's magnanimity or showcases a certain degree of *Schadenfreude* coupled with a subtle reminder that al-Muhallab himself had never fled from his enemy (or both). He reassures ʿAbd al-ʿAzīz that reinforcements will be sent soon. Curiously, it is also al-Muhallab who informs Khālid b. ʿAbdallāh of his brother's defeat instead of ʿAbd al-ʿAzīz himself; Khālid thereupon sends a letter to ʿAbd al-Malik about the fiasco. The caliph is not amused and chastises Khālid for sending his brother rather than al-Muhallab, "who is fortunate in judgment, good in management, skilful and experienced in war – a man of war and the son of men of war!"[43] He instructs Khālid to send al-Muhallab against the Khārijites in al-Ahwāz, saying that Bishr's Kufan troops will supplement al-Muhallab's Basran army, that al-Muhallab is to have supreme command over the mission and that all decisions fall to him. Predictably, as soon as al-Muhallab is back in charge, the tide turns and the Azāriqa are routed by the government troops.[44]

Ibn Aʿtham's report of this event is significantly longer than al-Ṭabarī's; it also emphasises Khālid's foolishness and al-Muhallab's wisdom and foresight much more strongly. In his version, al-Muhallab repeatedly offers Khālid advice on how to fight the Khārijites, but Khālid turns him down each time and only regrets his conduct when the Azāriqa prove to be superior.[45] Al-Muhallab also warns Khālid against sending his brother, but Khālid ignores him and goes so far as to conceal a letter from ʿAbd al-Malik that orders him to put al-Muhallab back in charge. The Basrans are worried because they "know" that Khālid's brother is incapable of fighting the Khārijites successfully; even from Syria (!) a poet sends words about the people's concerns, but to no avail.[46] As foreseen by everyone except Khālid, the Khawārij utterly defeat his brother's army, put him to flight and kill his wife, who had accompanied him for some unknown reason. Only then, and when confronted with the Basrans' fear of another Azraqī attack, does Khālid truly see the error of his ways and apologise to al-Muhallab for disregarding his counsel. Only al-Muhallab can withstand "this enemy of dogs", he states, and then asks him to "remove this sorrow from your land".[47] Al-Muhallab and his men agree enthusiastically and, as we can now predict, the Azāriqa suffer defeat after defeat once al-Muhallab is back in charge.

Finally, we also have several accounts of al-Ḥajjāj's initial impatience with al-Muhallab's course of action against the Khārijites. He repeatedly orders him to speed up his pursuit of the rebels and eventually sends envoys to report back on al-Muhallab's conduct in battle. As expected, they all confirm al-Muhallab's supreme struggle against a near invincible enemy and underline the admirable commitment not only of al-Muhallab, but also of his sons and troops. Al-Ḥajjāj eventually has to admit the unfairness of his accusations. Al-Muhallab, as usual, bears all of this with a stoicism of almost preternatural proportion. His careful approach to engaging the Azāriqa is shown to be borne of his strategic genius: rather than wasting men and resources through mindless bloodlust, he waits for the Khārijites' self-destructive tendencies to take effect and whittle down the number of enemies. His instinct is proven right when the Azāriqa finally split into various subgroups who are defeated one after the other.[48]

The point of these reports is evident. Apart from a few overambitious and spiteful individuals, everyone – including the intended audience – knows that al-Muhallab is unsurpassed as a military leader and battle strategist. Even the Khārijites are shown to acknowledge him as their only worthy opponent. When Bishr b. Marwān dismisses al-Muhallab from his post, the Khārijites rejoice and Qaṭarī sends Bishr a gleeful message to the effect that they are now free to roam the lands unchecked.[49] When Ibn Maʿmar is on his way to Sābūr to confront the Azāriqa, he sends them a poem[50] in which he boasts about his battle skills and derides al-Muhallab by accusing him of cowardice. He calls him a fraud whose popularity is down to his winning personality rather than any real achievements in combat. The Azraqī leader ʿUbayda b. Hilāl in turn mocks Ibn Maʿmar's pretensions:

> Hold on! Don't hasten towards us, Ibn Maʿmar / for you are even less than al-Muhallab;
> You have no business (*ḥazẓa*) in the art of war / and you have no loyal follower (lit. "who sacrifices their mother and father for you");
> . . .
> If you fought us – and you won't! – / you would suffer horribly from it;
> We are not weak, our spears are long / and we do not fear whoever approaches us.[51]

Unsurprisingly, the Khārijite prediction comes true and Ibn Maʿmar suffers a humiliating defeat. His boasting and ridicule of al-Muhallab are thus turned back on him, friend and foe alike confirming al-Muhallab's superiority.

The sources thus unanimously portray al-Muhallab as a skilled warrior, circumspect strategist and devout Muslim. He is presented as the only serious challenge to the Azāriqa capable of doing permanent damage to them. The decision to remove him from his position, based as it is on petty politics and personal grudges, therefore has disastrous ramifications that can only be remedied by reappointing al-Muhallab as commander-in-chief. His reputation is best exemplified in a poem recited by al-Muhallab's messenger to al-Ḥajjāj after the vanquishing of the main body of the Azāriqa:

> We caused the disease of the Azāriqa to perish forever / and they became [extinct] like ʿĀd and Thamūd;
> And we accomplished with al-Muhallab what / he wished for in his wisdom;
> . . .
> I achieved this with al-Muhallab / I am sure I did not thank him enough;
> All of us are like his own children to him / when asking us about our fallen;
> With his own hands he treats our wounded / and fixes us a feast like a birth feast;
> Every good thing that the people say about him / regarding [his] bravery and good morals is right;
> People [can] find an equal replacement for whom they lost / [but] not for the *shaykh* [al-Muhallab], he has no equal.[52]

Ibn Aʿtham in particular focuses on al-Muhallab to such an extent that the Azāriqa appears as a deliberate antithesis, set up to demonstrate al-Muhallab's many achievements and illustrate the ramifications of bad political decisions, especially when built on base motives. This is not peculiar to the figure of al-Muhallab, however, as the commonalities in the accounts of the Azāriqa and the rebel Shabīb b. Yazīd evince. Their stories are structured similarly: the Azraqites and Shabīb both travel around Iraq and Iran a lot and wreak havoc wherever they go; both are notorious for their ferociousness in battle; both are portrayed as promoting a rigid view of militant piety; and both can ultimately only be defeated by a particular commander (the Syrian Sufyān b. al-Abrad in Shabīb's case). These highly dramatised yet to an extent standardised narratives support the observation that literary Khārijism functions as a contrast agent throwing into relief superordinate socio-political and religious concerns.

"God Has Cast the Fierceness of the Khārijites in their Own Midst"[53] – Khārijite Volatility

The inherent volatility of Khārijism is another main concern of the early historical tradition.[54] The constant divisions among the various Khārijite factions are a major theme of the source material on this period, which leads to the inevitable conclusion that the explosive nature of Khārijism ultimately causes its downfall.[55] This is certainly true for the Azāriqa and the Najdiyya, and elements of this can also be observed in the story of Shabīb. As noted, the sources are much less concerned with the more moderate strands of Khārijism in this period, in part perhaps because they were significantly less prone to internal splits and thus less useful for instruction. It is telling that the only surviving branch of Khārijism today, the Ibāḍiyya (if one accepts their Khārijite ancestry, which is controversial among the Ibāḍīs themselves), is also the only Khārijite faction that largely came to reject violence and allowed its followers to live among non-Khārijite Muslims while making provisions even for important ritual acts like prayer, meals and inheritance.

The continuous internal tension characteristic of Khārijism is portrayed as primarily based on disagreements over doctrine. Khārijite inflexibility regarding matters of belief and practice is shown to cause an extraordinary amount of dissent. The most detailed accounts of the disagreements between the Basran Khārijites that ultimately led to their division into the four 'mother sects' (*uṣūl al-Khawārij*) – the Azāriqa, the Najdiyya, the Ṣufriyya and the Ibāḍiyya – are transmitted by al-Balādhurī and al-Ṭabarī. Curiously, Ibn Aʿtham has nothing at all on the doctrinal conflict between the Basran Khārijites and the resulting break. He does preserve reports of internal strife among the Azāriqa, but only in the context of their interactions with al-Muhallab and how he managed to take advantage of this weakness. Their discord in Ibn Aʿtham's rendering is also not caused by doctrinal issues but rather by disagreement over whether or not to flee from al-Muhallab.[56] Al-Masʿūdī once again, unfortunately, seems to have treated this part of Khārijite history in yet another work of his, *al-Maqālāt fī Uṣūl al-Diyānāt*,[57] which – like the *Akhbār al-Zamān* – is not extant, but judging from the title was probably a heresiographical work.

Al-Balādhurī and al-Ṭabarī's reports vary in the details. The former has the Khawārij split after their joint departure from Basra to al-Ahwāz whereas the latter places this event in Basra, followed by a letter exchange between the quietists in Basra and the militants in al-Ahwāz. Both nonetheless agree that the dissent is caused by the extremism of the Azraqīs, who maintain that *istiʿrāḍ* is lawful. Other bones of contention are the permissibility of *taqiyya* (concealment of one's beliefs under threat), the status of the *quʿūd* (quietists, 'those who remain sitting'), the killing of enemy children, the necessity of performing a *hijra* and, as a corollary, whether non-Khārijite territory should be considered *dār al-kufr*. The Khārijites argue fiercely with one another on the basis of the Qurʾān and illustrate beautifully how skilled rhetoricians can make just about anything work in their favour. Ultimately, their differences prove too great and they split, declare one another hypocrites and unbelievers and attack each other's views:

> Damn him! Whatever opinion he held, Nāfiʿ b. al-Azraq was sincere . . . But now he has lied and accused us of lying when he says that the people who have rejected the divine grace and ordinances are infidels, that they [Ibn al-Azraq's party] dissociate from polytheism, that we must shed the blood of the polytheists and act similarly with their property, something which has been forbidden to us.[58]

> God is quit of you [Ibn Ibāḍ], for you have fallen short, and God is quit of Ibn al-Azraq, for he has gone too far. God is quit of you both.[59]

> You have lost the men [ʿAṭiyya b. al-Aswad's followers], but you have not lost Islam! God has granted you rest from five things: from the worthlessness (*jufāʾ*) of Qaṭarī b. al-Fujāʾa, the stupidities (*akhlāṭ*) of ʿUbayda b. Hilāl, the haughtiness (*nakhwat*) of ʿAmr al-Qanāʾ, the deviation (*fisq*) of ʿAbd Rabbih al-Saghīr, and the *fitna* of ʿAṭiyya b. al-Aswad.[60]

> Najda wrote to Nāfiʿ and summoned him to return to his original beliefs and to leave behind what he had innovated . . .[61]

> Ibn Abāḍ [*sic*] and the Ṣufriyya wrote to Nāfiʿ rejecting his declaration that the quietists are unbelievers and his appropriation of property before battle and the killing of children.[62]

Another issue that causes frequent disagreement and secession among the Khawārij is the question of leadership: what characteristics and opinions qualify a man for the position of *imām*? While all agree that the best, most virtuous, courageous and pious of Khārijites should be in charge,[63] just who that person is, and whether certain actions or beliefs disqualify him for that position, is subject to heated and often lethal debate.[64] Even more so than doctrinal differences, this innate instability weakens the rebels significantly, especially as it is shown to arise at the most inopportune moments. The following rather comical episode set during Shabīb's rebellion demonstrates this.

The scene is the major clash between al-Ḥajjāj and his troops on one side and Shabīb's rebel group on the other, following the Khārijite's attack on Kufa. In the thick of battle, Shabīb is suddenly approached by one of his own men who wants to know: "What do you say about Ṣāliḥ b. Musarriḥ and how do you testify concerning him?" Shabīb, understandably, is a little confused as to whether that particular moment really is the right time to be getting into this: "Here and now, in the midst of this situation, with al-Ḥajjāj looking on?" Shabīb's companion insists and so Shabīb declares himself quit of Ṣāliḥ. In response, the man repudiates Shabīb and leaves with all remaining Khārijites in tow, except 40 of Shabīb's closest companions. Al-Ḥajjāj astutely observes, "[t]hey have a dispute", and orders his men to attack.

The consequences are disastrous as Ghazāla, Shabīb's wife, is killed in the confusion.[65]

Bothersome practical details such as how the other Khārijites could have just left the battlefield or how Shabīb's remaining 40 men could possibly have withstood al-Ḥajjāj's army of 4,000 even when allowing for a disproportionately high number of casualties among the governor's soldiers, remain unanswered and are clearly beside the point. The purpose of this report and others like it is to delineate the volatility of Khārijism which makes it prone to failure. The doctrinal content of the material is not in itself a main concern – it is sketchy at best and obviously schematised. The focus is rather on the potential for division and strife resulting from a far too unyielding and punctilious understanding of religion as advocated by the Azāriqa and other such militants. The constant disagreements over minute doctrinal details and the near-impossible requirements imposed on the leader present the Khārijite mindset as exceedingly petty. The inherent fallibility of Khārijism simultaneously discredits militant piety as a viable model for a Muslim way of life.

A corollary issue is one we have already come across in al-Ṭabarī's Khārijite material for the reign of Muʿāwiya, i.e. the threat of tribal and civil strife. We saw in Chapter Five that al-Ṭabarī is preoccupied with the repercussions of revolt for the social, political and religious cohesion of *umma* and empire. This concern re-emerges in the accounts of this period, not just in al-Ṭabarī's work. Here as well, it appears to be related to the development of the *jamāʿī* view.

Al-Balādhurī in particular preserves several reports that blame the Khārijites' initial success in Basra on the tribal strife that emerged there and all over Iraq after the death of Yazīd I in 63 H/683–4 CE. When ʿUbaydallāh b. Ziyād eventually had to flee Basra for Syria, the revolts and tribal strife that had simmered under his governorship broke out in earnest and threatened the safety of the garrison town and its hinterland. The Khawārij used the chaos to their advantage and escaped from prison following ʿUbaydallāh's flight; the Basrans were so distracted by tribal discord that the rebels were able to abscond undetected. These accounts are a clear warning: the ramifications of such discord can extend far beyond a simple feud between individual clans or tribal groups. Given the right circumstances, participation in any factional dispute carries the potential for bloodshed of an unforeseen magnitude, as shown by the situation in Basra: the reports have the Khārijites leave thousands of victims, soldiers and civilians alike, in their wake.[66]

There is a pronounced connection here to the theme of Khārijite fractiousness. As their propensity for internal splits debilitates them and ultimately causes their downfall, so does tribal conflict threaten social order and invite disaster to strike. The message is clear: factionalism must be avoided to safeguard the community. Reports like that of an Iraqi soldier who was only allowed to take part in the battle against Shabīb precisely because he and his men had "never participated in factionalism" illustrate this well.[67] When the Basrans disregard this fundamental premise, they suffer for it just like the Khawārij did.

The story of the murder of Masʿūd b. ʿAmr al-Azdī, ʿUbaydallāh's representative in Basra, exemplifies tribal strife as a major concern of scholarly discourse. The details vary, but the core of the story can be summarised thus: shortly after the death of the caliph Yazīd I, the Basrans rebelled against ʿUbaydallāh b. Ziyād, who fled to Syria after appointing Masʿūd as his deputy. The Tamīm and the Qays were dissatisfied with him for some reason, but Masʿūd refused to leave his post and was eventually murdered. The circumstances of his death are not at all clear. Al-Balādhurī alone transmits a plethora of different reports, but most extant accounts claim the involvement of both the Khawārij and the Tamīmī chief, al-Ahnaf b. Qays. A group of Khārijites had apparently left Basra but were encamped nearby. Al-Ahnaf sent a message to them in which he called Masʿūd their common enemy and disclosed the deputy's location. The Khārijites seized on this opportunity and entered Basra, where they killed Masʿūd and a number of his supporters. Masʿūd's enraged Azdī clansmen subsequently drove them out of town once more.[68]

The murder of Masʿūd clearly carried meaning: in the edition, al-Balādhurī devotes over 30 pages to various versions of this event. As usual, the focus is not on the Khārijites but here rests on the tribal discord ravaging Basra. The Khawārij are a convenient tool within the immediate context of the story and also with regard to its broader meaning. In the former, al-Ahnaf in his cunning uses them to get rid of his rival; in the latter, they illustrate the menace of civil strife. No statement of theirs regarding Masʿūd is found in the accounts, no indication at all as to why they would be doing al-Ahnaf's bidding; we learn nothing about their involvement in this episode apart from their role as Masʿūd's killers. The framing is what is important here: the Khārijites can only wreak such havoc because of the already chaotic circumstances in Basra caused by a dangerous focus on tribal factionalism.[69] To prevent such discord, scholars – here including al-Balādhurī – thought it necessary to unite as many people as possible under as wide an umbrella as was feasible: we are back at the *jamāʿī* mindset and the four-caliph thesis.[70]

The source material gives the impression that the status of ʿAlī and ʿUthmān remained a core issue of Khārijite dissent, despite the apparent formation of Khārijite groups with far more developed beliefs than the first protesters at Ṣiffīn or the lacklustre rebels of Muʿāwiya's reign. The historical tradition may have continued to associate Khārijism with this first cause because civil and religious strife were rife in the centuries when the source material was compiled and increasingly systematised.[71] As noted, civil discord and religious fervour constituted exactly the kind of milieu in which the Khawārij reportedly thrived; their dissociation from ʿUthmān, ʿAlī, or both, is a manifestation of this.[72] Still, this also illustrates how static the image of Khārijism is.

Ibn Aʿtham preserves a very telling story of al-Ḥajjāj interrogating a number of Khārijites after Shabīb's death. When the survivors of Shabīb's group are brought to him, al-Ḥajjāj questions them about their religious beliefs. Without fail, they all reply that they follow the religion of one Biblical or Qurʾānic prophet or another, from Noah to Muḥammad, and without fail, al-Ḥajjāj agrees with them. However, when he asks about their opinion on ʿAlī and ʿUthmān, each one of the rebels calls them both unbelievers. In response, al-Ḥajjāj orders their execution. This goes on for some time until he encounters the last Khārijite sent to him, who says that he follows Muḥammad, Abū Bakr and ʿUmar, but that he does not revile ʿUthmān and ʿAlī. Consequently, al-Ḥajjāj releases him.[73]

There are some odd elements to this story. Why would al-Ḥajjāj, a steadfast supporter of the Umayyads, care all that much about the reputation of ʿAlī? Why would this last rebel have joined the Khārijites if he did not believe ʿUthmān and ʿAlī to be sinners? The objective of this account as it is preserved in Ibn Aʿtham's *Futūḥ* appears to be to establish the soundness of both ʿUthmān and ʿAlī as caliphs alongside Abū Bakr and ʿUmar, and to denounce their rejection as deviant. The fact that al-Ḥajjāj is remembered for his loyalty to ʿAbd al-Malik only strengthens this point. The problem is not necessarily religious: al-Ḥajjāj approves of the Khārijites identifying themselves as followers of Hūd, Ṣāliḥ and so forth; what he is shown to take issue with are the socio-political consequences of rejecting various members of the *umma* as unbelievers.[74] The Khārijite definition of the *umma* is presented as too narrow and thus incapable of encompassing a large enough section of the population to avoid factional conflict.

A final example of this concern is an episode set during Shabīb's rebellion that underlines the irreconcilable differences between Khārijism and the *jamāʿī* approach. At some point during his adventures, Shabīb comes up against a combined army of Kufan soldiers under the supreme command of Zāʾida b. Qudāma. Before the battle, Zāʾida exhorts his troops to fight the Khārijites, whom he denounces as riffraff and deviators:

> O servants of God, you are the virtuous many, afflicted by a wicked few . . . Take a look at them, by God! They are not even two hundred – diners on a single head of cattle! They are nothing but bandits and renegades [*surrāq murrāq*], and they have come to you only to spill your blood and take your spoil . . . They are few, and you are many; *they belong to a sect, while you belong to a community*.[75]

In sum, Khārijite volatility and their fastidiousness regarding who they accept as believers constitutes a counterpoint to the *jamāʿī* approach, which seeks to unite as many sections of the *umma* as possible. Factionalism, religious extremism, a pedantic obsession with the letter of the Qurʾān and a radical insistence on minute doctrinal issues all lead to bloodshed and strife, which in turn threatens the stability of state and society. Khārijites stand accused of violating the precepts of *jamāʿī* politics and refusing to listen to reason, and so the response has to be just as fierce as their own behaviour towards non-Khārijites. The material discussing Khārijite attitudes towards ʿUthmān and ʿAlī fits well into the developing four-caliph frame; perhaps it was deliberately utilised to support its claims. The *isnāds* of the relevant *akhbār* and/or the authorities associated with such accounts[76] indicate a late eighth- to ninth-century Iraqi milieu. Both this dating and the fact that the ʿAlī-ʿUthmān issue is addressed in both proto-Sunnī and proto-Shīʿī works accords with the latest research, which has pushed back the formative period of the four-caliph thesis by about two generations and argues for a broad anchoring among different confessional groups.[77]

"The Hypocrites' Chief" – The Censure of Umayyad Governors Continued

In Chapter Five, we saw that al-Balādhurī in particular employed Khārijism to criticise the tyranny of the Umayyads as represented by their officials, especially ʿUbaydallāh b. Ziyād. The same mechanism is at work in the material for this period, epitomised in a statement by the Khārijite ascetic Ṣāliḥ b. Musarriḥ intended to exhort his companions to revolt:

> You see how injustice has become the rule and justice has been effaced. These [Umayyad] governors only increase in their excesses and arrogance toward the people, their remoteness from right, and their effrontery before the Lord. Ready yourselves, then, and send for your brethren who desire, as you do, to reject the wrong and summon to the right.[78]

The main focus here will be on the reputation of al-Ḥajjāj. The portrayal of this particular Iraqi governor is somewhat more complex than that of ʿUbaydallāh whom just about everybody appears to have disliked. Al-Ḥajjāj, on the other hand, is not exclusively cast as a villain; his support of the legitimacy of both ʿAlī and ʿUthmān against the Khārijites, for instance, puts him firmly within the *jamāʿī* camp. Most of the studied sources nonetheless convey an unfavourable image of him that ranges from mildly critical to wholly damning. The censure of al-Ḥajjāj in the context of Khārijite revolts is shored up by non-Khārijite reproach, which will be addressed at the end of this section. The discussion will show that despite different backgrounds, political views and religious affiliations, Khārijites and non-Khārijites make largely the same accusations against al-Ḥajjāj.

Al-Ḥajjāj's reputation in the relevant material is that of a harsh taskmaster who instils fear in his subordinates and is unreasonable and unjust in his decision-making. His religious credentials are called into question and it is implied that he cares more about worldly success than acting in accordance with God's provisions. This characterisation is observable in his interactions with Khārijites and non-Khārijites alike. The works of al-Ṭabarī and Ibn Aʿtham preserve the most detailed portrayal of al-Ḥajjāj in relation to Khārijism and will thus predominate the following discussion.

Ibn Aʿtham in particular transmits a range of accounts that attack al-Ḥajjāj's commitment to Islam. The account of al-Ḥajjāj interrogating the survivors of Shabīb's rebellion has already been outlined, but let us take another look. One of the questions al-Ḥajjāj is shown to ask is whether the rebel prefers this world to the next. A Khārijite *shaykh* replies: "No, O Ḥajjāj! Rather, I chose the Hereafter over this world with my *khurūj* against you and your transgressing companion [i.e., ʿAbd al-Malik]." In response, al-Ḥajjāj orders his head to be cut off, but the Khārijite asks him for a brief respite because he wants to recite two lines of poetry first. Al-Ḥajjāj grants his wish and the Khārijite declaims:

> Before God, I declare myself quit of ʿAmr [b. al-ʿĀṣ] and his party / and of ʿAlī and the people of Ṣiffīn;
> and of Muʿāwiya the deviator and his party / God does not bless the damned.[79]

Then he is killed and al-Ḥajjāj moves on to the next Khārijite.[80]

Not much needs to be said about the obviously literary character of this episode. The figure of the Khārijite rebel who does not beg for mercy but uses his last breath to dissociate himself from those he believes are transgressors is a classic staple in the depiction of Khārijism. He might be misguided, but his piety is a forceful contrast to al-Ḥajjāj's lack thereof, a point that will emerge most explicitly in the discussion of non-Khārijite reproach below. It is also apparent in his interactions with another captive Khārijite, a female rebel.

Following his release of the one Khārijite who did not revile ʿUthmān and ʿAlī, this Khārijite woman by the name of Umm ʿAlqama, one of the rebels' *mutakallimāt*, comes forward to confront al-Ḥajjāj. The governor exclaims: "O enemy of God! Praise be to God who killed your father, your brother and your husband [who were all Khārijites as well]!" Her reply follows immediately: "Yes, praise be to God who sent them to Paradise and placed me behind them."[81] They argue for a while; al-Ḥajjāj becomes increasingly irritated because she keeps averting her eyes, so eventually he orders her to look up at him. Umm ʿAlqama refuses: "Verily, I hate to look upon him who God does not lay his eyes on!" Overcome by anger, al-Ḥajjāj orders her execution and she dies by the sword, chanting *lā ḥukma illā li-llāh* until the very end.[82]

This, too, is a classic Khārijite martyrdom story. It is a standardised narrative as her demise, especially with regard to the element of pious dying words, resembles that of other (in)famous Khārijites from Ibn Muljam[83] to ʿUrwa b. Udayya[84] to Shabīb b. Yazīd,[85] continuing well beyond the period investigated in this study.[86] It serves to demonstrate the indomitable fortitude of the Khawārij, however misguided, which al-Ḥajjāj cannot hope to defeat or match, even if he is victorious from a military point of view. No matter how many Khārijites he has executed, ultimately he remains helpless against their unshakeable conviction. The implication here is that he falls short even in comparison with deviants like the Khawārij, which exacerbates his unfavourable image. This is a mechanism similar to the one we encountered in al-Ṭabarī's treatment of the Basran quietists discussed in Chapter Five.

A powerful example of Khārijite censure of al-Ḥajjāj is also found in Ibn Aʿtham's account of Shabīb's revolt. Having invaded Kufa, Shabīb eventually reaches al-Ḥajjāj's residence and calls out to him: "O enemy of God! O son of Abū Righāl! O brother of Thamūd! Come out to us!"[87] The "enemy of God" reference is universal, but the allusion to Abū Righāl certainly is not. There are two main traditions regarding Abū Righāl: he is identified either as the pre-Islamic Thaqafī tribesman who guided Abraha in his campaign against the Meccans or as the sole surviving member of the Thamūd who died after leaving the sanctuary of Mecca.[88] Ibn Aʿtham's report combines both versions here, as al-Ḥajjāj was from Thaqīf and Shabīb also calls him "brother of Thamūd". Neither comparison is particularly flattering. Three little phrases thus suffice to call al-Ḥajjāj's credentials into question. Al-Ḥajjāj tells his men not to react to this insult in the hope that God would destroy the Khārijites;[89] alas, God does not appear to be favourably disposed toward al-Ḥajjāj: following a fierce skirmish, al-Ḥajjāj and his men flee before Shabīb.[90] The account thus adds insult to injury by painting him as a failure and a coward. (Though al-Muhallab would probably console him on both points.)

Another way in which Ibn Aʿtham's work casts al-Ḥajjāj in a negative light is his disagreement with al-Muhallab over how best to combat the Azāriqa. While there is no explicit criticism of al-Ḥajjāj in these reports, his attitude towards al-Muhallab reflects badly on him within the framework of Ibn Aʿtham's glorification of the Muhallabids. Al-Ḥajjāj is shown to be impatient and dismissive of al-Muhallab's expertise: al-Muhallab wants to wait for the death of Qaṭarī b. al-Fujāʾa or for the Khārijites to split up before engaging them, but al-Ḥajjāj is unconvinced and even accuses al-Muhallab of prolonging the war with the Khawārij for his own enjoyment.[91] As we saw above, al-Ḥajjāj has to acknowledge al-Muhallab's efforts eventually and admit his own mistaken approach.[92] This depiction casts doubt on al-Ḥajjāj's abilities as a governor and contrasts his inadequacy with the patience and circumspection of al-Muhallab. In the context of Ibn Aʿtham's work the negative image of al-Ḥajjāj is thus particularly pronounced where it is juxtaposed with the hagiographical depiction of al-Muhallab.

Turning to al-Ṭabarī, his material on al-Ḥajjāj's shortcomings is mostly related to a non-Khārijite context. This fits the overall orientation of his work: wary of depicting rebellion as positive even when directed against oppression and impiety, Khārijite disapproval of al-Ḥajjāj lacks the full weight of non-rebel censure of the governor. As a result, there is only one instance in which al-Ḥajjāj is explicitly criticised in relation to Khārijism. Granted, there are reports of al-Ḥajjāj's cowardice vis-à-vis the Khawārij, going so far as to dress up some of his *mawālī* in his own clothes in order to escape Shabīb's notice.[93] Likewise, it takes him a few days to make up his mind about engaging Shabīb's rebels himself despite the havoc they wreak.[94] But al-Ḥajjāj's reputation comes off worst in the story of Muḥammad b. Mūsā b. Ṭalḥa, grandson of the famous Companion, and his death at the hands of Shabīb.

Al-Ṭabarī preserves three consecutive, but very different, versions of Muḥammad b. Mūsā's death in battle against the Khārijites, the first from Abū Mikhnaf, the second on the authority of "someone other than Abū Mikhnaf" and the third from ʿUmar b. Shabba. Abū Mikhnaf's report emphasises Muḥammad b. Mūsā's courage: while many of his comrades surrendered to Shabīb, Muḥammad continued to fight and stopped only for the call to prayer. When the Khārijites charged him after completing their own prayer, he recited Q 29:1–3 ('Alif. Lām. Mīm. Do the people reckon they will be left to say "we believe" and not be tried? We put to the test those who came before them, so that God may know those who were sincere and those who were lying') and fought them until he was killed.[95] This version focuses on Muḥammad as a pious and brave man who patiently endured his fate as God's will while vilifying the Khawārij. The death of such a righteous man is lamentable and highlights the dire consequences of (Shabīb's) *fitna*, but it is also a straightforward tale of martyrdom. The other two variants, however, are more complex and paint al-Ḥajjāj in a very undesirable light.

The report from "someone other than Abū Mikhnaf" is completely different from the first. Here, ʿAbd al-Malik appoints Muḥammad b. Mūsā as governor of Sīstān and sends him on his way, telling him to go through Kufa. The caliph advises al-Ḥajjāj to provision Muḥammad with troops and supplies. Muḥammad postpones his departure from Kufa, however, against the advice of his companions who worry that he might get embroiled in conflict if he does not leave.[96] Of course, those words prove 'prophetic' when Shabīb rebels against the Umayyads some time later and al-Ḥajjāj asks Muḥammad to fight Shabīb, which he agrees to do. Shabīb himself now beseeches Muḥammad not to engage the Khārijites because Muḥammad is Shabīb's neighbour in Kufa and thus entitled to his protection. He tells Muḥammad that al-Ḥajjāj only uses him to get rid of his opponents instead of taking them on himself,[97] but Muḥammad insists on fighting Shabīb and calls for single combat. Shabīb gives in, if only after pleading with him one last time not to throw away his life so needlessly. Muḥammad sadly persists and Shabīb kills him. Then he has Muḥammad dressed and buried according to custom, buys up the spoils taken from his camp and sends them to Muḥammad's family despite the protests of his fellow Khawārij.[98]

The positive depiction of Muḥammad b. Mūsā remains here, albeit with a focus on his (misguided) sense of duty rather than his piety. The blame for his death rests firmly on al-Ḥajjāj's manipulations, while Shabīb is portrayed as an honourable combatant who goes out of his way to avoid killing a good man, not as the bloodthirsty rebel other reports make him out to be. The third report from ʿUmar b. Shabba is similar in content, but stronger in its condemnation of al-Ḥajjāj.

The account begins by praising Muḥammad's valour against the Khārijite Abū Fudayk, whom he had fought in Arabia. Muḥammad, who was ʿAbd al-Malik's brother-in-law,[99] passed through Kufa on the way to taking up his governorship and "it was suggested to al-Ḥajjāj" that Muḥammad was a potential threat: because of his position and his proven bravery, he might not always do as told. Al-Ḥajjāj was told to greet him, praise his courage and then mention Shabīb's rebellion, stressing that he hoped God would rid them of the Khārijites through Muḥammad. Al-Ḥajjāj did as suggested and Muḥammad agreed to pursue Shabīb. The Khārijite tried to dissuade him by arguing that al-Ḥajjāj had set him up and that Shabīb himself valued Muḥammad too highly to see him die.[100] Muḥammad did not want to renege on his word, however, and was eventually killed by Shabīb in single combat.[101]

Here as well, Muḥammad and (to an extent) even Shabīb are painted as tragic heroes. Al-Ḥajjāj, on the other hand, is portrayed as an unsavoury, manipulative character who does not refrain from sending a righteous man to his death in order to secure his own power – his selfishness prevents him from considering the greater good. Even worse, he lets his actions and opinions be dictated by equally disreputable (if unidentified) elements. In consequence, doubt is cast on al-Ḥajjāj's suitability for the office of governor and a harsh judgement is passed on his personal qualities.

The criticism of al-Ḥajjāj in his interactions with the Khārijites is indeed mild when compared with reports of his dealings with non-Khārijites. Al-Balādhurī and al-Ṭabarī both transmit further stories that pit eminent members of the community against al-Ḥajjāj. This applies in particular to al-Balādhurī's portrayal of Ibn al-Zubayr's death and to al-Ṭabarī's depiction of activities in the Umayyad camp during Shabīb's uprising. Let us begin with al-Balādhurī's accounts of the interaction between al-Ḥajjāj and Ibn al-Zubayr's mother Asmāʾ bt. Abī Bakr after her son's death in battle against al-Ḥajjāj's troops.

We have already seen[102] that Asmāʾ is very outspoken in her censure of al-Ḥajjāj. Like Shabīb in Ibn Aʿtham's work, she is shown to insult al-Ḥajjāj by calling him 'Abū Righāl'.[103] This epithet is especially scathing as her son Ibn al-Zubayr was a revered Companion, the first child to be born after the *hijra*, grandson of Abū Bakr, son of one of Muḥammad's closest confidants and nephew of Muḥammad's beloved wife ʿĀʾisha; the contrast between al-Ḥajjāj and Ibn al-Zubayr is glaring. Even ʿAbd al-Malik reproaches al-Ḥajjāj for crucifying Ibn al-Zubayr after his death,[104] a punishment the latter had feared greatly in the event of his defeat[105] and that in Islamic legal discourse came to be associated with bandits and heretics.[106] Al-Ḥajjāj's actions as judged through the lens of this discourse thus appear disproportionate and unjust. The significance of punitive practice, especially in contradistinction to legal or theological classifications, as a communication tool on the part of the authorities as well as the reception of this practice by the audience (contemporary and of later generations) is made evident here and should not be underestimated.[107] On another level, the common use of the appellation 'Abū Righāl' by Khawārij and non-Khārijites alike underlines the prevalence of moving phrases that are not as much tied to one particular setting as they are to specific narrative purposes.[108] In this case, the point is to highlight universal dissatisfaction with al-Ḥajjāj's religious and political qualities.

Al-Balādhurī's section on Ibn al-Zubayr, including the conflict between his mother and al-Ḥajjāj, concludes with a harsh assessment of al-Ḥajjāj that remains the last word on this whole affair. Asmāʾ tells al-Ḥajjāj: "I heard God's messenger (ṣ) say: 'Among Thaqīf [al-Ḥajjāj's tribe] there are the excessive destroyer (*mubīr*) and the liar' . . . Regarding the destroyer, that is you!" Al-Ḥajjāj responds, "[I am] the destroyer of hypocrites, the destroyer of hypocrites (*mubīr al-munāfiqīn*)". Asmāʾ, however, retorts: "Nay, rather, their chief!"[109]

Al-Ṭabarī's work contains an equally negative appraisal of al-Ḥajjāj in a variant report on his battle with Shabīb in Kufa. It is an eyewitness account related from ʿUmar b. Shabba, on whose authority the third – and highly critical – version of al-Ṭabarī's account of Muḥammad b. Mūsā's death had been transmitted. It appears that at least some of ʿUmar b. Shabba's material as it relates to Khārijism was censorious of al-Ḥajjāj, apparently more so than Abū Mikhnaf's. The report in question stresses this: according to the eyewitness, al-Ḥajjāj summoned his advisors and military commanders after Shabīb had defeated the armies sent out against him. The governor asked for advice and told his companions to speak their mind even if they disagreed with him. The only one to speak up was Qutayba b. Muslim, who declared that al-Ḥajjāj had "neither feared God nor defended the Commander of the Faithful nor shown any commitment toward his subjects".[110] Enraged, al-Ḥajjāj asked who had spoken so boldly. Qutayba repeated his words and when the governor inquired what he meant by them, he told al-Ḥajjāj to go out against the enemy himself. Al-Ḥajjāj finally heeded his advice and defeated the Khārijites in a fierce battle shortly after.[111]

Another version of this episode follows immediately. Here, al-Ḥajjāj reprimands the Kufans for their hesitancy in fighting Shabīb and requests Syrian troops to be sent to him instead. At this point, Qutayba reproaches him: "You have shown commitment neither to God nor to the Commander of the Faithful in fighting them."[112] Al-Ḥajjāj asks Qutayba about his meaning and receives the response that al-Ḥajjāj had sent out noble commanders but only given them inadequate troops from the "riffraff". It is no surprise that they keep getting defeated, but the commanders are so ashamed that they fight to the death. Qutayba advises al-Ḥajjāj to go out against the rebels himself, with "men your equal, who will defend you as they do themselves".[113] Al-Ḥajjāj follows his suggestion and the rebels are finally vanquished.[114]

The point of this entire section on Shabīb's revolt is clearly the interaction between Qutayba and al-Ḥajjāj. Qutayba's courage in speaking up against a man who is feared by friend and foe alike as well as his strategic wisdom are certainly important aspects, but his criticism of al-Ḥajjāj is even more significant for our purposes. It fits in well with the preceding examples of al-Ḥajjāj's reputation: here, too, al-Ḥajjāj is chastised for his shortcomings as a Muslim and governor. His reprimand of the Kufan troops is turned back on him; his failure to equip his commanders with competent troops reflects badly on his decision-making and puts the blame for Shabīb's success on his own head. It is only when he follows the advice of a better man and commander than himself, the formidable general and later governor of Khurāsān, Qutayba b. Muslim,[115] that he is finally successful in his campaign against the Khārijites, who otherwise play a limited narrative role here.

The unfavourable image of al-Ḥajjāj is thus well-established. That such eminent members of the community as Asmāʾ bt. Abī Bakr and Qutayba b. Muslim condemn his conduct exacerbates the harsh assessment of his persona, which is shared by Khārijites and non-Khārijites alike. Lastly, the focus on al-Ḥajjāj reinforces the premise that Khārijism is not discussed as an end in itself. This is evident, for instance, in the reports of Qutayba's dealings with al-Ḥajjāj: here, Shabīb's revolt is a subsidiary issue that serves as a frame for the confrontation between al-Ḥajjāj and Qutayba. Likewise, Shabīb's Khārijism is essentially irrelevant for the tragedy of Muḥammad b. Mūsā.

"I Am a Friend of Ibn ʿAffān in This World and the Next"[116] – Ibn al-Zubayr and the Khawārij

ʿAbdallāh b. al-Zubayr is the other major figure of early Islamic history that the sources are concerned with, after al-Muhallab and al-Ḥajjāj. The interactions between Ibn al-Zubayr and the Khārijites are mostly limited to the early stages of his rule, at the time of the first siege of Mecca before the death of Yazīd I. There is no direct contact between them after that event other than Ibn al-Zubayr appointing military commanders, chief among them al-Muhallab, to fight the Azāriqa and the Najdiyya. The portrayal of Ibn al-Zubayr that emerges from these accounts is ambivalent, especially in the rendering of al-Balādhurī. His *Ansāb* and al-Ṭabarī's *Taʾrīkh* transmit the most detailed information on the conflict between Ibn al-Zubayr and the Khawārij.

Both al-Balādhurī and al-Ṭabarī mention that on the occasion of the first Umayyad siege of Mecca, the Khārijites (or Khārijites-to-be) decided to support Ibn al-Zubayr against the forces of the caliph Yazīd I.[117] Al-Ṭabarī explains the Khārijite involvement as follows: after the death of Abū Bilāl,[118] ʿUbaydallāh b. Ziyād became even more invested in the persecution of the Khawārij and strove to eradicate them completely. When the news of Ibn al-Zubayr's establishment in Mecca and the Syrian campaign against him reached Iraq, the Khārijites gathered to discuss their options. In this version of the story, related on the authority of Hishām b. Muḥammad al-Kalbī and Abū Mikhnaf, Nāfiʿ b. al-Azraq is given credit for convincing his fellow Khārijites to support Ibn al-Zubayr:

> God sent down the Book to you and in it He imposed *jihād* as an obligation upon you and remonstrated with you with clear eloquence. The swords of the evil ones and those with enmity and oppression [i.e., the Syrians] have been unsheathed against you. Now there is this one who has risen in Mecca [i.e., Ibn al-Zubayr], so let us go out together and we will come to the sanctuary and join this man. If he is of our opinions, we will join him in *jihād* against the enemy; if his opinions are different from ours, we will fight in defense of the sanctuary to the best of our ability and afterward consider our situation.[119]

Al-Ṭabarī's account states that Ibn al-Zubayr was pleased with the Khārijite support and even implied that he shared their views, thereby avoiding *istiʿrāḍ*. They fought together until the caliph Yazīd died and the Umayyad troops subsequently returned to Syria.

The hostilities having ceased, the Khārijites turn to discussing how to proceed; one faction maintains that they had been wrong to join Ibn al-Zubayr who not long ago had opposed them in his calls for vengeance for ʿUthmān. They decide to interrogate him about his views on ʿUthmān, but Ibn al-Zubayr is worried about his safety as only a few of his supporters are around and tells them to return later that evening. The Khārijites do so and are met by a large group of Ibn al-Zubayr's men armed and ready for conflict. Nevertheless, Nāfiʿ prompts ʿUbayda b. Hilāl (another leader of the future Azāriqa) to explain Khārijite views on Muḥammad and his successors up to ʿUthmān, so ʿUbayda informs Ibn al-Zubayr that they accept Abū Bakr and ʿUmar but not ʿUthmān because of his many transgressions, which he names in detail:

> ʿUthmān (. . .) created reserved areas, favored kinship, appointed youths to positions of authority, abolished the lash and laid aside the whip, destroyed the Book, shed the blood of the Muslim, beat those who rejected oppression, granted shelter to him whom the Messenger had expelled, and beat those with precedence in merit, drove them out and disposed them. Not content with that, he seized the spoils [*fay*ʾ] which God had given to them and shared it out among the godless ones of Quraysh and the shameless ones of the Arabs.[120]

Ibn al-Zubayr agrees with their assessment of Abū Bakr and ʿUmar but disagrees strongly with their censure of ʿUthmān, saying that he was the one person still alive who had in-depth knowledge of ʿUthmān. Upon hearing this, the Khārijites and Ibn al-Zubayr dissociate from each other and the Khārijites split into factions upon their return to Basra.[121]

Al-Balādhurī's reports of the Khārijites' initial support for Ibn al-Zubayr are shorter and exhibit a somewhat different emphasis. In agreement with al-Balādhurī's focus on moral questions and his depiction of the Khārijites as extremely pious (if extremely misguided, too), his narrative does not linger on Ibn al-Zubayr's potential as an ally but stresses the Khārijite desire to defend Mecca, "the Sanctuary of God and His House".[122] So a group of Khārijites, among them Najda b. ʿĀmir and ʿAṭiyya b. al-Aswad, make their way to Mecca. Of note, there is no mention at all of Nāfiʿ b. al-Azraq in his accounts of Khārijite interactions with Ibn al-Zubayr. When the Khārijites arrive in Mecca, a poet tells Ibn al-Zubayr that a people have arrived who had killed his father unlawfully – a reference to the Battle of the Camel that many future Khawārij had participated in on ʿAlī's side – and asks him whether he is satisfied with these people. Ibn al-Zubayr replies that even if the devil himself helped him against the Syrians, he would accept him.[123] The rest of the account resembles al-Ṭabarī's report: upon the Syrian retreat, the Khārijites decide to investigate Ibn al-Zubayr's stance on ʿUthmān as well as ʿAlī. When he disagrees with them, they return to Basra and divide into factions.[124]

Both al-Balādhurī and al-Ṭabarī's versions of these events reflect negatively on Ibn al-Zubayr. However, while his opportunism is pointed out clearly in al-Ṭabarī's rendering, it is not elaborated on, and he manages to redeem himself from a *jamāʿī* point of view with his outspoken support of ʿUthmān and dissociation from the Khārijites when their views on ʿUthmān are made explicit. Al-Balādhurī's account is more critical. Ibn al-Zubayr is not only presented as unscrupulous in his attempts to gather support, but also as an unprincipled cynic who does not mind relying on the same people who were involved in killing his father. Of course, the remark about the "devil" joining him does not reflect well on the Khārijites either. Nonetheless, al-Balādhurī also transmits a report that balances Ibn al-Zubayr's approach to an extent. The account is a little confused regarding the actual timeline as it seems to combine the first siege of Mecca with the second, in which Ibn al-Zubayr eventually lost his life.

Al-Balādhurī mentions that a group of Egyptians who later became Khawārij of great courage and strength fought for Ibn al-Zubayr, presumably during the first attack on Mecca, and inflicted great damage on the enemy. Ibn al-Zubayr was nevertheless troubled by their repudiation of ʿUthmān: "By God, I do not like that I seek assistance against my enemy among those who hate ʿUthmān."[125] The Khārijites in turn clarified that they did not fight for Ibn al-Zubayr, "a man who charged our forebears with unbelief"; rather, they only fought "for the inviolability of this house [i.e., the Kaʿba]".[126]

Then they dissociated from him. The account continues with allusions to fierce battles, now presumably during the second attack in 692, until Ibn al-Zubayr was in a dire situation. One of his men told him off for alienating the Khārijites, reminding him of his statement that he would accept help from the devil and claiming that even the Prophet himself asked for assistance from the hypocrites and the Jews in war.[127]

Here, then, Ibn al-Zubayr is shown to be somewhat more discerning in his choice of comrades. At the very least he is uncomfortable with the Khārijite rejection of ʿUthmān. In fact, this report contains two avenues of redemption for Ibn al-Zubayr. First, it is implied that Ibn al-Zubayr may have been under pressure from his men, who did not want to lose the support of the Khawārij because of their prowess. More importantly, the reference to Prophetic practice excuses him for accepting help from the Khārijites: Muḥammad himself was not averse to a little opportunism if the end justified the means. Likening the Khārijites to hypocrites and *dhimmīs* also calls into question their status as proper Muslims. Such allusion to Prophetic *sunna* as a method of redeeming suspect behaviour is a technique we already encountered with regard to ʿAlī – it is a very effective tool, one that often indicates a controversial discourse concerning a particular individual or subject.

Second, the Khārijite insistence that they do not fight for Ibn al-Zubayr but rather for God and His sanctuary emphasises their piety, but also frees Ibn al-Zubayr from accusations of collaboration with rebels and heretics. Most of the reports that address Khārijite involvement in the defence of Mecca highlight this aspect;[128] indeed, there is nothing to indicate that Ibn al-Zubayr agrees with any of their views apart from the universal acceptance of Abū Bakr and ʿUmar. Even al-Ṭabarī's reports make clear that Ibn al-Zubayr only implied his approval of Khārijite beliefs. While he can justifiably be called an opportunist – and did he really have a choice in the face of the Syrian march on Mecca? – nothing worse can be said about his dealings with the Khawārij. In point of fact, al-Ṭabarī also preserves a brief statement to the effect that the later pro-ʿAlid rebel al-Mukhtār rushed to the defence of the Kaʿba as well; both the Khawārij and al-Mukhtār would subsequently be fought by the Zubayrids. Reportedly, even some women joined Ibn al-Zubayr in his fight against the Syrians.[129] This indicates that protecting Mecca was not necessarily an act of support for Ibn al-Zubayr, but rather an act of piety performed by Muslims of all persuasions. The stories of Khārijite support for Ibn al-Zubayr can therefore also be read as a condemnation of the Umayyads and their Syrian armies who endangered and eventually even damaged the 'House of God'.

How to Wage War and Win Battles – Khārijite Revolts as a Military Aptitude Test

So far, we have looked at Khārijism as a tool for discussing matters of chief concern to the early historical tradition. The portrayal of Khārijite revolts operates as a means of (re)constructing the past according to the requirements of the present, as evidenced by such major themes as the vindication of ʿAlī, the condemnation of the Umayyads or the threat of social strife. The material for the period of the second *fitna* and ʿAbd al-Malik's rule also utilises Khārijite uprisings to get across points that appear comparatively minor, such as the issue of female rebels addressed already in Chapter Five. Not all of these can be dealt with here, but in this final section we will discuss one such concern: Khārijism as a military aptitude test for government troops. This theme is virtually exclusive to al-Ṭabarī.

A second look at the depiction of Khārijite rebellions in his work, especially the Shabīb story, reveals that much of the material reads like a military 'how-(not)-to' manual. It contains a plethora of remarks that have strategic or tactical relevance and together form a kind of 'mirror for commanders' that gives advice on warfare: always dig a trench around your camp;[130] do not split up your troops as the individual units are weaker than the combined whole;[131] wait for assistance whenever possible;[132] stay in battle formation;[133] be prepared for nightly attacks;[134] do not forget to put up sentries;[135] avoid disagreement between individual commanders;[136] make sure your soldiers are competent and loyal to avoid desertion;[137] avoid preconceptions and do not make hasty decisions, but prepare for all eventualities.[138] Khārijism here serves to assess the skills of the various government armies and in particular their commanders. The account of Shabīb's revolt specifically is largely a story of military failure on the part of the Umayyad troops. We have already encountered elements of this phenomenon in the reports of al-Muhallab's wars against the Azāriqa: whenever he is removed from his position, the Khārijites manage to regain the upper hand because his replacements are incompetent, prone to rashness or imprudent in judgement. 'Do not remove a successful commander' can be added to the above list of advice.

Two examples illustrate how a few comments on war strategy can convey a harsh evaluation of a commander or governor's capabilities. The first is taken from al-Ṭabarī's portrayal of the conflict between al-Muhallab and the Azāriqa. When Bishr b. Marwān arrived in Basra in 74 H/693–4 CE after his appointment as governor, the caliph, his brother ʿAbd al-Malik, ordered him to send al-Muhallab against the Azāriqa. Bishr should let him choose the best soldiers from Kufa and Basra, as ʿAbd al-Malik completely trusted al-

Muhallab to take care of the Khārijite problem. Bishr, however, was annoyed that his brother had chosen al-Muhallab instead of allowing him to pick his own commander, so he sent ʿAbd al-Raḥmān b. Mikhnaf – the great-uncle of Abū Mikhnaf, al-Ṭabarī's source here – to Kufa to select the most experienced men.[139] Instead of counselling ʿAbd al-Raḥmān on troops or strategy, Bishr tried to incite him against al-Muhallab, told him to question al-Muhallab whenever possible and to take over command if and when the situation presented itself. ʿAbd al-Raḥmān was outraged at Bishr's conniving, all the more so because he and al-Muhallab were fellow Azdīs.[140]

Bishr's death a short while later delayed the battle with the Azāriqa,[141] but the following year al-Muhallab and ʿAbd al-Raḥmān finally moved against the Khārijites in Rāmhurmuz and pursued them to Fārs. Both al-Muhallab and ʿAbd al-Raḥmān set up camp, but while al-Muhallab dug a defensive trench around his, ʿAbd al-Raḥmān was convinced that their swords would be sufficient defence against the Azāriqa. Consequently, when the Khawārij attacked at night, they found al-Muhallab's camp protected and therefore snuck into ʿAbd al-Raḥmān's instead; he was killed in the ensuing battle.[142]

This story of al-Muhallab and ʿAbd al-Raḥmān's collaboration against the Khārijites combines several aspects of the 'mirror for commanders': an attempt at sowing discord between two military leaders; a nightly attack; and the importance of digging a trench. While ʿAbd al-Raḥmān is an honourable man who withstands Bishr's attempts at manipulation, he is also shown to be imprudent in his decision to forego a defensive trench and so brings about his own death, which could have easily been avoided by following al-Muhallab's advice. Of course, this also serves to underline al-Muhallab's skills as a warrior. More generally, it is an example of recklessness in the face of a dangerous enemy and a warning to all military men to avoid such lethal mistakes. Lastly, it also reflects badly on Bishr, who not only foolishly objected to his brother's appointment of al-Muhallab out of hurt pride, but even tried to sabotage him. The way this episode unfolds confirms that al-Muhallab really was the best choice; ʿAbd al-Raḥmān's death is partly Bishr's fault as well.

The second example is taken from al-Ṭabarī's account of Shabīb's rebellion. Here, al-Ḥajjāj orders a certain Sufyān b. Abī al-ʿĀliya al-Khathʿamī to join forces with al-Ḥārith b. ʿUmayra, the commander who had just succeeded in killing Shabīb's companion/predecessor Ṣāliḥ b. Musarriḥ. Sufyān's army takes a while to assemble, but he is impatient and so ignores the message from the head of the cavalry scouts, Sawra b. Abjar al-Tamīmī, to wait for them. Sufyān sets off to pursue Shabīb and finally catches up with him, but he is so eager to fight the rebel that he dismisses the counsel of one of his unit commanders that he should be cautious and reconnoitre the area first.

Sufyān refuses to listen and leads his troops right into an ambush prepared by Shabīb's Khārijites. Sufyān and some of his men fight vigorously, but most of his soldiers are cut down without any effort on the part of the rebels. Sufyān only manages to escape because one of his servant boys sacrifices himself for him.[143]

This episode also contains several themes from the 'mirror for commanders'. Sufyān's decision to leave behind the cavalry scouts, of all army units, comes back to haunt him when he walks into Shabīb's trap and is responsible for getting most of his men killed. As in the first example, Sufyān's behaviour reflects badly not only on himself, but also on al-Ḥajjāj, whose ill-fated appointment of Sufyān calls into question his own capabilities as a judge of character, military commander and governor. The 'military aptitude test' motif may thus partly be read as a sub-theme to the criticism of Umayyad authorities. While elements of this 'mirror for commanders' are echoed in the other sources, particularly the discussion of al-Muhallab's conflict with the Azāriqa, the notable concern with military tactic is peculiar to al-Ṭabarī's rendering of the Khārijite wars.

One explanation for this might be al-Ṭabarī's heavy reliance on Abū Mikhnaf for the accounts of the Azāriqa and Shabīb's uprising. As noted, at least one of Abū Mikhnaf's ancestors appears to have been involved in the battles with the Khawārij. Al-Muhallab as an Azdī warrior will certainly have captured the imagination of his fellow tribesmen as well, so it is not surprising that Abū Mikhnaf had a particular interest in material of this kind. Furthermore, al-Balādhurī and Ibn Aʿtham as the author-compilers who preserve a similar amount of material to al-Ṭabarī do not seem to have relied on Abū Mikhnaf as much in their portrayal of Khārijism. This may explain why this theme is less prominent in their works, but it also makes it difficult to determine whether al-Ṭabarī quoted whatever accounts from Abū Mikhnaf he could access or whether this emphasis on military strategy results from al-Ṭabarī's conscious selection of the relevant reports from Abū Mikhnaf's material.[144] Focusing on warfare might have offered al-Ṭabarī a way to criticise the Umayyad authorities without being too obvious, as his objective of condemning social strife and emphasising the importance of political stability did not necessarily invite open censure.

Conclusions

This chapter has demonstrated the use of Khārijism as a narrative tool with which to illustrate topics and actors of great significance for historiographical and doctrinal discourse leading to a first tentative scholarly consensus. 'Consensus' should not be taken to mean that all of the works under examination display unanimous agreement on how to approach each and every individual subject. Such perfect accord is impossible considering the range of ideological, political, occupational, religious, socio-economic and educational backgrounds not only of the author-compilers themselves, but also of their sources and the sources' sources. Nevertheless, the preceding discussion has shown that certain issues were of particular interest to early Muslim scholars. The complex and controversial historical memory of the second *fitna* and its ramifications, as well as the growth of Khārijism over the 25 years since its alleged inception at Ṣiffīn, mean that more topics could be identified in the reports of Khārijism here than for the preceding two periods. The predominant themes that emerged from the analysis of the source material were (1) the martial skills of al-Muhallab and his family; (2) the volatility of Khārijism as an antithesis to the importance of communal cohesion in an increasingly fragmented polity; (3) the condemnation of Umayyad agents as illustrated by the criticism of the Iraqi governor al-Ḥajjāj; and (4) the relationship between Ibn al-Zubayr and the Khawārij that joined his ranks to defend Mecca and the Kaʿba from the Syrians. The final topic was included in the discussion because of its marked prevalence in al-Ṭabarī's material on the armed conflicts between the Khārijites and their various opponents: extensive passages in his accounts of the Azāriqa and Shabīb b. Yazīd read like a manual of military strategy outlining the consequences of both prudent and foolish decision-making in war.

The historiographical focus was mostly on the activist Khārijites in this period. This is not surprising, as recounting the *umma*'s internal conflicts had historical, literary and doctrinal significance. Nevertheless, the selected sources' almost total disregard for the more moderate or outright quietist factions of the Khawārij is noteworthy. Even the Najdiyya, who – if we can trust the record – were politically more successful than the Azāriqa, occupy very little space compared with their militant counterparts. The mid-680s are commonly regarded as the beginnings of the *uṣūl al-khawārij*, the four main groups within Khārijism that all later subdivisions are reportedly descended from.[145] While the heresiographers preserve the largest amount of material on the Azāriqa,[146] they also discuss the 'doctrines' of the moderate or quietist Khārijites at great length. This is not reflected in the early historical tradition and underlines the different concerns expressed in both genres: unlike historiography, heresiography is explicitly intended to depict, dissect and classify controversial beliefs that ultimately lead to a negative definition of right belief and practice – orthodoxy. The Azāriqa may have been a particularly thrilling subject of study, but the moderates and quietists were (almost) as important for this endeavour.

Based on the specific concerns that emerge from the material on Khārijism during this period, doctrine does not seem to have been a terribly important issue for the historians in the works studied here. On the whole, the early historical tradition appears more interested in Khārijism in terms of the problem of rebellion and how to keep together the wider community; it also makes for some exciting adventure stories. The quietists were less useful in this regard than militant Khārijites such as Nāfiʿ b. al-Azraq, Qaṭarī b. al-Fujāʾa or Shabīb b. Yazīd. The issue of rebellion was certainly also a concern of the heresiographers, as expressed in al-Shahrastānī's famous dictum that everyone who had at any point in the history of mankind rebelled against the rightful ruler of their time is considered a Khārijite.[147] However, a host of other doctrinal matters was similarly important to the heresiographers, like the different Khārijite opinions on marriage and inheritance or the status of the children of unbelievers. Ultimately, however, heresiographers and historians approached Khārijism in similar ways: not as an end in itself, but as a tool that illustrates the correct way of being Muslim by virtue of its embodiment of deviation from the right path.

Notes

1. Muṭarrif's rebellion against al-Ḥajjāj and ʿAbd al-Malik is a curious episode that actually does not fit all that well into the Khārijite template. For a detailed discussion of this episode from a historical as well as historiographical perspective, see Hagemann, "Muṭarrif".
2. Al-Ṭabarī, *Taʾrīkh*, II, 881–1003.
3. See, for example, the remarks in Rowson, *Marwānid Restoration*, translator's foreword and 60, 69 n. 283, 93, 112, 118.
4. For the explicit characterisation of the founders of those two Khārijite groups as quietist, see al-Ṭabarī, *Taʾrīkh*, II, 518.
5. Al-Masʿūdī, *Murūj*, III–IV, 100. Regrettably, this applies to a lot of his Khārijite material.
6. Ibid., 126.
7. Al-Yaʿqūbī, *Taʾrīkh*, II, 264.
8. See, for example, al-Masʿūdī, *Murūj*, III–IV, 126; al-Dīnawarī, *Akhbār*, 280; Ibn Aʿtham, *Futūḥ*, VI, 11; al-Balādhurī, *Ansāb*, IV/2, 422; al-Ṭabarī, *Taʾrīkh*, II, 583, 765.
9. See, for example, al-Ṭabarī, *Taʾrīkh*, II, 580, 581–2; Ibn Khayyāṭ, *Taʾrīkh*, I, 251, 252; al-Masʿūdī, *Murūj*, III–IV, 126; al-Dīnawarī, *Akhbār*, 279, 280; al-Balādhurī, *Ansāb*, IV/2, 406, 407, 408–10. Ibn Aʿtham, *Futūḥ*, VI skips the pre-Muhallabid battles against the Azāriqa altogether and focuses on al-Muhallab's exploits.
10. Ibn Aʿtham, *Futūḥ*, VI, 11 (where the Basran governor writes the letter to

al-Muhallab on the authority of Ibn al-Zubayr); al-Dīnawarī, *Akhbār*, 281; al-Balādhurī, *Ansāb*, IV/2, 423.

11. Al-Muhallab had been appointed as governor of Khurāsān and was on his way to the province when he passed through Basra.
12. Al-Ṭabarī, *Taʾrīkh*, II, 583–4; Hawting, *Collapse*, 167.
13. See, for example, al-Yaʿqūbī, *Taʾrīkh*, II, 265; al-Dīnawarī, *Akhbār*, 282, 284; Ibn Aʿtham, *Futūḥ*, VI, 16, 19, 29, 32, 34–5 and VII, 29, 31, 33, 41, 45; al-Balādhurī, *Ansāb*, IV/2, 424, 426, 430; al-Ṭabarī, *Taʾrīkh*, II, 584–5, 588, 1006.
14. Al-Ṭabarī, *Taʾrīkh*, II, 587.
15. See, for example, al-Ṭabarī, *Taʾrīkh*, II, 825, 855; Ibn Aʿtham, *Futūḥ*, VII, 17, 78; al-Yaʿqūbī, *Taʾrīkh*, II, 272, 275; al-Masʿūdī, *Murūj*, III–IV, 126.
16. Ibn Aʿtham, *Futūḥ*, VII, 32.
17. Al-Dīnawarī, *Akhbār*, 284. See also ibid., 286; Ibn Aʿtham, *Futūḥ*, VI, 29 and VII, 43, 67.
18. Ibn Aʿtham, *Futūḥ*, VII, 58–9, 63, 69.
19. Ibid., 55. But see a very similar report on 57 according to which Qaṭarī's critic says he would renounce Qaṭarī if he fled. This fits the usual representation of Khārijite attitude better than the account cited above, but it is precisely this apparent discordance that is interesting because it further illuminates Ibn Aʿtham's stance on the Azraqīs vis-à-vis al-Muhallab.
20. Al-Dīnawarī, *Akhbār*, 284, 286 (where his flight from al-Muhallab costs Qaṭarī his leadership); Ibn Aʿtham, *Futūḥ*, VI, 34 and VII, 27, 28, 31, 43, 44, 67, 69; al-Ṭabarī, *Taʾrīkh*, II, 588.
21. Ibn Aʿtham, *Futūḥ*, VII, 27.
22. Ibid., 44.
23. Ibid., 24.
24. See, for example, ibid., 24–5, 31, 40–1, 45, 53–5, 61, 66.
25. Ibid., 33–4.
26. Ibid., 37, 43.
27. Robinson, *Historiography*, 42.
28. See also Lynch, *Arab Conquests*, 181 n. 33. For the dating of Ibn Aʿtham and his work, see Chapter Seven below.
29. On the *futūḥ* works of al-Azdī and ps.-Wāqidī in comparison to Ibn Aʿtham's compilation, see Scheiner, "Writing the History", 154–6. Al-Balādhurī's *Futūḥ* was edited as early as 1866 and translated into English in 1916–24 (Hitti and Murgotten, *Origins of the Islamic State*). On this work and its author, see Lynch, *Arab Conquests*.
30. See above, 95, 97.
31. Al-Ṭabarī, *Taʾrīkh*, II, 589; Hawting, *Collapse*, 173.
32. Al-Dīnawarī, *Akhbār*, 288. See also Ibn Aʿtham, *Futūḥ*, VII, 29.
33. Ibn Aʿtham, *Futūḥ*, VI, 24.
34. Ibid., 30–1.

35. Ibn Aʿtham, *Futūḥ*, VII, 65.
36. See, for example, Ibn Aʿtham, *Futūḥ*, VI, 316; al-Ṭabarī, *Taʾrīkh*, II, 855, 856.
37. Donner, *Narratives*, 255–60; Robinson, *Historiography*, 15–19, 36, 83–97. Towards the end of the ninth century, the predominance of 'traditionist historiography' began to wane, however. Historians increasingly dropped the *isnād* and harmonised disparate accounts into one flowing narrative. Khalidi, *Islamic Historiography*, 23–7. The last great representative of traditionist historiography was al-Ṭabarī, for whose status as "imam" of this form of historical writing see Khalidi, *Arabic Historical Thought*, 73–81.
38. Donner, *Narratives*, 266.
39. In addition to the examples cited below, see Ibn Aʿtham, *Futūḥ*, VI, 316–18, where Bishr b. Marwān removes al-Muhallab from office against ʿAbd al-Malik's orders.
40. Ibn Aʿtham, *Futūḥ*, VI, 41–7.
41. Ibid., 44.
42. Al-Ṭabarī, *Taʾrīkh*, II, 822–5. See also Ibn Aʿtham's report of the same event, *Futūḥ*, VI, 298–312.
43. Al-Ṭabarī, *Taʾrīkh*, II, 825; Fishbein, *Victory*, 203.
44. Al-Ṭabarī, *Taʾrīkh*, II, 826–7.
45. Ibn Aʿtham, *Futūḥ*, VI, 300–2.
46. Ibid., 302–4.
47. Ibid., 310.
48. For all this, see al-Ṭabarī, *Taʾrīkh*, II, 1003–7; al-Dīnawarī, *Akhbār*, 285, 287–8; Ibn Aʿtham, *Futūḥ*, VII, 17–26.
49. Ibn Aʿtham, *Futūḥ*, VI, 316.
50. As to how he would have passed it along to them, Ibn Aʿtham provides no information.
51. Ibn Aʿtham, *Futūḥ*, VI, 43.
52. Ibn Aʿtham, *Futūḥ*, VII, 74–6.
53. Al-Ṭabarī, *Taʾrīkh*, II, 1007.
54. For example al-Dīnawarī, *Akhbār*, 286; Ibn Aʿtham, *Futūḥ*, VII, 17, 55, 63; al-Balādhurī, *Ansāb*, VI/1, 395 and IV/2, 462, 463, 465, 466, 467; al-Yaʿqūbī, *Taʾrīkh*, II, 272–3, 275; al-Ṭabarī, *Taʾrīkh*, II, 518–20, 1006.
55. See, for example, al-Balādhurī, *Ansāb*, IV/2, 457–9 (Najda's followers split from him, whereupon the subject population of his territory rises against and kills him); al-Ṭabarī, *Taʾrīkh*, 1007.
56. Ibn Aʿtham, *Futūḥ*, VII, 57–60, 63–4.
57. Al-Masʿūdī, *Murūj*, III–IV, 100.
58. Al-Ṭabarī, *Taʾrīkh*, II, 519.
59. Ibid.
60. Ibn Aʿtham, *Futūḥ*, VII, 63–4. A few lines down on the same page we find al-Muhallab's statement about these five Khārijite leaders being the "five companions of the devil" (see also n. 55 on 108). This is another nice example of

the parallelism Noth identified as one of the literary features of early Islamic historiography (see 149 and n. 76 thereto).

61. Al-Balādhurī, *Ansāb*, VI/2, 403–4.
62. Ibid., 406.
63. E.g., al-Balādhurī, *Ansāb*, IV/2, 441, 446; al-Ṭabarī, *Taʾrīkh*, II, 985–6; and the election episodes discussed above.
64. E.g., al-Balādhurī, *Ansāb*, IV/2, 462; Ibn Aʿtham, *Futūḥ*, VII, 57–8, 63; al-Ṭabarī, *Taʾrīkh*, II, 1006–7.
65. Al-Ṭabarī, *Taʾrīkh*, II, 967; Rowson, *Marwānid Restoration*, 117.
66. Al-Ṭabarī, *Taʾrīkh*, II, 517–18, 581; al-Balādhurī, *Ansāb*, IV/2, 105–6, 401.
67. Al-Ṭabarī, *Taʾrīkh*, II, 956.
68. For all this, see al-Ṭabarī, *Taʾrīkh*, II, 461; al-Balādhurī, *Ansāb*, VI/1, 396–427.
69. Haider, *Rebel and Imām*, 71–2, 85–6, 102–4, 110 identified a similar interpretive framework focused on tribalism and ethnicity in al-Balādhurī, al-Dīnawarī and al-Ṭabarī's narratives of the rebellion of al-Mukhtār, which further illustrates the importance of this particular framework for the imposition of meaning on conflicts from the early Islamic past.
70. For this, the reader is referred back to Chapter Five, 193.
71. See above, 105 and the notes thereto.
72. See, for example, al-Ṭabarī, *Taʾrīkh*, II, 515, 516–17, 882–3, 900; al-Masʿūdī, *Murūj*, III–IV, 138; Ibn Khayyāṭ, *Taʾrīkh*, I, 248; Ibn Aʿtham, *Futūḥ*, VII, 92, 93–4; al-Balādhurī, *Ansāb*, IV/1, 395. This issue had already cropped up in the account of al-Mustawrid's rebellion in the early days of Muʿāwiya's rule.
73. Ibn Aʿtham, *Futūḥ*, VII, 92–5.
74. Some of the Khārijites also reject Ṭalḥa and al-Zubayr; Abū Mūsā and ʿAmr b. al-ʿĀṣ are reviled by the Khawārij by default. Ibn Aʿtham, *Futūḥ*, VII, 93; al-Masʿūdī, *Murūj*, III–IV, 138.
75. Al-Ṭabarī, *Taʾrīkh*, II, 923; Rowson, *Marwānid Restoration*, 75 [emphasis added]. Note the stress on the Khārijites being the "wicked few" opposing the "virtuous many" – this is a direct reference to the Qurʾānic 'small group'/'large group' dichotomy so often employed in Khārijite rhetoric, but Zāʾida reverses it to decry the much smaller rebel party as inferior to the large group, i.e., 'the community'.
76. Al-Ṭabarī relates the relevant accounts on the authority of Abū Mikhnaf, one also from Hishām b. Muḥammad al-Kalbī. Ibn Aʿtham does not provide individual *isnāds*, but the authorities listed in his introduction to the *Futūḥ* are all firmly late-eighth to mid-ninth-century transmitters, such as al-Madāʾinī.
77. Su, "Early Shiʿi".
78. Al-Ṭabarī, *Taʾrīkh*, II, 884; Rowson, *Marwānid Restoration*, 36.
79. Reading "*al-qawm al-malāʿīn*" instead of "*al-qawm al-mayāmīn*" for "the damned".
80. Ibn Aʿtham, *Futūḥ*, VII, 92.
81. Ibid., 95.

82. Ibn Aʿtham, *Futūḥ*, VII, 96.
83. For his death scene, see Chapter Seven.
84. See Chapter Five, 199–200.
85. Al-Ṭabarī, *Taʾrīkh*, II, 973–5. During his drowning, Shabīb apparently recited some Qurʾān verses (Q 8:42, 44; 6:96/36:38/41:12). There are different renditions of his death by drowning in al-Ṭabarī, but this is the first, most detailed and – according to Abū Mikhnaf – the standard one. Ibid., 976. Al-Masʿūdī, *Murūj*, III–IV, 140 has Shabīb sent to al-Ḥajjāj and executed there, with no further details forthcoming.
86. See, for example, the story of the execution of the Khārijite rebel Wazīr al-Sakhtiyānī in 119 H/737 CE, discussed in Marsham, "Attitudes", 111, 118–19.
87. Ibn Aʿtham, *Futūḥ*, VII, 88.
88. EI², "Abū Righāl" (S. A. Bonebakker). For more variants of the Abū Righāl story, see Stetkevych, *Muhammad and the Golden Bough*, 36–49.
89. Ibn Aʿtham, *Futūḥ*, VII, 88.
90. Ibid., 90. See also al-Masʿūdī, *Murūj*, III–IV, 139.
91. Ibn Aʿtham, *Futūḥ*, VII, 18.
92. Ibid., 17–26. See also al-Ṭabarī, *Taʾrīkh*, II, 1004–5; al-Dīnawarī, *Akhbār*, 287.
93. Al-Ṭabarī, *Taʾrīkh*, II, 966, 967; Ibn Khayyāṭ, *Taʾrīkh*, I, 274.
94. Al-Ṭabarī, *Taʾrīkh*, II, 963, 966. For the entire story of Shabīb's second invasion of Kufa and the ensuing battle with al-Ḥajjāj, see ibid., 956–68. Al-Ṭabarī is the only source to report two invasions of Kufa; all other works only list the one that includes the battle between Shabīb and al-Ḥajjāj. See Rowson, *Marwānid Restoration*, 70 n. 283.
95. Al-Ṭabarī, *Taʾrīkh*, II, 926–7.
96. Ibid., 920.
97. Reasoning we also encountered before the battle of al-Nukhayla between Khārijites and Kufan troops just after Muʿāwiya's accession. See Chapter Five, 177–8.
98. Al-Ṭabarī, *Taʾrīkh*, II, 927–8.
99. The caliph was married to Muḥammad's sister. Madelung, *Succession to Muḥammad*, 379.
100. Of note, there is no indication in the account that Shabīb viewed Muḥammad as an enemy or held a grudge against him because of his previous battles against the Arabian Khawārij.
101. Al-Ṭabarī, *Taʾrīkh*, II, 928.
102. See Chapter Three, 118.
103. Al-Balādhurī, *Ansāb*, IV/2, 386.
104. Ibid., 385.
105. Ibid., 377.
106. See above, 201–2.

107. Marsham, "Public Execution", 104–5.
108. See also above, 68, 73–5, 118.
109. Al-Balādhurī, *Ansāb*, IV/2, 387.
110. Al-Ṭabarī, *Taʾrīkh*, II, 962; Rowson, *Marwānid Restoration*, 112.
111. Al-Ṭabarī, *Taʾrīkh*, II, 962–3.
112. Ibid., 963; Rowson, *Marwānid Restoration*, 114–15.
113. Al-Ṭabarī, *Taʾrīkh*, II, 964; Rowson, *Marwānid Restoration*, 115.
114. Al-Ṭabarī, *Taʾrīkh*, II, 963–4. For an earlier example of al-Ḥajjāj being advised by a prominent Muslim – here Zuhra b. Ḥawiyya, a veteran of the conquest of Iraq and a hero of al-Qādisiyya – see al-Ṭabarī, *Taʾrīkh*, II, 942.
115. EI², "Ḳutayba b. Muslim" (C. E. Bosworth); Stark, "Arab Conquests"; Haug, *Eastern Frontier*, 114–23.
116. Al-Ṭabarī, *Taʾrīkh*, II, 516.
117. Ibid., 425–6, 514–7, 529; al-Balādhurī, *Ansāb*, IV/1, 394–5 and IV/2, 401, 372–3, 455.
118. See Chapter Five.
119. Al-Ṭabarī, *Taʾrīkh*, II, 514; Hawting, *Collapse*, 98.
120. Al-Ṭabarī, *Taʾrīkh*, II, 516; Hawting, *Collapse*, 99–100.
121. For this entire episode, see al-Ṭabarī, *Taʾrīkh*, II, 513–17. See also Ibn Khayyāṭ, *Taʾrīkh*, I, 248.
122. Al-Balādhurī, *Ansāb*, IV/1, 394.
123. Ibid., 395.
124. Ibid.
125. Al-Balādhurī, *Ansāb*, IV/2, 372.
126. Ibid., 373.
127. Ibid.
128. See the references listed at notes 117 and 121.
129. Al-Balādhurī, *Ansāb*, IV/2, 107.
130. Al-Ṭabarī, *Taʾrīkh*, II, 975, 890, 903, 930, 932.
131. Ibid., 903, 942.
132. Ibid., 896–7.
133. Ibid., 930, 932, 959, 970.
134. Ibid., 875, 892, 903–4, 969.
135. Ibid., 900, 960.
136. Ibid., 761, 856, 877, 878, 897, 908, 913–14, 933.
137. Ibid., 587, 853, 857, 888, 898, 902, 926, 930, 948, 952–3, 954, 957, 964, 970, 973.
138. Ibid., 897, 909–10, 933, 943–6, 960.
139. Ibid., 855–6.
140. Ibid., 856.
141. Ibid., 857.
142. Ibid., 875.
143. Ibid., 896–8.

144. On this, see also the comments on 32.
145. Lewinstein, "Making and Unmaking", 77.
146. Lewinstein, *Studies*, 37 n. 9 and "Azāriqa", 252.
147. Al-Shahrastānī, *al-Milal*, I, 132. See also Abou el Fadl, *Rebellion and Violence*, 248 and Kenney, *Muslim Rebels*, 30–1. Al-Ṭabarī preserves an account in which ʿUbaydallāh b. Ziyād accuses someone of having 'turned Khārijite' (*ḥarūrī*) when he refused to follow an order. It is uncertain whether this reflects early uses of the term or later developments, but it underlines in any case the governor's own immoderation in his treatment of subjects and opponents – killing said person, he reasons, is now permissible. Al-Ṭabarī, *Taʾrīkh*, II, 253.

PART IV

OBSERVATIONS AND CONCLUSIONS

7

Observations Regarding the Historiographical Tradition on Khārijism

The works selected for this study cover a wide range of political, religious and occupational affiliations. They are all examples of Iraqi historiography in a broad sense, but nevertheless transmit diverse material and employ narrative devices in different ways. The volume of material on Khārijite history in the individual works as well as the particular accounts they preserve vary as well. Some reports are almost identical in phrasing but differ in the *isnād*; sometimes the same version of an account appears in several different sources, but the placement and emplotment differ considerably. Overall, the study of the portrayal of Khārijism has revealed certain characteristics that warrant a closer look.

Is There a Historiographical Tradition on Early Khārijite History?

The short answer is yes, however the longer answer starts with a 'yes, but . . .' and requires some qualification. As the preceding chapters have shown, the sources often differ regarding the details of early Khārijite history. Nonetheless, there are no major deviations from the story of Khārijism as outlined in the historical overview in Part I. Even Ibn Aʿtham's rather distinctive portrayal does not present a radically different view of early Khārijite history: the overall framework of events is the same across the board. This applies not just to the major events of Khārijite history but also to their meaning for the construction of the early Islamic past. This consensus is particularly evident in the conflict between ʿAlī and the Khawārij, but similar commonalities can be discerned in the material for the other two periods as well. In all of the sources studied here, the primary narrative purpose of Khārijite rebellion is the provision of cautionary tales against the perils of an exclusionist definition of true belief that directs militant piety inward and thus endangers the very community that it claims to protect. This broad accord, which is not exclusive to historiography but perceptible in early Islamic scholarship more generally, enables us to speak of an early historiographical tradition on Khārijism.

At the same time, however, there are some marked differences in the way the various authors engage with literary Khārijism. These differences are not primarily related to the events themselves, but rather to their significance within a particular narrative unit. The discussion in Chapter Five illustrated this nicely: here, al-Balādhurī and al-Ṭabarī used similar material to come to different conclusions regarding the validity of Khārijite opposition. Another example is Ibn Aʿtham's treatment of the Muhallabid wars against the Azāriqa, where his primary objective is to build up a heroic narrative around the figure of al-Muhallab, whose literary presence far outweighs that of his Khārijite opponents. While other sources show a similar tendency, they also emphasise other issues, like Azraqī atrocities against other Muslims.

Evidently, the historians had distinct individual concerns beside their participation in the formation and continuation of a Khārijite master narrative. Al-Balādhurī as a courtier and caliphal boon companion, for instance, certainly had his audience to consider when he gathered his material, and it is thus not surprising that he transmits many more edifying or entertaining stories than, say, al-Ṭabarī or al-Yaʿqūbī. His *Ansāb* exhibits *adab* traits and is therefore concerned with questions of good conduct, with morals and ethics, characteristics that are also reflected in his treatment of Khārijism. Al-Ṭabarī as a more or less independent scholar who was primarily a jurist appears interested more in issues of statecraft, of communal cohesion and the dangers of *ʿaṣabiyya*. Ibn Aʿtham's work is the most decidedly pro-ʿAlid among the analysed sources and makes no pretence of his sympathies: his depiction of ʿAlī, for example, turns the caliph into an almost semi-divine figure who is able to predict the future and has access to special knowledge.[1] In light of the discussions of al-Yaʿqūbī's potential Shīʿism,[2] this is a particularly interesting point to note.

Such individual concerns influenced the interpretation of Khārijism in early Islamic historiography. While the Khārijite master narrative was broadly adhered to across the spectrum of political and religious affinities, the nuances in the way this narrative was presented are often not acknowledged. One problem is the (sometimes unavoidable) overreliance on the *History* of al-Ṭabarī,[3] but the consensus regarding the broad outline of Khārijite history also tends to obscure the finer points of how the sources shape literary Khārijism. This is all the more regrettable as a closer analysis allows for a greater understanding of the narrative techniques and individual concerns of early Islamic authors.

Proto-Sunnī and Proto-Shīʿī Sources

Four of the works under consideration, the *Taʾrīkh* by al-Yaʿqūbī, Naṣr b. Muzāḥim's *Waqʿat Ṣiffīn*, Ibn Aʿtham's *Kitāb al-Futūḥ* and al-Masʿūdī's *Murūj al-Dhahab* are often regarded as (proto-)Shīʿī sources.[4] The distinction between proto-Sunnī and proto-Shīʿī sources overall is murky at best, not least because of the polyphonic and compilatory character of the "tumultuous sea of contested historical memory" that is early Islamic historiography.[5] This can also be observed with regard to the portrayal of Khārijite history, as we shall see shortly. Generally speaking, a systematic or exclusionary distinction between so-called proto-Sunnī and proto-Shīʿī scholars and works does not have much value for the period and events investigated here. The formation processes of Sunnism and the various strands of Shīʿism continued until well after the youngest scholar considered here, al-Masʿūdī, had died in the mid-tenth century. ʿAlī and the Prophet's family held a revered position among many believers, ʿAlids, ʿAbbāsids and *jamāʿī*-minded alike; even the commemoration of al-Ḥusayn's death at Karbalāʾ was upheld by some Sunnīs as well.[6] And while their interpretations of certain events and protagonists may have differed, proto-Sunnī and proto-Shīʿī authors essentially approached history-writing according to the same structural and narrative conventions.[7]

The preceding analysis has shown that both proto-Sunnī and proto-Shīʿī works follow the same basic framework of Khārijite history and often transmit similar or identical material across 'denominational' lines. This is a well-known feature of early Islamic historiography: "wherever one turns, one finds compilers of different dates, origin and doctrinal persuasions presenting the same canon in different arrangements and selections".[8] Concerning the initial protest against the arbitration (or its outcome), for instance, al-Ṭabarī, al-Balādhurī, al-Yaʿqūbī and al-Masʿūdī all name ʿUrwa b. Udayya as originator of the *la ḥukma*-phrase. The remaining works offer a selection of accounts of this episode.[9] As regards the events immediately following the request for arbitration, Naṣr b. Muzāḥim, al-Dīnawarī and Ibn Aʿtham report that the Syrian and Iraqi *qurrāʾ* met after the Syrian call for armistice, discussed the *maṣāḥif* and then jointly agreed on the appointment of two arbiters.[10] The other sources do not record a particular involvement of the *qurrāʾ*.

Al-Dīnawarī has been called a pro-ʿAlid[11] or even (within limits) a Shīʿī historian,[12] but others have argued for a different understanding of his work.[13] I would agree with the latter at least in the context of this study: al-Dīnawarī betrays no particular proto-Shīʿī tendencies in his portrayal of Khārijism, and while his decidedly favourable coverage of ʿAlī far exceeds that of the first three caliphs in volume and detail, his sympathies for ʿAlī did not motivate al-Dīnawarī to depict the caliph along proto-Shīʿī lines of argument.[14] Moreover, as illustrated in Chapter Four, all sources are agreed on the justification of ʿAlī's conduct at Ṣiffīn and afterwards. The most recent study of al-Dīnawarī's *Akhbār* locates author and work in a *shuʿūbī* context because of the text's interest in Iranian history (much of it pre-Islamic) and the Persian language,[15] but this is controversial as well.[16] An Iranian or *shuʿūbī* perspective is in any case not evidence for potential Shīʿī sympathies, of course.

The transmission of very similar material across all selected sources indicates that the author-compilers indeed had access to more or less the same pool of information from which they selected their reports; some form of consensus regarding early Khārijite history must have crystallised at the latest by the early ninth century. This selection process reveals more about the sources' particular sympathies and concerns than simply labelling them as proto-Sunnī or proto-Shīʿī would, much the same way that a scholar's audience or occupation (where these are known) can often tell us more than classifying a work as belonging to a particular genre of literature.

Indeed, the question of (proto-)Sunnī vs. (proto-)Shīʿī sources is tricky. Take someone like Ibn Aʿtham, for instance. Conrad has argued that he was a "strident Shīʿī" and his material "virulently anti-Umayyad".[17] At the same time, however, the work also contains many accounts quoted on the authority of proto-Sunnī scholars and on several occasions he does not advance pro-ʿAlid claims even though the material would have given him ample opportunity to do so.[18] Likewise, al-Masʿūdī transmitted material from and studied with non-Shīʿī scholars like al-Ṭabarī and Ibn Durayd.[19] The same applies to al-Yaʿqūbī: he is called a Shīʿī historian by many,[20] but he, too, mainly quotes authorities that are not known for their particular Shīʿī tendencies and his *History* compares well to al-Balādhurī's *Ansāb* and al-Ṭabarī's *Taʾrīkh*.[21] Crone famously judged that "Yaʿqūbī gives us nothing like the Shīʿite experience of Islamic history, merely the same body of tradition as the Sunnī Ṭabarī with curses in appropriate places";[22] Daniel maintained that there was "no *prima facie* evidence at all of al-Yaʿqūbī's Shīʿism",[23] a view that has recently been challenged by Anthony, who considers him a *rāfiḍī* Shīʿī.[24] Al-Masʿūdī's exceedingly favourable depiction of ʿAlī and the clear redirection of blame towards his so-called supporters for the arbitration disaster and ultimate failure of his caliphate have been used to build up the argument that he was solidly in the (Twelver) Shīʿī camp,[25] but the discussion in Chapter Four demonstrated clearly that there is little difference in how the selected works treat the ʿAlī-Khawārij conflict. ʿAlī's harsh condemnation of Muʿāwiya and ʿAmr b. al-ʿĀṣ as 'the worst of children and worst of men', to give but one example, is not peculiar to al-Masʿūdī or the pro-ʿAlīd works, but likewise transmitted in al-Ṭabarī's *History*.

Even if we allow for strong ʿAlid or Shīʿī sympathies among historians like Ibn Aʿtham and al-Yaʿqūbī, is that then enough to qualify their entire works as Shīʿī? And if so, what does that signify, really, for our understanding of these texts?[26] What do we even mean by Shīʿism in this context, exactly? Shīʿī Islam is certainly no monolith and in the early period especially encompassed all sorts of groups and beliefs;[27] not even all ʿAlids were Shīʿīs.[28] Scholarship in the early Islamic period in particular transcended communal boundaries of all kinds, as also noted above.[29] And finally, in light of the editorial work done to texts by scribes, copyists, teachers, students and, importantly, modern editors, a good deal of caution concerning the labelling of texts according to denominational categories seems prudent.[30]

When it comes to the subject of the present book, it is also apparent that there are many disparities between these 'proto-Shīʿī' sources, too many to speak of a separate take on Khārijism. The term 'proto-Shīʿī' may make things worse here as it has a strong doctrinal and ideological undertone and suggests a tradition (in the making, at least). Ibn Aʿtham and al-Masʿūdī in particular can probably be regarded as part of a developing Shīʿī identity and so we might call them proto-Shīʿīs with some justification. Overall, however, the 'proto-Shīʿī' works examined here for the most part do not display a distinctly Shīʿī influence or common perspective when it comes to early Khārijite history, or rather, they share a broad perspective with proto-Sunnī historiography. Classifying such works as 'pro-ʿAlid' or as having pronounced sympathies for ʿAlid legitimist claims may work better here. We thus arrive at a distinction between proto-Shīʿī authors and their broadly pro-ʿAlid works.

A few examples from the period of ʿAlī's reign, where we might expect proto-Shīʿī influence or perspectives to manifest most clearly, will suffice to illustrate the broad overlap between proto-Sunnī and pro-ʿAlid historiography. Al-Yaʿqūbī, for instance, does present the conflict between ʿAlī and the Khawārij from a markedly pro-ʿAlid point of view, but this is much less obvious in the other three pro-ʿAlid works; interestingly, while al-Masʿūdī is more outspokenly pro-ʿAlid overall than al-Yaʿqūbī, whose work sometimes betrays an ʿAbbāsid-friendly stance even to the disadvantage of the ʿAlids,[31] this tendency is not reflected in the *Murūj*'s material on early Khārijism. As we saw in Chapter Four, al-Yaʿqūbī preserves a unique argument between the Khārijites and ʿAlī regarding the latter's status as *waṣī*, but al-Masʿūdī does not – at least not in his extant works. There are more such differences in the pro-ʿAlid works: the material on Ṣiffīn from the call to arbitration onward as preserved by Ibn Muzāḥim, for example, does not contain decidedly pro-ʿAlid (or proto-Shīʿī) material and was seamlessly incorporated into the proto-Sunnī histories of al-Ṭabarī and al-Dīnawarī in particular. As noted, the accounts of the originator(s) of the *lā ḥukma*-slogan and the role of the *qurrāʾ* in *Waqʿat Ṣiffīn* are practically identical in content (and the former also in phrasing) to the material in al-Dīnawarī's *Akhbār*.[32] Now, the reconstructed *Waqʿat Ṣiffīn* does not address the events after ʿAlī's departure from Ṣiffīn, which include the vast majority of his interactions with the Khawārij. Ibn Muzāḥim's work as we have it therefore does not contain the elaborate speeches ascribed to ʿAlī or Ibn ʿAbbās in their confrontations with the rebels and offers less opportunity for the propagation of decidedly pro-ʿAlid material. In any case, Ibn Muzāḥim's alleged pro-ʿAlid sympathies were not an issue for the later historical tradition that utilised his reports.

The depiction of the events leading to ʿAlī's agreement to the arbitration also varies. Whereas Ibn Muzāḥim and Ibn Aʿtham emphasise the role of the *qurrāʾ* in forcing ʿAlī to accept the arbitration and in choosing Abū Mūsā, al-Yaʿqūbī does not mention the *qurrāʾ* in connection with the Khawārij at all; al-Masʿūdī only mentions in passing that there were *qurrāʾ* among the rebels who withdrew to Ḥarūrāʾ. He in turn primarily blames al-Ashʿath b. Qays for the arbitration. All four sources furthermore disagree concerning the origin of the *lā ḥukma* phrase. Ibn Muzāḥim and Ibn Aʿtham are rather more outspoken in their criticism of the violent piety of the *qurrāʾ*/future Khārijites than al-Yaʿqūbī and al-Masʿūdī. Finally, Ibn Aʿtham, al-Masʿūdī and al-Yaʿqūbī all transmit distinct and unrelated descriptions of the murder of ʿAlī by Ibn Muljam. A broad consensus regarding the main events of Khārijite history and its interpretation can thus be discerned across the range of sources under study, but there is no evidence for a specific proto-Shīʿī/pro-ʿAlid sub-tradition on early Khārijism here.

Yet the pro-ʿAlid works have one thing in common: they have a lot less to say on Khārijism than their proto-Sunnī counterparts. They do not discuss internal Khārijite events and debates at any length, for instance. Where al-Ṭabarī, al-Dīnawarī and al-Balādhurī each preserve a relatively long passage detailing the election of Ibn Wahb al-Rāsibī as Khārijite leader and his speeches, the pro-ʿAlid sources contain hardly more than a reference to his name and rank. Khārijite arguments are not elaborated upon as a general rule, with the limited exception of al-Balādhurī's material on intra-Khārijite discord in Basra in the mid-680s. But there is virtually nothing in the pro-ʿAlid works that would allow the reader to get a glimpse of Khārijite thought and motivation beyond the generic call for abandonment of the arbitration process, repentance towards God and the necessity of *jihād*. In al-Masʿūdī's case at least, this may be due to much of the relevant information having been included in works that did not survive. But it is striking that it is up to al-Balādhurī and especially al-Ṭabarī to highlight the particular enmity between Khārijites and ʿAlids noted in Chapter Five.

This dearth of information on the Khawārij in the pro-ʿAlid sources is somewhat unexpected. At least in Ibn Aʿtham's case, space cannot have been an issue. He devotes over 100 pages (in the edition) to the events from the call to arbitration at Ṣiffīn until the murder of ʿAlī, for example – about as much as al-Ṭabarī. However, where al-Ṭabarī provides comparatively many details on internal Khārijite affairs, Ibn Aʿtham gives an endless stream of speeches, sermons and letters attributed to ʿAlī, much more so than any other source. Of course, this is not unusual for a proto-Shīʿī historian. The occupation with ʿAlī and ʿAlid matters might also partially explain why these works generally have little interest in Khārijite history after ʿAlī's caliphate. Ibn Aʿtham is the only one to transmit a significant amount of material on later Khārijism, for the period of the second *fitna* and ʿAbd al-Malik's caliphate, but the vast majority of his accounts are concerned with al-Muhallab and his family, not known to be particular champions of the ʿAlid cause. If Ibn Aʿtham was indeed an Azdī himself,[33] this might explain his engagement with and praise of al-Muhallab at least partly. His almost hagiographical take on this family stands out among the selected sources and warrants further study.

In sum, the pro-ʿAlid sources do not represent a specific and separate pro-ʿAlid tradition on Khārijism other than displaying a decided disinterest in the Khawārij beyond the portrayal of ʿAlī's superiority. Moreover, whereas Khārijism serves a range of narrative purposes in the other sources, it seems that the pro-ʿAlid works have little use for Khārijites where they do not fulfil the function of vindicating ʿAlī – again with the exception of Ibn Aʿtham's Muhallabid hagiography. This might be connected to the memory of Khārijism as a wholly misguided reaction to ʿAlī and ultimately as the caliph's downfall. Pro-ʿAlid historians may have been more hesitant to use the Khawārij as a means of criticising the Umayyads so as to avoid all positive connotations of the former. At the same time, they were perhaps less concerned with the issue of communal cohesion – one of al-Ṭabarī's main foci, for instance – as it appears to have first originated in the reaction among proto-Sunnīs to the formation of Shīʿism.[34]

Finally, let us look at the most peculiar of the historians examined in this study, Ibn Aʿtham. Some of his work's idiosyncrasies have already been pointed out, but it is worth investigating further.

The Case of Ibn Aʿtham's Kitāb al-Futūḥ

Very little is known about Ibn Aʿtham al-Kūfī. Details such as his birth and death date, early life, scholarly career and place of residence remain unknown or controversial. While his *nisba* maintains an affiliation with Kufa, it is not clear in what way he was connected to the city. Conrad has argued that his obscurity was a result of him being a Shīʿī *qāṣṣ*, or storyteller, rather than a *ḥadīth* transmitter or serious scholar of another profession.[35] The entry on

Ibn Aʿtham in the EI[2] comprises a mere 486 words[36] and very little research has been carried out on his fascinating *Kitāb al-Futūḥ*.[37] There has been some renewed interest recently, with the long-awaited publication of Conrad's piece and works by Schönléber and Lindstedt.[38] Overall, however, much remains to be done.

The *Kitāb al-Futūḥ* stands out from the other sources because its treatment of early Khārijite history, while adhering to the same basic framework, differs substantially. Ibn Aʿtham transmits a lot of material that is not found in the other works and much of what he preserves seems to have been disregarded by the later historical tradition. There are numerous examples of this, including the long 'debate' between Ibn ʿAbbās and a Khārijite opponent discussed in Chapter Four.[39]

Another instance is Ibn Aʿtham's rendering of the murder of ʿAlī. The standard version has it that Ibn Muljam, sometimes accompanied by two fellow Khārijites,[40] decided to kill ʿAlī to punish him for his transgressions. The variants that include two other Khārijites claim that it was their stated aim to kill Muʿāwiya and ʿAmr b. al-ʿĀṣ as well, but they both fail in their assignments. Not so Ibn Muljam: having arrived at Kufa, he spends some time in the city and encounters his bride-to-be, Qaṭāmi, who wants him to murder ʿAlī to avenge her family members, who died at Nahrawān. Ibn Muljam attacks and strikes the caliph while he is the mosque leading the morning prayer. ʿAlī succumbs to his wounds a few days later and Ibn Muljam is – depending on the source – either executed or tortured to death.[41] Some reports emphasise his immense piety and stoicism under torture: he remained silent until his executioners removed his tongue and then cried out only because he did not want to be alive for even an hour without being able to praise God.[42] Other accounts just state that he was executed after ʿAlī's death.[43] Here, too, there is no clear division of content between proto-Sunnī and pro-ʿAlid sources.

Ibn Aʿtham's description of Ibn Muljam's murderous enterprise adds many details unique to him among the selected sources. In his version, Ibn Muljam does not travel to Kufa specifically to kill ʿAlī, but during his stay there he falls in love with Qaṭāmi. It is she who incites him to murder ʿAlī by demanding this deed as part of her dowry. While her request for ʿAlī's blood is part of the standard version of this episode, Ibn Muljam is usually shown to have already decided to kill ʿAlī. In Ibn Aʿtham's rendering, however, Ibn Muljam is reluctant and unsure about the rightness of killing the caliph.[44]

Ibn Muljam also encounters the caliph in Kufa prior to the assassination attempt and is deeply impressed by ʿAlī's prediction of his death, to the precise day, by the hands of a Murādī; Ibn Muljam, of course, belongs to Banū Murād.[45] Yet more surprisingly, he calls ʿAlī by his title of *amīr al-muʾminīn*, which is in stark contrast to the other sources that make a point of Ibn Muljam's refusal to greet ʿAlī as *amīr al-muʾminīn*.[46] In Ibn Aʿtham's version, Ibn Muljam voices his doubts to Qaṭāmi right up until the moment he leaves the house to attack ʿAlī. On his way to the mosque, he even quotes a Prophetic *ḥadīth* according to which

> the most miserable [man] of the [pre-Islamic] ancestors (*al-awwalīn*) is Qadār b. Sālif, the slayer of Ṣāliḥ's camel,[47] and the most miserable [man] of the Islamic generations (*al-ākhirīn*) is the slayer of ʿAlī b. Abī Ṭālib.[48]

Ibn Aʿtham appears to have focused on ʿAlī as the most pious and excellent of his contemporaries much more so than the other historians. He transmits the largest number of speeches attributed to ʿAlī and he portrays the caliph as sharing in divine knowledge by having him predict certain events that promptly take place, such as the manner of his own death.[49] These elements are much more pronounced than in the other works with a pro-ʿAlid slant. While we cannot speak of a fully-fledged Shīʿī vision in Ibn Aʿtham's work, in terms of the material for the period studied here it is the most clearly pro-ʿAlid source.

It is noteworthy that these predictions are not found in the other historiographical sources, nor are the accounts of Ibn ʿAbbās' lengthy debate with the Khārijites at Nahrawān or the version of the Ibn Muljam narrative we find in Ibn Aʿtham's *Futūḥ*. His hagiographical treatment of al-Muhallab sets him apart as well. We do, however, find at least the prediction stories in another type of literature. Al-Mubarrad's *adab* work *al-Kāmil*, for example, cites both Muḥammad's prediction that ʿAlī will experience his own 'Day of al-Ḥudaybiyya' and ʿAlī's prediction concerning the number of men who will fall in battle against the Khārijites.[50] It also contains elements of Ibn Aʿtham's Ibn Muljam episode: Qaṭāmi has a very active role in exhorting Ibn Muljam to attack ʿAlī; the caliph and his assassin meet before the murder takes place; and ʿAlī predicts his death at the hand of Ibn Muljam.[51] The fluid boundaries of early Islamic literature and knowledge production are confirmed here once more.

Ibn Aʿtham's *Futūḥ* generally does not appear to have conformed too well to the evolving consensus of the early historical tradition. Aaron Hagler argued in his 2011 PhD dissertation on the portrayal of Ṣiffīn in Islamic historiography that the work was deliberately excluded from the agreed-upon framework of early Islamic history in order to explain the lack of interest that historians displayed regarding Ibn Aʿtham's work. Hagler maintained that there were two contemporary and competing early versions of the Ṣiffīn narrative, Ibn Muzāḥim's *Waqʿat Ṣiffīn* and the relevant chapters in Ibn Aʿtham's *Kitāb al-Futūḥ*; the former eventually became "the historical vulgate text" for the Ṣiffīn episode.[52] The reason for choosing Ibn Muzāḥim's work over Ibn Aʿtham's, he argues, can be found in the literary conventions of the ninth century: while Naṣr b. Muzāḥim adhered to the established *akhbārī* mode of historical writing, meaning that he provided *isnād*s and structured his narrative in small-scale *khabar* units of text, Ibn Aʿtham chose to depart from this mode and instead composed his work in the *muʾarrikhī* style, which mostly avoids *isnād*s in favour of an uninterrupted flow of narrative. He was ahead of his time and thus suffered the indignation of his contemporaries, who preferred the more "scholarly" style of his colleague Ibn Muzāḥim.[53]

Hagler's argument is based on his assumption of Ibn Aʿtham's contemporaneity with Ibn Muzāḥim. This leads to a controversial issue, namely the dating of *Kitāb al-Futūḥ* and its author. Many now maintain, based mostly on Conrad's work on the subject, that Ibn Aʿtham worked and died in the early to mid-ninth century[54]. Earlier scholars had argued for a later death date, around the year 926.[55] In his entry on Ibn Aʿtham in the *Encyclopedia of Arabic Literature*, Conrad called this later date "an old Orientalist error", although there he did not explain how it had come about. A detailed overview and critique of the tenth-century dating can now be found in his recently published study.[56] He argues for a 'tiered' dating of the work, with the first recension – covering only the period up to Karbalāʾ – completed in 204 H/819–20 CE. According to Conrad, Ibn Aʿtham later returned to the work and brought it down to the reign of Hārūn al-Rashīd; [57] one or two later (proto-?)Sunnī scholars then continued the work until the reign of al-Muqtadir (170–320 H/786–932 CE), although this continuation is not fully extant today.[58] Conrad's reconstruction of the work's composition process had circulated among scholars unofficially since 1992 and has proven highly influential.[59]

The suggested composition date of 204 H/819 CE for Ibn Aʿtham's *Kitāb al-Futūḥ* is quite early, especially so for a work of that volume and complexity. Shaban's EI^2 entry for Ibn Aʿtham, which advances this early dating, does not clarify on what basis he arrived at this date, or elaborate on his claim that Ibn Aʿtham was a contemporary of al-Madāʾinī (135–225 H/752–840 CE) other than Ibn Aʿtham's use of early Iraqi and Ḥijāzī authorities such as al-Madāʾinī, Abū Mikhnaf or al-Zuhrī,[60] which, taken on its own, is not a sound argument. Later scholars such as al-Ṭabarī clearly had access to the same material in some form or other, and in the absence of an original text that can safely be attributed to Abū Mikhnaf or another early transmitter, it is next to impossible to tell whether Ibn Aʿtham's reports were closer to this supposed original than a later version. Moreover, Ibn Aʿtham quotes this material in a haphazard manner, indicating that he referred to "a general collection of informants" rather than (his) teachers of the preceding generation.[61] Shaban's contention that Ibn Aʿtham's work can be used as a corrective for al-Ṭabarī's *Taʾrīkh* is thus problematic.[62] Shaban also suggested as *terminus ante quem* for the compilation of *Kitāb al-Futūḥ* the year 596 H/1199–1200 CE, the date given for the first partial Persian translation of the work. Several copies of this translation have survived, while only one complete manuscript of the Arabic work has come down to us.[63] We shall turn to this in a moment.

In his *ʿAbbāsid Revolution*, Shaban provides more information on his decision to classify Ibn Aʿtham as an early ninth-century historian. He argues that Ibn Aʿtham's use of the phrase *ḥaddathanī* ("he told me") in relation to al-Madāʾinī indicates that he was a contemporary of his. Shaban also accepts as authentic a note by the earliest Persian translator of the first part of the *Kitāb al-Futūḥ*, which states that Ibn Aʿtham composed his work in 204 H/819 CE.[64]

Establishing the composition date as 819 on the basis of these two factors is difficult, though. Shaban assumes that the historian mentioned by Ibn Aʿtham as his source is al-Madāʾinī because of the frequent recurrence of al-Madāʾinī's name as an important authority for historical traditions. However, the name actually given in the *Kitāb al-Futūḥ* is not Abū al-Ḥasan Muḥammad b. ʿAlī al-Madāʾinī, but Abū al-Ḥusayn ʿAlī b. Muḥammad al-Qurashī. Shaban dismisses this as a mere scribal error,[65] which is likely. His uncritical acceptance of the composition date given by the Persian translator, on the other hand, is more problematic: the date of the translation is given as approximately 596 H/1199–1200 CE,[66] but the oldest surviving Persian manuscript is from the sixteenth century.[67] There are no major deviations between the Persian translations and the oldest Arabic manuscript of the work available to us, but the latter is from the fifteenth century and thus not much earlier.[68] The manuscript evidence is thus late and also quite thin, not least because of several lacunae.[69] It may be true that in the late twelfth century "no useful purpose would have been served by forging [the date of 204 H/819 CE]", but the fact remains that the early date only appears on very few (and late) manuscripts and that it is curious why the Persian translator was the only one to know of it;[70] possibly it was (erroneously) inserted by a later copyist.[71] Conrad's detailed study of Ibn Aʿtham and his *Futūḥ* does not discuss the late dates of the extant manuscripts and makes much of the headings and other paratexts but, as in the previously discussed case of al-Yaʿqūbī, the fact remains that we do not know exactly what happened in the several hundred years between the composition of the work and the copying of the oldest available manuscript. That we need to be extremely cautious regarding the organisation of the text as we encounter it in the surviving manuscripts of the *Futūḥ* was briefly pointed out by Daniel already[72] and Schönléber's recent study has only reinforced this.[73] Also, if Ibn Aʿtham really was a "strident Shīʿī" as argued by Conrad, why, under what circumstances and for what purpose would a (proto-)Sunnī scholar produce a *dhayl* of an obscure Shīʿī *qiṣaṣ* work? Conrad's study does not address this issue.

Scheiner has argued that the later date of 926 must be incorrect because al-Balādhurī, who is commonly thought to have died in 892, quotes Ibn Aʿtham.[74] The date of 892 is not clearly attested anywhere, however, but only implied by Yāqūt, whose sources (for example, al-Jahshiyārī, Ibn al-Nadīm, al-Ṣūlī) do not give a specific date.[75] Perhaps al-Balādhurī was an older contemporary of Ibn Aʿtham who cited the latter's work among a host of other sources? Balʿamī (d. 363 H/974 CE) may have used Ibn Aʿtham's work in his 'translation' of al-Ṭabarī's *Taʾrīkh* and so perhaps narrows down the *terminus ante quem* to the decade from 352–63 H/963–74 CE, the former being the year in which Balʿamī began his work.[76] It must be noted here, however, that Peacock holds the passages from Ibn Aʿtham to be interpolations of later (post-eleventh century) copyists and editors.[77]

The later dating of Ibn Aʿtham and his *Futūḥ* has recently been defended against Shaban and Conrad. The exact date of 314 H/926–7 CE is almost certainly incorrect because it is not supported by primary source material,[78] but Lindstedt has shown on the basis of a range of Arabic and Persian biographical literature – some of which was not taken into account by Shaban and Conrad – that a tenth-century date is more likely.[79] Among the pieces of evidence he presents is the observation that Ibn Aʿtham was apparently a teacher of Ibn ʿAdī, who died in c. 365 H/976 CE, which thus makes an early ninth-century date for Ibn Aʿtham unlikely.[80]

Assigning a later death date to Ibn Aʿtham would also solve some of the problems Hagler encountered in trying to make him fit into the *akhbārī-muʾarrikhī* framework employed in his dissertation. What he considers unusual stylistic choices and anachronistic features, such as the flowing style of his narration or the occurrence of reports and themes that can usually only be found in later works of historiography,[81] are quite easily explained by a composition date in the late ninth/early tenth century. We thus might have an explanation for Hagler's observation that Ibn Aʿtham's work was excluded from the developing historiographical consensus of the ninth century as it was articulated in the works of Ibn Khayyāṭ, al-Balādhurī or al-Dīnawarī – it did not yet exist.

Notes

1. See the discussion below as well as Chapter Four.
2. See below.
3. Judd, "Narratives and Character Development", 224; Haider, *Rebel and Imām*, 13 and n. 50.
4. On Ibn Muzāḥim, see, for example, Brockelmann, "Naṣr ibn Muzāḥim" and the EI^2 entry (C. E. Bosworth); on Ibn Aʿtham, see, for example, Rosenthal, *Muslim Historiography*, 230 and Conrad, "Ibn Aʿtham"; on al-Masʿūdī, see, for example, Khalidi, *Islamic Historiography* and Bray, "ʿAbbāsid Myth", 43. Al-Yaʿqūbī's case is more controversial: scholars have argued at length about the extent of his Shīʿī tendencies. See, for a range of opinions, Millward, "Al-Yaʿqūbī's Sources"; Humphreys, *Islamic History*, 102; Marquet, "Šiʿisme"; Daniel, "Al-Yaʿqūbī"; EI^2, "al-Yaʿkūbī" (M. Q. Zaman); and now the biographical introduction in vol. I of the monumental translation of al-Yaʿqūbī's extant works edited by Matthew Gordon et al. Haider, *Rebel and Imām*, 139–42, 151–2 considers both al-Yaʿqūbī and al-Masʿūdī Twelver Shīʿīs; Anthony, "Ibn Wāḍiḥ", 17, 27 argues that there is not enough evidence in biographical notices or his extant works to determine which particular Shīʿī denomination al-Yaʿqūbī may have belonged to, a position restated in Anthony and Gordon, "Biographical Sketch", 21–2.
5. Anthony, "Ibn Wāḍiḥ", 34. See also Conrad, "Ibn Aʿtham", 96–7, 117.
6. Peacock, *Medieval Islamic Historiography*, 127, 136.
7. On this last point see now Haider, *Rebel and Imām*, 22–3, 191, *passim*.
8. Crone, *Slaves*, 11.
9. See the section on *awāʾil* in Chapter One.
10. Ibn Muzāḥim, *Waqʿat Ṣiffīn*, 571–2; al-Dīnawarī, *Akhbār*, 204–5; Ibn Aʿtham, *Futūḥ*, IV, 1–3.
11. See the very brief discussion in Tayyara, "Origin Narratives", 55.
12. Cahen, "History and Historians", 198. Petersen, *ʿAlī and Muʿāwiya*, 168 suggests he was a moderate Shīʿī who combined this tendency with "soundly orthodox views" in his work.
13. Tayyara, "Origin Narratives", 55–6 and *passim*; Khalidi, *Islamic Historiography*, 126–7.
14. Khalidi, *Islamic Historiography*, 126.
15. M. R. J. Bonner, *Historiographical Study*, 58–69.
16. Roberts, *Early Islāmic Historiography*, 174.
17. Conrad, "Ibn Aʿtham", 91; see also 96 and *passim*. Conrad based his claim of Ibn Aʿtham's Shīʿism on a remark by Yāqūt (d. 636 H/1229 CE), but this information is not mentioned anywhere else. See Lindstedt, "Biography", 304 n. 26. Lindstedt thinks that this is Yāqūt's own deduction and probably correct. We cannot know for sure, however, and while the tone of some of Ibn Aʿtham's material does suggest ʿAlid/proto-Shīʿī partisanship, the following discussion highlights some of the issues inherent in such a classification.

18. Conrad, "Ibn Aʿtham", 97. Similarly, al-Iṣfahānī's proto-Shīʿī inclinations did not prevent him from casting events in a manner largely acceptable to (proto-) Sunnīs in both his *Maqātil al-Ṭālibiyyīn* and the *Kitāb al-Aghānī*. Günther, *Quellenuntersuchungen*, 5–6; Su, *Shīʿī Past*, chapters one and five.
19. Khalidi, *Islamic Historiography*, 148–9.
20. See, for example, Madelung, *Succession*, 90, 100; Marquet, "Šiʿisme", very explicitly on 138; Cahen, "History and Historians", 198; and the brief overview in Anthony, "Ibn Wāḍiḥ", 15–17.
21. Daniel, "Al-Yaʿqūbī", 213–14 (discussing Millward's findings), 223–4.
22. Crone, *Slaves*, 11.
23. Daniel, "Al-Yaʿqūbī", 227.
24. Anthony, "Ibn Wāḍiḥ", 17–18, 27–33, 34. This impression is based only on al-Yaʿqūbī's *History*, however; his other extant works do not hint at his potential Shīʿī affiliation. Anthony and Gordon, "Biographical Sketch", 21.
25. Khalidi, *Islamic Historiography*, 120–6.
26. A question rarely pursued in detail, as pointed out by Anthony, "Ibn Wāḍih", 15–16. Anthony himself argues that ignoring what he understands to be al-Yaʿqūbī's Shīʿī perspective leads the reader to disregard his "authorial vision and, therefore, a key contribution of his chronicle to Islamic historiography" (ibid., 35).
27. Van Ess, *Theologie und Gesellschaft*, I, 233–4; Kennedy, *Early ʿAbbāsid Caliphate*, 198–9; Hurvitz, "Where Have All the People Gone"; Haider, *Origins of the Shiʿa*, 11.
28. Bernheimer, *The ʿAlids*, 2, 9.
29. A good example of this is the tenth-century scholar Ibn ʿUqda, for whom see Brown, "Man for All Seasons".
30. Daniel's excellent study of al-Yaʿqūbī throws the dangers of interpretation based on rubrics (headings), pious formulae and other text 'ingredients' into sharp relief. See his "Al-Yaʿqūbī", 224–7. On the manuscripts of al-Yaʿqūbī's *Taʾrīkh*, see also Rowson, "Manuscripts", 23–6 (esp. 25–6 for later interventions in the text). Modern editions of Balʿamī's *Tārīkhnāma* are likewise problematic, in some cases resulting in "an ahistorical text that never existed until the late twentieth century" (Peacock, *Medieval Islamic Historiography*, 6). Conrad makes much of what is presumably the only personal information given in Ibn Aʿtham's *Futūḥ*, which implies that he may have been associated with a *rāfiḍī* or at least strongly Shīʿī milieu. We cannot exclude the possibility, however, that this is an insertion by a later copyist. Lindstedt, "Biography", 301.
31. Khalidi, *Islamic Historiography*, 127–8, 132–3. For a brief analysis of al-Masʿūdī's depiction of the caliphs up until the mid-tenth century, see ibid., 120–36.
32. For the originator of the *lā ḥukma*-phrase, compare al-Dīnawarī, *Akhbār*, 210 with Ibn Muzāḥim, *Waqʿat Ṣiffīn*, 588; for the role of the *qurrāʾ* in negotiat-

ing the arbitration agreement and choosing Abū Mūsā, compare al-Dīnawarī, *Akhbār*, 204–5 with Ibn Muzāḥim, *Waqʿat Ṣiffīn*, 571.

33. Lindstedt, "Biography", 308.
34. Berkey, *Formation of Islam*, 141–3. But see Su, "Early Shiʿi", for the involvement of Kufan Zaydīs and other proto-Shīʿīs in the distribution of *ḥadīth* propagating the notion of the four rightly-guided caliphs.
35. Conrad, "Ibn Aʿtham", 101–2.
36. EI², "Ibn Aʿtham al-Kūfī" (M. A. Shaban).
37. E.g., Massè, "La Chronique"; Togan, "Ibn Aʿtham al-Kufi"; U. Sezgin, "Abū Miḫnaf".
38. Conrad, "Ibn Aʿtham"; Schönléber, "Textual Tradition"; Lindstedt, "Biography".
39. Ibn Aʿtham, *Futūḥ*, IV, 90–5. See Chapter Four of the present book, section on 'pragmatic justifications' (141–6).
40. Sometimes, the other two Khawārij are said to have been Ibn Muljam's brothers: al-Balādhurī, *Ansāb*, II, 447–8 (on the authority of al-Madāʾinī); al-Kindī, *Wulāt wa-quḍāt*, 31–2 (less detailed). Al-Balādhurī's account calls this version into question (*khabar*^{un} *shādh*^{un}) – only some Khārijites believe it (447). Al-Kindī, being focused on Egyptian history, only narrates the tale of the brother who attacked (or tried to attack) ʿAmr b. al-ʿĀṣ, the governor of Egypt at the time. The basic story elements are the same as elsewhere, however; the difference is only in the identity of ʿAmr's would-be assassin.
41. Al-Masʿūdī, *Murūj*, I–II, 411–17; Ibn Saʿd, *Ṭabaqāt*, III, 35–9; al-Yaʿqūbī, *Taʾrīkh*, II, 212; al-Ṭabarī, *Taʾrīkh*, I, 3457–65; al-Dīnawarī, *Akhbār*, 227–9; al-Balādhurī, *Ansāb*, II, 430–2, 432–7, 446.
42. Ibn Saʿd, *Ṭabaqāt*, III, 39; al-Dīnawarī, *Akhbār*, 228–9; al-Balādhurī, *Ansāb*, II, 446.
43. Al-Yaʿqūbī, *Taʾrīkh*, II, 214; al-Ṭabarī, *Taʾrīkh*, I, 3464.
44. Ibn Aʿtham, *Futūḥ*, IV, 136–9.
45. Ibid., 136, 137. Ibn Saʿd (ed. ʿUmar), III, 31–3 has ʿAlī reject Ibn Muljam's oath of allegiance twice because of his misgivings about him and express foreboding regarding his own death; his sons shiver in the presence of Ibn Muljam even before he plots ʿAlī's death. This adumbration of the caliph's murder is not as explicit as in Ibn Aʿtham's depiction, however. Al-Balādhurī, *Ansāb*, II, 441–4 provides much the same material, some of it explicitly on the authority of Ibn Saʿd.
46. See, for example, Ibn Saʿd, *Ṭabaqāt*, III, 37; al-Masʿūdī, *Murūj*, I–II, 412; al-Dīnawarī, *Akhbār*, 228; al-Balādhurī, *Ansāb*, II, 434, 437.
47. In the Qurʾān Ṣāliḥ is a pre-Islamic prophet who was sent to the people of Thamūd. They rejected his teachings, however, and slaughtered the camel that God had sent to them as a sign or test despite Ṣāliḥ's warnings. They were all killed in retribution for their transgression of God's commandment. See EI², "Ṣāliḥ" (A. Rippin).

48. Ibn Aʿtham, *Futūḥ*, IV, 139. Ibn Saʿd (ed. ʿUmar), III, 32 also has the *ḥadīth* but here Muḥammad tells ʿAlī directly. Al-Balādhurī, *Ansāb*, II, 441–2 quotes the same *ḥadīth* in the same setting explicitly on the authority of Ibn Saʿd.
49. For other predictions by ʿAlī, see the notes to p. 148.
50. Rescher, *Kharidschitenkapitel*, 19, 23.
51. Ibid., 31, 32, 35.
52. Hagler, *Echoes of Fitna*, 19, 30–4.
53. Ibid., 90–1.
54. See, for example, EI^2, "Ibn Aʿtham" (Shaban); Conrad, "Ibn Aʿtham", 314; Scheiner, "Writing the History", 162.
55. See, for example, Brockelmann, *GAL, Supplement,* I, 220 (5c); Sezgin, *GAS,* I, 329 (33); Fraehn, *Indications bibliographiques*, 16; Rosenthal, *Muslim Historiography*, 230.
56. Conrad, "Ibn Aʿtham", 90–6.
57. Ibid.,112–14.
58. Ibid.,103–8. See also his summary of the compilation process on 121–2.
59. See, for example, the discussions in Bowen-Savant, *New Muslims*, 200; Borrut, *Entre mémoire et pouvoir*, 91–3.
60. EI^2, "Ibn Aʿtham" (Shaban).
61. Conrad, "Ibn Aʿtham", 116.
62. EI^2, "Ibn Aʿtham" (Shaban); Shaban, *ʿAbbāsid Revolution*, xix.
63. EI^2, "Ibn Aʿtham" (Shaban).
64. Shaban, *ʿAbbāsid Revolution*, xviii.
65. Ibid.
66. On Shaban's reasoning for the early ninth-century date, see Conrad, "Ibn Aʿtham", 93–4.
67. Kurat, "Abū Muḥammad", 276–7.
68. Ibid., 275–7.
69. On the latter point, see Conrad, "Ibn Aʿtham", 88–9, 108. For an overview of the 'discovery' of the manuscripts of Ibn Aʿtham's work and the modern editions, see Schönléber, "Textual Tradition", 427–31.
70. Conrad, "Ibn Aʿtham", 94.
71. Lindstedt, "Biography", 304.
72. Daniel, "Al-Yaʿqūbī", 224 n. 79.
73. Schönléber, "Textual Tradition", 431–8.
74. Scheiner, "Writing the History", 162.
75. Lynch, *Arab Conquests*, 38.
76. Balʿamī's engagement with al-Ṭabarī's chronicle is another great example of the complexity of early Islamic authorship. For his comprehensive reworking, far beyond a 'mere' translation, see Peacock, *Medieval Islamic Historiography*, esp. 73–136; Meisami, *Persian Historiography*, 28–37.
77. Peacock, *Medieval Islamic Historiography*, 91–3.
78. Conrad, "Ibn Aʿtham", 92–3.

79. Lindstedt, "Biography".
80. Ibid., 302, 308.
81. Hagler, *Echoes of Fitna*, e.g. 34, 46–7, 56, 63, 65.

Conclusion

This study has analysed the representation of Khārijite history in the early Islamic historical tradition. Unlike previous studies of Khārijism, the approach here was based on an understanding of the sources as literary artefacts (texts), not as databanks of hard facts to be utilised for a reconstruction of historical circumstances 'as they really were'. Issues of factual authenticity and historicity were thus of little consequence for the objective of this study. This approach to the source material instead allowed us to investigate the narrative function of Khārijites in the early Islamic historical tradition and point out specific concerns of the various historians as they emerge from their portrayals of literary Khārijism.

Two main findings arose from the literary analysis: first, literary Khārijism is characterised by stereotypes that associate the Khawārij with specific attributes, predominantly a proclivity for militant piety that exceeds all bounds of moderation. These stereotypes permeate the reports of Khārijite rebellions to such an extent that the individual circumstances of a particular rebel or revolt are largely inconsequential, which results in the impression that Khārijism was a wholly unchanging and unchanged phenomenon. The occasionally very detailed reports of Khārijite activities cannot conceal that there is actually little substance to these accounts once structural components and recurrent motifs are stripped away. The feeling of monotony is reinforced by the fact that Khārijite utterances and doctrines are just as static and hence predictable, which accords them the status of stock phrases.

This characteristic of the material is rooted in the second main conclusion put forward by this study: despite the frequent appearance of Khārijites in the accounts of early Islamic history, Khārijism is portrayed not just for its own sake, but also in order to illustrate and debate other protagonists and subjects. Khārijite rebels serve as mouthpieces for unpopular, flawed or plainly heretical statements, thereby providing a convenient foil for the discussion and rejection of certain ideas. Their main purpose is to demonstrate the inherent dangers of extreme religious devotion. We saw that the early historical tradition presents the Khawārij as strict adherents of the divine provisions enshrined in the Qur'ān. However, the lack of moderation they display distorts their piety: by rebelling against 'Alī, they separate from the community; by claiming the right to kill non-Khārijite Muslims as unbelievers, they transgress Islamic norms and social boundaries. Excessive piety is thereby shown to end in depravity and the resulting bloodshed threatens the very fabric of Muslim society. In sum, literary Khārijism serves as a cautionary tale.

That militant piety was an important and controversial issue is demonstrated by its ubiquity in the reports of Khārijite history. The period in which these were composed, collected and narrated witnessed heated cross-confessional debates that occasionally led to violent conflict, most famously perhaps in tenth-century Baghdad. These debates may have had an impact on the extant form of the material. In any case, Khārijism as remembered by the early historical tradition reflects the scholarly unease with rebellion and emphasis on communal cohesion prevalent at the time, notions that were perpetuated by the increasing religious and political fragmentation of the *umma* in the ninth and tenth century. It comes as no surprise, then, that the sources make a point of condemning Khārijite exclusionist definitions of Islam. Deviations from this pattern only occur where the censure of militant piety clashes with another concern: reproaching unjust rule. Here, Khārijite piety is sometimes employed as a foil for Umayyad tyranny.

The material also betrays various concerns peculiar to specific periods. As regards the reign of 'Alī, stories of Khārijism serve mainly to explain and justify the caliph's actions from the call to arbitration at Ṣiffīn onwards. For the reign of Mu'āwiya, the two main sources for this period – al-Balādhurī's *Ansāb* and al-Ṭabarī's *Ta'rīkh* – are divided in their focus: al-Balādhurī is mostly concerned with presenting Khārijite piety as a counterexample to Umayyad iniquity as represented by their agents, while al-Ṭabarī follows the established pattern of condemning Khārijism, but restricts his criticism largely to its activist form. The final period, the second *fitna* and 'Abd al-Malik's rule, reveals the most comprehensive set of themes related to the portrayal of Khārijism. The two main issues here were al-Muhallab's war with the Azāriqa and the volatility of Khārijism, a motif that is related to the theme of militant piety but concentrates on intra-Khārijite conflict and connects back to the issue of communal togetherness. Literary Khārijism thus serves as a counterpoint to the evolving *jamā'ī* view.

The form and content of the material studied in this book also grant us some insight into the developing framework of early Islamic history. A fairly well-formed agreement regarding Ṣiffīn and the course of 'Alī's conflict with the Khārijites was in place by the early ninth century at the latest, for example.

The details may differ, but the story's overall framework was firmly established. There was nonetheless considerable room for manoeuvre within this tradition regarding the selection and framing of the material. The last period under study in particular revealed great variance: Ibn Aʿtham, for instance, focused predominantly on al-Muhallab's battles with the Azāriqa and preserved the only account of ʿImrān b. Ḥiṭṭān's flight from al-Ḥajjāj, which features broadly in the types of literature that preserve his poetry (mostly *adab*, but also anthologies and heresiography); al-Ṭabarī engaged mostly with Shabīb's revolt. Al-Balādhurī provided the most in-depth engagement with Khārijite doctrinal disagreements and the most detailed section on the Najdiyya, while al-Dīnawarī's treatment of Khārijism in this period consists of a mere eleven pages in the printed edition, almost exclusively dedicated to the Azāriqa. The broad outline of Khārijite history is nonetheless the same in all sources.

With regard to the three periods studied in this book, Muʿāwiya's reign stands out from the other two. Much less material is available for Khārijite activities in that period, to the extent that the analysis had to focus on al-Balādhurī and al-Ṭabarī because they alone provided sufficient accounts for an analysis of literary Khārijism. Unlike the first (Chapter Four) and third (Chapter Six) period, engagement with the rebels from a decidedly religious perspective is muted here – Qurʾānic references and allusions to Prophetic *sunna* are largely absent from the material, for example. Khārijites continue to be censured for their misguided understanding of Islam and excessive use of force, but religious argumentation of the kind encountered in the depiction of ʿAlī's confrontation with the Khawārij features very little. The stakes were different: when the Khārijites articulated their allegations against ʿAlī, they attacked his (retrospective) status as rightful and rightly-guided caliph, eminent Companion and even as a believer. Such accusations needed to be refuted on religious grounds, which is where Qurʾān and *sunna* come into play. The period of the second *fitna* and ʿAbd al-Malik's reign (Chapter Six), on the other hand, is remembered as the moment when the four main Khārijite subdivisions arose. The main narrative foci here are the doctrinal strife among and volatility of these divisions vis-à-vis more community-minded attempts at defining an *umma* ravaged by civil war and its aftermath. Accordingly, the connection between excessive piety, violence and social discord is most pronounced in the material for this period.

Finally, it should be noted that the condemnation of Khārijism in the early historical tradition is based primarily on deeds, not words. This is evident in the distinction between activist and quietist Khārijites discussed in Chapter Five, but it is also illustrated by the fact that apart from a few reports in al-Balādhurī's *Ansāb* that deal with internal disagreements, we do not encounter any extended discussions or arguments about Khārijite beliefs and doctrines. The debates at Ḥarūrāʾ and Nahrawān are a different matter because they justify ʿAlī's conduct at Ṣiffīn and subsequent to the adjudication; due to the schematisation of these accounts, there is little substance to the arguments put forward by the Khawārij. What appears to have mattered most to our historians is the specifically Khārijite brand of piety that causes violence and bloodshed within the community. Unlike in heresiographical works, the elaboration of individual doctrines seems to have been surplus to requirements. At the same time, this emphasises further the stereotypical depiction of Khārijism: individual traits are curtailed as much as possible in favour of creating a Khārijite typecast that can be re-employed irrespective of distinct circumstances and that evokes in the audience an immediate association with particular characteristics. In that way, literary Khārijism operates as another building block in the narrative repertoire of early Muslim storytelling.

Much research remains to be done in terms of the literary portrayal of both Khārijite and early Islamic history. A first step in that direction is the acknowledgment that our sources are literary constructs that have to be studied as such and cannot merely be mined for the data they contain. This book examined a segment of the early historical tradition consisting mostly of major chronicles. Future scholarship might pursue a literary study of Khārijism focusing on other types of historical writing or periods of history. Later historiography, particularly with the reappearance of the Syrian historical tradition in the shape of Ibn ʿAsākir (d. 571 H/1176 CE) or Ibn Kathīr (d. 774 H/1373 CE), promises intriguing insight especially in comparison with the older works examined here. The study of literary Khārijism could (and should) also be extended to other genres, such as *adab*. A comparative analysis of the depiction of Khārijism in various types of literature would also shed light on the particularities of different genres and allow for comprehensive synchronic and/or diachronic analyses of the discourse on Khārijism. Such studies would not only broaden our understanding of how the Khawārij were remembered, but also illuminate processes of composition and redaction, which in turn advances our knowledge of the formation and continuity of the Islamic literary tradition.

While it is certainly not impossible to reconstruct the events of the early period of Islam, this book sought to contribute to a better understanding of the perils of a particular positivist approach that chooses one set of reports over another without studying the literary aspects of the subject matter as it is portrayed in the sources. This is an acute concern because the scarce evidence we have for the first century of Islamic history in particular poses an immense epistemological challenge: "As long as our evidence remains so weak, the models we choose to apply will exert disproportionate power on our explanations."[1] By casting the Khawārij alternately as disgruntled tribesmen pining for the Bedouin ways of old or as religious zealots expecting the immediate end of the world, we may create plausible interpretations of a highly complex phenomenon. We can only do so by leaving out evidence that does not fit our 'model', however, or by arguing for or defending perspectives that might not reflect actual conditions on the historic ground. In constructing such plausible interpretations, we do not give (enough) credit to the complex rhetorical functions of Khārijism that tell us more about the particular concerns of individual authors and the literary conventions of early Islamic historiography than about the 'true' intentions of those individuals who were remembered as Khawārij. The recurring themes, schematised narratives and replicated material that make up literary Khārijism point to the fact that we need to be more careful in our attempts at understanding historical Khārijism: the stereotyping inherent in its depiction requires us to seriously reconsider what we think we know about Khārijite history and how much we can ever reasonably expect to know.

Note

1. Robinson, "Reconstructing", 131.

Bibliography

Sources

ʿAbbās, Ihsān, ed. *Diwān shiʿr al-khawārij*. 3rd edition. Beirut, 1974.

Abū Dāwūd, Sulaymān b. al-Ashʿath al-Sijistānī. *Sunan*. 4 vols. Cairo, 1988.

Abū Zurʿa al-Dimashqī, ʿAbd al-Raḥmān b. ʿAmr. *Taʾrīkh*, ed. Kh. al-Manṣūr. Beirut, 1996.

al-Balādhurī, Aḥmad b. Yaḥyā. *Ansāb al-ashrāf*. Vol. II, ed. W. Madelung. Beirut, 2003.

al-Balādhurī, Aḥmad b. Yaḥyā. *Ansāb al-ashrāf*. Vol. IV/1, ed. I. ʿAbbās. Wiesbaden, 1979.

al-Balādhurī, Aḥmad b. Yaḥyā. *Ansāb al-ashrāf*. Vol. IV/2, ed. ʿA. ʿA. al-Dūrī and ʿI. ʿUqla. Beirut, 2001.

al-Balādhurī, Aḥmad b. Yaḥyā. *Liber Expugnationis Regionum: Futūḥ al-buldān*, ed. M. J. de Goeje. Leiden, 1866. Translated into English as *The Origins of the Islamic State* by Philip K. Hitti (vol. I) and Francis C. Murgotten (vol. II). New York: Columbia University, 1916–24.

al-Bukhārī, Muḥammad b. Ismāʿīl. *Ṣaḥīḥ al-Bukhārī. Al-Mujallad 4: al-aḥādīth 5640–7563*, ed. Ṣ. J. al-ʿAttār. Beirut, 2003.

al-Dīnawarī, Abū Ḥanīfa Aḥmad b. Dāwūd. *Kitāb al-Akhbār al-ṭiwāl*, ed. I. Kratchkovsky. Leiden, 1912.

Ibn ʿAbd Rabbih, Aḥmad b. Muḥammad al-Andalusī. *al-ʿIqd al-Farīd*. 9 vols, ed. M. M. Qamīḥa. Beirut, 1983. Translated into English as *The Unique Necklace* by Issa J. Boullata. 3 vols. Reading: Garnet, 2006–11.

Ibn Abī Shayba, Abū Bakr ʿAbdallāh b. Muḥammad: *al-Kitāb al-Muṣannaf fī l-aḥādīth wa-l-āthār*. Vol. 8, ed. S. al-Laḥḥām. Beirut, 1989.

Ibn Aʿtham al-Kūfī, Aḥmad. *Kitāb al-Futūḥ*, ed. M. Khān. Hyderabad, 1968–75.

Ibn Ḥabīb, ʿAbd al-Malik. *Kitāb al-Taʾrīkh*, ed. J. Aguadé, *Kitāb al-Taʾrīj (La Historia)*. Madrid, 1991.

Ibn Ḥanbal, Aḥmad b. Muḥammad. *Musnad*. 8 vols, ed. S. T. al-Majdhūb. Beirut, 1993.

Ibn Hishām, Abū Muḥammad ʿAbd al-Malik. *al-Sīra al-nabawiyya*. 4 vols, ed. ʿU. ʿA. Tadmuri. Beirut, 1987.

Ibn Khayyāṭ, Khalīfa. *Taʾrīkh Khalīfa b. Khayyāṭ*. 2 vols, ed. S. Zakkār. Damascus, 1967–8.

Ibn Khayyāṭ, Khalīfa. *Taʾrīkh Khalīfa b. Khayyāṭ*, ed. A. Ḍ. al-ʿUmarī. 2nd edition. Riyadh, 1985.

Ibn al-Nadīm, Abū al-Faraj Muḥammad b. Isḥāq. *Kitāb al-Fihrist*, ed. R. Tajaddud. Tehran, 1971.

Ibn Qutayba, Abū Muḥammad ʿAbdallāh b. Muslim. *Kitāb al-Maʿārif*, ed. T. ʿUkāsha. 2nd edition. Cairo, 1969.

Ibn Saʿd, Abū ʿAbdallāh Muḥammad. *Kitāb al-Ṭabaqāt al-kubrā*. Beirut, 1958.

Ibn Saʿd, Abū ʿAbdallāh Muḥammad. *Kitāb al-Ṭabaqāt al-kabīr*. 11 vols, ed. ʿA. M. ʿUmar. Cairo, 2001.

Ibn al-Saghīr. *Akhbār al-aʾimma al-rustumiyyīn*, ed. M. Nāṣir and I. Baḥāz. Beirut, 1986.

Ibn Sallām al-Ibāḍī. *Kitāb Fīhi badʿ al-islām wa-sharāʾiʿ al-dīn*, ed. W. Schwartz and S. b. Yaʿqūb, *Kitāb Ibn Sallām: Eine ibāḍitisch-maghribinische Geschichte des Islams aus dem 3./9. Jahrhundert*. Wiesbaden, 1986.

al-Jāḥiẓ, Abū ʿUthmān ʿAmr b. Baḥr. *Kitāb al-Ḥayawān*. 8 vols, ed. ʿA. M. Hārūn. 2nd edition. Cairo, 1965–9.

Kāshif, Sayyida Ismāʿīl, ed. *al-Siyar wa-l-jawābāt li-ʿulamāʾ wa-aʾimmat ʿUmān*. 2 vols. Cairo, 1986.

al-Kindī, Abū ʿUmar Muḥammad b. Yūsuf. *Kitāb al-Wulāt wa-Kitāb al-Quḍāt*, ed. R. Guest. Leiden, 1912.

al-Maqdisī, al-Muṭahhar b. Ṭāhir. *Kitāb al-Badʿ wa-l-taʾrīkh*. 6 vols, ed. and translated into French by C. Huart as *Le livre de la création et de l'histoire*. Paris, 1899–1919.

al-Masʿūdī, Abū al-Ḥasan ʿAlī b. al-Ḥusayn b. ʿAlī. *Murūj al-dhahab wa-maʿādin al-jawhar*. 4 vols in 2. 3rd edition. Beirut, 1978.

al-Masʿūdī, Abū al-Ḥasan ʿAlī b. al-Ḥusayn b. ʿAlī. *Kitāb al-Tanbīh wa-l-ishrāf*, ed. ʿA. I. al-Ṣāwī. Cairo, 1938.

al-Minqarī, Naṣr b. Muzāḥim. *Waqʿat Ṣiffīn*, ed. M. Hārūn. Cairo, 1945 or 1946.

Muslim, Abū al-Ḥusayn b. al-Ḥajjāj al-Qushayrī al-Naysābūrī. *Ṣaḥīḥ Muslim*. 5 vols, ed. M. F. ʿAbd al-Bāqī. Cairo, 1955–6.

al-Shahrastānī, Muḥammad b. ʿAbd al-Karīm. *Kitāb al-Milal wa-l-niḥal*, ed. A. ʿA. Muhannā and ʿA. Ḥ. Fāʿūr. Beirut, 1992.

al-Shaybānī, Abū Bakr al-Ḍaḥḥāk b. Makhlad. *Kitāb al-Sunna*. 2 vols, ed. M. N. al-Albānī. Beirut, 1993.

al-Ṭabarī, Abū Jaʿfar Muḥammad b. Jarīr. *Taʾrīkh al-rusul wa-l-mulūk*. 3 parts in 16 vols, ed. M. J. de Goeje et al. Leiden, 1879–1901.

al-Yaʿqūbī, Aḥmad b. Abī Yaʿqūb. *Taʾrīkh al-Yaʿqūbī*. Beirut, 1960. Translated into English by Matthew Gordon et al. in *The Works of Ibn Wāḍiḥ al-Yaʿqūbī: An English Translation*. 3 vols, here vols II–III. Leiden: Brill, 2018.

Studies

Abou el Fadl, Khaled. *Rebellion and Violence in Islamic Law*. Cambridge: Cambridge University Press, 2001.

Ahsan, Talha. "The Life and Works of Qaṭarī b. al-Fujāʾah (d. c. 79/699), Poet and Leader of the Azraqites: An Application of Critical-Source Methodologies in Khārijite Historiography". M.A. dissertation, University of London (SOAS), 2018.

Alshaar, Nuha, ed. *The Qurʾan and* Adab. *The Shaping of Literary Traditions in Classical Islam*. Oxford: Oxford University Press, in association with The Institute of Ismaili Studies (London), 2017.

Alshaar, Nuha. "Introduction: The Relation of *Adab* to the Qurʾan: Conceptual and Historical Framework", in N. Alshaar, ed., *The Qurʾan and* Adab. *The Shaping of Literary Traditions in Classical Islam*. Oxford: Oxford University Press, in association with The Institute of Ismaili Studies (London), 2017, 1–58.

Alshaar, Nuha. "The Qurʾan in Literary Anthologies: A Case Study of *al-ʿIqd al-Farīd* by Ibn ʿAbd Rabbih al-Andalusī (d. 328/940)", in N. Alshaar, ed., *The Qurʾan and* Adab. *The Shaping of Literary Traditions in Classical Islam*. Oxford: Oxford University Press, in association with The Institute of Ismaili Studies (London), 2017, 381–400.

Althoff, Gerd, Johannes Fried, and Patrick J. Geary, eds. *Medieval Concepts of the Past. Ritual, Memory, Historiography*. Cambridge: Cambridge University Press, 2002.

Andersen, Elizabeth et al., eds. *Autor und Autorschaft im Mittelalter*. Tübingen: Niemeyer, 1998.

Andersson, Tobias S. *Early Sunnī Historiography. A Study of the Tārīkh of Khalīfa b. Khayyāṭ*. Leiden: Brill, 2018.

Ansari, Mahsheed. "Said Nursi's Non-Violent Social Activism as a Refutation and Response to the Re-Emergent Neo-Kharijite Sect in Islam", in F. Mansouri and Z. Keskin, eds, *Contesting the Theological Foundations of Islamism and Violent Extremism*. Cham: Palgrave Macmillan, 2019, 185–206.

Anthony, Sean. *Crucifixion and Death as Spectacle: Umayyad Crucifixion in its Late Antique Context*. New Haven, CT: American Oriental Society, 2014.

Anthony, Sean. "Was Ibn Wāḍiḥ al-Yaʿqūbī a Shiʿite Historian? The State of the Question", *ʿUW* 24 (2016), 15–41.

Anthony, Sean, and Matthew S. Gordon. "Ibn Wāḍiḥ al-Yaʿqūbī: A Biographical Sketch", in M. Gordon et al., trans., *The Works of Ibn Wāḍiḥ al-Yaʿqūbī: An English Translation*. 3 vols, Leiden/Boston: Brill, 2018, I, 9–22.

Antúnez, Juan Carlos, and Ioannis Tellidis. "The Power of Words: The Deficient Terminology Surrounding Islam-Related Terrorism", *Critical Studies on Terrorism* 6/1 (2013), 118–39.

Aṭfayyish, Abū Isḥāq Ibrāhīm. *al-Farq bayna al-ibāḍiyya wa-l-khawārij*. Muscat: Maktabat al-istiqāma, 1980.

ʿAthamina, Khalil. "The Sources of al-Balādhurī's *Ansāb al-Ashrāf*", *JSAI* 5 (1984), 237–62.

Aillet, Cyrille, ed. *L'ibadisme dans l'Islam médiéval: modèles et interactions*. Berlin: De Gruyter, 2018.

Bacharach, Jere L. "Signs of Sovereignty: The *Shahāda*, Qurʾanic Verses, and the Coinage of ʿAbd al-Malik", *Muqarnas* 27 (2010), 1–30.

Bathish, Ghada H. *Discourse Strategies: The Persuasive Power of Early Khārijī Poetry*. PhD dissertation, University of Washington, 1988.

Barthes, Roland. "The Death of the Author", *Aspen* 5–6 (1967).

Baugh, Carolyn. "Revolting Women? Early Kharijite Women in Islamic Sources", *JIMS* 2/1 (2017), 36–55.

Beaumont, Daniel. "Hard-Boiled: Narrative Discourse in Early Muslim Traditions", *SI* 83 (1996), 5–31.

Behzadi, Lale, and Jaako Hämeen-Anttila, eds. *Concepts of Authorship in Pre-Modern Arabic Texts*. Bamberg: University of Bamberg Press, 2015.

Bellamy, James A. "Pro-Umayyad Propaganda in Ninth-Century Baghdad in the Works of Ibn Abī 'l-Dunyā", in G. Makdisi et al., eds, *Prédication et propaganda au Moyen Age: Islam, Byzance, Occident*. Paris: Presses Universitaires de France, 1983, 71–86.

Bently, Lionel. "Review: Copyright and the Death of the Author in Literature and Law", *The Modern Law Review* 57/6 (1994), 973–86.

Berkey, Jonathan. *The Formation of Islam. Religion and Society in the Near East, 600–1800*. Cambridge: Cambridge University Press, 2003.

Bernheimer, Teresa. *The ʿAlids. The First Family of Islam, 750–1200*. Edinburgh: Edinburgh University Press, 2011.

Bernheimer, Teresa. "'Kharijism' and 'the Kharijites': The Case of Early Islamic Iran". Unpublished conference paper, Deutscher Orientalistentag, University of Jena, 2017.

Bonebakker, Seeger A. "*Adab* and the Concept of *Belles-Lettres*", in J. Ashtiany et al., eds, *The Cambridge History of Arabic Literature. Vol. II: ʿAbbasid Belles-Lettres*. Cambridge: Cambridge University Press, 1990, 16–30.

Bonner, Michael. *Aristocratic Violence and Holy War. Studies in the Jihad and the Arab-Byzantine Frontier*. New Haven, CT: American Oriental Society, 1996.

Bonner, Michael R. J. *An Historiographical Study of Abū Ḥanīfa Aḥmad b. Dāwūd b. Wanand al-Dīnawarī's* Kitāb al-Akhbār al-ṭiwāl. PhD dissertation, University of Oxford, 2013.

Borrut, Antoine. *Entre mémoire et pouvoir. L'espace syrien sous les derniers Omeyyades et les premiers Abbassides (v. 72–193/692–809)*. Leiden: Brill, 2011.

Borrut, Antoine. "La *memoria* omeyyade: les Omeyyades entre souvenir et oubli dans les sources narratives islamiques", in A. Borrut and P. Cobb, eds, *Umayyad Legacies. Medieval Memories from Syria to Spain*. Leiden: Brill, 2010, 25–61.

Borrut, Antoine. "The Future of the Past: Historical Writing in Early Islamic Syria and Umayyad Memory", in A. George and A. Marsham, eds, *Power, Patronage, and Memory in Early Islam: Perspectives on Umayyad Elites*. Oxford: Oxford University Press, 2018, 275–300.

Borrut, Antoine. "Review of Judd, Steven C. *Religious Scholars and the Umayyads. Piety-Minded Supporters of the Marwānid Caliphate* (London and New York: Routledge, 2014)", *Islamic Law and Society* 25/4 (2018), 473–5.

Bosworth, Clifford Edmund. *Sistan under the Arabs*, Rome: IsMEO, 1968

Bray, Julia, ed. *Writing and Representation in Medieval Islam. Muslim Horizons*. London: Routledge, 2006.

Bray, Julia. "ʿAbbāsid Myth and the Human Act: Ibn ʿAbd Rabbih and Others", in P. Kennedy, ed., *On Fiction and* Adab *in Medieval Arabic Literature*. Wiesbaden: Harrassowitz, 2005, 1–54.

Bray, Julia. "Lists and Memory: Ibn Qutayba and Muḥammad b. Ḥabīb", in F. Daftary and J. W. Meri, eds, *Culture and Memory in Medieval Islam. Essays in Honour of Wilferd Madelung*. London: I. B. Tauris, in association with The Institute of Ismaili Studies (London), 2003, 210–31.

Brockelmann, Carl. *Geschichte der arabischen Litteratur. Supplement*. Leiden: Brill, 1937–42.

Brockelmann, Carl. "Naṣr ibn Muzāḥim: der älteste Geschichtsschreiber der Schia", *Zeitschrift für Semitistik und verwandte Gebiete* IV (1926), 1–23.

Brockopp, Jonathan E. "Islamic Origins and Incidental Normativity", *JAAR* 84/1 (2016), 28–43.

Brown, Jonathan. "A Man for All Seasons: Ibn ʿUqda and Crossing Sectarian Boundaries in the 4th/10th Century", *ʿUW* 24 (2016), 139–44.

Burnyeat, Abigail. "'Wrenching the Club from the Hand of Hercules': Classical Models for Medieval Irish *compilatio*", in R. O'Connor, ed., *Classical Literature and Learning in Medieval Irish Narrative*. Cambridge: D. S. Brewer, 2014, 196–207.

Burnyeat, Abigail. "*Córugud* and *compilatio* in Some Manuscripts of *Táin Bó Cúailnge*", in B. Ó Catháin and R. Ó hUiginn, eds, *Ulidia 2: Proceedings of the Second International Conference on the Ulster Cycle of Tales*. Maynooth: An Sagart, 356–74.

Burrow, John A. *Medieval Writers and Their Work: Middle English Literature and Its Background, 1100–1500*. Oxford: Oxford University Press, 1982.

Cahen, Claude. "History and Historians", in M. J. L. Young et al., eds, *The Cambridge History of Arabic Literature. Religion, Learning, and Science in the ʿAbbāsid Period*. Cambridge: Cambridge University Press, 1990, 188–233.

Cameron, Averil. "Introduction: The Writing of History", in A. Cameron, ed., *History as Text. The Writing of Ancient History*. London: Duckworth, 1989, 1–10.

Cascio, Roberto. "Il Kharigismo come concetto politico nel mondo contemporaneo: riflessioni sullo scontro ideologico tra Al-Azhar e Sayyid Quṭb", *Occhialì* 3 (2018), 34–44.

Challet, Vincent. "Violence as a Political Language: The Uses and Misuses of Violence in Late Medieval French and English Popular Rebellions", in J. Firnhaber-Baker and D. Schoenaers, eds, *The Routledge History Handbook of Medieval Revolt*. London: Routledge, 2017, 279–91.

Chamberlain, Michael. *Knowledge and Social Practice in Medieval Damascus, 1190–1350*. Cambridge: Cambridge University Press, 1994.

Cheddadi, Abdessalam. *Les arabes et l'appropriation de l'histoire: émergence et premiers développements de l'historiographie musulmane jusqu'au IIe-VIIIe siècle*. Arles: Sindbad-Actes Sud, 2004.

Clark, Elizabeth A. *History, Theory, Text: Historians and the Linguistic Turn*. Cambridge, MA: Harvard University Press, 2004.

Clarke, Nicola. ""They are the Most Treacherous of People": Religious Difference in Arabic Accounts of Three Early Medieval Berber Revolts", *eHumanista* 24 (2013), 510–25.

Cobb, Paul. "Review of Tayeb El-Hibri's *Reinterpreting Islamic Historiography: Hārūn al-Rashīd and the Narrative of the ʿAbbāsid Caliphate*", *JAOS* 121/1 (2001), 109–10.

Conermann, Stephan, ed. *Mamluk Historiography Revisited – Narratological Perspectives*. Göttingen: V&R Unipress/Bonn University Press, 2018.

Conrad, Lawrence. "Abraha and Muhammad: Some Observations a propos of Chronology and Literary *Topoi* in the Early Arabic Historical Tradition", *BSOAS* 50/2 (1987), 225–40.

Conrad, Lawrence. "Seven and the Tasbīʿ: On the Implications of Numerical Symbolism for the Study of Medieval Islamic History", *JESHO* 31/1 (1988), 42–73.

Conrad, Lawrence. "Ibn Aʿtham al-Kūfī", in J. S. Meisami and P. Starkey, eds, *Encyclopedia of Arabic Literature*, volume I. London: Routledge, 1998, 314.

Conrad, Lawrence. "ʿUmar at Sargh: The Evolution of an Umayyad Tradition on Flight from the Plague", in S. Leder, ed., *Story-Telling in the Framework of Non-Fictional Arabic Literature*. Wiesbaden: Harrassowitz, 1998, 488–528.

Conrad, Lawrence. "The Conquest of Arwād. A Source-Critical Study in the Historiography of the Early Medieval Near East", in A. Cameron and L. I. Conrad, eds, *The Byzantine and Early Islamic Near East. Vol. I: Problems in the Literary Source Material*. Princeton: Darwin, 1992, 317–401.

Conrad, Lawrence. "Theophanes and the Arab Historical Tradition", *Byzantinische Forschungen* 15 (1990), 1–44.

Conrad, Lawrence. "Ibn Aʿtham and His History", *ʿUW* 23 (2015), 87–125.

Conti, Aidan. "Scribes as Authors, Transmission as Composition: Towards a Science of Copying", in S. Rankovic, ed., *Modes of Authorship in the Middle Ages*. Toronto: Pontifical Institute of Mediaeval Studies, 2012, 267–88.

Cook, David. *Martyrdom in Islam*. Cambridge: Cambridge University Press, 2007.

Cook, Michael. *Early Muslim Dogma. A Source-Critical Study*. Cambridge: Cambridge University Press, 1981.

Cook, Michael. *Commanding Right and Forbidding Wrong in Islamic Thought.* Cambridge: Cambridge University Press, 2000.

Cook, Michael. *Muhammad.* Oxford: Oxford University Press, 1983.

Cook, Michael. "'Anan and Islam: The Origins of Karaite Scripturalism", *JSAI* 9 (1987), 161–82.

Cooperson, Michael. *Classical Arabic Biography. The Heirs of the Prophets in the Age of al-Ma'mūn.* Cambridge: Cambridge University Press, 2000.

Cooperson, Michael. "Probability, Plausibility, and "Spiritual Communication" in Classical Arabic Biography", in P. Kennedy, ed., *On Fiction and* Adab *in Medieval Arabic Literature.* Wiesbaden: Harrassowitz, 2005, 69–84.

Crone, Patricia. *Medieval Islamic Political Thought.* Edinburgh: Edinburgh University Press, 2004.

Crone, Patricia. *Slaves on Horses: The Evolution of the Islamic Polity.* Cambridge: Cambridge University Press, 1980.

Crone, Patricia. *Meccan Trade and the Rise of Islam.* Princeton: Princeton University Press, 1987.

Crone, Patricia. "Ninth-Century Muslim Anarchists", *Past & Present* 167 (2000), 3–28.

Crone, Patricia. "On the Meaning of the 'Abbasid Call to al-Riḍā", in C. E. Bosworth et al., eds, *The Islamic World from Classical to Modern Times. Essays in Honor of Bernard Lewis.* Princeton: Darwin, 1989, 95–111.

Crone, Patricia. "A Statement by the Najdiyya Khārijites on the Dispensability of the Imamate", *SI* 88 (1998), 55–76.

Crone, Patricia. "The Khārijites and the Caliphal Title", in G. Hawting et al., eds, *Studies in Islamic and Middle Eastern Texts and Traditions in Memory of Norman Calder.* Oxford: Oxford University Press, 2000, 85–91.

Crone, Patricia, and Fritz Zimmermann, eds, trans. *The Epistle of Sālim b. Dhakwān.* Oxford: Oxford University Press, 2001.

Crone, Patricia, and Martin Hinds. *God's Caliph. Religious Authority in the First Centuries of Islam.* Cambridge: Cambridge University Press, paperback ed., 2003.

Crone, Patricia, and Michael Cook. *Hagarism: The Making of the Muslim World.* Cambridge: Cambridge University Press, 1977.

Cubitt, Catherine. "Memory and Narrative in the Cult of Early Anglo-Saxon Saints", in Y. Hen and M. Innes, eds, *The Uses of the Past in the Early Middle Ages.* Cambridge: Cambridge University Press, 2000, 29–66.

Custers, Martin. *Al-Ibadiyya. A Bibliography.* 3 vols. 2nd, rev. and enlarged edition. Hildesheim: Olms, 2017.

Dähne, Stephan. "Zu den ḫutab des Abū Ḥamza aš-Šārī in der klassischen arabischen Literatur", in W. Beltz and S. Günther, eds, *Erlesenes: Sonderheft . . . anläßlich des 19. Kongresses der Union Européenne d'Arabisants et Islamisants.* Halle: Institut für Orientalistik, 1998, 30–45.

Dähne, Stephan. "Context Equivalence: A Hitherto Insufficiently Studied Use of the

Quran in Political Speeches from the Early Period of Islam", in S. Günther, ed., *Ideas, Images, and Methods of Portrayal. Insights into Classical Arabic Literature and Islam*. Leiden: Brill, 2005, 1–17.

Daniel, Elton. "Al-Yaʿqūbī and Shīʿism Revisited", in J. E. Montgomery, ed., *ʿAbbasid Studies. Occasional Papers of the School of ʿAbbasid Studies*. Leuven: Peeters, 2004, 209–32.

Daniel, Elton. "Balʿamī's Account of Early Islamic History", in F. Daftary and J. W. Meri, eds, *Culture and Memory in Medieval Islam. Essays in Honour of Wilferd Madelung*. London: I. B. Tauris, in association with The Institute of Ismaili Studies (London), 2003, 163–89.

Dehgani Farsani, Yoones. *Text und Kontext des al-Wāqidī zugeschriebenen* Futūḥ aš-Šām*: Ein Beitrag zur Forschungsdebatte über frühe* Futūḥ-*Werke*. PhD dissertation, Universität Göttingen, 2017.

Del Río, José Ramírez. "Un paradigma guerrero feminino en el Islam: Las combatientes jāriŷíes", in F. Roldán Castro, ed., *La mujer musulmana en historia*. Huelva: Universidad de Huelva, 2007, 141–60.

Donner, Fred M. *Narratives of Islamic Origins – The Beginnings of Islamic Historical Writing*. Princeton: Darwin, 1990.

Donner, Fred M. *Muhammad and the Believers. At the Origins of Islam*. Cambridge, MA/London: The Belknap Press of Harvard University Press, 2010.

Donner, Fred M. "Modern Approaches to Early Islamic History", in C. Robinson, ed., *The New Cambridge History of Islam. Vol. I: The Formation of the Islamic World, Sixth to Eleventh Centuries*. Cambridge: Cambridge University Press, 2010, 623–47.

Donner, Fred M. "Piety and Eschatology in Early Kharijite Poetry", in M. al-Saʿafin, ed., *Fī Mihrāb al-Maʿrifa. Festschrift for Ihsan ʿAbbas*. Beirut: Dār ṣādir, 1997, 13–19 [English Section].

Donner, Fred M. "The Problem of Early Arabic Historiography in Syria", in M. A. Bakhit, ed., *Proceedings of the 2nd Symposium on the History of Bilād al-Shām – Early Islamic Period*. Amman: al-Jāmiʿa al-Urdunniyya, 1987, 1–27.

Donner, Fred M. "ʿUthmān and the Rāshidūn Caliphs in Ibn ʿAsākir's *Taʾrīkh madinat Dimashq*: A Study in Strategies of Compilation", in J. Lindsay, ed., *Ibn ʿAsākir and Early Islamic History*. Princeton: Darwin, 2001, 44–61.

Donner, Fred M. "Qurʾānicization of Religio-Political Discourse in the Umayyad Period", *REMMM* 129 (2011), 79–92.

Drout, Michael D. C. "'I am Large, I Contain Multitudes": The Medieval Author in Memetic Terms", in S. Rankovic, ed., *Modes of Authorship in the Middle Ages*. Toronto: Pontifical Institute of Mediaeval Studies, 2012, 30–51.

al-Dūrī, ʿAbd al-ʿAzīz. *The Rise of Historical Writing Among the Arabs*. Translated into English by L. Conrad, introduction by F. Donner. Princeton: Princeton University Press, 1983.

Eisener, Reinhard. *Zwischen Faktum und Fiktion. Eine Studie zum Umayyadenkalifen*

Sulaimān b. ʿAbdalmalik und seinem Bild in den Quellen. Wiesbaden: Harrassowitz, 1987.

Eisener, Reinhard, ed. *Today's Perspectives on Ibadi History and the Historical Sources*. Hildesheim: Olms, 2017.

El-Hibri, Tayeb. *Parable and Politics in Early Islamic History: The Rashidun Caliphs*. New York: Columbia University Press, 2010.

El-Hibri, Tayeb. *Reinterpreting Islamic Historiography: Hārūn al-Rashīd and the Narrative of the ʿAbbāsid Caliphate*. Cambridge: Cambridge University Press, 1999.

El-Hibri, Tayeb. "Review of *The Early Arabic Historical Tradition: A Source-Critical Study* (A. Noth / L. I. Conrad; trans. M. Bonner)", *JAOS* 18/1 (1998), 114–18.

El-Hibri, Tayeb. "The Redemption of Umayyad Memory by the ʿAbbāsids", *JNES* 61/4 (2002), 241–65.

Eley, Geoff. "Is All the World a Text? From Social History to the History of Society Two Decades Later", in G. Spiegel, ed., *Practicing History: New Directions in Historical Writing after the Linguistic Turn*. New York: Routledge, 2005, 35–61.

Encyclopaedia of Islam, Second Edition. Edited by P. Bearman, Th. Bianquis, C. E. Bosworth, E. van Donzel and W. P. Heinrichs. Available at www.brillonline.com.

Encyclopaedia of Islam, THREE. Edited by K. Fleet, G. Krämer, D. Matringe, J. Nawas and E. Rowson. Available at www.brillonline.com.

Ende, Werner. *Arabische Nation und islamische Geschichte: Die Umayyaden im Urteil arabischer Autoren des 20. Jahrhunderts*. Wiesbaden: Steiner, 1977.

Ennami, Amr K. *Studies in Ibāḍism*. Benghazi Faculty of Arts, 1972.

Fiaccadori, Gianfranco. "Kharidjites et donatistes", *Annales. Histoire, Sciences Sociales* 38/2 (1983), 470–4.

Fierro, Maribel. "Heresy in al-Andalus", in S. Jayyusi, ed., *The Legacy of Muslim Spain*, vol. II. Leiden: Brill, 1992, 895–908.

Firnhaber-Baker, Justine. "Introduction", in J. Firnhaber-Baker and D. Schoenaers, eds, *The Routledge History Handbook of Medieval Revolt*. London: Routledge, 2017, 1–15.

Fishbein, Michael, trans. *The History of al-Ṭabarī. Volume XXI: The Victory of the Marwānids*. Albany: State University of New York Press, 1990.

Fisher, Matthew: *Scribal Authorship and the Writing of History in Medieval England*. Columbus, OH: Ohio State University Press, 2012.

Foss, Clive. "Islam's First Terrorists", *History Today*, December 2007, 12–17.

Foss, Clive. "The Kharijites and Their Coinage", *ONS* 171 (2002), 24–34.

Foss, Clive. "A New and Unusual Kharijite Dirham", *ONS* 182 (2005), 11–13.

Foucault, Michel. "What is an Author?", in J. V. Harari, ed., *Textual Strategies. Perspectives in Post-Structuralist Criticism*. Ithaca: Cornell University Press, 1979, 141–60.

Fraehn, Christian M. *Indications bibliographiques . . . à nos employés et voyageurs en Asie*. St Petersburg: Imprimerie de l'Académie Impériale des Sciences, 1845.

Francesca, Ersilia. "The Formation and Early Development of the Ibāḍī Madhhab", *JSAI* 28 (2003), 260–77.

Francesca, Ersilia, ed. *Ibadi Theology. Rereading Sources and Scholarly Works.* Hildesheim: Olms, 2015.

Franz, Kurt. *Kompilation in arabischen Chroniken. Die Überlieferung vom Aufstand der Zanǧ zwischen Geschichtlichkeit und Intertextualität vom 9. bis ins 15. Jahrhundert.* Berlin: De Gruyter, 2004.

Freimark, Peter. *Das Vorwort als literarische Form in der arabischen Literatur.* PhD dissertation, University of Münster (Westfalen), 1967.

Friedlaender, Israel. "Muhammedanische Geschichtskonstruktionen", *Beiträge zur Kenntnis des Orients* 9 (1911), 17–34.

Fulton, Helen. "History and *historia*: Uses of the Troy Story in Medieval Ireland and Wales", in R. O'Connor, ed., *Classical Literature and Learning in Medieval Irish Narrative.* Cambridge: D. S. Brewer, 2014, 40–57.

Gabrieli, Francesco. "La poesia ḫārigita nel secolo degli Omayyadi", *RSO* 20 (1943), 331–72.

Gaddis, Michael. *There Is No Crime for Those Who Have Christ. Religious Violence in the Christian Roman Empire.* Berkeley, CA: University of California Press, 2005.

Gaiser, Adam. *Muslims, Scholars, Soldiers: The Origin and Elaboration of the Ibāḍī Imāmate Traditions.* Oxford: Oxford University Press, 2010.

Gaiser, Adam. *Shurāt Legends, Ibāḍī Identities. Martyrdom, Asceticism, and the Making of an Early Islamic Community.* Columbia: University of South Carolina Press, 2016.

Gaiser, Adam. "What Do We Learn about the Early Khārijites and the Ibāḍiyya from Their Coins?", *JAOS* 130/2 (2010), 167–87.

Gaiser, Adam. "Source-Critical Methodologies in Recent Scholarship on the Khārijites", *History Compass* 7/5 (2009), 1376–90.

Gaiser, Adam. "Tracing the Ascetic Life and Very Special Death of Abū Bilāl: Martyrdom and Early Ibāḍī Identity", in A. Ziaka, ed., *On Ibadism.* Hildesheim: Olms, 2014, 59–72.

Gaiser, Adam. " 'In Them Are Good Models': Ibāḍī Depictions of the Muḥakkima", in R. Eisener, ed., *Today's Perspectives on Ibadi History and the Historical Sources.* Hildesheim: Olms, 2017, 75–82.

Gaiser, Adam. "*Takfīr* Re-Examined: Polemic and Ambiguity in the Sources on the Muḥakkima", in B. Michalak-Pikulska and R. Eisener, eds, *Ibadi Jurisprudence. Origins, Developments and Cases.* Hildesheim: Olms, 2015, 31–9.

Gaiser, Adam. "North African and Omani Ibāḍī Accounts of the *Munāẓāra* [*sic*]: A Preliminary Comparison", *REMMM* 132, 63–73.

Geary, Patrick J. *Phantoms of Remembrance: Memory and Oblivion at the End of the First Millennium.* Princeton: Princeton University Press, 1994.

Geissinger, Aisha. *Gender and Muslim Constructions of Exegetical Authority. A Re-Reading of the Classical Genre of Qurʾān Commentary.* Leiden: Brill, 2015.

Ghazal, Amal. "Politics and Polemics: Ibāḍī Theology in North Africa in the Modern

Period", in E. Francesa, ed., *Ibadi Theology. Rereading Sources and Scholarly Works*. Hildesheim: Olms, 2015, 271–80.

Gilliot, Claude. "The Scholarly Formation of al-Ṭabarī (224–310/838–923)", in C. Gilliot, ed., *Education and Classical Learning the Early Islamic World.* Farnham/Burlington, VT: Ashgate Variorum, 2012, 113–47.

Gilliot, Claude. "Portrait 'mythique' d'Ibn ʿAbbās", *Arabica* 33 (1985), 127–184.

Görke, Andreas. "Die frühislamische Geschichtsüberlieferung zu Hudaibiya", *ISL* 74 (1997), 193–237.

Görke, Andreas. "Authorship in the *Sīra* Literature", in L. Behzadi and J. Hämeen-Anttila, eds, *Concepts of Authorship in Pre-Modern Arabic Texts*. Bamberg: University of Bamberg Press, 2015, 63–92.

Goldziher, Ignaz. *Muhammedanische Studien. Theil 2.* Halle: Niemeyer, 1890.

Gruendler, Beatrice. "Abbasid Poets and the Qurʾan", in N. Alshaar, ed., *The Qurʾan and* Adab. *The Shaping of Literary Traditions in Classical Islam*. Oxford: Oxford University Press, in association with The Institute of Ismaili Studies (London), 2017, 137–69.

Gruendler, Beatrice. "'Pardon Those Who Love Passionately': A Theologian's Endorsement of *Shahādat al-ʿIshq*", in F. Pannewick, ed., *Martyrdom in Literature. Visions of Death and Meaningful Suffering in Europe and the Middle East from Antiquity to Modernity*. Wiesbaden: Reichert, 2004, 189–236.

Günther, Sebastian. *Quellenuntersuchungen zu den "Maqātil aṭ-Ṭālibiyyīn" des Abū 'l-Farağ al-Iṣfahānī (gest. 356/967)*. Hildesheim: Olms, 1991.

Günther, Sebastian, ed. *Ideas, Images, and Methods of Portrayal. Insights into Classical Arabic Literature and Islam*. Leiden: Brill, 2005.

Guo, Li. "Mamluk Historiographic Studies – The State of the Art", *Mamluk Studies Review* 1 (1997), 15–43.

Gwynne, Rosalind W. *The "Tafsir" of Abu ʿAli al-Jubbaʾi: First Steps Toward a Reconstruction, with Texts, Translation, Biographical Introduction and Analytical Essay*. PhD dissertation, University of Washington, 1982.

Hämeen-Anttila, Jaako. "ʿAmr b. Hawbar and His Poem on Crucifixion", *StOrE* 82 (1997), 159–66.

Hagemann, Hannah-Lena. "Challenging Authority: Al-Balādhurī and al-Ṭabarī on Khārijism During the Reign of Muʿāwiya b. Abī Sufyān", *al-Masāq* 28/1 (2016), 36–56.

Hagemann, Hannah-Lena. "Review of *Shurāt Legends, Ibāḍī Identities: Martyrdom, Asceticism, and the Making of an Early Islamic Community*, by Adam R. Gaiser, Columbia, SC: The University of South Carolina Press, 2016", *ICMR* 29/4 (2018), 534–6.

Hagemann, Hannah-Lena. "Was Muṭarrif b. al-Mughīra al-Thaqafī a Khārijite? Rebellion in the Early Marwānid Period", *ʿUW*, forthcoming.

Hagemann, Hannah-Lena and Peter Verkinderen. "Kharijism in the Umayyad Period", in A. Marsham, ed., *The Umayyad World*. London: Routledge, 2020, 489–517.

Hagler, A. M. *The Echoes of Fitna: Developing Historiographical Interpretations of the*

Battle of Siffin. PhD dissertation, University of Pennsylvania, 2001. Retrieved from https://repository.upenn.edu/cgi/viewcontent.cgi?article=1500&context=edissertations, last accessed 4 February 2020.

Hagler, A. M. "Repurposed Narratives: The Battle of Ṣiffīn and the Historical Memory of the Umayyad Dynasty", *Mathal. Journal of Islamic and Middle Eastern Multidisciplinary Studies* 3/1 (2013), 1–27.

Hagler, A. M. "Unity through Omission: Literary Strategies of Recension in Ibn al-Aṯīr's *al-Kāmil fī l-Taʾrīḫ*", *Arabica* 65 (2018), 285–313.

Haider, Najam. *The Rebel and the Imām in Early Islam. Explorations in Muslim Historiography*. Cambridge: Cambridge University Press, 2019.

Haider, Najam. *The Origins of the Shīʿa. Identity, Ritual, and Sacred Space in Eighth-Century Kūfa*. Cambridge: Cambridge University Press, 2011.

Haider, Najam. "The Community Divided: A Textual Analysis of the Murders of Idrīs b. ʿAbd Allāh (d. 175/791)", *JAOS* 128/3 (2008), 459–75.

Hamori, Andras. "Ascetic Poetry (Zuhdiyyāt)", in J. Ashtiany et al., eds, *The Cambridge History of Arabic Literature. Vol. II: ʿAbbasid Belles-Lettres*. Cambridge: Cambridge University Press, 1990, 265–74.

Hasson, Isaac. "Ansāb al-ašrāf d'al-Balāḏurī est-il un livre de *taʾrīḫ* ou d'*adab*?", *IOS* 19 (1999), 479–93.

Haug, Robert. *The Eastern Frontier: Limits of Empire in Late Antique and Early Medieval Central Asia*. London: I. B. Tauris, 2019.

Hawting, Gerald R. *The First Dynasty of Islam. The Umayyad Caliphate AD 661–750*. London: Croom Helm, 1986.

Hawting, Gerald R. *The Idea of Idolatry and the Emergence of Islam: From Polemic to History*. Cambridge: Cambridge University Press, 1999.

Hawting, Gerald R., trans. *The History of al-Ṭabarī. Volume XX: The Collapse of Sufyānid Authority and the Coming of the Marwānids*. Albany: State University of New York Press, 1989.

Hawting, Gerald R., trans. *The History of al-Ṭabarī. Volume XVII: The First Civil War*. Albany: State University of New York Press, 1996.

Hawting, Gerald R. "The Significance of the Slogan "lā ḥukma illā li-llāh" and the References to the "Ḥudūd" in the Traditions about the Fitna and the Murder of ʿUthmān", *BSOAS* 41 (1978), 453–63.

Hawting, Gerald R. "'Has God Sent a Mortal as a Messenger?" (Q 17:95): Messengers and Angels in the Qurʾān", in G. S. Reynolds, ed., *The Qurʾān in Its Historical Context, Volume 2: New Perspectives on the Qurʾān*. London: Routledge, 2011, 372–90.

Hawting, Gerald R. "Two Citations of the Qurʾān in "Historical" Sources for Early Islam", in G. Hawting and A.-K. A. Shareef, eds, *Approaches to the Qurʾān*. London: Routledge, 1993, 260–8.

Hawting, Gerald R. "The *Tawwābūn*, Atonement and ʿĀshūrāʾ", *JSAI* 17 (1994), 166–81.

Hawting, Gerald R. "The Case of Jaʿd b. Dirham and the Punishment of "Heretics" in the Early Caliphate", in C. Lange and M. Fierro, eds, *Public Violence in Islamic Societies. Power, Discipline, and the Construction of the Public Sphere, 7th–19th Centuries* CE. Edinburgh: Edinburgh University Press, 2009, 27–41.

Heck, Paul L. *The Construction of Knowledge in Islamic Civilization: Qudāma b. Ja'far and His* Kitāb al-Kharāj wa-ṣināʿat al-kitāba. Leiden: Brill, 2002.

Heck, Paul L. "Jihād Revisited", *Journal of Religious Ethics* 32/1 (2004), 95–128.

Heck, Paul L. "Eschatological Scripturalism and the End of Community: The Case of Early Kharijism", *Archiv für Religionsgeschichte* 7 (2005), 137–52.

Heijer, Johannes den and Perinne Pilette. "Transmission et diffusion de l'historiographie copto-arabe: nouvelles remarques sur les recensions primitive et vulgate de l'Histoire des Patriarches d'Alexandrie", in S. Torallas Tovar and J. P. Monferrer-Sala, eds, *Cultures in Contact: Transfer of Knowledge in the Mediterranean Context.* Cordoba: CNERU, 2013, 103–40.

Heilman, Elizabeth G. *Popular Protest in Medieval Baghdad, 295–334* A.H.*/908–946.* PhD dissertation, Princeton University, 1978.

Hen, Yitzhak and Matthew Innes, eds. *The Uses of the Past in the Early Middle Ages.* Cambridge: Cambridge University Press, 2000.

Higgins, Annie C. *The Qur'ānic Exchange of the Self in the Poetry of Shurāt (Khārijī) Political Identity 37–132* A.H.*/657–750* A.D. PhD dissertation, University of Chicago, 2001.

Higgins, Annie C. "Faces of Exchangers, Facets of Exchange in Early *Shurāt* (Khārijī) Poetry", *BRIIFS* 7/1 (2005), 7–38.

Hinds, Martin. "Kufan Political Alignments and Their Background in the Mid-Seventh Century A.D.", *IJMES* 2 (1971), 346–67.

Hinds, Martin. "The Murder of the Caliph ʿUthmān", *IJMES* 3 (1972), 450–69.

Hirsch, Eric D. *Validity in Interpretation.* New Haven, CT: Yale University Press, 1967.

Hirschler, Konrad. *Medieval Arabic Historiography: Authors as Actors.* London: Routledge, 2006.

Hirschler, Konrad. "Studying Mamluk Historiography. From Source-Criticism to the Cultural Turn", in S. Conermann, ed., *Ubi Sumus? Quo Vademus? Mamluk Studies – State of the Art.* Göttingen: V&R Unipress/Bonn University Press, 2013, 159–86.

Hobsbawm, Eric J. *Primitive Rebels: Studies in Archaic Forms of Social Movement in the 19th and 20th Centuries.* Manchester: Manchester University Press, 1959.

Hobsbawm, Eric J. *Bandits.* Harmondsworth: Pelican, 1972.

Hobsbawm, Eric J. "Social Banditry", in H. A. Landsberger, ed., *Rural Protest: Peasant Movements and Social Change.* London: Palgrave Macmillan, 1974, 142–57.

Hodgson, Marshall G. S. "Two Pre-Modern Muslim Historians: Pitfalls and Opportunities in Presenting them to Moderns", in J. Nef, ed., *Towards World Community.* The Hague: Junk, 1968, 53–69.

Hoffman, Valerie. *The Essentials of Ibāḍī Islam.* Syracuse: Syracuse University Press, 2012.

Hoffman, Valerie. "Historical Memories and Imagined Communities. Modern Ibadi Writings on Khārijism", in A. Ziaka, ed., *On Ibadism*. Hildesheim: Olms, 2014, 137–50.

Hoffman, Valerie. "Ibāḍism: History, Doctrines, and Recent Scholarship", *Religion Compass* 9/9 (2015), 297–307.

Hoyland, Robert. "History, Fiction and Authorship in the First Centuries of Islam", in J. Bray, ed., *Writing and Representation in Medieval Islam: Muslim Horizons*. London: Routledge, 2006, 16–46.

Hoyland, Robert. "Review of *The Early Arabic Historical Tradition* (A. Noth/ L. I. Conrad; trans. M. Bonner)", *BSOAS* 60/1 (1997), 130–1.

Hoyland, Robert. *Seeing Islam as Others Saw It: A Survey and Evaluation of Christian, Jewish and Zoroastrian Writings on Early Islam*. Princeton: Darwin, 1997.

Hoyland, Robert. "Arabic, Syriac and Greek Historiography in the First Abbasid Century: An Inquiry into Inter-Cultural Traffic", *Aram* 3/1–2 (1991), 211–33.

Hoyland, Robert. "New Documentary Texts and the Early Islamic State", *BSOAS* 69/3 (2006), 395–416.

Humphreys, R. Stephen. *Islamic History. A Framework for Inquiry*. Rev. edition. Princeton: Princeton University Press, 1991.

Humphreys, R. Stephen. "Qurʾānic Myth and Narrative Structure in Early Islamic Historiography", in F. M. Clover and R. S. Humphreys, eds, *Tradition and Innovation in Late Antiquity*. Madison: University of Wisconsin Press, 1989, 271–90.

Hurvitz, Nimrod. "Early Hanbalism and the Shiʿa", in O. Bengio and M. Litvak, eds, *The Sunna and Shiʿa in History. Division and Ecumenism in the Muslim Middle East*. New York: Palgrave Macmillan, 2011, 37–50.

Hurvitz, Nimrod. "Where Have All the People Gone? A Critique of Medieval Islamic Historiography", in D. Zeevi and E. R. Toledano, eds, *Society, Law, and Culture in the Middle East. Modernities in the Making*. Berlin: De Gruyter, 2015, 60–73.

Hylén, Torsten. "The Date of the Story of the *Tawwābūn*", *SI* 112/2 (2017), 175–205.

Ibrahim, Mahmood. "Religious Inquisition as Social Policy: The Persecution of the *Zanadiqa* in the Early Abbasid Caliphate", *ASQ* 16/2 (1994), 53–72.

Iggers, Georg G. "The Intellectual Foundations of Nineteenth-Century 'Scientific' History: The German Model", in S. Macintyre, J. Maiguashca and A. Pók, eds, *The Oxford History of Historical Writing. Volume 4: 1800–1945*. Oxford: Oxford University Press, 2015, 41–58.

Jacobi, Renate. "Das Fiktive und das Imaginäre in der klassischen arabischen Dichtung", in S. Leder, ed., *Story-Telling in the Framework of Non-Fictional Arabic Literature*. Wiesbaden: Harrassowitz, 1998, 20–33.

Johns, Jeremy. "Archaeology and the History of Early Islam: The First Seventy Years", *JESHO* 46/4 (2003), 411–36.

al-Jomaih, Ibrahim A. *The Use of the Qurʾān in Political Argument: A Study of Early Islamic Parties (35–86 A.H./656–705)*. PhD dissertation, University of California (Los Angeles), 1988.

Judd, Steven C. *Religious Scholars and the Umayyads. Piety-Minded Supporters of the Marwānid Caliphate*. London: Routledge, 2014.

Judd, Steven C. "Narratives and Character Development: Al-Ṭabarī and al-Balādhurī on Late Umayyad History", in S. Günther, ed., *Ideas, Images, and Methods of Portrayal. Insights into Classical Arabic Literature and Islam*. Leiden: Brill, 2005, 209–25.

Judd, Steven C. "Muslim Persecution of Heretics during the Marwānid Period (64–132/684–750)", *al-Masāq* 23/1 (2011), 1–14.

Juynboll, G. H. A. "The Qurrā' in Early Islamic History", *JESHO* 16 (1973), 113–29.

Juynboll, G. H. A. "The Qur'ān Reciters on the Battlefield and Concomitant Issues", *ZDMG* 125 (1975), 11–27.

Keaney, Heather. "The First Islamic Revolt in Mamlūk Collective Memory: Ibn Bakr's (d. 1340) Portrayal of the Third Caliph 'Uthmān", in S. Günther, ed., *Ideas, Images, and Methods of Portrayal. Insights into Classical Arabic Literature and Islam*. Leiden: Brill, 2005, 375–402.

Keaney, Heather. *Medieval Islamic Historiography: Remembering Rebellion*. New York: Routledge, 2013.

Keaney, Heather. "Confronting the Caliph: 'Uthmān b. 'Affān in Three 'Abbasid Chronicles", *SI* 1 (2011), 37–65.

Kelsay, John. "Al-Qaida as a Muslim (Religio-Political) Movement: Remarks on James L. Gelvin's 'Al-Qaeda and Anarchism: A Historian's Reply to Terrorology'", *Terrorism and Political Violence* 20/4 (2008), 601–5.

Kennedy, Hugh. *The Prophet and the Age of the Caliphates*. 2nd edition. Harlow: Pearson Longman, 2004.

Kennedy, Hugh. *The Early 'Abbāsid Caliphate: A Political History*. London: Croom Helm, 1981.

Kennedy, Philip, ed. *On Fiction and* Adab *in Medieval Arabic Literature*. Wiesbaden: Harrassowitz, 2005.

Kenney, Jeffrey T. "The Emergence of the Khawārij: Religion and the Social Order in Early Islam". M. A. dissertation, *JUSŪR* 5 (1989), 1–29.

Kenney, Jeffrey T. *Heterodoxy and Culture: The Legacy of the Khawārij in Islamic History*. PhD dissertation, University of California (Santa Barbara), 1991.

Kenney, Jeffrey T. "Jews, Kharijites and the Debate over Religious Extremism in Egypt", in R. L. Nettler and S. Taji-Farouki, eds, *Muslim-Jewish Encounters: Intellectual Traditions and Modern Politics*. Amsterdam: Harwood Academic, 65–86.

Kenney, Jeffrey T. *Muslim Rebels: Khārijites and the Politics of Extremism in Egypt*. Oxford: Oxford University Press, 2006.

Khalek, Nancy. *Damascus After the Muslim Conquest: Text and Image in Early Islam*. New York: Oxford University Press, 2011.

Khalek, Nancy. "Medieval Biographical Literature and the Companions of Muḥammad", *ISL* 91/2 (2014), 272–94.

Khalidi, Tarif. *The Qur'an*. London: Penguin, 2008.

Khalidi, Tarif. *Islamic Historiography: The Histories of Mas'ūdī*. Albany: State University of New York Press, 1975.

Khalidi, Tarif. *Arabic Historical Thought in the Classical Period*. Cambridge: Cambridge University Press, 1994.

Khalidi, Tarif. "The Poetry of the Khawārij: Violence and Salvation", in Th. Scheffler, ed., *Religion between Violence and Reconciliation*. Würzburg: Ergon, 2002, 109–22.

Kilito, Abdelfattah. *The Author and His Doubles. Essays on Classical Arabic Culture*. Translated into English by Michael Cooperson. Syracuse: Syracuse University Press, 2001.

Kilito, Abdelfattah. *Thou Shalt Not Speak My Language*. Translated into English by Waïl S. Hassan. Syracuse: Syracuse University Press, 2008.

Kilito, Abdelfattah. *Arabs and the Art of Storytelling: A Strange Familiarity*. Translated into English by Mbarek Sryfi and Eric Sellin. Syracuse: Syracuse University Press, 2014.

Kilpatrick, Hilary. "Adab", in J. S. Meisami and P. Starkey, eds, *Encyclopedia of Arabic Literature*, vol. I. London: Routledge, 1998, 54–6.

Kinberg, Leah. "What is Meant by Zuhd", *SI* 61 (1985), 27–44.

Kittang, Atle. "Authors, Authorship, and Work. A Brief Theoretical Survey", in S. Rankovic, ed., *Modes of Authorship in the Middle Ages*. Toronto: Pontifical Institute of Mediaeval Studies, 2012, 17–29.

Klein, Dorothea. "Zwischen Abhängigkeit und Autonomie: Inszenierungen inspirierter Autorschaft in der Literatur der Vormoderne", in R. Schlesier and B. Trinca, eds, *Inspiration und Adaptation: Tarnkappen mittelalterlicher Autorschaft*. Hildesheim: Weidmann, 2008.

Knysh, Alexander. "'Orthodoxy' and 'Heresy' in Medieval Islam: An Essay in Reassessment", *MW* 83 (1993), 48–67.

Kraemer, Joel L. "Apostates, Rebels and Brigands", *IOS* 10 (1980), 34–73.

Kruk, Remke. *The Warrior Women of Islam: Female Empowerment in Arabic Popular Literature*. London: I. B. Tauris, 2014.

Kurat, Akdeş N. "Abū Muḥammad Aḥmad b. A'tham al-Kūfī's Kitāb al-Futūḥ and Its Importance Concerning the Arab Conquest in Central Asia and the Khazars", *Dil ve Tarih-Coğrafya Fakültesi Dergisi* 7/2 (1949), 274–82.

Lahoud, Nelly. *Political Thought in Islam. A Study in Intellectual Boundaries*. London: RoutledgeCurzon, 2005.

Lahoud, Nelly. *The Jihadi's Path to Self-Destruction*. New York: Columbia University Press, 2010.

Lahoud, Nelly. "The Early Kharijites and Their Understanding of *Jihād*", *Mélanges de l'Université Saint-Joseph* 62 (2009), 283–305.

Landau-Tasseron, Ella. "Sayf b. 'Umar in Medieval and Modern Scholarship", *ISL* 67 (1990), 1–26.

Landau-Tasseron, Ella. "New Data on an Old Manuscript: An Andalusian Version of the Works Entitled *Futūḥ al-Shām*", *Al-Qantara* 21/2 (2000), 361–80.

Landau-Tasseron, Ella. "On the Reconstruction of Lost Sources", *al-Qanṭara* XXV/1 (2004), 45–91.

Landau-Tasseron, Ella. "Processes of Redaction: The Case of the Tamīmite Delegation to the Prophet Muḥammad", *BSOAS* 49/2 (1986), 253–70.

Lane, Edward W. *An Arabic-English Lexicon*. London: Williams and Norgate, 1863–1893.

Lang, Kate. "Review of Tayeb El-Hibri, *Reinterpreting Islamic Historiography: Hārūn al-Rashīd and the Narrative of the ʿAbbāsid Caliphate*", *JNES* 62/2 (2003), 111–12.

Lassner, Jacob. *Islamic Revolution and Historical Memory: An Inquiry into the Art of ʿAbbāsid Apologetics*. New Haven, CT: American Oriental Society, 1986.

Lassner, Jacob. "'Doing' Early Islamic History: Brooklyn Baseball, Arabic Historiography, and Historical Memory", *JAOS* 114/1 (1994), 1–10.

Lecker, Michael. "Biographical Notes on Abū ʿUbayda Maʿmar b. al-Muthannā", *SI* 81 (1995), 71–100.

Leder, Stefan. *Das Korpus al-Haiṯam b. ʿAdī (st. 207/822). Herkunft, Überlieferung, Gestalt früher Texte der Aḫbār-Literatur*. Frankfurt am Main: Klostermann, 1991.

Leder, Stefan, ed. *Story-Telling in the Framework of Non-Fictional Arabic Literature*. Wiesbaden: Harrassowitz, 1998.

Leder, Stefan. "Features of the Novel in Early Historiography: The Downfall of Xālid al-Qasrī", *Oriens* 32 (1990), 72–96.

Leder, Stefan. "The Literary Use of the *Khabar*: A Basic Form of Historical Writing", in A. Cameron and L. I. Conrad, eds, *The Byzantine and Early Islamic Near East. Vol. I: Problems in the Literary Source Material*. Princeton: Darwin, 1992, 277–315.

Leder, Stefan. "Authorship and Transmission in Unauthored Literature", *Oriens* 31 (1988), 67–81.

Leder, Stefan. "The Use of Composite Form in the Making of the Islamic Historical Tradition", in P. Kennedy, ed., *On Fiction and* Adab *in Medieval Arabic Literature*. Wiesbaden: Harrassowitz, 2005, 125–48.

Leder, Stefan and Hilary Kilpatrick. "Classical Arabic Prose Literature: A Researchers' Sketch Map", *JAL* 23/1 (1992), 2–26.

Leder, Stefan. "Grenzen der Rekonstruktion alten Schrifttums nach den Angaben im Fihrist", in *Ibn al-Nadim und die mittelalterliche arabische Literatur. Beiträge zum ersten Johann Wilhelm Fück-Kolloqium*. Wiesbaden: Harrassowitz, 1996, 21–31.

Leder, Stefan. "Conventions of Fictional Narration in Learned Literature", in S. Leder, ed., *Story-Telling in the Framework of Non-Fictional Arabic Literature*. Wiesbaden: Harrassowitz, 1998, 34–60.

LeGoff, Jacques. *Die Intellektuellen im Mittelalter*. Translated into German by Christiane Kayser. 2nd edition. Stuttgart: Klett-Cotta, 1987.

Lethbridge, Emily. "Authors and Anonymity, Texts and Their Contexts: The Case of Eggertsbok", in S. Rankovic, ed., *Modes of Authorship in the Middle Ages*. Toronto: Pontifical Institute of Mediaeval Studies, 2012, 343–64.

Leube, Georg. *Kinda in der frühislamischen Geschichte. Eine prosopographische Studie auf Basis der frühen und klassischen arabisch-islamischen Geschichtsschreibung*. Würzburg: Ergon, 2017.

Lewinstein, Keith. *Studies in Islamic Heresiography: The Khawārij in Two* Firaq *Traditions*. PhD dissertation, Princeton University, 1989.

Lewinstein, Keith. "Making and Unmaking a Sect: The Heresiographers and the Ṣufriyya", *SI* 76 (1992), 75–96.

Lewinstein, Keith. "The Azāriqa in Islamic Heresiography", *BSOAS* 54/2 (1991), 251–68.

Lewinstein, Keith. "Notes on Eastern Ḥanafite Heresiography", *JAOS* 114/4 (1994), 583–98.

Lewis, Bernard. *The Arabs in History*. 6th edition. Oxford: Oxford University Press, 2002.

Lewis, Bernard. "The Significance of Heresy in Islam", *SI* 1 (1953), 43–63.

Lewis, Bernard. "On the Quietist and Activist Traditions in Islamic Political Writing", *BSOAS* 49/1 (1986), 141–7.

Lindorfer, Bettina. "Der Diskurs der Geschichte und der Ort des Realen: Roland Barthes' Beitrag zum Linguistic Turn der Geschichtsschreibung", in J. Trabant, ed., *Sprache der Geschichte*. München: Oldenbourg, 2005, 87–105.

Lindsay, James, ed. *Ibn ʿAsākir and Early Islamic History*. Princeton: Darwin, 2001.

Lindsay, James. "Ibn ʿAsakir, His Taʾrīkh madinat Dimashq and its Usefulness for Early Islamic History", in J. Lindsay, ed., *Ibn ʿAsākir and Early Islamic History*. Princeton: Darwin, 2001, 1–23.

Lindstedt, Ilkka. *The Transmission of al-Madāʾinī's Material: Historiographical Studies*. PhD dissertation, University of Helsinki, 2013.

Lindstedt, Ilkka. "Sources for the Biography of the Historian Ibn Aʿtham al-Kūfī", in J. Hämeen-Anttila et al., eds, *Contacts and Interaction. Proceedings of the 27th Congress of the Union Européenne des Arabisants et Islamisants*. Leuven: Peeters, 2017, 299–309.

Lingelbach, Gabriele. "The Institutionalization and Professionalization of History in Europe and the United States", in S. Macintyre, J. Maiguashca and A. Pók, eds, *The Oxford History of Historical Writing. Volume 4: 1800–1945*. Oxford: Oxford University Press, 2015, 78–96.

Livne-Kafri, Ofer. "Early Muslim Ascetics and the World of Christian Monasticism", *JSAI* 20 (1996), 105–29.

Love, Paul M. *Ibadi Muslims of North Africa. Manuscripts, Mobilization, and the Making of a Written Tradition*. Cambridge: Cambridge University Press, 2018.

Luce, T. James. *The Greek Historians*. London: Routledge, 1997.

Lynch, Ryan J. *Arab Conquests and Early Islamic Historiography. The Futuh al-Buldan of al-Baladhuri*. London: I. B. Tauris, 2020.

Lynch, Ryan J. "Sons of the Muhājirūn: Some Comments on Ibn al-Zubayr and Legitimizing Power in Seventh-Century Islamic History", in A. Gnasso, E. E. Intagliata and T. J. MacMaster, eds, *The Long Seventh Century: Continuity and Discontinuity in an Age of Transition*. Oxford: Peter Lang, 2014, 251–67.

Madelung, Wilferd. *The Succession to Muḥammad. A Study of the Early Caliphate*. Cambridge: Cambridge University Press, 1997.

Madelung, Wilferd. *Religious Trends in Early Islamic Iran*. Albany: Persian Heritage Foundation, 1988.

Madelung, Wilferd. "Abū ʿUbayda Maʿmar b. al-Muthannā as a Historian", *JIS* 3/1 (1992), 47–56.

Malti-Douglas, Fedwa. "Texts and Tortures: The Reign of al-Muʿtaḍid and the Construction of Historical Meaning", *Arabica* 46 (1999), 313–36.

Marincola, John. *Authority and Tradition in Ancient Historiography*. Cambridge: Cambridge University Press, 1997.

Marquet, Yves. "Le Shiʿisme au IXe siècle à travers l'histoire de Yaʿqubi", *Arabica* XIX (1972), 1–45, 101–38.

Marsham, Andrew. *Rituals of Islamic Monarchy. Accession and Succession in the First Muslim Empire*. Edinburgh: Edinburgh University Press, 2009.

Marsham, Andrew. *The Umayyad Empire (644–750)*. Edinburgh: Edinburgh University Press, forthcoming.

Marsham, Andrew, ed. *The Umayyad World*. London: Routledge, 2020.

Marsham, Andrew. "Attitudes to the Use of Fire in Executions in Late Antiquity and Early Islam: The Burning of Heretics and Rebels in Late Umayyad Iraq", in R. Gleave and I. T. Kristo-Nagy, eds, *Violence in Islamic Thought from the Qurʾān to the Mongols*. Edinburgh: Edinburgh University Press, 2015, 106–27.

Marsham, Andrew. "Public Execution in the Umayyad Period: Early Islamic Punitive Practice and Its Late Antique Context", *JAIS* 11/4 (2011), 101–36.

Marsham, Andrew. "Those Who Make War on God and His Messenger: Some Implications of Recent Scholarship on Rebellion, Banditry and State Formation in Early Islam", *ʿUW* 17/2 (2005), 29–31.

Marsham, Andrew. "Universal Histories in Christendom and the Islamic World, c.700-c.1400", in S. Foot and C. Robinson, eds, *The Oxford History of Historical Writing. Volume 2: 400–1400*. Oxford: Oxford University Press, 2012, 431–56.

Martin, B. G. "Unbelief in the Western Sudan: ʿUthmān dan Fodio's *Taʿlīm al-ikhwān*", *Middle Eastern Studies* 4/1 (1967), 50–97.

Masullo, Mariangela. "Laylà bint Ṭarīf's *riṯāʾ*: An Example of Kharijite Female Poetry", in A. Cilardo, ed., *Islam and Globalisation: Historical and Contemporary Perspectives*. Leuven: Peeters, 2013, 281–91.

Mattock, John N. "History and Fiction", *Occasional Papers of the School of Abbasid Studies* 1 (1986), 80–97.

McKitterick, Rosamund. *The Carolingians and the Written Word*. Cambridge: Cambridge University Press, 1989.

Meisami, Julie S. *Persian Historiography to the End of the Twelfth Century*. Edinburgh: Edinburgh University Press, 1999.

Meisami, Julie S. "Masʿūdī on Love and the Fall of the Barmakids", *JRAS* 2 (1989), 252–77.

Meisami, Julie S. "Masʿūdī and the Reign of al-Amīn: Narrative and Meaning in Medieval Muslim Historiography", in P. Kennedy, ed., *On Fiction and* Adab *in Medieval Arabic Literature*. Wiesbaden: Harrassowitz, 2005, 149–76.

Meisami, Julie S. "History as Literature", *Iranian Studies* 33/1–2 (2000), 15–30.

Melchert, Christopher. "Aḥmad b. Ḥanbal's Book of Renunciation", *ISL* 85/2 (2011), 345–59.

Melve, Leidulf. "'. . . to distil the excellence of their genius': Conceptions of Authorship in Eleventh- and Twelth-Century Polemical Literature", in S. Rankovic, ed., *Modes of Authorship in the Middle Ages*. Toronto: Pontifical Institute of Mediaeval Studies, 2012, 133–50.

Mez, Adam. *Die Renaissance des Islāms*. Heidelberg: Carl Winters Universitätsbuchhandlung, 1922.

Mikati, Rana. "Fighting for the Faith? Notes on Women and War in Early Islam", *JNES* 78/2 (2019), 201–13.

Millward, William. "Al-Yaʿqūbī's Sources and the Question of Shīʿa Partiality", *Abī-Nahrain* xii (1971–2), 47–74.

Mommsen, Wolfgang J., ed. *Leopold von Ranke und die moderne Geschichtswissenschaft*. Stuttgart: Klett Cotta, 1988.

Montgomery, James E. "Editor's Introduction", in J. E. Montgomery, ed., *ʿAbbasid Studies. Occasional Papers of the School of ʿAbbasid Studies*. Leuven: Peeters, 2004, 1–22.

Montgomery, James E. "Serendipity, Resistance, and Multivalency: Ibn Khurradādhbih and His *Kitāb al-Masālik wa-l-Mamālik*", in P. Kennedy, ed., *On Fiction and* Adab *in Medieval Arabic Literature*. Wiesbaden: Harrassowitz, 2005, 177–232.

Morony, Michael G. *Iraq after the Muslim Conquest*. Princeton: Princeton University Press, 1984.

Morony, Michael G., trans. *The History of al-Ṭabarī, volume XVIII: Between Civil Wars: The Caliphate of Muʿāwiyah*. Albany: State University of New York Press, 1987.

Motzki, Harald. "The Collection of the Qurʾān: A Reconsideration of Western Views in Light of Recent Methodological Developments", *ISL* 78/1 (2001), 1–34.

Motzki, Harald. "The Author and His Work in Islamic Literature of the First Centuries. The Case of ʿAbd al-Razzāq's Muṣannaf", *JSAI* 28 (2003), 171–203.

Munslow, Alan. "Authority and Reality in the Representation of the Past", *Rethinking History* 1 (1997), 75–87.

Munt, Harry. "Mamluk Historiography Outside of Egypt and Syria: ʿAlī b. ʿAbd Allāh al-Samhūdī and His Histories of Medina", *ISL* 92/2 (2015), 413–41.

Muranyi, Miklos. *The First Compendium of Ibadi Law. The "Mudawwana" of Abu Ghanim Bishr b. Bishr al-Khurasani*. Hildesheim: Olms, 2018.

Nadler, Rajaa. *Die Umayyadenkalifen im Spiegel ihrer zeitgenössischen Dichter*. PhD dissertation, University of Erlangen-Nürnberg, 1990.

Neuwirth, Angelika. "From Sacrilege to Sacrifice. Observations on Violent Death in Classical and Modern Arabic Poetry", in F. Pannewick, ed., *Martyrdom in Literature. Visions of Death and Meaningful Suffering in Europe and the Middle East from Antiquity to Modernity*. Wiesbaden: Reichert, 2004, 259–81.

Neuwirth, Angelika. "Die *Masāil Nāfi' b. al-Azraq* – Element des "Portrait mythique d'Ibn 'Abbās" oder ein Stück realer Literatur? Rückschlüsse aus einer bisher unbeachteten Handschrift", *ZAL* 25 (1993), 233–50.

Nirenberg, David. "The Rhineland Massacres of Jews in the First Crusade: Memories Medieval and Modern", in G. Althoff, J. Fried, and P. J. Geary, eds, *Medieval Concepts of the Past. Ritual, Memory, Historiography*. Washington, DC: German Historical Institute and Cambridge: Cambridge University Press, 2002, 279–309.

Noth, Albrecht. *Heiliger Krieg und Heiliger Kampf in Islam und Christentum. Beiträge zur Vorgeschichte und Geschichte der Kreuzzüge*. Bonn: Röhrscheid, 1966.

Noth, Albrecht. *Quellenkritische Studien zu Themen, Formen und Tendenzen frühislamischer Geschichtsüberlieferung*. Habilitationsschrift, University of Bonn, 1973.

Noth, Albrecht. *The Early Arabic Historical Tradition – A Source-Critical Study*. 2nd edition. Princeton: Darwin Press, 1994.

Noth, Albrecht. "Fiktion als historische Quelle", in S. Leder, ed., *Story-Telling in the Framework of Non-Fictional Arabic Literature*. Wiesbaden: Harrassowitz, 1998, 472–87.

Noth, Albrecht. "Iṣfahān-Nihāwand. Eine quellenkritische Studie zur frühislamischen Historiographie", *ZDMG* 118 (1968), 274–96.

Noth, Albrecht. "Der Charakter der ersten grossen Sammlungen von Nachrichten zur frühen Kalifenzeit", *ISL* 47 (1971), 168–99.

Noth, Albrecht. "Zum Verhältnis von Recht und Geschichte im Islam", *Saeculum* 26 (1975), 341–346.

O'Connor, Ralph. "Irish Narrative Literature and the Classical Tradition, 900–1300", in R. O'Connor, ed., *Classical Literature and Learning in Medieval Irish Narrative*. Cambridge: D. S. Brewer, 2014, 1–22.

Orfali, Bilal and Maurice Pomerantz. "'I See a Distant Fire': Tha'ālibī's (d. 429/1030) *Kitāb al-Iqtibās min al-Qur'ān al-karīm*", in N. Alshaar, ed., *The Qur'an and* Adab. *The Shaping of Literary Traditions in Classical Islam*. Oxford: Oxford University Press, in association with The Institute of Ismaili Studies (London), 2017, 191–215.

Oskarsdottir, Svanhildur. "The Resourceful Scribe: Some Aspects of the Development of Reynistadarbok (AM 764 4to)", in S. Rankovic, ed., *Modes of Authorship in the Middle Ages*. Toronto: Pontifical Institute of Mediaeval Studies, 2012, 325–42.

Osti, Letizia. "Tailors of Stories: Biographers and the Lives of the *khabar*", *Synergies Monde Arabe* 6 (2009), 283–91.

Palmer, Andrew, Sebastian P. Brock and Robert Hoyland, eds, trans. *The Seventh Century in the West-Syrian Chronicles*. Liverpool: Liverpool University Press, 1993.

Pampus, Karl-Heinz. *Über die Rolle der Ḫāriǧīya im frühen Islam*. Wiesbaden: Harrassowitz, 1980.

Pampus, Karl-Heinz. "Historische Minderheitenforschung am Beispiel einer Neubetrachtung der frühen Ḫāriǧītenbewegung – Diskussion eines neuen Forschungsansatzes", in W. Voigt, ed., *Vorträge. XIX. Deutscher Orientalistentag vom 28. September bis 4. Oktober 1975 in Freiburg im Breisgau*. Wiesbaden: Steiner, 1977, 572–8.

Pannewick, Friederike. "Introduction", in F. Pannewick, ed., *Martyrdom in Literature. Visions of Death and Meaningful Suffering in Europe and the Middle East from Antiquity to Modernity*. Wiesbaden: Reichert, 2004, 1–25.

Paret, Rudi. "Die legendäre Futūḥ-Literatur, ein arabisches Volksepos?", in *La poesia epica e la sua formazione*. Rome: Accademia Nazionale dei Lincei, 1970, 735–49.

Peacock, Andrew. *Medieval Islamic Historiography and Political Legitimacy: Balʿamī's Tārīkhnāma*. London: Routledge, 2007.

Pellat, Charles. "Was al-Masʿūdī an Historian or an *adīb*?", *Journal of the Pakistan Historical Society* 9 (1961), 231–4.

Pellat, Charles. "Djāḥiẓ et les Khāridjites", *FO* 12 (1970), 195–209.

Petersen, Erling L. *ʿAlī and Muʿāwiya in Early Arabic Tradition: Studies of the Genesis and Growth of Islamic Historical Writing Until the End of the Ninth Century*. Copenhagen: Munksgaard, 1964.

Potter, David S. *Literary Texts and the Roman Historian*. London/New York: Routledge, 1999.

Pratsch, Thomas. *Der hagiographische Topos. Griechische Heiligenviten in mittelbyzantinischer Zeit*. Berlin: De Gruyter, 2005.

Prevost, Virginie. "Les dernières communautés chrétiennes autochtones d'Afrique du Nord", *Revue de l'histoire des religions* 4 (2007), 461–83, open access at https://journals.openedition.org/rhr/5401 (last access 9 October 2020).

al-Qāḍī, Wadād. "The Limitations of Qurʾānic Usage in Early Arabic Poetry: The Example of a Khārijite Poem", in W. Heinrichs and G. Schoeler, eds, *Festschrift Ewald Wagner zum 65. Geburtstag. Band II: Studien zur Arabischen Dichtung*. Stuttgart: Steiner, 1994, 162–81.

al-Qāḍī, Wadād. "The Impact of the Qurʾan on the Epistolography of ʿAbd al-Ḥamīd b. Yaḥyā al-Kātib (d. 132/750)", in N. Alshaar, ed., *The Qurʾan and* Adab. *The Shaping of Literary Traditions in Classical Islam*. Oxford: Oxford University Press, in association with The Institute of Ismaili Studies (London), 2017, 341–79.

al-Qāḍī, Wadād. "Abū Ḥayyān al-Tawḥīdī: A Sunni Voice in the Shiʿi Century", in F. Daftary and J. W. Meri, eds, *Culture and Memory in Medieval Islam. Essays in Honour of Wilferd Madelung*. London: I. B. Tauris, in association with The Institute of Ismaili Studies (London), 2003, 128–59.

al-Qāḍī, Wadād. "Biographical Dictionaries: Inner Structure and Cultural Significance", in G. N. Atiyeh, ed., *The Book in the Islamic World. The Written Word and Communication in the Middle East*. Albany: State University of New York Press, 1995, 93–122.

al-Qāḍī, Wadād, and Mustansir Mir. "Literature and the Qur'an", in J. D. McAuliffe, ed., *Encyclopaedia of the Qur'ān*. 6 vols. Leiden: Brill, 2006, vol. III, 205–27.

Qutbuddin, Tahera. "Qur'an Citation in Early Arabic Oration (*Khuṭba*): Mnemonic, Liturgical and Testimonial Functions", in N. Alshaar, ed., *The Qur'an and* Adab. *The Shaping of Literary Traditions in Classical Islam*. Oxford: Oxford University Press, in association with The Institute of Ismaili Studies (London), 2017, 315–40.

Radtke, Andreas. *Offenbarung zwischen Gesetz und Geschichte. Quellenstudien zu den Bedingungsfaktoren frühislamischen Rechtsdenken*. Wiesbaden: Harrassowitz, 2003.

Radtke, Bernd. *Weltgeschichte und Weltbeschreibung im mittelalterlichen Islam*. Stuttgart: Steiner, 1992.

Rankovic, Slavica. *The* Distributed Author *and the* Poets of Complexity*: A Comparative Study of the Sagas of Icelanders and Serbian Epic Poetry*. PhD dissertation, University of Nottingham, 2006.

Rankovic, Slavica, ed. *Modes of Authorship in the Middle Ages*. Toronto: Pontifical Institute of Mediaeval Studies, 2012.

Rankovic, Slavica. "Introduction", in S. Rankovic, ed., *Modes of Authorship in the Middle Ages*. Toronto: Pontifical Institute of Mediaeval Studies, 2012, 1–14.

Reinfandt, Lucian. "Bewaffneter Raub und Kreuzigung im frühen Islam", in R. Rollinger et al., eds, *Strafe und Strafrecht in den antiken Welten*. Wiesbaden: Harrassowitz, 2012, 249–59.

Rescher, Oskar, trans. *Die Kharidschitenkapitel aus dem Kāmil (nach der Ausgabe William Wright's) – ein Specimen der älteren arabischen Adab-Literatur*. Stuttgart: n.p., 1922.

Rich, J. W. "Dio on Augustus", in A. Cameron, ed., *History as Text. The Writing of Ancient History*. London: Duckworth, 1989, 86–110.

Riffaterre, Michael. *Fictional Truth*. Baltimore: The Johns Hopkins University Press, 1990.

Rippin, Andrew. "Review of *Islamic Revolution and Historical Memory: An Inquiry into the Art of 'Abbāsid Apologetics* by Jacob Lassner", *BSOAS* 51/3 (1988), 552–3.

Rippin, Andrew. "The Place of the Qur'an in 'The Sermons and Exhortations' of Abū 'Ubayd (d. 224/838)", in N. Alshaar, ed., *The Qur'an and* Adab. *The Shaping of Literary Traditions in Classical Islam*. Oxford: Oxford University Press, in association with The Institute of Ismaili Studies (London), 2017, 219–37.

Roberts, Joseph B. *Early Islāmic Historiography: Ideology and Methodology*. PhD dissertation, The Ohio State University, 1986.

Robinson, Chase F. *Empire and Elites after the Muslim Conquest: The Transformation of Northern Mesopotamia*. Cambridge: Cambridge University Press, 2000.

Robinson, Chase F. *Islamic Historiography*. Cambridge: Cambridge University Press, 2003.

Robinson, Chase F. *ʿAbd al-Malik*. Oxford: Oneworld, 2007.

Robinson, Chase F. "The Study of Islamic Historiography: A Progress Report", *JRAS* 7/2 (1997), 199–227.

Robinson, Chase F. "History and Heilsgeschichte in Early Islam: Some Observations on Prophetic History and Biography", in B.-C. Otto et al., eds, *History and Religion. Narrating a Religious Past*. Berlin: De Gruyter, 2015, 119–50.

Robinson, Chase F. "Reconstructing Early Islam: Truths and Consequences", in H. Berg, ed., *Method and Theory in the Study of Islamic Origins*. Leiden/Boston: Brill, 2003, 101–34.

Robinson, Chase F. "Crone and the End of Orientalism", in A. Q. Ahmed et al., eds, *Islamic Cultures, Islamic Contexts. Essays in Honor of Professor Patricia Crone*. Leiden: Brill, 2014, 597–620.

Roded, Ruth, ed. *Women in Islam and the Middle East: A Reader*. London: I. B. Tauris, 1999.

Rorty, Richard. *The Linguistic Turn: Recent Essays in Philosophical Method*. Chicago: University of Chicago Press, 1967.

Rosenthal, Franz. *A History of Muslim Historiography*. 2nd, rev. edition. Leiden: Brill, 1968.

Rotter, Gernot. "Abū Zurʿa ad-Dimašqī (st. 281/894) und das Problem der frühen arabischen Geschichtsschreibung in Syrien", *WO* 6 (1971), 80–104.

Rotter, Gernot. "Zur Überlieferung einiger historischer Werke Madāʾinīs in Ṭabarīs *Annalen*", *Oriens* 23–24 (1974), 103–33.

Rotter, Gernot. *Die Umayyaden und der Zweite Bürgerkrieg*. Wiesbaden: Steiner, 1982.

Rowson, Everett K. *The History of al-Ṭabarī. Vol. XXII: The Marwānid Restoration*. Albany: State University of New York Press, 1989.

Rowson, Everett K. "Manuscripts, Printed Editions, and Translations of al-Yaʿqūbī's Work", in M. S. Gordon et al., trans., *The Works of Ibn Wāḍiḥ al-Yaʿqūbī: An English Translation*. 3 vols. Leiden: Brill, 2018, I, 23–7.

Rubanovich, Julia. "Metaphors of Authorship in Medieval Persian Prose: A Preliminary Study", *Middle Eastern Literatures* 12/2 (2009), 127–35.

Rubinacci, Roberto. "Political Poetry", in J. Ashtiany et al., eds, *The Cambridge History of Arabic Literature. Vol. II: ʿAbbasid Belles-Lettres*. Cambridge: Cambridge University Press, 1990, 185–201.

Sabari, Simha. *Mouvements populaires à Bagdad à l'époque ʿAbbasside, ixe -xie siècle*. Paris: Librairie d'Amérique et d'Orient, Adrien Maisonneuve, 1981.

al-Sābiʿī, Nāṣir b. Sulaymān b. Saʿīd. *al-Khawārij wa-l-ḥaqīqa al-ghāʾiba*. Muscat: n.p., 1999.

Salem, Elie A. *Political Theory and Institutions of the Khawārij*. Baltimore: The Johns Hopkins University Press, 1956.

Salem, Feryal E. *ʿAbd Allāh b. al-Mubārak between* Ḥadīth, Jihād, *and* Zuhd: *An Expression of Early Sunni Identity in the Formative Period*. PhD dissertation, University of Chicago, 2013.

al-Ṣāliḥī, ʿAzmī Muḥammad. *The Society, Beliefs and Political Theory of the Khārijites as Revealed in Their Poetry of the Umayyad Era*. PhD dissertation, University of London (SOAS), 1975.

al-Sālimī, ʿAbd al-Raḥmān. "Ibadi Studies and Orientalism", in A. Ziaka, ed., *On Ibadism*. Hildesheim: Olms, 2014, 23–34.

al-Ṣallābī, ʿAlī Muḥammad. *al-Ibāḍiyya. Madrasa islāmiyya baʿīda ʿan al-khawārij*. Beirut: Dār Ibn Kathīr, 2019.

Sahner, Christian. ""The Monasticism of My Community is Jihad": A Debate on Monasticism, Sex, and Warfare in Early Islam", *Arabica* 64 (2017), 149–83.

al-Samuk, Sadun Mahmud. *Die historischen Überlieferungen nach Ibn Isḥāq. Eine synoptische Untersuchung*. PhD dissertation, University of Frankfurt (Main), 1978.

Sanagustin, Florèal. "Une poésie de combat: la poésie kharédjite", in F. Sanagustin, ed., *L'Orient au coeur: en l'honneur d'André Miquel*. Paris: Maisonneuve & Larose, 2001, 45–52.

Sauer, Rebecca. *Rebellion und Widerstand: politisch-religiös motivierte Gewalt im innerislamischen Diskurs. Eine Untersuchung vormoderner und moderner Korankommentare*. Würzburg: Ergon, 2013.

Savage, Elizabeth. *A Gateway to Hell, a Gateway to Paradise: The North African Response to the Arab Conquest*. Princeton: Darwin, 1997.

Savage, Elizabeth. "Survival through Alliance: The Establishment of the Ibadiyya", *BRISMES* 17/1 (1990), 5–15.

Savage, Elizabeth. "Iraqi Christian Links with an Early Islamic Sect", *Aram* 6/1–2 (1994), 179–92.

Sayyid, Riḍwān. *Die Revolte des Ibn al-Ašʿaṯ und die Koranleser: Ein Beitrag zur Religions- und Sozialgeschichte der frühen Umayyadenzeit*. Freiburg: Schwarz, 1977.

Scarcia, Gianroberto, "Lo scambio di lettere tra Hārūn al-Rashīd e Ḥamza al-Khārijī secondo il "Taʾrīkh-I Sīstān"", *AIUON* 14 (1964), 623–45.

Schacht, Joseph. *The Origins of Muhammedan Jurisprudence*. Oxford: The Clarendon Press, 1950.

Scheiner, Jens. "Writing the History of the *futūḥ*: The *futūḥ*-works of al-Azdī, Ibn Aʿtham and al-Wāqidī", in P. M. Cobb, ed., *The Lineaments of Islam. Studies in Honor of Fred McGraw Donner*. Leiden: Brill, 2012, 151–76.

Schlesier, Renate and Beatrice Trinca, eds. *Inspiration und Adaptation. Tarnkappen mittelalterlicher Autorschaft*. Hildesheim: Weidmann, 2008.

Schmitt, Stefanie. *Inszenierungen von Glaubwürdigkeit. Studien zur Beglaubigung im späthöfischen und frühneuzeitlichen Roman*. Tübingen: Niemeyer, 2005.

Schoeler, Gregor. "Die Frage der schriftlichen oder mündlichen Überlieferung der Wissenschaften im frühen Islam", *ISL* 62/2 (1985), 201–30.

Schoeler, Gregor. "Weiteres zur Frage der schriftlichen oder mündlichen Überlieferung der Wissenschaften im Islam", *ISL* 66/1 (1989), 38–67.

Schoeler, Gregor. "Mündliche Thora und Ḥadīṯ: Überlieferung, Schreibverbot, Redaktion", *ISL* 66/2 (1989), 213–51.

Schoeler, Gregor. "Schreiben und Veröffentlichen. Zur Verwendung und Funktion der Schrift in den ersten islamischen Jahrhunderten", *DI* 69/1 (1992), 1–43.

Schoeler, Gregor. "Gesprochenes Wort und Schrift. Mündlichkeit und Schriftlichkeit im frühislamischen Lehrbetrieb", in P. Gemeinhardt and S. Günther, eds, *Von Rom nach Baghdad: Bildung und Religion von der römischen Kaiserzeit bis zum klassischen Islam*. Tübingen: Mohr Siebeck, 269–89.

Schoeler, Gregor. "Theorien zu den Quellen der den Isnād verwendenden kompilatorischen Werke der arabisch-islamischen Wissenschaften", in *Ibn al-Nadim und die mittelalterliche arabische Literatur. Beiträge zum ersten Johann Wilhelm Fück-Kolloqium*. Wiesbaden: Harrassowitz, 1996, 118–26.

Schoeler, Gregor. *The Genesis of Literature in Islam: From the Aural to the Read*. Translated by S. Toorawa. Edinburgh: Edinburgh University, 2009.

Schönléber, Monika. "Notes on the Textual Tradition of Ibn Aʿtham's *Kitāb al-Futūḥ*", in J. Hämeen-Anttila et al., eds, *Contacts and Interaction. Proceedings of the 27th Congress of the Union Européenne des Arabisants et Islamisants*. Leuven: Peeters, 2017, 427–38.

Schöttler, Peter. *Nach der Angst. Geschichtswissenschaft vor und nach dem Linguistic Turn*. Münster: Westfälisches Dampfboot, 2018.

Schwartz, Werner. *Ǧihād unter Muslimen*. Wiesbaden: Harrassowitz, 1980.

Sears, Stuart. "Umayyad Partisan or Khārijite Rebel? The Issue of ʿAbd al-ʿAzīz b. MDWL (?)", *StIr* 31/1 (2002), 71–8.

Segovia, Carlos A. "John Wansbrough and the Problem of Islamic Origins in Recent Scholarship: A Farewell to the Traditional Account", in B. Lourié and C. A. Segovia, eds, *The Coming of the Comforter: Where, When, and to Whom? Studies on the Rise of Islam and Various Other Topics in Memory of John Wansbrough*. Piscataway, NJ: Gorgias Press, 2012, xix–xxviii.

Seidensticker, Tilman. "Responses to Crucifixion in the Islamic World (1st–7th/7th–13th Centuries)", in C. Lange and M. Fierro, eds, *Public Violence in Islamic Societies: Power, Discipline, and the Construction of the Public Sphere, 7th–19th Centuries* CE. Edinburgh: Edinburgh University Press, 2009, 203–16.

Sewell, William H. *Logics of History. Social Theory and Social Transformation*. Chicago: University of Chicago Press, 2005.

Sezgin, Fuat. *Geschichte des arabischen Schrifttums. Bd. I: Qurʾānwissenschaften, Ḥadīṯ, Geschichte, Fiqh, Dogmatik, Mystik bis circa 430* H. Leiden: Brill, 1967.

Sezgin, Fuat. *Geschichte des arabischen Schrifttums. Bd. II: Poesie bis circa 430 H.* Leiden: Brill, 1975.

Sezgin, Ursula. *Abū Miḫnaf: Ein Beitrag zur Historiographie der umaiyadischen Zeit.* Leiden: Brill, 1971.

Shaban, Muḥammad A. *Islamic History. A New Interpretation. Volume I: A.D. 600–750 (A.H. 132).* Cambridge: Cambridge University Press, 1971.

Shaban, Muḥammad A. *The ʿAbbāsid Revolution.* Cambridge: Cambridge University Press, 1970.

Shaddel, Mehdy. "ʿAbd Allāh ibn al-Zubayr and the Mahdī: Between Propaganda and Historical Memory in the Second Civil War", *BSOAS* 80/1 (2017), 1–19.

Shah, Mustafa. "The Quest for the Origins of the qurraʾ in the Classical Islamic Tradition", *JQS* 7/2 (2005), 1–35.

Shah, Mustafa. "Kalām: Rational Expressions of Medieval Theological Thought", in H. Touati, ed., *Encyclopedia of Mediterranean Humanism*, Spring 2014, available at http://encyclopedie-humanisme.com/?Islamic-Kal%C4%81m, last accessed 3 April 2020.

Shahin, Aram A. "In Defense of Muʿāwiya ibn Abī Sufyān: Treatises and Monographs on Muʿāwiya from the Eighth to the Nineteenth Centuries", in P. M. Cobb, ed., *The Lineaments of Islam. Studies in Honor of Fred McGraw Donner.* Leiden: Brill, 2012, 177–208.

Sharon, Moshe. "The Umayyads as *Ahl al-Bayt*", *JSAI* 14 (1991), 115–52.

Sharon, Moshe. "*Ahl al-Bayt* – People of the House", *JSAI* 8 (1986), 169–84.

Sharon, Moshe. "The Development of the Debate around the Legitimacy of Authority in Early Islam", *JSAI* 5 (1984), 121–42.

Shoshan, Boaz. *Poetics of Islamic Historiography: Deconstructing Ṭabarī's History.* Leiden: Brill, 2004.

Sigurdsson, Gisli. "Poet, Singer of Tales, Storyteller, and Author", in S. Rankovic, ed., *Modes of Authorship in the Middle Ages.* Toronto: Pontifical Institute of Mediaeval Studies, 2012, 227–35.

Sizgorich, Thomas. *Violence and Belief in Late Antiquity – Militant Devotion in Christianity and Islam.* Philadelphia: University of Philadelphia Press, 2009.

Sonnesyn, Sigbjorn Olsen. "Obedient Creativity and Idiosyncratic Copying: Tradition and Individuality in the Works of William of Malmesbury and John of Salisbury", in S. Rankovic, ed., *Modes of Authorship in the Middle Ages.* Toronto: Pontifical Institute of Mediaeval Studies, 2012, 113–32.

Spannaus, Nathan. "The Azāriqa and Violence among the Khawārij". A. M. dissertation, Harvard University, 2007.

Spiegel, Gabrielle. *The Past as Text: The Theory and Practice of Medieval Historiography.* Baltimore: The Johns Hopkins University Press, 1997.

Spiegel, Gabrielle. "History, Historicism, and the Social Logic of the Text", in G. Spiegel, *The Past as Text: The Theory and Practice of Medieval Historiography.* Baltimore: The Johns Hopkins University Press, 1997, 3–28.

Spiegel, Gabrielle. "In the Mirror's Eye: The Writing of Medieval History in North

America", in G. Spiegel, *The Past as Text: The Theory and Practice of Medieval Historiography*. Baltimore: The Johns Hopkins University Press, 1997, 57–80.

Spiegel, Gabrielle. "Political Utility in Medieval Historiography: A Sketch", in G. Spiegel, *The Past as Text: The Theory and Practice of Medieval Historiography*. Baltimore: The Johns Hopkins University Press, 1997, 83–98.

Spiegel, Gabrielle, ed. *Practicing History: New Directions in Historical Writing after the Linguistic Turn*. New York: Routledge, 2005.

Spiegel, Gabrielle. "The Task of the Historian", *AHR* 114/1 (2009), 1–15.

Spiegel, Gabrielle. "Introduction", in G. Spiegel, ed., *Practicing History: New Directions in Historical Writing after the Linguistic Turn*. New York: Routledge, 2005, 1–32.

Stark, Sören. "The Arab Conquest of Bukhārā: Reconsidering Qutayba b. Muslim's Campaigns 87–90 H/706–709 CE", *ISL* 95/2 (2018), 367–400.

Stauth, Georg. *Die Überlieferung des Korankommentars Muǧāhid b. Ǧabrs: Zur Rekonstruktion der in den Sammelwerken des 3. Jh. d. H. benutzten frühislamischen Quellenwerke*. PhD dissertation, University of Giessen, 1969.

Stetkevych, Jaroslav. *Muhammad and the Golden Bough. Reconstructing Arabian Myth*. Bloomington, IN: Indiana University Press, 1996.

Stetter, Eckart. *Topoi und Schemata im Ḥadīṯ*. PhD dissertation, University of Tübingen, 1965.

Stillinger, Jack. *Multiple Authorship and the Myth of Solitary Genius*. New York: Oxford University Press, 1991.

Su, I-Wen. *The Shīʿī Past in the* Great Book of the Songs: *A New Perspective on the* Kitāb al-Aghānī *by Abū al-Faraj al-Iṣfahānī and Shīʿī Islam in the Tenth Century*. Piscataway, NJ: Gorgias, 2021.

Su, I-Wen. "The Early Shiʿi Kufan Traditionists' Perspective on the Rightly Guided Caliphs", *JAOS* 141–1 (2021), 27–47.

Surkis, Judith. "When was the Linguistic Turn? A Genealogy", *AHR* 117/3 (2012), 700–22.

Tayob, Abdelkader I. "Ṭabarī on the Companions of the Prophet: Moral and Political Contours in Islamic Historical Writing", *JAOS* 119/2 (1999), 203–10.

Tayyara, Abed el-Rahman. "Origin Narratives and the Making of Dynastic History in al-Dīnawarī's Akhbār", *DMES* 23 (2014), 54–75.

Tillier, Mathieu. "Le règne du calife Ḥasan bar Alī d'après une source syriaque", *Les Carnet de l'Ifpo. La recherche en train de se faire à l'Institut français du Proche-Orient* (Hypothesis.org), 29 novembre 2013, available online at https://ifpo.hypotheses.org/5489 (accessed 4 August 2020).

Tillschneider, Hans Thomas. "*Asbāb wurūd al-ḥadīṯ* - eine wenig beachtete Gattung der islamischen Traditionsliteratur", *ZDMG* 165 (2015), 63–91.

Thomson, Rodney L. "The Khawārij and Religious Identity Formation in Early Islam". M. A. dissertation, California State University (Chico), 2017.

Thomson, William. "Kharijitism and the Kharijites", *The MacDonald Presentation Volume*. Princeton: Princeton University Press, 1933, 373–89.

Timani, Hussam S. *Modern Intellectual Readings of the Khārijites*. New York: Lang, 2007.

Toews, John E. "Intellectual History After the Linguistic Turn", *AHR* 92/4 (1987), 879–907.

Treiger, Alexander. "Origins of *Kalām*", in S. Schmidtke, ed., *The Oxford Handbook of Islamic Theology*. Oxford: Oxford University Press, 2016, 27–43.

Tucker, William F. *Mahdis and Millenarians. Shīʿite Extremists in Early Muslim Iraq*. Cambridge: Cambridge University Press, 2008.

Tyler, Elizabeth and Ross Balzaretti, eds. *Narrative and History in the Early Medieval West*. Turnhout: Brepols, 2006.

Ullmann, Manfred. *Das Motiv der Kreuzigung in der arabischen Poesie des Mittelalters*. Wiesbaden: Harrassowitz, 1995.

Vacca, Alison. "The Fires of Naxčawan: In Search of Intercultural Transmission in Arabic, Armenian, Greek, and Syriac", *Le Muséon* 129/3–4 (2016), 323–62.

Vajda, Georges. "The Oral Transmission of Knowledge in Traditional Islam", in C. Gilliot, ed., *Education and Classical Learning the Early Islamic World*. Farnham/Burlington, VT: Ashgate Variorum, 2012, 163–72.

Van Ess, Josef. *The Flowering of Muslim Theology*. Trans. J. M. Todd. Cambridge, MA: Harvard University Press, 2006.

Van Ess, Josef. *Theologie und Gesellschaft im 2. und 3. Jahrhundert Hidschra: Eine Geschichte des religiösen Denkens im frühen Islam*. Vol. I. Berlin: De Gruyter, 1991.

Van Ess, Josef. *Theologie und Gesellschaft im 2. und 3. Jahrhundert Hidschra: Eine Geschichte des religiösen Denkens im frühen Islam*. Vol. II. Berlin: De Gruyter, 1992.

Van Ess, Josef. "The Beginning of Ibadi Studies", in A. Ziaka, ed., *On Ibadism*. Hildesheim: Olms, 2014, 35–41.

Van Ess, Josef. "Unfertige Studien I: Wer sind und was bedeutet al-māriqa?", *ASIA* 70/4 (2016), 1389–431.

Van Ess, Josef. "Das *Kitāb at-Taḥrīš* des Ḍirār b. ʿAmr. Einige Bemerkungen zu Ort und Anlaß seiner Abfassung", in H. Biesterfeldt, ed., *Kleine Schriften* by Josef van Ess, vol. III. Leiden: Brill, 2018, 2461–500.

Van Ess, Josef. "Das Bild der Ḫāriǧiten im *Kitāb at-Taḥrīš* des Ḍirār b. ʿAmr", in H. Biesterfeldt, ed., *Kleine Schriften* by Josef van Ess, vol. III. Leiden: Brill, 2018, 2534–601.

Van Steenbergen, Jo. "Truth and Politics in Late Medieval Arabic Historiography: The Formation of Sultan Barsbāy's State (1422–1438) and the Narratives of the Amir Qurqumās al-Shaʿbānī (d. 1438)", *ISL* 95/1 (2018), 147–87.

Vansina, Jan. *Oral Tradition as History*. London: Heinemann, 1985.

Vernon, James. "Who's Afraid of the 'Linguistic Turn'? The Politics of Social History and Its Discontents", *Social History* 19/1 (1994), 81–97.

Vollmann, Benedikt K. "Autorenrollen in der lateinischen Literatur des 13. Jahrhunderts", in M. Meyer and H.-J. Schiewer, eds, *Literarische Leben.*

Rollenentwürfe in der Literatur des Hoch- und Spätmittelalters. Tübingen: Niemeyer, 2002, 813–27.

Von Grunebaum, Gustave. *Medieval Islam. A Study in Cultural Orientation*. 2nd edition. Chicago/London: University of Chicago Press, 1961.

Wagemakers, Joas. "'Seceders' and 'Postponers'? An Analysis of the 'Khawarij' and 'Murji'a' Labels in Polemical Debates between Quietist and Jihadi-Salafists", in J. Deol and Z. Kazmi, eds, *Contextualizing Jihadi Thought*. London: Hurst, 145–64.

Waldman, Marion R. *Toward a Theory of Historical Narrative. A Case Study in Perso-Islamicate Historiography*. Columbus, OH: Ohio State University Press, 1980.

Wansbrough, John E. *The Sectarian Milieu: Content and Composition of Islamic Salvation History*. Oxford: Oxford University Press, 1978.

Wansbrough, John E. "Res Ipsa Loquitur: History and Mimesis", in H. Berg, ed., *Method and Theory in the Study of Islamic Origins*. Leiden/Boston: Brill, 2003, 3–19.

Warden, W. "A Very Rare Kharijite Propaganda Silver Drahm", *ONS* 92–3 (1984), 4.

Watt, William M. *Islamic Political Thought - The Basic Concepts*. Edinburgh: Edinburgh University Press, 1968.

Watt, William M. *The Formative Period of Islamic Thought*. Edinburgh: Edinburgh University Press, 1973.

Watt, William M. *Muḥammad at Mecca*. Oxford: Clarendon Press, 1953.

Watt, William M. "The Study of the Development of the Islamic Sects", in P. W. Pestman, ed., *Acta Orientalia Neerlandica: Proceedings of the Congress of the Dutch Oriental Society, held in Leiden on the Occasion of its 50th Anniversary 8th–9th May 1970*. Leiden: Brill, 1971, 82–91.

Watt, William M. "The Significance of the Sects in Islamic Theology", in *Actas do IV Congresso des Estudos Árabes e Islámicos*. Leiden: Brill, 1971, 169–76.

Watt, William M. "The Great Community and the Sects", in G. E. von Grunebaum, ed., *Theology and Law in Islam*. Wiesbaden: Harrassowitz, 1971, 25–36.

Watt, William M. "Was Wāṣil a Khārijite?", in M. W. Watt, ed., *Early Islam. Collected Articles*. Edinburgh: Edinburgh University Press, 1990, 129–34.

Watt, William M. "The Significance of Khārijism under the ʿAbbāsids", in M. W. Watt, ed., *Early Islam. Collected Articles*. Edinburgh: Edinburgh University Press, 1990, 135–9.

Watt, William M. "Khārijite Thought in the Umayyad Period", *ISL* 36/3 (1961), 215–31.

Wellendorf, Jonas. "Scriptorial Scruples: The Writing and Rewriting of a Hagiographical Narrative", in S. Rankovic, ed., *Modes of Authorship in the Middle Ages*. Toronto: Pontifical Institute of Mediaeval Studies, 2012, 289–308.

Wellhausen, Julius. *Die religiös-politischen Oppositionsparteien im alten Islam*. Berlin: Weidmann, 1901.

Wheeldon, M. J. "'True Stories': The Reception of Historiography in Antiquity", in A. Cameron, ed., *History as Text. The Writing of Ancient History*. London: Duckworth, 1989, 33–63.

White, Hayden. *The Content of the Form: Narrative Discourse and Historical Representation*. Baltimore: The Johns Hopkins University Press, 1987.

White, Hayden. *Tropics of Discourse: Essays in Cultural Criticism*. Baltimore: The Johns Hopkins University Press, 1978.

White, Hayden. "The Discourse of History", *Humanities in Society* 2 (1979), 1–15.

Widengren, Geo. *Muhammad, the Apostle of God, and His Ascension*. Uppsala: Lundequist, 1955.

Wilkinson, John C. "The Early Development of the Ibāḍī Movement in Basra", in G. H. A. Juynboll, ed., *Studies in the First Century of Islamic Society*. Carbondale, IL: Southern Illinois University Press, 1982, 125–44.

Wilkinson, John C. *Ibadism. Origins and Early Development in Oman*. Oxford: Oxford University Press, 2010.

Woodmansee, Martha. "The Genius and the Copyright: Economic and Legal Conditions of the Emergence of the 'Author'", *Eighteenth-Century Studies* 17/4 (1984), 425–48.

Zaman, Muhammad Qasim. *Religion and Politics under the Early ʿAbbāsids: The Emergence of the Proto-Sunnī Elite*. Leiden: Brill, 1997.

Zarrou, Mohamed. *Les thèmes réligieux et les réminiscences coraniques chez les poètes de l'ancien islam et les poètes Khārijites*. PhD dissertation, University of Paris, 1992–3.

Ziaka, Angeliki, ed. *On Ibadism*, Hildesheim: Olms, 2014.

Zubaidi, A. M. "The Impact of the Qur'ān and *Ḥadīth* on Medieval Arabic Literature", in A. F. L. Beeston et al., eds, *The Cambridge History of Arabic Literature. Vol. I: Arabic Literature to the End of the Umayyad Period*. Cambridge: Cambridge University Press, 1983, 322–43.

Index

ʿAbbāsid–ʿAlid relations, 135–6, 151–3, 156
ʿAbd al-ʿAzīz b. ʿAbdallāh, 225
ʿAbd al-Malik
  appointment of Bishr b. Marwān, 224
  appointment of Muḥammad b. Mūsā, 237
  confidence in al-Muhallab, 220
  death of Ibn al-Zubayr, 49
  death of Muṣʿab b. al- Zubayr, 115–16, 117, 118
  Khārijism during the reign of, 217–48
  Khārijite rebellions against, 49–51
ʿAbd al-Qays, 46, 193–5
ʿAbd al-Raḥmān b. Mikhnaf, 245
ʿAbdallāh b. ʿAbbās (Ibn ʿAbbās)
  ʿAbbāsid–ʿAlid relations, 135–7, 151–3, 156
  confrontation with the Khārijites, 138–41, 142–3, 145–6, 148–9, 152, 154
  status in Islamic historiography, 151
ʿAbdallāh b. al-Kawwāʾ, 86, 141, 142–5, 148
ʿAbdallāh b. al-Zubayr (Ibn al-Zubayr)
  caliphate of, 19 n.8, 47–8, 217
  conflict with Umayyads, 19 n.8, 47, 48, 49, 118, 224, 238–9
  death of, 49, 220, 238
  forged letter to al-Muhallab, 220
  relations with the Khārijites, 47, 48, 240–4
  removal of al-Muhallab, 224
  use of Khārijite language, 115–16, 117
ʿAbdallāh b. Āmir, 45–7, 165, 182, 195–6, 201
ʿAbdallāh b. Khabbāb, 99, 101–3, 150, 157, 182, 201
ʿAbdallāh b. Wahb al-Rāsibī (Ibn Wahb al-Rāsibī), 44, 73, 88, 122, 123, 131 n.75, 189, 190, 204, 262
Abū Bilāl Mirdās b. Udayya
  as a Basran quietist, 70, 197, 198–9
  disapproval of female warriors, 184–5, 210 n.107
  elegies for, 116, 172–3
  imprisonment by ʿUbaydallāh b. Ziyād, 47, 200
  in the Islamic tradition, 36 n.24, 82 n.104, 169, 178, 185, 199, 202, 204, 207 n.35, 210 n.107, 214 n.189
  opposition to *istiʿrāḍ*, 183, 202
  (militant) piety of, 168–9, 170–3, 200, 202, 204, 214 n.189
  rebellion by, 47, 168–9, 170–3, 215 n.192
  see also ʿUrwa b. Udayya al-Tamīmī
Abū Fudayk, 237
Abū Mikhnaf
  ʿAlid sympathies, 32, 153
  as al-Ṭabarī's source, 32, 96, 115, 153, 163 n.123, 185, 205, 211 n.118, 214 n.174, 236, 239, 241, 245, 246, 252 n.85
  scholarship on, 27
Abū Mūsā al-Ashʿarī
  as arbiter at Ṣiffīn, 43, 141–2, 144, 151, 152, 155, 162 n.95, 262
  as an unbeliever, 142, 144, 251 n.74
Abū Sufyān, 139
Abū al-Wāziʿ, 170, 174

adab
Ansāb al-Ashrāf as an example of, 25, 204, 258
genre classification, 25, 26, 35 n.7
Khārijism in, 4, 277
overlap of material with Ibn Aʿtham's *Kitāb al-Futūḥ*, 265, 276
ʿAdī b. Ḥātim, 111 n.92, 194–5
al-Akhbār al-Ṭiwāl (al-Dīnawarī) *see* al-Dīnawarī, Abū Ḥanīfa
ʿAlī b. Abī Ṭālib
ʿAbbāsid–ʿAlid relations, 135–7, 151–3, 156
arbitration of Ṣiffīn in historiography, 42–4, 69–71, 135–57, 259
assassination of, 103, 187–8, 264–5
debates with the Khārijites, 136–57, 168, 191–2
ḥadīths on Khārijites, 99–101
Khārijite allegations against, 136–7, 139
Khārijite attitudes towards, 42–4, 135–51, 231–2, 233
on the *lā ḥukma* slogan, 93–4
refusal to recommence fighting during the arbitration, 136, 146–7
rule of, 4, 42–4
status in Islamic law and tradition, 135, 151
see also ʿAbdallāh b. ʿAbbās; Battle of Ṣiffīn; Battle of Nahrawān
ʿAlids
(pro-)ʿAlid–Khārijite enmity, 179, 193–6, 262
ʿAbbāsid–ʿAlid relations, 135–7, 151–3, 156
pro-ʿAlid historiography, 45, 139, 258–68
relations with the Umayyads, 44–5, 177–8, 194, 260
ʿAmr b. al-ʿĀṣ, 42, 104, 138, 139, 144, 152, 156, 234, 251 n.74, 260, 264
Ansāb al-Ashrāf (al-Balādhurī) *see* al-Balādhurī, Aḥmad b. Yaḥyā
ascetic poetry (*zuhdīyāt*), 118–20
al-Ashʿath b. Qays, 42–3, 69–70, 151, 155, 162 n.97, 194–5, 262
Asmāʾ bt. Abī Bakr, 118, 238–9, 240
authorship, 27–33, 61, 180, 191, 272 n.76
Azāriqa
conflicts with al-Muhallab, 48–9, 50, 91, 94, 97, 117, 219–23, 225–7, 244–5
militancy of, 217–18, 228
see also Nāfiʿ b. al-Azraq; Qaṭarī b. al-Fujāʾa

al-Balādhurī, Aḥmad b. Yaḥyā
Ansāb al-Ashrāf, 4, 24–5, 26, 32, 179–80, 205, 206 n.19, 222, 258
approval of Khārijite resistance to the Umayyads, 17, 169–80, 203, 204, 233, 275
criticism of the Khawārij, 99–101, 180–5
criticism of the Umayyads, 118, 167, 169–70, 175–8, 238–9
on Khārijism during the reign of Muʿāwiya, 165–85, 202–4
narrative techniques for Khārijite confrontations, 167–9, 178–80, 190
personal background, 25, 36 n.13, 258
portrayal of Khārijite women, 183, 184–5
on revolts and tribal strife, 230, 231, 251 n.69
Basra
Khārijite division into four sects in, 48, 218, 228, 241, 242
Khārijite revolts in, 48–9, 182–3, 201–2, 219–20, 230, 231
persecution of the Khārijites in, 46–7, 168, 170–1, 173–6
quietist Khārijites in, 47, 197–201, 218
ʿUbaydallāh b. Ziyād's flight from, 230, 231
Battle of Nahrawān
ʿAlī's discussions with the Khārijites at, 138–40, 142, 145, 147, 149–51
ʿAlī's use of *ḥadīth* at, 99–100
events of, 44, 71–3, 149–51
Ibn ʿAbbās as ʿAlī's arbitrator at, 73, 152
Battle of Ṣiffīn, 42–3; *see also* Ṣiffīn arbitration
Battle of the Camel, 137, 147, 242
Bishr b. Marwān, 224, 225, 226, 244–5
Brünnow, Rudolf Ernst, 9–10, 13

Christians/Christianity, 50, 79 n.38, 84 n.133, 86, 103, 109 n.59, 119, 121, 130 n.54
Conrad, Lawrence, 260, 263, 264, 266, 268
Cook, Michael, 12, 60, 125
Crone, Patricia, 12, 60, 61, 71
crucifixion, 47, 175, 176, 182, 184, 201–2, 215 n.201, 238

al-Ḍaḥḥāk b. Qays, 126, 127
al-Dīnawarī, Abū Ḥanīfa
  al-Akhbār al-Ṭiwāl, 24, 25, 26, 160 n.55
  as pro-ʿAlid or proto-Sunnī historian, 259–60, 261, 262
  censure of Khārijism, 94–5
  depiction of conflict between ʿAlī and the Khārijites, 142, 145–6
  depiction of conflict between al-Muhallab and the Azāriqa, 97
Donner, Fred, 7–9, 12, 13

early Islamic historiography
  ʿAbbāsid–ʿAlid relations, 135–7, 151–3, 156
  aurality and, 37 n.32, 60–1, 67
  authorship, 27–33, 61, 180, 191, 272 n.76
  challenges of the historical tradition, 3, 27–9, 59–61, 73–5
  denunciation of militant piety, 86, 103–5, 187, 257
  as a genre, 24–6
  Ibāḍī, 26–7
  interpretations of Khārijism, 257–8
  as literature, 5–6, 14–15, 29–33, 41–2, 59–75, 114
  proto-Shīʿī and proto-Sunnī sources, 258–63
  scholarship on, 5, 59–61
  universal histories, 26
  see also *schemata*/*schema*; *topoi*/*topos*
El-Hibri, Tayeb, 64, 157

ḥadīth
  critical of Khārijism, 93, 99–102, 104, 110 n.76, 187, 265
  historiography and, 18 n.7, 26, 60, 74, 84 n.134, 223
  Khārijite zealotry in, 99–102
  quoted by ʿAli, 99–101
  topoi and *schemata* in, 65–7
Hagler, Aaron, 265–6, 268
Haider, Najam, 5, 60
al-Ḥajjāj b. Yūsuf
  al-Muhallab and, 97, 220, 226–7, 236
  Asmāʾ's criticism of, 118, 238
  clash with Shabīb, 50, 229–30
  governorship of Iraq, 49–51, 217
  Ibn al-Zubayr's conflict with, 118, 238–9
  interrogation of Khārijites, 232, 234–5
  and Muḥammad b. Mūsā, 236–8
  reputation of, 17, 55 n.72, 118, 233–40, 245–6
  suppression of Khārijite revolts, 49–51, 229–30, 232, 234–5
Ḥarūrāʾ, 36 n.24, 44, 70, 73, 137, 138, 141, 143, 145, 148, 150, 153, 154, 155, 262
Ḥarūrites, 44, 106 n.7
al-Ḥasan al-Baṣrī, 115
al-Ḥasan b. ʿAlī, 44–5, 155–6, 177–8
Hawthara b. Wadāʿ al-Asadī, 181–2
Hawting, Gerald, 11–12, 13, 60
Ḥayyān b. Ẓabyān al-Sulamī, 91–2, 123, 187–8, 189, 190, 196, 197, 204
Heck, Paul, 13
Hinds, Martin, 11
Hodgson, Marshall, 62, 63
al-Ḥudaybiyya, treaty of, 139, 148, 154, 265
Ḥujr b. ʿAdī, 194–5

Ibāḍism, 7, 20 n.21–2, 26–7, 36 n.24, 48, 109 n.59, 111 n.97, 154, 162 n.110, 199, 207 n.35, 209 n.93, 210 n.107, 214 n.189, 218, 228, 229
Ibn ʿAbbās *see* ʿAbdallāh b. ʿAbbās
(Ibn) ʿAbd Rabbih, 91, 229
Ibn ʿAbd Rabbih, Aḥmad b. Muḥammad, 30–1, 212 n.137
Ibn Aʿtham al-Kūfī
  dating of the work of, 265–8

Kitāb al-Futūḥ, 24, 25, 26, 28, 222, 251 n.76, 263–8
portrayal of al-Ḥajjāj, 234–6
portrayal of al-Muhallab, 94–5, 117, 219–27, 228, 236, 257, 263, 265
portrayal of the murder of ʿAlī, 264–5
pro-ʿAlid stance, 139, 161 n.85, 258–63
Ibn al-Mubārak, 119, 120–1
Ibn Muljam, 43, 44, 88, 103, 148, 187, 188, 199, 262, 264–5
Ibn Qutayba, ʿAbdallāh b. Muslim, 119
Ibn Saʿd, Muḥammad, 24, 26, 271 n.45
Ibn Wahb al-Rāsibī *see* ʿAbdallāh b. Wahb al-Rāsibī
Ibn al-Zubayr *see* ʿAbdallāh b. al-Zubayr
ʿImrān b. Ḥiṭṭān, 51, 106 n.14, 116, 119–20, 172–3, 276

al-Jazīra (Northern Mesopotamia)
Khārijite revolts in, 13, 33–4 n.1, 50
see also Ṣāliḥ b. Musarriḥ; Shabīb b. Yazīd
jihād
militant piety in Khārijism, 13, 89–93, 99–101, 104–5, 169–75, 188–9, 191–7, 218
pious warriors in early Islam, 120–2
Judd, Steven, 166–7, 179

kalām (dialectical reasoning), 143, 144, 154
khabar (report), 29, 59–60, 118, 266
Khālid b. ʿAbbād/ʿUbbād, 168, 173–4
Khālid b. ʿAbdallāh (governor of Basra), 224–5
Khalīfa b. Khayyāṭ
Taʾrīkh, 24, 28, 180, 205
Khārijism
censorship of, 93–105
desire for *jihād*, 89–93
doctrine, 75, 95–6, 124–7, 228–30, 231–3, 247, 248, 277
four mother sects of, 48, 218, 228, 241, 242
Khārijite revolts as military aptitude tests, 244–6
lā ḥukma slogan, 3, 8, 11–12, 42, 43, 55 n.76, 69–70, 86–7, 93–4, 100, 136, 150, 185, 201, 235, 259, 261, 262
literary approach to, 4–5, 14–15, 61–75
scholarship on, 6–13
al-shurāt epithet, 36 n.24, 87, 115, 117, 224
significance of eschatology for, 12, 13
as a transgression of Islam, 89, 93–5, 100, 102–3, 104, 148, 182, 275
volatility of, 48, 95–7, 218, 227–33, 241, 242
Khārijite origins
scholarship on, 6–7, 9–14
source materials, 3–6, 7–8, 277–8
term, 4–5
Khārijites/Khawārij
collective identity of, 218–19
emergence of the Khārijites, 42–4
executions of, 118, 124, 168, 170, 171, 173–4, 199–200, 201–2, 205, 232, 235, 264
murder of Companions by, 99, 101–2, 150, 157, 182–3, 201, 216 n.210
non-Muslims and, 50, 51, 95, 103, 183, 243
outward appearances of, 87–8, 94, 173–4, 181, 234
poetry, 7–8, 12, 51, 87, 89–90, 91, 116, 172–3, 176, 183, 226
pro-ʿAlid opposition to, 193–6
see also Ḥarūrites; *al-shurāt*
Kitāb al-Futūḥ (Ibn Aʿtham) *see* Ibn Aʿtham al-Kūfī

Leder, Stefan, 59–60
linguistic turn, 61–3

al-Madāʾinī, Muḥammad b. ʿAlī, 251 n.76, 266, 267
Maʿqil b. Qays, 46, 91, 191–2, 195, 196–7
martyrdom, 7, 64, 86, 98, 100, 116, 118, 120–1, 181, 198, 199, 200, 202, 203, 235, 237
Marwān b. al-Ḥakam, 49
Masʿūd b. ʿAmr al-Azdī, 231

al-Mas'ūdī, 'Alī b. al-Ḥusayn
Murūj al-Dhahab wa-Ma'ādin al-Jawhar, 24
Shī'ism of, 258–63
works of, 18–19 n.7, 24, 212 n.137, 219, 228
Morony, Michael, 8, 127
Mu'ādh b. Juwayn, 91, 123, 190, 196, 197
Mu'āwiya b. Abī Sufyān
accounts of Khārijism under, 165–205
caliphate of, 4, 44–7
conflict with 'Alī, 42–4, 136–7, 138, 139, 141, 150, 151, 152, 156–7
criticism of, 177–8
death of, 47
Khārijite assassination plot against, 264
al-Mughīra b. Shu'ba, 45, 46–7, 91–2, 165, 175, 181, 184, 187, 190, 191–2, 195, 196
muhājirūn, term, 91
al-Muhallab b. Abī Ṣufra
al-Ḥajjāj's attitude towards, 50, 236
conflicts with the Azāriqa, 48–9, 50, 91, 94, 97, 117, 219–23, 225–7, 244–5
Ibn al-Zubayr's forged letter to, 220
piety of, 222–3
reinstatement, 225–7
removal from office, 223–4, 244
sons of, 221, 223
use of Khārijite language, 115, 223
Muḥammad
condemnation of Khārijism by, 99–100, 101, 111–12 n.97, 265
ḥadīth and *sunna* of, 99–100, 104, 138–40, 147, 148, 243
Prophetic precedence for Ṣiffīn arbitration, 138–40, 154
Muḥammad b. Mūsā, 236–7
al-Mukhtār b. Abī 'Ubayd, 47, 243, 251 n.69
Murūj al-Dhahab wa-Ma'ādin al-Jawhar (al-Mas'ūdī) *see* al-Mas'ūdī, 'Alī b. al-Ḥusayn
Muṣ'ab b. al-Zubayr, 115–16, 117, 220
al-Mustawrid b. 'Ullafa al-Taymī
conflict with Simāk b. 'Ubayd, 97–8, 192
election of, 122–3, 189–90
in Kufa, 193–4
rebellion by, 46, 88, 91, 97-8, 185, 189–90, 191–2, 193–4, 195, 196–7
Muṭarrif b. al-Mughīra b. Shu'ba, 217

Nāfi' b. al-Azraq, 47, 48–9, 90, 95, 107 n.33, 109–10 n.68, 161 n.91, 170, 229, 241, 242, 247; *see also* Azāriqa
Najda b. 'Āmir, 47, 49, 96, 108 n.47, 209–10 n.93, 229, 242, 250 n.55; *see also* Najdiyya
Najdiyya, 21 n.36, 47–8, 49, 207 n.35, 218, 227–8, 240, 247, 276
Naṣr b. Muzāḥim al-Minqarī, 24, 70, 258, 259, 261–2, 266
Noth, Albrecht, 65, 67–8, 74, 114, 183, 250–1 n.60

piety, militant
Abū Bilāl's militant piety, 168–9, 170–3, 200, 202, 204, 214 n.189
denunciation of militant piety, 86, 103–5, 187, 257
Khārijite piety as a threat, 86, 103–5, 121–2, 186, 188–9, 191–7, 200–2, 203–4, 230, 274–5
see also *jihād*; *umma*

Qaṭarī b. al-Fujā'a, 14, 33–4 n.1, 50, 51, 96, 117, 127, 221, 224, 225, 226, 229, 236, 248; *see also* Azāriqa
Qur'ān
in Khārijite discourse, 88–9
shirā' (exchange) concept in, 87
use in debates about Ṣiffīn arbitration, 138, 140, 144, 146
used to condemn Khārijism, 96–9
qurrā', 9, 10, 13, 42, 43, 86, 94, 104, 151, 155, 259, 261, 262
Qutayba b. Muslim, 239–40

Robinson, Chase, 12–13, 59, 62, 222

Sahm b. Ghālib al-Ḥujaymī, 182, 201, 210 n.111, 216 n.210
Ṣāliḥ (prophet), 232, 265
Ṣāliḥ b. Mukhrāq, 107 n.25, 221

Ṣāliḥ b. Musarriḥ, 50, 90, 96, 107 n.28, 124–5, 217, 229
Sālim b. Dhakwān, 209–10 n.93, 210 n.107
Sālim b. Rabī' al-'Absī, 188
Ṣa'ṣa'a b. Ṣūḥān, 73, 152, 187, 193–4, 195
Scheiner, Jens, 268
schemata/schema
  appointment *schema*, 122–4, 189–90, 204, 262
  awā'il (firsts), 68, 69–71, 183
  concept of, 65–6, 68
  in *ḥadīth* literature, 66–7
Schoeler, Gregor, 34–5 n.5, 37 n.32, 76 n.14
Sezgin, Fuat, 34–5 n.5, 37 n.32, 76 n.14
Shaban, Muḥammad A., 10–11, 266–7
Shabath b. Rib'ī, 73
Shabīb b. Bajara al-Ashjā'ī, 181
Shabīb b. Yazīd al-Shaybānī
  al-Ṭabarī's portrayal of, 51, 90, 96, 237–8
  in non-Muslim sources, 50, 51
  pro-*isti'rāḍ* sentiments, 96
  rebellion by, 50–1, 98–9, 217–18, 227, 229–30, 231, 232–3, 235, 236, 237, 239–40, 244, 245–6
Sharīk b. al-A'war al-Ḥārithī, 196
shirā', 87; see also *al-shurāt*
al-shurāt, Khārijite epithet, 36 n.24, 87, 115, 117, 224
Shurayḥ b. Awfā al-'Absī, 70–1, 72, 88–9, 106 n.20, 131 n.75
Ṣiffīn arbitration
  Abū Mūsā as an arbiter, 43, 141–2, 144, 151, 152, 251 n.74, 262
  'Alī's acceptance of, 42–4, 136–7
  'Alī's refusal to recommence fighting during the arbitration, 146–7
  in early Islamic historiography, 42–4, 163 n.123
  emergence of the Khārijites, 3, 4, 42–4, 69
  justifications for, 136–49, 154–5
  Khārijite protest at, 3, 8, 42, 69–71, 94, 136, 141, 142, 185, 232, 259
  Mu'āwiya's role in, 42–4, 136–7, 138, 139
Simāk b. 'Ubayd, 54 n.40, 97–8, 192, 193, 196
Sizgorich, Thomas, 64
Stetter, Eckart, 65–7, 68, 211 n.123
Ṣūfism, 119, 121
Ṣufriyya, 48, 96, 218, 228, 229
Sufyān b. Abī al-'Āliya al-Khath'amī, 245–6
Sufyān b. al-Abrad, 227

al-Ṭabarī, Muḥammad b. Jarīr
  Abū Mikhnaf as a source for, 32, 96, 115, 153, 163 n.123, 185, 205, 211 n.118, 214 n.174, 236, 239, 241, 245, 246, 252 n.85
  on Khārijism during the reign of Mu'āwiya, 185–205
  on Khārijite piety as a threat, 186, 188–9, 191–7, 200–2, 203–4, 230
  on Khārijite rebellions as tests of military aptitude, 244–6
  narrative techniques, 191–7
  portrayal of al-Ḥajjāj, 234, 236, 239–40
  portrayal of Shabīb, 50–1, 96, 98–9, 217–18, 229–30, 237–8, 244, 245–6, 247, 252 n.85
  portrayal of the Umayyads, 187, 194–6
  as a scholar, 32, 33, 203, 211 n.123, 258
  Ta'rīkh al-Rusul wa-l-Mulūk, 24, 28–9, 32, 59, 205, 258
Ta'rīkh (Khalīfa b. Khayyāṭ) *see* Khalīfa b. Khayyāṭ
Ta'rīkh (al-Ya'qūbī) *see* al-Ya'qūbī, Aḥmad b. Abī Ya'qūb
Ta'rīkh al-Rusul wa-l-Mulūk (al-Ṭabarī) *see* al-Ṭabarī, Muḥammad b. Jarīr
topoi/topos
  battle order topos, 71–3, 150
  concept of, 65–6, 68, 74
  in *ḥadīth* literature, 65–6
  Khārijite-specific, 86–93, 105, 114, 127–8, 154, 199
  mission topos, 125

'Ubāda b. Qurṣ al-Laythī, 182, 216 n.210
'Ubayda b. Hilāl, 72, 94, 131 n.72, 221, 226, 229, 241
'Ubaydallāh b. Ziyād
  Basran quietists and, 118, 197, 198–9

ʿUbaydallāh b. Ziyād (*cont.*)
execution of ʿUrwa b. Udayya, 118, 170, 172, 174, 198, 199–200, 205
flight from Basra, 48, 230, 231
governorship of, 48
imprisonment of Abū Bilāl, 200
Khārijite revolts against, 168, 170–4, 175–6, 200–2
persecution of female Khārijites, 175, 184
persecution of the Khārijites, 47, 48, 118, 173–4, 182, 198–9, 200, 240
tyranny of, 175–6, 184, 197, 198, 233
ʿUmar b. Shabba, 115, 236, 237, 239
ʿUmar b. ʿUbaydallāh b. Maʿmar, 224, 226
Umayyads
criticism of, 17, 118, 167, 169–80, 186, 187, 233–40, 243, 246, 275
Khārijite criticism of the injustice of, 50, 125, 136–7, 168, 169–70, 171, 198, 233
the pro-ʿAlids and, 187, 193–4, 195, 263
during the second *fitna*, 47–8, 49–50, 217
umma
calls on the Khārijites to return to, 98, 104, 144, 168, 178–9, 191–2
development of four-caliph thesis, 193, 197, 233
development of *jamāʿī* view, 193, 231, 232–3, 234
Khārijite zealotry as a threat to, 86, 103–5, 121–2, 186, 192, 230, 257, 274–5
Khārijites as outside of, 93, 98, 104, 182
under threat from tribal strife, 230–1
ʿUrwa b. Udayya al-Tamīmī
argument with ʿUbaydallāh b. Ziyād, 118, 199
as a Basran quietist, 185, 197, 198–9
opposition to the Ṣiffīn arbitration, 69–70
originator of *lā ḥukma* slogan, 69–70, 71
pious fortitude of, 199–200
ʿUbaydallāh b. Ziyād's execution of, 118, 170, 172, 174, 198, 199–200, 205
see also Abū Bilāl Mirdās b. Udayya
ʿUthmān b. ʿAffān
Khārijite attitudes towards, 11, 47, 98, 125, 126, 127, 141, 192, 197, 231–2, 233, 235, 241, 242, 243
murder of, 13, 42, 43, 141, 155, 157

Van Ess, Josef, 8, 105, 111 n.92

Waqʿat Ṣiffīn (Naṣr b. Muzāḥim) *see* Naṣr b. Muzāḥim al-Minqarī
Watt, W. Montgomery, 3, 8, 11, 13
Wellhausen, Julius, 10
women
Khārijite murder of, 93, 101–3, 181
as Khārijite rebels, 175, 183–5, 204, 235
as poets, 173, 183
portrayal of Khārijite women, 183–5, 235
al-Thabjā''s execution, 171, 184
Ziyād b. Abīhi's cruelty against, 175, 184

al-Yaʿqūbī, Aḥmad b. Abī Yaʿqūb
focus on ʿAlī, 145, 156, 159–60 n.53
Shīʿism of, 137, 140–1, 258–63
specific Khārijite accusations against ʿAlī, 137, 140–1
Taʾrīkh al-Yaʿqūbī, 24, 25, 28, 76 n.3, 136, 205
Yazīd b. Mālik (al-Khaṭīm al-Bāhilī), 182, 201, 210 n.111, 216 n.210
Yazīd I, 47, 48, 215 n.192, 217, 230, 231, 240, 241

Ziyād b. Abīhi/b. Abī Sufyān
conflicts with the Khārijites, 47, 168, 175, 182, 184, 197, 198, 201
governorship of, 46, 165
tyranny of, 46–7, 175, 184, 198

EU representative:
Easy Access System Europe
Mustamäe tee 50, 10621 Tallinn, Estonia
Gpsr.requests@easproject.com

www.ingramcontent.com/pod-product-compliance
Lightning Source LLC
Chambersburg PA
CBHW051559230426
43668CB00013B/1914
* 9 7 8 1 4 7 4 4 5 0 8 9 8 *